Victims, Atrocity and International Criminal Justice

While international criminal courts have often been declared as bringing 'justice' to victims, their procedures and outcomes historically showed little reflection of the needs and interests of victims themselves. This situation has changed significantly over the last sixty years; victims are increasingly acknowledged as having various 'rights', while their need for justice has been deployed as a means of justifying the establishment of international criminal courts. However, it is arguable that the goals of political and legal elites continue to be given precedence, and the ability of courts to deliver 'justice to victims' remains contested. This book contributes to this important debate through an examination of the role of victims as civil parties within the Extraordinary Chambers in the Courts of Cambodia. Drawing on a series of interviews with civil parties, court practitioners and civil society actors, the book explores the ways in which both the ECCC and the role of victims within it are shaped by specific political, economic and legal contexts, examining the 'gap' between the legitimising value of the 'imagined victim' and the extent to which victims are able to further their interests within the courtroom.

Rachel Killean is a lecturer at Queen's University Belfast.

part of the
TRANSITIONAL JUSTICE
series

Series Editor:
Kieran McEvoy, Queen's University Belfast

for information about the series and details of previous and forthcoming titles, see www.routledge.com/Transitional-Justice/book-series/TRANJ

A GlassHouse Book

Victims, Atrocity and International Criminal Justice

Lessons from Cambodia

Rachel Killean

Routledge
Taylor & Francis Group
LONDON AND NEW YORK

First published 2018 by Routledge

2 Park Square, Milton Park, Abingdon, Oxfordshire OX14 4RN
52 Vanderbilt Avenue, New York, NY 10017

Routledge is an imprint of the Taylor & Francis Group, an informa business

First issued in paperback 2019

British Library Cataloguing-in-Publication Data
A catalogue record for this book is available from the British Library

Library of Congress Cataloging-in-Publication Data
A catalog record for this book has been requested

ISBN: 978-1-138-73776-1 (hbk)
ISBN: 978-0-367-89547-1 (pbk)

Typeset in Galliard
by Apex CoVantage, LLC

Contents

Acknowledgements

Profoundest thanks to Professors Kieran McEvoy and Anne-Marie MacAlinden for their assistance, encouragement, constructive comments and sympathetic ears throughout my PhD journey. Two better supervisors I could not imagine. Thank you to my examiners, Professor Jonathan Doak and Dr Cheryl Lawther, for their close reading and helpful feedback. I would also like to thank the many people who provided feedback on earlier drafts and extracts, including Dr Anna Bryson, Dr Graham Ellison, Professor Shadd Maruna, Dr Marny Requa, Dr Lauren Dempster, Dr Stephen Smith Cody and Ms Silke Studzinsky. Special thanks to Dr Luke Moffett for being such a pragmatic and hilarious mentor and colleague. I am grateful to the staff at the ECCC, the civil society actors and the civil parties who so graciously gave up their time in order to share their thoughts and experiences with me. Thanks to the civil parties in particular, I hope I have done your views justice. Thanks go to Beini Ye, ANG Chanrith and the ECCC's Victim Support Section for their practical assistance, as well as to Alex Batesmith for his help in establishing initial contacts. Thank you to Nayheak for her invaluable interpreting assistance, and for the pleasure of her company during fieldwork. Thanks go to Anna Killean, David and Yvonne Killean, Barry Connolly, the County Antrim Jury, the Socio-legal Studies Association, the Department of Employment and Learning and the Planethood Foundation for their contributions to the funding of my time in Cambodia. For their solidarity and encouragement, thank you to my delightful PhD cohort, and in particular to Amanda, Ivanka, Lauren and Eithne for their camaraderie over the past few years. For their love and support, thanks to Yvonne, David, Angus and Nell. Finally, I thank Barry for the agreeable fact of his continuing presence, which in six years I have never presumed to expect.

Abbreviations

ADHOC	The Cambodian Human Rights and Development Association
CAE	Chambres Africaines Extraordinaires
CDP	Cambodian Defenders Project
CHRAC	Cambodian Human Rights Action Committee
CIJ	Co-Investigating Judges
DC-Cam	Documentation Center of Cambodia
DK	Democratic Kampuchea
DRC	Democratic Republic of the Congo
ECCC	Extraordinary Chambers in the Courts of Cambodia
ECtHR	European Court of Human Rights
FIDH	International Federation for Human Rights
IACtHR	Inter-American Court of Human Rights
ICC	International Criminal Court
ICL	International Criminal Law
ICTR	International Criminal Tribunal for Rwanda
ICTY	International Criminal Tribunal for the Former Yugoslavia
LCL	Lead Co-Lawyers
NGO	Non-Governmental Organisation
PTC	Pre-Trial Chamber
RGC	Royal Government of Cambodia
SCC	Supreme Court Chamber
SCSL	Special Court for Sierra Leone
SGBV	Sexual- and Gender-Based Violence
STL	Special Tribunal for Lebanon
TC	Trial Chamber
UN	United Nations
UNGA	United Nations General Assembly
UNOHCHR	United Nations Office of the High Commissioner of Human Rights
UNSC	United Nations Security Council
VSS	Victim Support Services

1 Introduction

> The participation of legal representatives of victims of the Khmer Rouge crimes in the ECCC proceedings is considered to be a historic day in international criminal law. To date, no international or hybrid tribunal mandated to investigate war crimes, crimes against humanity or genocide has involved victims as civil parties, giving them full procedural rights.[1]

At 9 a.m. on the 21 November 2011, 16 kilometres outside Phnom Penh in a building situated within the grounds of the Royal Cambodian Armed Forces, the curtains opened on what has been called 'the most important trial in the world'.[2] The ECCC was commencing its second trial, against three of the most senior leaders of the infamous Khmer Rouge regime: Ieng Sary, Nuon Chea and Khieu Samphan. Had you managed to secure yourself a seat in the Court's large viewing gallery,[3] the opening of the curtain would have revealed a courtroom of particularly grand proportions. On the back wall, you would have seen the emblems of the two forces responsible for the ECCC's unique hybrid structure[4] – the United Nations (UN) and the RGC – with the emblem of the ECCC symbolically placed between them. You would have observed the range of Cambodian and international actors present: from the judges in their robes to the multitude of lawyers on either side of the courtroom. Your eyes might have been drawn to the elderly Cambodian men at the centre of the trial: the three accused. But they may also have been drawn to an additional group of 11 Cambodian individuals sitting in the room. These individuals and their lawyers sat as living representatives of those who survived the Khmer Rouge's brutal regime and of 'one of the areas in which the ECCC is breaking new ground'[5]: the recognition of the Khmer Rouge's victims as civil parties.

Over the last 70 years, there has been a growing impetus to prosecute mass atrocities as international crimes.[6] Yet while international(ised) criminal courts[7] have often been declared as bringing 'justice' to victims, their procedures and outcomes historically showed little reflection of the needs and interests of victims themselves.[8] Such an approach is reflective of the traditional position of the victim within many domestic legal systems;[9] one consequence of the emergence of modern criminal law has been what Christie has termed the 'theft of the conflict' from the victim,[10] with the state prosecuting alleged perpetrators for crimes perceived to be against the state rather than against an individual.[11] This situation has changed significantly over the last 70 years both nationally and internationally.[12] The inclusion of victim-centric provisions at the ECCC, as well as the permanent ICC, the STL and the Extraordinary African Chambers (EAC)[13] are indicators of what some have described as a shift towards a more 'victim-orientated justice'.[14] Victims are increasingly acknowledged as having various 'rights', including the rights to protection, participation and reparation.[15] The international acknowledgement of such rights, while often vague and non-prescriptive,[16] has led to Aldana-Pindell identifying an evolving 'universality of victims' rights'.[17]

Nonetheless, to return to the ECCC's viewing gallery, the first days of trial soon revealed that while both the prosecution and the defence were permitted to make opening statements, the lawyers representing the victims were not. Fiercely resisted by the victims' lawyers, this contest is emblematic of a much larger struggle which has existed within the court since it began operations.[18] The unprecedented role given to victims within the ECCC has been subjected to a number of modifications and restrictions as the court has progressed.[19] The court has struggled to balance the involvement of large numbers of victims and their lawyers with the need to ensure expedient trials and the rights of the accused.[20] Such struggles are not unique to the ECCC, and the purpose and feasibility of victim participation remain subject to rigorous debate amongst practitioners and academics alike.[21] The variety of views spans from those who express practical fears as to the impact of victim participation on efficiency and fair trial rights[22] to those who adopt more normative arguments about the need to place victims at the centre of proceedings, with criminal trials acting as the locus to give effect to the needs of victims.[23]

While the extent to which international(ised) criminal courts can and should be amenable to victims' interests is increasingly contested,[24] the 'imagined victim'[25] of atrocity[26] has grown in prominence within the speeches of those seeking to legitimise those same courts.[27] The predominance of victim-centric language within ICL discourse has increased significantly with the advent of the ICC, with victims being described as that court's *raison d'être*.[28] Similarly, the ECCC has utilised victim-centric language since its inception,[29] with the 'imagined victim' appearing in the public pronouncements of the court's practitioners,[30] of donor state representatives[31] and of monitoring non-governmental organisations (NGOs) and academics.[32] The apparent dissonance between such statements and the actual protection of victims' interests has led some commentators to claim that victims are being instrumentalised by proponents of international criminal justice while receiving little of substance in return.[33] Yet as 'justice for victims' rhetoric becomes increasingly entrenched in ICL's normative framework,[34] the support of victim populations and perceived legitimacy[35] are increasingly heralded as crucial to the success of ICL as a legitimate system of law.[36] It is therefore clear that the relationship between victims and international(ised) criminal courts remains contested amongst practitioners and academics alike. At the heart of the debate lie fundamental questions with regards to the legitimacy of ICL, the role of victim communities and the ability of international(ised) criminal courts to deliver 'justice to victims'. Much of this debate is at times quite theoretical in nature, and it is therefore important that the discussion is accompanied by empirical research into how victim participation is being performed in practice.[37] It is such an approach that this book seeks to contribute to the discussion.

1. Aim and approach: a multi-perspective analysis

This book draws from qualitative field research conducted in 2013 and 2014, during which semi-structured interviews were conducted with 18 lawyers, judges and administrative staff employed by the court; seven lawyers and civil society actors engaged in work related to the court's functions; and 27 Cambodian citizens who were either currently, or had previously been, accepted as civil parties at the ECCC. Ethical approval was obtained from my institution beforehand, respondents were fully informed about the project, and informed consent was obtained before beginning the interviews. In order to ensure anonymity, interviewees are identified by either their job description (e.g. judge) or their relationship to the court (e.g. civil party). As it is primarily a qualitative study, no claims are made as to the study being statistically representative. Rather, it is an exploration of how particular people, at a particular time, have understood their actions and experiences.[38] In addition to drawing on interviews, the book features textual analysis of the ECCC's judgement and pronouncements, particularly in the context of Chapter 5, which considers the role of judges in shaping civil party participation. The interview schedule is included in the Appendix.

This study seeks to make three contributions to the existing literature on international criminal justice: (1) utilising a multi-perspective, actor-oriented analysis,[39] it will shed light on the way in which both the ECCC and the role of victims within it were shaped by specific political, economic and legal contexts; (2) it will provide an empirical contribution to the discussion surrounding the perceived 'gap' between the legitimising value of the abstract 'imagined victim' and the extent to which victims are able to further their interests within international criminal courts; (3) it will analyse the impact, if any, that victim participation has had on the ECCC's ability to deliver 'justice' and garner legitimacy in the eyes of civil parties. These will each be outlined in turn.

The first contribution takes as its starting point Douglas's argument that institutions cannot 'think' for themselves. Rather, they are constructed, interpreted and guided by the approaches and attitudes of those engaged in their work.[40] Similarly, the rule of law is not an objective and finite entity but, rather, a site of contest and struggle, often interpreted in many different ways by different actors.[41] As victims of international crime have received enhanced roles within ICL, it has fallen on lawyers, court officials, outreach workers, intermediaries and others to implement these policies in practice.[42] The new and evolving nature of ICL as a legal system grants practitioners an influence that would not often be found within domestic jurisdictions. The mobility of professionals between and within international criminal institutions, as well as their movement between roles as scholars, advocates and practitioners, potentially expands their sphere of influence.[43] In placing these actors in a key position within the analysis, we 'get the sense of law as a dynamic and, in some ways, even contingent process'.[44] The book therefore considers the ECCC's historical and political context and analyses the extent to which the definitions, visibility and benefits granted to victims of the Khmer Rouge within the ECCC are influenced by a myriad of heterogeneous actors pursuing (not necessarily aligned) goals.[45] Accordingly, it seeks to provide a 'thicker' understanding of victim participation at the ECCC,[46] by exploring how the system has (a) been shaped by the specific context in which it was created and (b) continues to be 'produced, perceived and interpreted' by the various actors engaged in the work of the court.[47] The actor-oriented nature of the research allows for an exploration of the different stakeholders within the system, of their interest in the system and of their influence over it,[48] while utilising a multi-perspective analysis offers the potential for a more comprehensive understanding of a complex system.[49]

This analysis is situated within broader criminological and victimological debates. As explored in greater detail within Chapter 2, victimology has grown from a study of 'victim-proneness' and 'victim-culpability' within Western domestic contexts, to a diverse discipline encompassing a range of radical and critical approaches. This book draws from state crime victimology, which explores the role of state actors in causing and responding to harm, and particularly from critical victimology,[50] which considers how terms such as *victim* and *victimisation* are manipulated by elites pursuing a range of agendas.[51] Drawing from these radical and critical perspectives, the book explores how political and legal elites have produced and legitimised certain narratives of victimisation, how these actors have shaped responses to those victimisations and what considerations have influenced those determinations.

While pointing out the weaknesses in the construct of 'victims' rights',[52] critical victimologists continue to advocate for 'a justice-based approach', moving towards notions of victims as citizens with rights.[53] Similarly, this book acknowledges that 'victimhood' is subjective, and there is an inherent gap between what law can provide and the illusive rhetorical 'justice'.[54] Yet, as noted by Moffett, justice can be utilised as a framework with which to explore the 'results which victims can expect from domestic and international mechanisms in redressing international crimes'.[55] In adopting such an approach, this book utilises a theory of 'justice for victims' as a benchmark against which to analyse the influence of different actors and contexts on the ECCC's ability to respond to the needs and interests of victims.[56]

In line with Moffett and others,[57] this book considers justice for victims as including procedural and substantive elements. The specific criteria that inform perceptions of procedural justice are disputed amongst scholars, and it appears that the criteria will vary depending on the situation[58] and context.[59] However, certain key elements have consistently emerged in the literature, which can be classified into two categories: the quality of decision making and the quality of interpersonal treatment.[60] Quality of decision making includes concepts such as neutrality and ethicality, consistency and the correctability of decisions,[61] while quality of interpersonal treatment incorporates dignity and respect, participation through representation and the exercising of voice[62] within proceedings and the provision of information.[63] While victims are by no means a homogeneous group,[64] research has shown that they often have a multitude of informational, emotional and practical needs,[65] which can become intensified for victims of international crime because of the grave and widespread nature of the crimes perpetrated against them.[66] They may require protection, emotional support, recognition of their harm and participation in a justice process.[67] Procedural justice has value in its ability to address some of these needs. It can also assist victims in pursuing their legitimate interests within the courtroom,[68] prevent secondary victimisation[69] and affirm victims' dignity and agency.[70] Substantive justice refers to the outcomes of decision-making bodies such as courts. Human rights law has established the need to provide substantive justice through an effective remedy to victims of crime.[71] These remedies have been interpreted as encompassing truth, accountability, and reparations,[72] with reparations, in turn, comprising compensation, rehabilitation, guarantees of non-repetition and satisfaction.[73] These factors can therefore be taken as comprising substantive justice.[74] Throughout this book, these two elements of justice are utilised as a framework in order to assess the extent to which the ECCC is responsive to the interests of victims in its proceedings and outcomes and to analyse the extent to which this responsiveness has been influenced by the various stakeholders and contexts explored throughout the book.

The second contribution of this book is to provide an empirical perspective to the debate surrounding the 'gap' between the legitimising value of the 'imagined victim' in ICL discourse, and the willingness of international(ised) criminal institutions to respond to the interests of 'actual' victims.[75] The architects and supporters of ICL have long been engaging in 'legitimation work',[76] by which is meant the rituals and claims used to justify the activities and purposes of an industry. Victims increasingly feature in this legitimation work[77] yet are often denied ownership of their conflicts[78] and have arguably found themselves instrumentalised by political and legal elites, who have utilised abstract notions of victims to legitimise the pursuit of goals that may not accurately reflect the wishes of actual victim populations.[79] While most attention is paid to legitimation work directed at outside actors, whether donors, subjects or monitoring organisations, less attention has been paid to the ways in which those within the system seek to legitimise it to *themselves*.[80] Barker's original and seminal work on processes of self-legitimation focused on such processes in the context of governance and rulers,[81] but similar processes of self-legitimation can be found within legal systems, particularly amongst those engaged in humanitarian work or other 'worthy' causes.[82] This book therefore seeks to explore the attitudes of those who 'argue the law, make decisions and implement the judgments' within the ECCC,[83] analysing the use of the 'imagined victim' in self-legitimation practices as well as attitudes towards the civil-party participation mechanism. Garland has argued that inquiring as to how legal staff understand their work reveals 'the structures of social action and the webs of cultural meaning'[84] within an institution. Such an approach may assist in the provision of a thick descriptive basis for normative judgements,[85] enabling a critical examination of the ways in which victim participation has been influenced by the ECCC's legal culture. The language used by ECCC staff when seeking to legitimise the ECCC's work will both reflect and constitute these webs of cultural meaning and help to explain the court's approach to victim participation.[86]

The third contribution of this study is also linked to issues of legitimacy. While international(ised) criminal institutions and practitioners may engage in self-legitimising practices, they also continue to be evaluated against the interests and beliefs of the people subordinate to their authority.[87] Within international(ised) criminal courts generally, perceived legitimacy amongst the victim population is often held up as crucial to the court's success.[88] Indeed, Beetham's seminal study on legitimacy has found that to be legitimate, the exercise of any power must (1) conform to established rules, (2) the rules must be justified by reference to beliefs shared by both dominant and subordinate parties in the power relation and (3) there must be evidence of consent by the subordinate to that particular relationship.[89] Perceived legitimacy is linked to this last requirement; the exercise of power must be seen as legitimate by those subject to that power. This book therefore considers how the ECCC and its civil party system were viewed by the participants themselves. Such an account is in keeping with a 'bottom-up' approach as recommended by Rhodes and Bevir and others.[90] It provides an account of the ECCC and the role of victims within it 'from below',[91] examining the interpretations provided by those who are subject to the authority of the court. Insights from these individuals allow for a discussion of how interpretations of justice are 'reproduced, or disrupted, by – the everyday consciousness and conversations'[92] of the Cambodians who interact with the court's civil-party participation system.[93] Such an approach allows for conclusions to be based on the victims' reality, avoiding a top-down prescriptive approach which considers the work of the court solely through the eyes of 'experts'.[94]

This is not the first study to explore the opinions of the ECCC's civil parties.[95] However, in conducting research before and after the ECCC's second trial judgement, it allows for an exploration of the impact, if any, this judgement made on civil party attitudes. By utilising the 'justice for victims' theory outlined earlier, and using it to assess perceived legitimacy, it also constitutes a novel approach to analysing civil party perceptions. This analysis adopts a more subjective investigation into 'justice for victims', drawing particularly on procedural justice theory.[96] It explores the extent to which procedural justice elements influence the overall judgements made by the civil parties. In particular, it considers the claims made by proponents of procedural justice that procedural elements can actually be of greater value and importance to participants than substantive outcomes[97] and that by enhancing procedural justice, institutions can promote perceived legitimacy[98] and cushion negative outcomes.[99] This theory is of significant potential value to international(ised) criminal courts; while they cannot guarantee victims of mass crimes the outcomes they might seek, they may be able to take tangible steps towards ensuring the victims perceive the proceedings as fair. While this proposition has been explored theoretically, there has been limited empirical research conducted to explore the extent to which the claims of procedural justice are borne out in an international criminal context.[100] This contribution seeks to address this gap, by focusing on the attitudes of victim participants, their conceptions of justice, and the extent to which elements of procedural justice influence their overall perceptions of the ECCC's legitimacy.

Overall, these three interlinked contributions create a thicker description of the civil party model utilised at the ECCC. Using theories of justice and legitimacy to analyse this thicker description, the book draws conclusions as to how different contexts and actors have had an impact on the legitimacy of the court in the eyes of victims and the ability of that court to deliver justice to victim communities.

2. Chapter outlines

The rest of this book proceeds as follows.

Chapter 2 provides some historical context to the study. It highlights the various factors that have influenced the growth of the victims' rights movement in domestic criminal justice settings and traces the growth of a multitude of victimological theories, including positivist, radical, feminist and state crime victimologies. In introducing state crime victimology, it provides an introduction to the international criminal focus of the book. It then turns to briefly explore the approaches towards victims taken by the first international criminal trials after World War II before detailing the various factors which have led to changing attitudes towards victims' rights amongst those engaged in the practice of ICL and transitional justice more generally. It highlights the recent growth of more reparative approaches to justice and the corresponding increased victim-orientation of ICL. Thus, it briefly explores the approaches adopted in the ad hoc tribunals for Rwanda and the former Yugoslavia and at the permanent ICC, considering the extent to which these institutions were able to deliver procedural and substantive justice to victim populations. The symbolic value of the 'victim' in the legitimation practices of proponents of ICL is highlighted and explored.

Chapter 3 begins to focus on the ECCC, in particular, and on the various actors who have influenced its response to victimisation. It focuses on the role of politics and politicians, beginning with an outline of the various political factors which contributed to the Khmer Rouge's rise to power. After briefly detailing some of the violence which was perpetrated against the Cambodian population, it moves on to explain how the regime ended and how Cold War politics and Cambodian political instability fed a culture of impunity for decades. The chapter then moves to consider the negotiations between the RGC and the UN which led to the creation of the ECCC. It will be argued that the court is the result of a series of compromises and concessions, primarily on the part of the UN, many of which have had an impact on the structure of the court. The ways in which the negotiations have had an impact on the ability of the court to bring procedural and substantive justice to victims are explored, and the extent to which politics continue to shape the court's work is exposed.

Chapter 4 moves the analysis more particularly onto civil party participation and specifically onto the role of the ECCC's judges in the creation of the civil party system. Drawing on theories of judicial performance, it analyses the different creational, external and internal factors which contributed to the attitudes and strategies adopted by the ECCC's judges with regards to victim participation. It finds that through their creation of the Internal Rules, the ECCC's judges granted themselves unusual legislative powers, which have had a significant impact on the role of victims within the proceedings. This chapter explores the expansive civil party participation mechanism originally envisaged in the first Internal Rules, finding that the very creation of such a mechanism was an example of judicial activism.

Chapter 5 continues the focus on the role of judges in shaping the civil party system by exploring which victims were recognised as civil parties in Cases 001 and 002/01, what form participation took in the first two trials and the extent to which those trials delivered substantive justice through judgements and reparations. It notes that the judges' initial desire to involve victims quickly became an urge to contain their role and demonstrates the ways in which the civil party system was modified and restricted as the judges pursued these changing strategies.

Chapter 6 adopts a more subjective analysis, exploring the self-legitimising practices and attitudes towards victim participation amongst ECCC practitioners. The distinction being made amongst practitioners between a symbolic notion of the victim as someone deserving of justice and the actual victims seeking to participate in the work of the court is explored. It is found that many practitioners utilise 'justice for victims' rhetoric in their self-legitimising practices and in the language used to justify the ECCC and ICL more generally. However, it is also found that this desire to do justice for victims rarely translates to a wish to see enhanced rights for victims within the courtroom. The reasons for this are explored, with a particular focus on the role of practitioners' positions within the courtroom, their desire to exercise control or power within the proceedings and their preference for their own domestic legal culture. The impact these perspectives have had on the actual practice of the court and its ability to deliver justice to victims are analysed.

Chapter 7 considers the various roles that have been played by professional civil society since the ECCC began its operations. The role of donors, the limits placed on the court's finances and the belated creation of the Victim Support Services (VSS) are demonstrated as factors which inevitably led to civil society adopting an expansive role in the court's practice. After outlining these roles, the chapter considers how the work of civil society, particularly through its engagement with the civil party participation mechanism, has influenced the court's ability to deliver justice to victims. The role of civil society in drawing attention to the experiences of more typically marginalised categories of victims is highlighted as a valuable contribution. However, the dangers of an over-reliance on professional civil society as the 'mouthpieces' or representatives of victim populations are also critiqued.

Chapter 8 then turns to the civil parties themselves in order to consider their experiences of participation in their own words. Similar to Chapter 6, this chapter adopts a more subjective analysis, exploring the civil parties' understanding of the court's work, their expectations as to what the court can deliver and the level of support they have for the Court. Utilising procedural justice theory and Beetham's theory of legitimacy, this chapter assesses to what extent the ECCC is considered legitimate by civil parties and what role procedural justice has in those considerations. It analyses the values placed by civil parties on the different elements of both procedural and substantive justice in order to provide a bottom-up analysis of whether the ECCC can be considered capable of delivering 'justice' to victims.

Chapter 9 concludes the study, drawing together the key themes of the previous chapters. The chapter has three main conclusions: first, that the role of the victim within the ECCC has been constructed, understood and enacted through a legal process which involves a range of actors, judges, lawyers, civil society and the victims themselves. The combined efforts of these actors have resulted in an incomplete justice being delivered to victim participants. The second is that while the 'imagined victim' and the notion of delivering 'justice to victims' have significant roles within the legitimising practices of the court, the actual victims of the Khmer Rouge are frequently denied ownership over the process, finding themselves sidelined by international criminal justice professionals. Third, while the court engages in an active process of self-legitimation, its legitimacy also continues to be evaluated against the beliefs and wishes of the victim participants. This legitimacy could be significantly enhanced by paying attention to what this group is asking for. While there is much to critique in the practice of the ECCC, there are also valuable lessons that can be learned for future institutions seeking to bring justice to victims of international crime. The book concludes by summarising these lessons.

Notes

1 'Historic Achievement in International Criminal Law: Victims of Khmer Rouge Crimes Fully Involved in Proceedings of the ECCC' Statement by the Victims Unit, ECCC Website, 4 February 2008, www.eccc.gov.kh/sites/default/files/media/Victim_Unit_Press_Release.pdf (accessed 09/02/18).

2 S.J. Rapp, United States Ambassador at Large for War Crimes Issues, cited in T. De Langis, '"This Is Now the Most Important Trial in the World": A New Reading of Code #6, the Rule Against Immoral Offenses Under the Khmer Rouge Regime' 3 *The Cambodia Law and Policy Journal* (2014) 39.

3 The ECCC has the largest viewing gallery of any international(ised) criminal court, see R. Jeffery and H. Joon Kim (eds.), *Transitional Justice in the Asia Pacific* (Cambridge University Press, 2013) 132.

4 A hybrid court is one which features a combination of national and international law, procedure or staff. See for example L. Raub, 'Positioning Hybrid Tribunals

in International Criminal Justice' 41 *New York University Journal of International Law and Politics* (2008–2009) 1013.

5 'Germany Pledges More Financial Support to Maximise Victims' Participation in KR Trials' ECCC Website, 17 June 2010, www.eccc.gov.kh/en/articles/germany-pledges-more-financial-support-maximise-victims-participation-kr-trials (accessed 09/02/18).

6 L. Moffett, *Justice for Victims at the International Criminal Court* (Routledge, 2014) 1.

7 The term *international(ised) criminal court* is used throughout to refer to any international or hybrid court engaged in the prosecution of international crimes such as genocide, war crimes and crimes against humanity.

8 R. Hodžić, 'Living the Legacy of Mass Atrocities: Victims' Perspectives on War Crimes Trials' 8(1) *Journal of International Criminal Justice* (2010) 113; S. Kutnjak Ivković and J. Hagan, *Reclaiming Justice: The International Tribunal for the Former Yugoslavia and Local Courts* (Oxford University Press, 2011); E. Stover, *The Witnesses: War Crimes and the Promise of Justice in The Hague* (University of Pennsylvania Press, 2005); H. Weinstein and E. Stover (eds.), *My Neighbor, My Enemy: Justice and Social Reconstruction in Rwanda and the Former Yugoslavia* (Cambridge University Press, 2004).

9 T. Booth and K. Carrington, 'A Comparative Analysis of the Victim Policies Across the Anglo-speaking World' in S. Walklate (ed.), *Handbook of Victims and Victimology* (Routledge, 2007) 380–417.

10 N. Christie, 'Conflict as Property' 17(1) *British Journal of Criminology* (1977) 1.

11 T. Bonacker and C. Safferling, 'Introduction' in T. Bonacker and C. Safferling (eds.), *Victims of International Crimes: An Interdisciplinary Discourse* (Asser Press, 2013) 5; T. Kearon and B. Godfrey, 'Setting the Scene: A Question of History' in S. Walklate (ed.), *Handbook of Victims and Victimology* (Routledge, 2007) 17–37.

12 For a comprehensive overview, see for example S. Walklate (ed.), *Handbook of Victims and Victimology* (Routledge, 2007).

13 L. Catani, 'Victims at the International Criminal Court' 10 *Journal of International Criminal Justice* (2012) 905; J. de Hemptinne, 'Challenges Raised by Victims' Participation in the Proceedings of the Special Tribunal for Lebanon' 8(1) *Journal of International Criminal Justice* (2010) 16; C. Sperfeldt, 'The Trial Against Hissène Habré: Networked Justice and Reparations at the Extraordinary African Chambers' 21(9) *The International Journal of Human Rights* (2017) 1243.

14 S. Vasiliev, 'Article 68(3) and the Personal Interests of Victims in the Emerging Practice of the ICC' in C. Stahn and G. Sluiter (eds.), *The Emerging Practice of the International Criminal Court* (Brill, 2009) 635–691.

15 See for example *UN Declaration of Basic Principles of Justice for Victims of Crime and Abuse of Power*, UNGA Res. 40/34, 29 November 1985; UNOHCHR, *The Right to Restitution, Compensation and Rehabilitation for Victims of Gross Violations of Human Rights and Fundamental Freedoms, Final Report of the Special Rapporteur, Mr M.Ch Bassiouni*, UN Doc. E/CN.4/2000/62, 5 March 1993; UNOHCHR, *Updated Set of Principles for the Protection and Promotion of Human Rights through Action to Combat Impunity*, UN Doc. E/CN.4/2005/102/Add.1, 18 February 2005; *UN Basic Principles and Guidelines on the Right to a Remedy and Reparation for Victims of Gross Violations of International Human Rights Law and Serious Violations of International Humanitarian Law*, UNGA Res. 60/147, 16 December 2005.

16 J. Doak, 'Participatory Rights for Victims of Crime: In Search of International Consensus' 15(1) *Canadian Criminal Law Review* (2011) 43.

17 R. Aldana-Pindell, 'An Emerging Universality of Justiciable Victims' Rights in the Criminal Process to Curtail Impunity for State-Sponsored Crimes' 26(3) *Human Rights Quarterly* (2004) 605.

18 Case 001, Decision on the Request of the Co-Lawyers for Civil Parties Group 2 to Make an Opening Statement During the Substantive Hearing, 001/18-7-2007-ECCC/TC, 27 March 2009; Case 002/01, Trial Chamber Response to Lead Co-Lawyers and Civil Party lawyers' Request to Make a Brief Preliminary Remarks on Behalf of Civil Parties, 002/19-9-2007-ECCC/TC, 15 November 2011; Case 002/02, Decision on Civil Party Lead Co-Lawyers' Request to Make Opening Remarks, 002/19-9-2007-ECCC/TC, 14 October 2014.

19 S. Studzinsky, 'Participation Rights of Victims as Civil Parties and the Challenges of Their Implementation before the Extraordinary Chambers in the Courts of Cambodia' in T. Bonacker and C. Safferling (eds.), *Victims of International Crimes: An Interdisciplinary Discourse* (Asser Press, 2013) 175–189.

20 D. Sokol, 'Reduced Victim Participation: A Misstep by the Extraordinary Chambers in the Courts of Cambodia' 10 *Washington University Global Studies Law Review* (2011) 167.

21 REDRESS, *The Participation of Victims in International Criminal Court Proceedings: A Review of the Practice and Consideration of Options for the Future* (REDRESS Trust, 2012); V. Spiga, 'No Redress without Justice: Victims and International Criminal Law' 10 *Journal of International Criminal Justice* (2012) 1377; C. van den Wyngaert, 'Victims before International Criminal Courts. Some Views and Concerns of an ICC Trial Judge' 44 *Case Western Reserve Journal of International Law* (2011) 475; B. McGonigle Leyh, *Procedural Justice? Victim Participation in International Criminal Proceedings* (Intersentia, 2011).

22 B. McGonigle Leyh, 'Victim-Oriented Measures at International Criminal Institutions: Participation and its Pitfalls' 12 *International Criminal Law Review* (2012) 375; C. Trumbull IV, 'The Victims of Victim Participation in International Criminal Proceedings' 29(4) *Michigan Journal of International Law* (2008) 777; C. Chung, 'Victims' Participation at the International Criminal Court: Are Concessions of the Court Clouding the Promise?' 6(3) *Northwestern Journal of International Human Rights* (2008) 459; M. Damaska, 'What is the Point of International Criminal Justice?' 83 *Chicago Kent Law Review* (2008) 329.

23 R. Henham and M. Findlay, 'Introduction: Rethinking International Criminal Justice' in R. Henham and M. Findlay (eds.), *Exploring the Boundaries of International Criminal Justice* (Ashgate Publishing, 2011) 1–27; M. Findlay, 'Activating a Victim Constituency in International Criminal Justice' 3 *International Journal of Transitional Justice* (2009) 183.

24 L. Moffett, 'Meaningful and Effective? Considering Victims' Interests through Participation at the International Criminal Court' 26 *Criminal Law Forum* (2015) 255.

25 S. Walklate, *Imagining the Victim of Crime* (McGraw-Hill, 2006).

26 L.E. Fletcher, 'Refracted Justice: The Imagined Victim and the International Criminal Court' in C. De Vos, S. Kendall and C. Stahn (eds.), *Contested Justice: the Politics and Practice of International Criminal Court Interventions* (Cambridge University Press, 2015) 302–326; S. Kendall and S. Nouwen, 'Representational Practices at the International Criminal Court: The Gap between Juridified and Abstract Victimhood' 76 *Law and Contemporary Problems* (2013) 235; K. McEvoy and K. McConnachie, 'Victims and Transitional Justice: Voice, Agency and Blame' 22 *Social and Legal Studies* (2013) 489.

27 For example ICTY, Annual Report to the UNGA, A/50/365-S/1995/728, 23 August 1995, paras. 1 and 198–199; ICTR, Annual Report to the UNGA, A/53/429-S/1998/857, 23 September 1998, para. 160.

28 ICC, 'Statement to the Press by the Prosecutor of the International Criminal Court' (Abidjan, Côte d'Ivoire, 20 July 2013), www.icc-cpi.int/iccdocs/PIDS/wu/ED181_ENG.pdf (access 09/02/18).
29 *Report of the Group of Experts for Cambodia Established Pursuant to General Assembly Resolution 52/135*, UN Doc. A/53/850, 15 March 1999.
30 'Opening Speech by the Plenary's President Judge KONG Srim During the 8th Plenary of the Extraordinary Chambers in the Courts of Cambodia' ECCC Website, 13 September 2010, www.eccc.gov.kh/sites/default/.../8th_plenary_president_speech_EN.pdf (last accessed 26/11/15).
31 'Statement by the Principal Donors Group for the Extraordinary Chambers in the Courts of Cambodia' ECCC Website, 27 June 2014, www.eccc.gov.kh/en/articles/statement-principal-donors-group-extraordinary-chambers-courts-cambodia (accessed 09/02/18).
32 M. Guiraud, *Victims' Rights before the Extraordinary Chambers in the Courts of Cambodia (ECCC): A Mixed Record for Civil Parties* (FIDH, November 2012); K. Yesberg, 'Accessing Justice Through Victim Participation at the Khmer Rouge Tribunal' 40 *Victoria University of Wellington Law Review* (2009) 555.
33 Fletcher, n.26; Kendall and Nouwen, n.26; McEvoy and McConnachie, n.26; S. Nouwen 'Justifying Justice' in J. Crawford and M. Koskennieme (eds.), *The Cambridge Companion to International Law* (Cambridge University Press, 2012) 327–352.
34 Kendall and Nouwen, n.26 at 6.
35 Perceived legitimacy relates only to how the institution is viewed subjectively and does not speak to whether the institution *should* be perceived as legitimate; see S. Ford, 'A Social Psychology Model of the Perceived Legitimacy of International Criminal Courts: Implications for the Success of Transitional Justice Mechanisms' 45 *Vanderbilt Journal Transnational Law* (2012) 405.
36 J. Doak, 'The Therapeutic Dimension of Transitional Justice: Emotional Repair and Victim Satisfaction in International Trials and Truth Commissions' 11 *International Criminal Law Review* (2011) 263 at 52; J. Ramji-Nogales, 'Designing Bespoke Transitional Justice: A Pluralist Process Approach' 32(1) *Michigan Journal of International Law* (2010) 1; J.E. Stromseth, 'Pursuing Accountability for Atrocities after Conflict: What Impact on Building the Rule of Law?' 38 *Georgetown Journal of International Law* (2007) 251.
37 L. Nguyen and C. Sperfeldt, 'Victim Participation and Minorities in Internationalised Criminal Trials: Ethnic Vietnamese Civil Parties at the Extraordinary Chambers in the Courts of Cambodia' 14 *Macquarie Law Journal* (2014) 97.
38 N. Palmer, *Courts in Conflict* (Oxford University Press, 2015) 15.
39 See C. Nyamu-Musembi, 'Towards an Actor-Oriented Perspective on Human Rights' *Working Paper 169* (Surrey Institute of Development Studies, 2002); N. Long and A. Long (eds.), *Battlefields of Knowledge: The Interlocking of Theory and Practice in Social Research and Development* (Routledge, 1992); N. Long, 'From Paradigm Lost to Paradigm Regained? The Case for an Actor-Oriented Sociology of Development' 49 *European Review of Latin American and Caribbean Studies* (1990) 3.
40 M. Douglas, *How Institutions Think* (Routledge and Kegan Paul Ltd., 1987).
41 C. Smart, *Feminism and the Power of Law* (Routledge, 1989).
42 J. Eisenstein and H. Jacob, *Felony Justice: An Organisational Analysis of Criminal Courts* (Little, Brown and Company, 1977).
43 L. Vinjamuri and J. Snyder, 'Advocacy and Scholarship in the Study of International War Crime Tribunals and Transitional Justice' 7 *Annual Review of Political Science* (2004) 345 at 359.
44 Palmer, n.38 at 15; R.A. Wilson, *Writing History in International Criminal Trials* (Cambridge University Press, 2011) 109.

45 S. Walklate, 'Reframing Criminal Victimization: Finding a Place for Vulnerability and Resilience' 15(2) *Theoretical Criminology* (2011) 179 at 189.
46 C. Geertz, 'Thick Descriptions: Toward an Interpretive Theory of Culture' in C. Geertz (ed.), *The Interpretation of Cultures: Selected Essays* (Fontana Press, 1973) 3–30. See also K. McEvoy, 'Beyond Legalism: Towards a Thicker Understanding of Transitional Justice' 24 *Journal of Law and Society* (2007) 411; M. Coppedge, 'Thickening Thin Concepts and Theories: Combining Large-N and Small-N in Comparative Politics' 31 *Comparative Politics* (1999) 465.
47 Geertz, ibid., at 7.
48 Thus, drawing from stakeholder analysis as well as social theory; see for example R. Ramirez, 'Stakeholder Analysis and Conflict Management' in D. Buckles (ed.), *Cultivating Peace: Conflict and Collaboration in Natural Resource Management* (World Bank, 1999) 101–129; Long and Long, n.39.
49 Such an approach draws from organisation culture research, see C. Daymon, 'Culture Formation in a New Television Station: A Multi-Perspective Analysis' 11 *British Journal of Management* (2000) 121; M.W. Lewis and A.J. Grimes, 'Metatriangulation: Building Theory from Multiple Paradigms' 24(4) *Academy of Management Review* (1999) 672; D. Gioia and E. Pitre, 'Multiparadigm Perspectives on Theory Building' 15 *Academy of Management Review* (1990) 584.
50 R. Mawby and S. Walklate, *Critical Victimology* (Sage, 1994).
51 J. Dignan, *Understanding Victims and Restorative Justice* (Oxford University Press, 2005).
52 Mawby and Walklate, n.50 at 178–179.
53 *Idem.*
54 K.M. Clarke, *Fictions of Justice: The International Criminal Court and the Challenge of Legal Pluralism in Sub-Saharan Africa* (Cambridge University Press, 2009); E. Haslam, 'Law, Civil Society and Contested Justice' in M. Dembour and T. Kelly (eds.), *Paths to International Justice: Social and Legal Perspectives* (Cambridge University Press, 2007) 57–82; C. Douzinos, *The End of Human Rights: Critical Legal Thought at the Turn of the Century* (Hart Publishing, 2002).
55 Moffett, n.6 at 30.
56 UN Basic Principles, n.15.
57 Moffett, n.6; G. Mettraux, 'Victims' Participation in International Criminal Law' 8(1) *Journal of International Criminal Justice* (2010) 75; D. Shelton, *Remedies in International Human Rights Law* (2nd edn) (Oxford University Press, 2005).
58 T. Tyler, 'Procedural Justice, Legitimacy, and the Effective Rule of Law' 30 *Crime and Justice* (2003) 283.
59 T. Tyler, 'Social justice: Outcome and Procedure' 35(2) *International Journal of Psychology* (2000) 117; K. Leung and E.A. Lind, 'Procedural Justice and Culture: Effects of Culture, Gender, and Investigator Status on Procedural Preferences' 50(6) *Journal of Personality and Social Psychology* (1986) 1134; G. Leventhal, 'What Should be Done with Equity Theory' in K.J. Gergen et al. (eds.), *Social Exchange: Advances in Theory and Research* (Plenum, 1980); G. Leventhal, J. Karuza and W. Fry, 'Beyond Fairness: a Theory of Allocation Preferences' in G. Miluka (ed.), *Justice and Social Interaction* (Springer-Verlag, 1980) 167–218.
60 Tyler, n.59.
61 J. Shapland, 'Victims, the Criminal Justice System and Compensation' 24(2) *British Journal of Criminology* (1984) 136.
62 For a discussion on the contests concerning the meaning of victims' 'voice' see for example S. Robins, 'Towards a Victim-Centred Transitional Justice: Understanding the Needs of Families of the Disappeared in Postconflict Nepal' 5 *The International Journal of Transitional Justice* (2011) 75; T. Madlingozi, 'On Transitional Justice Entrepreneurs and the Production of Victims' 2 *Journal of Human Rights Practice* (2010) 208.

63 J. Wemmers, *Victims in the Criminal Justice System* (Kugler Publications, 1996); L. Musante, M.A. Gilbert and J. Thibaut, 'The Effects of Control on Perceived Fairness of Procedure and Outcome' 19 *Journal of Experimental Social Psychology* (1983) 223.
64 L. Mallinder, *Amnesty, Human Rights and Political Transitions: Bridging the Peace and Justice Divide* (Hart Publishing, 2008) 360–366.
65 S. Walklate, *Victimology: The Victim and the Criminal Justice Process* (Unwin Hyman, 1989) 133–136.
66 C. Lawther, 'Victims Needs and Dealing with the Past' in O. Lynch and J. Argomaniz (eds.), *Victims of Terrorism: A Comparative and Interdisciplinary Study* (Routledge, 2015) 31–58.
67 Moffett, n.6 at 28.
68 Wemmers, n.64; E.A. Lind and T.R. Tyler, *The Social Psychology of Procedural Justice* (Springer, 1988).
69 UN Office on Drugs and Crime, *Handbook on Justice for Victims*, 1999 at 9–10, describing secondary victimisation as 'the harm that may be caused to a victim by the investigation and prosecution of the case or by publicizing the details of the case in the media'.
70 UN Victims Declaration, n. 15, Principle 6(b).
71 M.C. Bassiouni, 'International Recognition of Victims' Rights' 6 *Human Rights Law Review* (2006) 203.
72 *Universal Declaration of Human Rights* ('UDHR'), UNGA Res. 217 A (III), 10 December 1948, Article 8; Council of Europe, *European Convention for the Protection of Human Rights and Fundamental Freedoms, as amended by Protocols Nos. 11 and 14* ('ECHR'), ETS 5, 4 November 1950, Article 13; UNGA, *International Covenant on Civil and Political Rights* ('ICCPR'), UNGA Resolution 2200A (XXI), 16 December 1966, Article 2(3); Organization of American States, *American Convention on Human Rights* ('ACHR'), 'Pact of San Jose', Costa Rica, 22 November 1969, Article 25.
73 UN Basic Principles, n. 15.
74 E. Kiza, C. Rathgeber and H. Rohne, *Victims of War: An Empirical Study on War Victimization and Victims' Attitudes towards Addressing Atrocities* (Hamburger Edition, 2006); Moffett, n.6 at 35.
75 While a distinction is being drawn here between the abstract and actual victims, this does not mean to imply that there is an authentic category of actual victims that can be objectively identified. Any understanding of victims will always occur through acts of interpretation. However, creating this distinction allows for an exploration of the discourse surrounding victim participation and the practical implications of this discourse.
76 R. Barker, *Legitimating Identities: The Self-Presentation of Rulers and Subjects* (Cambridge University Press, 2001); A. Thumula, B. Goold and I. Loader, 'A Tainted Trade? Moral Ambivalence and Legitimation Work in the Private Security Industry' 62 *British Journal of Sociology* (2011) 283.
77 Kendall and Nouwen, n.26 at 6.
78 Christie, n.10.
79 Fletcher, n.26; Kendall and Nouwen, n.26; McEvoy and McConnachie, n.26; Nouwen, n.33.
80 Barker, n.77 at 5.
81 Ibid.
82 A. Sarat and S. Scheingold (eds.), *The Cultural Lives of Cause Lawyers* (Cambridge University Press, 2008); A. Sarat and S. Scheingold (eds.), *Cause Lawyering and Social Movements* (Stanford University Press, 2006); A. Sarat and S. Scheingold (eds.), *The Worlds Cause Lawyers Make: Structure and Agency in Legal Practice* (Stanford University Press, 2005); S. Scheingold and A. Sarat, *Something to Believe In: Politics, Professionalism, and Cause Lawyering* (Stanford

University Press, 2004); A. Sarat and S. Scheingold (eds.), *Cause Lawyering and the State in a Global Era* (Oxford University Press, 2001); A. Sarat and S. Scheigold (eds.), *Cause Lawyering: Political Commitments and Professional Responsibilities* (Oxford University Press, 1998).

83 Palmer, n.38 at 59; see also J. Wemmers, 'Victims and the International Criminal Court: Evaluating the Success of the ICC with Respect to Victims' 16 *International Review of Victimology* (2009) 221.

84 D. Garland, *Punishment and Modern Society: A Study in Social Theory* (Oxford University Press, 1990) 10.

85 Geertz, n.44.

86 Palmer, n.38 at 54; Garland, n.85 at 210.

87 Palmer, n.38.

88 J. Doak, 'Enriching Trial Justice for Crime Victims in Common Law Systems: Lessons from Transitional Environments' 21(2) *International Review of Victimology* (2015) 139; L.A. Dickinson, 'The Promise of Hybrid Courts' 97 *American Journal of International Law (*2003) 295.

89 D. Beetham, *The Legitimation of Power*, P. Jones and A. Weale (eds.) (MacMillan, 1991) 15–16.

90 R. Rhodes and M. Bevir, 'Defending Interpretation' 5 *European Political Science* (2006) 69. See also H. Rombouts, 'Importance and Difficulties of Victim-Based Research in Post-Conflict Societies' 10 *European Journal of Crime, Criminal Law and Criminal Justice* (2002) 216.

91 K. McEvoy and L. McGregor (eds.), *Transitional Justice from Below: Grassroots Activism and the Struggle for Change* (Hart Publishing, 2007) 2–5.

92 I. Loader and A. Mulcahy, *Policing and the Condition of England: Memory, Politics and Culture* (Oxford University Press, 2003).

93 Palmer, n.38 at 16.

94 Rombouts, n.910.

95 See also for example J. Herman, *Local Voices in Internationalised Justice: The Experience of Civil Parties at the Extraordinary Chambers in the Courts of Cambodia* (Centre on Human Rights in Conflict, University of East London, May 2014); E. Hoven, M. Feiler and S. Scheibel, 'Victims in Trials of Mass Crimes: A Multi-Perspective Study of Civil Party Participation at the Extraordinary Chambers in the Courts of Cambodia' 3 *Cologne Occasional Papers on International Peace and Security Law* (2013); P. Pham et al., *After the First Trial: A Population-Based Survey on Knowledge and Perception of Justice and the Extraordinary Chambers in the Courts of Cambodia* (Human Rights Center, Berkeley, 2011); N. Stammel et al., *The Survivors' Voices: Attitudes on the ECCC, the Former Khmer Rouge and Civil Party Participation* (Berlin Center for the Treatment of Torture Victims, December 2010); P. Pham et al., *So We Will Never Forget: A Population-Based Survey on Attitudes About Social Reconstruction and the Extraordinary Chambers in the Courts of Cambodia* (Human Rights Center, Berkeley, 2009).

96 J. Thibaut and L. Walker, *Procedural Justice: A Psychological Analysis* (Erlbaum, 1975).

97 Y. Huo and T. Tyler, *Trust in the Law: Encouraging Public Cooperation with the Police and Courts* (Russell-Sage Foundation, 2002); Thibaut and Walker, ibid.

98 U. Orth, 'Secondary Victimization of Crime Victims by Criminal Proceedings' 15(4) *Social Justice Research* (2002) 313.

99 E.A. Lind et al., 'Procedure and Outcome Effects on Reactions to Adjudicated Resolution of Conflicts of Interests' 39 *Journal of Personality and Social Psychology* (1980) 643; S. LaTour, 'Determinants of Participant and Observer Satisfaction with Adversary and Inquisitorial Modes of Adjudication' 36(12) *Journal of Personality and Social Psychology* (1978) 1531.

100 Kutnjak Ivković and Hagan, n.8.

2 Victimology, victims' rights and the politicised victim

1. Introduction

This chapter provides some historical and theoretical context to the study of victims within the ECCC. It begins by briefly exploring the emergence of victimology as a distinct branch of criminology, and its development into a rich theoretical discipline. Although much of victimology theory originally developed within the context of Western democracies, acknowledging the similarities, as well as the differences, between 'ordinary' and 'exceptional' justice can allow transitional justice research to benefit from the rich theoretical base which has emerged within criminology and victimology in particular.[1] Indeed, victimology has increasingly been applied to the study of mass victimisation and ICL[2] and forms some of the theoretical underpinnings of this book.

The chapter then considers the various factors that have influenced the growth of an 'evolving universality of victims' rights'.[3] It begins by exploring the development of victims' services and rights within settled Western democracies. There are obvious differences between the experience of victimhood in cases of international[4] and domestic crime, including the extent of victimisation, the multitude of perpetrators, the ideological motivations behind victimisation, the organised and systemic involvement of state actors and the frequent impunity of perpetrators.[5] That said, when considering the ways in which victims are defined, treated and utilised by ICL practitioners, one can draw on particular themes from the experiences of domestic criminal proceedings to better understand the dynamics at work in ICL settings.[6] Furthermore, ICL institutions are operated by individuals whose beliefs about criminal justice and victims' rights have been informed by their experiences within their domestic jurisdictions. Indeed, as will be seen in subsequent chapters, legal traditions have played a significant role in shaping judicial and legal attitudes towards the civil party system at the ECCC. Thus, while there is a need to be aware of the distinct and aggravated nature of international crime,[7] an understanding of the development of victims' rights and policies within domestic legal jurisdictions provides valuable context to an exploration of victims' roles within international criminal proceedings.

The influence of human rights law on victims' rights is particularly examined. The framing of state-sponsored atrocity as both a breach of human rights law and a criminal act has allowed 'access to justice for victims' to become a central demand of human rights advocates,[8] blurring the distinction between victims of crimes by private actors and victims of crimes by a public actor.[9] As a result, human rights have informed both domestic responses to crime, and international responses to international crime. Indeed, the origins of transitional justice can be found within human rights movements,[10] and the role of international human rights in shaping victim-centred responses to atrocity is therefore highly relevant to an analysis of the role of victims within international criminal law.

Finally, the chapter traces the changing approaches towards victims within international criminal institutions, focusing on the tribunals established in the aftermath of World War II, the ad hoc tribunals for Rwanda and the former Yugoslavia, the permanent ICC, the STL and the Chambres Africaines Extraordinaires. The chapter concludes that despite the growing sense of moral and legal obligation towards victims, a gap remains between the 'imagined victim' as a motivating force for action[11] and the benefits victims of harm receive from official responses to their harm.

2. The growth of victimology

The origins of victimology, or the study of victims of crime,[12] have been credited to a number of eclectic scholars but particularly to Von Hentig and Mendelsohn, who are often described as the 'founding fathers' of victimology.[13] Both focused on notions of 'victim proneness'[14] and 'victim culpability'.[15] Their work formed the core of 'positivist' victimology,[16] an approach which focused on the identification of factors that could contribute to patterns of criminal victimisation,[17] as well as the determination of lifestyle choices and structural variables which could place individuals at high risk of victimisation.[18] Methodologically, positivists drew largely on crime surveys, which produced unprecedented amounts of crime data,[19] and challenged narratives about how, where and when victimisation occurred.[20] However, surveys could not explain why certain groups were more vulnerable to crime, and their reliance on victims being aware of and willing to report their victimisation meant much harm went unquantified.[21] Positivist victimology has since been critiqued for its reliance on a number of contestable assumptions, for example that a consensus exists about the aetiology, definition and consequences of crime or that the home is a safe place.[22] The separation of an analysis of crime from the workings of the state was also criticised for overlooking state crime[23] and depicting the state as the self-evidently legitimate punisher of crime and protector of victims.[24]

Such criticisms soon led to the development of alternative radical and critical victimological theories.[25] For example, the 1970s saw attention being drawn to categories of victim who had traditionally been neglected by criminal law.[26] While positivist victimology had been characterised by a separation of research and advocacy,[27] the two were merged by feminists who attempted to expose harms that occurred within the home,[28] the lack of protection available to victims of SGBV and the impact of sexism on experiences of victimisation.[29] Rising out of this activism, feminist victimologists sought to provide a gendered lens with which to examine crime, the law and the criminal justice system.[30] Other branches of radical victimology also emerged at this time, drawing from Marxist and left realist–based theories.[31] Responding to positivist victimology's failure to engage with relationships of power,[32] radical victimologists began to consider victims of 'political crime',[33] where the state is directly involved in the act of victimisation, and 'structural victimisation', where victimisation reflects the economic and power structures of a society.[34]

These developments have led to the recent emergence of state crime victimology.[35] Still in its infancy, state crime victimology appears to draw from two distinct approaches. Some have adopted a legalistic approach,[36] arguing in favour of establishing state illegality using domestic, international and human rights legal frameworks.[37] Within this framework, victims of state crime are identified as 'individuals or groups of individuals who have experienced economic, cultural, or physical harm, pain, exclusion, or exploitation because of tacit or explicit state actions or policies which violate law or generally defined human rights'.[38] Reflecting this focus on accountability, one emerging branch has been the victimology of international criminal justice,[39] which examines the circumstances and results of mass victimisation and the relationships victims have with accountability mechanisms.[40] While this legalistic approach demonstrates a definitional expansion of criminal victimisation, encompassing human rights, humanitarian law and international law, it also frames victimisation using legal definitions, thereby potentially overlooking harms which fall outside legal parameters. Other scholars have acknowledged this limitation, and have focused instead on the concept of social harms.[41] This approach frames state crime as 'state organisational deviance involving the violation of human rights', with human rights defined as morally valid claims made by virtue of being human,[42] and 'deviant' acts as those considered as contravening a widely accepted social rule.[43] Reflecting this focus on social harm, Hillyard et al. have argued for the abandonment of a criminal focus in favour of zemiology, the study of harm.[44] Such an approach considers harms beyond what would be considered 'criminal' and seeks to develop policies that move away from punishment and towards prevention.[45]

While radical victimology challenged many positivist assumptions around the role of the state and the nature of power, it failed to offer a framework for critiquing the victim/offender dichotomy and the image of the 'ideal' victim[46] which prevailed within victim-related policy and practice. In response to these continued stereotypes, a critical victimology emerged in the 1990s[47] as a framework for critiquing who has the power to apply the label 'victim' and what considerations influence that determination.[48] Highlighting 'hierarchies of victimhood',[49] which distinguish between those victims who are 'innocent'[50] or 'good'[51] and therefore 'worthy' and those that are not,[52] critical victimologists argue that who acquires the label of victim depends both on the individual's experiences and characteristics and, in part, on the reactions of others.[53] Highlighting the political dimension to victim legitimacy, they argue that the very term *victim* is not universal but is shaped by context[54] and is open to manipulation.[55] Although critical victimology developed in the context of Western domestic criminal justice systems, it has evolved as a framework used to explore state crime,[56] responses to atrocity[57] and the emergence of victim hierarchies and the 'imagined victim' within transitional justice contexts.[58]

This overview has demonstrated how the study of victims has exponentially expanded since its inception in the 1940s, from a positivist examination of victim characteristics to a diverse area of research encompassing multiple methodologies and theoretical approaches. This book seeks to make a contribution to victimology's growing focus on incidences of state crime and the role of victims within responses to such crimes. In doing so, it draws from radical and critical perspectives to explore how political and legal elites have produced and legitimised certain narratives of victimisation, how a diverse range of actors have shaped responses to those victimisations and what considerations and contexts have influenced those determinations.

3. Victims' rights, human rights and the 'imagined victim'

Since the 1950s, discourse and practice around victims' rights within domestic criminal justice systems have changed significantly. However, the ways in which victims' rights discourse and practice have emerged have varied amongst different 'legal families',[59] in part as a result of diverse understandings as to the appropriate role for victims within criminal law. While distinctions between states must be acknowledged, in broad terms, common law systems have tended to frame criminal trials as an adversarial contest between the state and the accused,[60] restricting the victims' role to that of a witness.[61] In his famous critique of common law systems, Christie argued that the common law and its host of criminal justice professionals stole the conflict from victims, leaving them 'reduced to the triggerer-off of the whole thing'.[62] However, as a result of sustained advocacy and research, there have been significant developments in victim-related policies since the end of World War II. The 1950s and 1960s saw the introduction of victim compensation across numerous jurisdictions,[63] while the 1970s and 1980s brought a growing awareness of secondary victimisation and the ways in which criminal justice systems were failing victims,[64] leading to the introduction of victim-related services and support groups.[65] The increased visibility and political currency this gave victims prompted the creation of victims' movements,[66] who were able to advocate for additional rights and services.[67] Many common law states now provide a variety of services to address victims' medical, psychological and financial needs[68] and have introduced victim charters, bills of rights and codes of conduct for criminal justice practitioners.[69] However, as non-binding documents, they highlight that increased victim-centric rhetoric does not necessarily translate into legally enforceable rights.[70] Similarly, although many jurisdictions have introduced victim impact statements,[71] they are often framed in such a way as to protect the traditional adversarial focus of the trial.[72] Outside the courtroom, restorative justice mechanisms, focusing on inclusivity, non-coerciveness and future-oriented accountability,[73] have been increasingly used as effective and cheaper alternatives to retributive focused disposals.[74] Mechanisms have expanded from 'predominantly victim-focused mediation to a comprehensive approach',[75] encompassing family group conferences, sentencing circles and citizen boards.[76] While heralded as offering a more participant-led reaction to crime, the emphasis on offender reintegration has led some commentators to doubt whether restorative justice mechanisms truly benefit victims.[77]

In contrast, civil and Islamic law jurisdictions have historically encompassed victim participatory rights, allowing them to claim compensation alongside criminal trials.[78] However, empirical research conducted within European continental (civil law) jurisdictions suggests that while many victims would like to play an active role in criminal prosecutions,[79] their access is sometimes restricted by legal professionals' reluctance to advise them of their rights or actively promote their interests.[80] The reason for this seems to be that legal professionals consider the victims' role to be primarily that of a witness or an 'assistant' to the prosecutor.[81] Thus, while the inquisitorial procedure of such systems allows for greater participation, victims may nonetheless find their rights restricted by the attitudes of those involved in the process. Outside the courtroom, victim service provisions have also developed within several European civil law countries.[82] In contrast to common law systems, where victim-orientated developments have been driven by activism and victimological study, these developments have been largely motivated by a number of Europe-wide initiatives from the Council of Europe and the European Union.[83] These transnational bodies have issued a number of binding and non-binding documents covering issues such as compensation, the position of the victim within the criminal justice system and victim assistance.[84]

This overview demonstrates that while victims' participatory rights vary amongst legal families, responses to crime are often viewed as the business of the state and legal actors. However, victims are increasingly able to access a range of services outside the courtroom and have gained in both political weight and visibility. These developments have been further enhanced and influenced by the emergence of human rights law, particularly as the divisions between human rights (concerned with individuals victimised by the state) and criminal law (concerned with crimes committed by private individuals) have become blurred.[85] As a result, moves to bestow similar human rights safeguards on victims of state and private actors are evident at a domestic and international level.[86]

The development of human rights norms requiring that victims' procedural and substantive rights be legally protected is reflected in a multitude of international instruments.[87] The UN's 1985 Declaration on the Basic Principles of Justice for Victims demonstrates an expansion of notions of victimhood,[88] outlining the rights of both 'Victims of Crime' and 'Victims of Abuses of Power' to respect and recognition, information, representation, privacy, protection, compensation and support.[89] Subsequent international instruments have built on the declaration's recognition of procedural and substantive justice, citing victims' rights to express their views, access equal and effective justice, obtain reparations and acquire information concerning violations and reparation mechanisms.[90] While

UN declarations are important statements of victims' rights, they are non-binding and are often drafted in purposefully vague language to appease the state actors involved in their creation.[91] However, some instruments have outlined specific victims' rights,[92] while others have included binding obligations, providing that victims *shall* be permitted to present their views and concerns.[93] While the latter provide rare examples of treaties requiring specific state action, their vague wording means states can interpret the provisions to suit their own legal context.[94]

The blurring of human rights and criminal law has been furthered by regional human rights courts such as the IACtHR and the ECtHR. Both courts have interpreted their conventions as providing for victims' rights within criminal proceedings.[95] They have found that under human rights law, gross violations of human rights require reparations and the investigation,[96] prosecution[97] and punishment of those responsible.[98] The courts have further found that impunity is a harm distinct from the original crime,[99] which also requires remedying.[100] They have also argued in favour of participation as a means of protecting victims' legitimate interests and ensuring effective proceedings,[101] even finding that the right to a fair trial may extend to victims.[102] However, they have failed to specify what that participation might look like, a restraint that is likely because of the varied legal systems of their member states.[103]

The combination of victim advocacy, victimological research and the merging of human rights and criminal law has demonstrably contributed to the emergence of a broader 'victims' rights' discourse, a significant, if often still largely theoretical, development.[104] However, despite significant developments in victims' rights and services, it is arguable that a gap exists between the value placed on the 'imagined victim' of crime as a political figure[105] and the meaningful benefits delivered to those who experience harm. The 'imagined victim' has only gained in rhetorical power, becoming a valuable figure for justifying and legitimising policy reform for those on both the political left and right.[106] As a result, victimisation has been increasingly seized by a criminal justice industry,[107] including not only politicians and policy makers but also pressure groups, charities, lawyers, insurance companies and the security industry.[108] Symbolic constructions of Christie's 'ideal victims' provide powerful stereotypes,[109] which can galvanise change but can also work to exclude less 'worthy' victims from victim-centric resources.[110] The offender/victim dichotomy which emerges from notions of 'ideal' victimhood has been further accentuated by a growing media interest and sensationalisation of victimhood, which increasingly casts victims as hero survivors and political figures in mainstream public discourse.[111] Thus, the definitions, visibility and corresponding benefits granted to those defined as a 'victim' are neither neutral nor independent from broader ideological, economic or political goals. As a result, and as noted within critical victimological literature, victim hierarchies emerge, with some more able to access political voice, rights and services than others.[112]

In contrast to the value placed on the imagined victims, actual victims can still struggle to access procedural and substantive justice. Indeed, even amongst those whose victimisations are recognised and legitimised within law and policy, it is questionable to what extent victim-centric developments have enhanced their experience of the criminal justice system. As a result of the commodification of victimhood, victims' rights and services may not reflect victims' needs and wishes, but rather 'other people's ideas of what victims want or should want'.[113] Victim-orientated policies appear to often be introduced without sufficient research and evaluation[114] or, as submitted by Sanders et al., *in spite* of evaluations.[115] This lack of evaluation and reflection is problematic: incorrect assumptions or inadequate knowledge may lead to inappropriate or misplaced service provision.[116] Indeed, studies at the domestic, regional and international levels have revealed that enhanced rights and services have frequently failed to prevent secondary victimisation, particularly amongst those who are already vulnerable.[117]

These sections have provided an overview of key developments in victim-centric research, discourse and practice within a number of domestic legal systems. As noted previously, there are obvious differences between the experience of victimhood in cases of international crime and victims of domestic crimes, and this is also true when considering the legal and theoretical responses to these victimisations. However, many of the trends identified earlier have been mirrored on the international criminal stage. In a similar vein to modern domestic criminal law, the creation of international(ised) criminal courts has facilitated the 'theft of the conflict'[118] away from victim communities and into the hands of politicians and legal professionals,[119] who have continuously shaped victims' access to justice through decisions as to what crimes to prosecute, what institutions to use for the process and what laws and procedures to use within them.[120] Thus, the critical victimological argument that definitions of and responses to victimisation will be influenced by a variety of contexts, actors and motivations remains highly applicable to an analysis of ICL.[121] The following section explores these issues within the context of a number of international criminal tribunals.

4. The rise of the victim in ICL

Justice as a faraway concept

Victims and their interests were not a prevalent concern of ICL in its early stages of development.[122] Rather, offender focused rationales for punishment such as retribution and deterrence were seen as the central goals, and to the extent that victims' interests were given consideration, they were assumed to coincide with these goals.[123] This can be evidenced in the approach taken in the post–World War II tribunals in Nuremberg[124] and Tokyo.[125] Neither the Nuremberg nor Tokyo tribunals provided any procedural rights to victims; indeed, the term *victim* did not appear in either statute.[126] The prosecution chose to primarily rely on documentary evidence,[127] expressing the belief that witness testimony might be simply too monstrous to be believed.[128] Nonetheless, some victims did participate as witnesses, with 14 victim-witnesses testifying at Nuremberg and 27 before Tokyo.[129] The experience was often fraught with re-traumatising incidents, with victims coming into contact with high-ranking Nazi and SS officers in the witness room[130] and facing interruptions, questions, requests to stay away from 'irrelevant' details and attacks on their credibility during their testimony.[131] With a lack of voice and strong risks of re-traumatisation, the tribunals cannot be considered as having delivered the quality of interpersonal treatment necessary to render procedural justice to victims.

In respect of substantive justice, although the tribunals provided some accountability, neither allowed for reparations; while the Nuremberg Charter provided for the restoration of stolen property, the tribunal failed to make any orders of the kind.[132] Perhaps unsurprisingly then, it seems that the tribunals failed to have much meaning for victims and their re-emerging communities.[133] In the words of Frederick Terna, a survivor of the concentration camps,

> [t]he Nuremberg trials were a distant happening, important for the abstract concept of international law, but did not touch us personally then.[134]

Danieli has held that this lack of impact not only prevented the tribunals from having meaning for survivors but also resulted in denial, self-blame and psychological trauma amongst those directly affected.[135] Further evidence of victim dissatisfaction can be found in the decades spent by victims seeking accountability and justice through other institutions, including the prosecution of Barbie, Touvier and Papon in France;[136] the Eichmann trial in Israel;[137] and the Women's Tribunal on Japanese Military Sexual Slavery,[138] all of which were to prove more responsive to their needs.

Despite the lack of victim-centricity in the tribunals' procedure and outcome, victims were frequently cited as justification for the punishment of individuals. The Nuremberg judges were beseeched by the French prosecutor to 'heed the voice of innocent blood crying for justice',[139] while the American chief prosecutor called on the tribunal to find the defendants guilty in order to ensure that 'justice may be done to . . . their countless victims'.[140] This language appeared to serve two purposes. First, it sought to equate the work of the tribunal with 'justice for victims', meaning a symbolic sense of justice through the punishment of individuals.[141] Second, the image of an innocent victim was used to justify retributive punishment and affirm the moral legitimacy of ICL, in general, and of the tribunals, in particular.[142] Thus, the 'imagined victims' were appropriated by the Allied powers and legal professionals to legitimise a retributive and politicised international criminal process, while the combination of common law procedures and the lack of a human rights or victims' rights discourse led to procedures which paid little heed to the needs or interests of victims.

Bearing witness

It was not until the end of the Cold War that ICL was utilised again as a response to atrocity. The ICTY was established by the UNSC in 1993, in response to the widespread violence taking place in the former Yugoslavia.[143] It was followed in 1994 by the ICTR, in response to the ongoing slaughter of Tutsis and moderate Hutu by the Hutu majority.[144] In the interim since the World War II tribunals, significant developments had occurred in the visibility of victims of crime.[145] As discussed earlier, victimological research had developed to include a multitude of methodologies and theoretical frameworks. The victims' rights movements within many common law states had resulted in enhanced service provision and voice for victims, and human rights law had received increased international recognition. A period of democratic transitions, beginning in Latin America and extending across Eastern Europe, Africa and Central America, had introduced more restorative conceptions of transitional justice, which were often characterised by a central role for victims.[146] There was also a desire amongst proponents of ICL to move away from the criticisms relating to the marginalisation of victims that had characterised the Nuremberg and Tokyo trials.[147]

In light of these developments, a number of states advocated for increased victim-centredness within the tribunals.[148] While common law procedures were adopted by both tribunals,[149] articles granting victims protection, support and restitution were included within the statutes.[150] Yet, in practice, protective measures often failed, with the revealing of victim identities in court leading to ostracisation,[151] threats, intimidation and even murder.[152] Within the courtrooms, the role of a witness was found to be 'ill-suited for the sort of expansive and nuanced story-telling so many witnesses yearned to engage in'.[153] Studies amongst victims who testified have suggested that the lawyers' use of adversarial examination techniques, such as cutting off witnesses when they deviated from the line of questioning,[154] challenging their testimony and attacking their credibility often contributed to secondary victimisation.[155] Many victims from Rwanda, in particular, expressed frustration at the adversarial methods used, which felt foreign to their own methods of conflict resolution.[156] Again, neither tribunal were equipped to provide reparations; although the trial chambers could make orders of restitution for victims of property theft,[157] victims could not initiate claims for them,[158] and the tribunals appeared unwilling to use their authority in this way.[159]

Studies into the perceptions of inhabitants in both the former Yugoslavia and Rwanda revealed a general lack of information about and satisfaction with the work of the tribunals.[160] In the case of the ICTY, perceptions have varied amongst the different ethnicities,[161] but overall many appear to consider the ICTY as unfair, both in terms of its decisions and its perceived lack of neutrality.[162] Other common criticisms from both populations have included the lack of accessibility to the tribunals,[163] the lack of a restorative justice focus and the relatively small number of persons prosecuted.[164] Nonetheless, the 'imagined victim' has featured heavily in the legitimising practices of the tribunals. This has been evident from their inception, as demonstrated for example by the language utilised by the US ambassador on the creation of the ICTY:

> [T]o the victims we declare by this action that your agony, your sacrifice, and your hope for justice have not been forgotten . . . the voices of the groups most victimized will be heard by the tribunal.[165]

Judges and lawyers have also cited the symbolic value of victims in their exploration of the purposes of punishment. The ICTY trial chamber has described the prosecution and punishment of perpetrators as being in 'recognition of the harm and suffering caused to victims',[166] while the chief prosecutor of the ICTR has spoken of the tribunal as constituting 'part of a truly global process of bringing justice to victims and survivors'.[167] Victims, therefore, continue to be utilised to legitimise justice processes, with their needs being assumed to coincide with the prosecution and punishment of perpetrators.[168] However, the common law procedures and retributive focus have meant that for the most part, victims have been considered an 'object matter or an instrument'[169] in the tribunal proceedings: justice is done in their name but without recognising them as individuals with needs and a legitimate interest in the process.[170]

Introducing participation and redress

The negative reactions of victims to the ad hoc tribunals, combined with the continued growth of victimology, human rights law and victims' rights, fulled calls for greater victim participation within international(ised) criminal courts.[171] Despite the negative reactions, proponents of increased victim-centredness continued to claim that courts' acknowledgement of victimisation could have a cathartic effect,[172] aid recovery from the psychological impact of victimisation, re-establish self-respect[173] and help victims regain control of their lives.[174] Such arguments signalled a definitive shift within international criminal discourse from the traditional retributive accused-focused justice towards a more restorative approach, with a greater focus on addressing the harm suffered by the victimised population.[175]

This change in discourse was reflected in the Rome Statute of the ICC. Ratified in 2002,[176] it created the first permanent ICL institution, as well as the first international(ised) criminal court to provide for the direct and active participation of victims. The ICC's procedural framework is the result of a complex compromise brokered between the 160 states and numerous international organisations who attended the negotiations which led to its statute.[177] As a result, it draws from civil, common and Islamic legal cultures,[178] while leaving a large amount of discretion to the judges in determining how best to balance the adversarial and inquisitorial elements.[179] In addition to balancing different legal traditions, the framework represents an attempt to address the criticisms levied at the ad hoc tribunals,[180] reflect the growth of alternative justice theories[181] and bring ICL in line with modern international standards on victims in criminal proceedings and human rights law.[182]

The court's Rules of Procedure and Evidence contain provisions for victim recognition, participation, protection and support,[183] and a trust fund has been created to administer reparations and generally assist victims.[184] For those recognised as victims,[185] the right to participate occurs predominantly through legal representation and involves the 'views and concerns' of the victims being presented and considered at stages of the proceedings, when the victims' personal interests are affected and the court deems it appropriate.[186] A high level of discretion is therefore left to the judges as to how participation should be implemented, and participation has been determined on a largely case-by-case basis.[187]

This has occasionally led to an expansion of victims' rights, for example through the decision to allow victims to lead and challenge evidence.[188] However, the discretionary element has led to inconsistencies, as different chambers appear to be influenced by their judges' legal backgrounds, experiences and personal views on the purpose and usefulness of victim participation.[189] This is problematic as it creates inequality amongst victims and infringes the defendants' right to legal certainty.[190] Furthermore, limited resources have made incorporating thousands of victims' views into the ICC's proceedings almost impossible. Staff and external observers have noted that current levels of outreach, care and support are inadequate, while members of the prosecution, defence and judiciary have raised queries as to the impact of victim participation on fair-trial rights.[191]

Concerns over these issues, as well as over the inefficiency of victim participation, have resulted in a number of streamlining measures being introduced. Victims are now organised into groups with common representation, the court has introduced collective applications[192] and participation rights are unlikely to be granted if a similar interest has already been raised.[193] These measures raise questions about whether victims are really being granted meaningful participation or if their role has been reduced to a more symbolic one, used as an instrument for condemnatory purposes.[194] Indeed, only 4 per cent of the victim applicants were given the opportunity to participate in the Lubanga trial,[195] and former prosecutor Christine Chung has described the system as fundamentally unworkable.[196] There is validity in the argument that without common representation, the large numbers of victims participating would have a negative impact on the court's expediency and efficiency. However, this highlights the disjuncture between the needs of a court system and the interests of victims,[197] while the limited influence granted to victims demonstrates the power dynamics at play in international courts.[198] Thus, while the ICC's provisions have been referred to as a 'high water mark'[199] by placing victims at the 'heart of international criminal justice',[200] the effectiveness of the system, both for victims and for the ICC itself, remains contested by academics and practitioners alike.[201]

The ICC has the ability to grant reparations and has done so in three cases so far, ordering both collective and individual reparations.[202] While the provision of reparations has been praised as an innovative development, the system has also been criticised for taking too long to implement (five years passed between the first decision in Lubanga and implementation on the ground);[203] for having a 'perpetrator centred' vision[204] which links reparations to the charges, thus excluding certain harms (particularly SGBV);[205] and for blurring the line between reparation and more general forms of assistance, thereby diluting victims' rights to reparation.[206] The reliance on the trust fund to deliver reparations and the increased focus on delivering 'transformative reparations' which address structural inequalities within states have also been critiqued for shifting the focus away from victims' wishes and for failing to redress the harm of those who suffered most.[207] These critiques go beyond the solely academic; 47 victims withdrew their participation in the Ruto and Sang case in 2013 (before it collapsed) on the grounds that collective reparations would benefit the same communities that had contributed to their victimisation,[208] demonstrating distrust amongst victims that the ICC is able to respond appropriately to their harm. Indeed, inadequate consultation on victims' wishes has led to the ICC being rejected by numerous victims and civil society organisations within Uganda.[209]

While the ability of the ICC to deliver meaningful procedural and substantive justice has been critiqued, the 'imagined victim' has only grown in importance in the legitimisation work that is conducted within and around the ICC. Victims have been cited as the court's raison d'étre,[210] while the statute recognises that 'during this century millions of children, women and men have been victims of unimaginable atrocities that deeply shock the conscience of humanity'.[211] Civil society, UN officials and lawyers alike have invoked 'the victims' to justify the ICC's work and even as a means of shielding it from criticism and challenges to its legitimacy.[212] For example, when faced with the claim that the ICC targets the African continent exclusively, the prosecutor responded,

> If we are thinking about the victims of these crimes, the victims of these atrocities who are also vulnerable African victims, then we would not think about targeting Africans. We will be thinking about, working for and supporting the victims of these crimes.[213]

In short, the moral currency of victimhood is firmly established as a means of legitimising the acts of international(ised) criminal courts.[214] This use of victims to deflect criticism is particularly effective not only because it is impossible for third parties to argue against those who act on behalf of the 'imagined victims' but also because the 'imagined victim' cannot argue either; as noted by Kendall and Nouwen, an abstraction cannot speak for itself.[215] In the event that specific victims do disagree with the work done in their name, the 'imagined victim' can be utilised to counter those criticisms.[216] Thus, it seems that despite the significant developments in victim-centrism at the ICC when compared to previous tribunals, there continues to be a significant gap between the rhetoric of delivering 'justice to victims' and the actual procedural and substantive justice offered by the institution.[217]

It is worth briefly noting that the establishment of the permanent ICC has not prevented the creation of additional international(ised) criminal courts. While no further courts have followed the ad hoc model, a number of 'hybrid' institutions have been created to respond to specific periods of violence.[218] Two of these are of particular note to this chapter because of their involvement of victims. The STL, created in 2006, has followed the ICC's approach, allowing victims to express their views and concerns at stages of the proceedings determined to be appropriate by the judges in a manner that is not inconsistent with the rights of the accused.[219] As of August 2017, 72 individuals were participating in the *Ayyash et al.* case, where they are represented as a single group.[220] More recently, the Chambres Africaines Extraordinaires (CAE) in Senegal has allowed the victims of Hissène Habré to participate as civil parties[221] and, in 2017, awarded tens of thousands of dollars in compensation to Habré's victims. While these developments are, in part, reflective of the hybrid nature of the courts – both Senegal and Lebanon's legal systems allow for civil party participation – they also reflect the growing trend towards victim-centric provisions within international(ised) criminal courts. Indeed, the CAE explicitly built and expanded on the jurisprudence of the ECCC when establishing its victim participation system.[222]

This section has explored how the growth of victimology, human rights law and victims' rights advocacy has also influenced the increased victim-orientation within ICL discourse and practice. The influence of international norms can be seen in the gradual introduction of more restorative and reparative conceptions of justice within the courts, leading to enhanced rights of participation, protection and reparation. However, the continued focus on the prosecution of individuals has meant that in practice, victims have continued to find themselves sidelined by legal elites who claim ownership over their conflicts.[223]

5. Conclusion

This chapter has sought to provide a historical and theoretical backdrop to this book's analysis by exploring the growth of diverse victimological theories, and the rise in victim-centric rhetoric and practice within domestic, regional and international criminal justice systems. By tracing these developments, it has highlighted how the victims' rights movement, victimology, human rights and transitional justice are united by underlying themes of victim-centrality and increasing demands for states to be responsive to victims' needs. However, the four are also united by the reality that victimhood is 'produced, perceived and interpreted' by a variety of invested actors,[224] who have themselves been influenced by a range of political, legal, social and economic factors, pursuing a variety of goals.

One strong critique that has emerged within the literature is that international crimes are often viewed as being first and foremost a breach of an abstract legal order, with the wrong committed against particular individuals being of secondary importance. Indeed, while the 'imagined victim' has developed as a key figure in the legitimating practices of ICL's proponents, courts and tribunals have found their procedures and outcomes subject to criticism from commentators and victim populations alike. Such reactions bring to mind the critique highlighted earlier: that the victims' movement has not been based on victims' interests but has been instrumentalised in the pursuit of other goals. The following chapters of this book consider this critique within the context of the ECCC, analysing how the ECCC and the role of victims within it have been both moulded by specific contexts and actors and considering the impact that these actors and contexts have had on the ability of the ECCC to deliver justice (both procedural and substantive) to victims. The following chapter begins this analysis, detailing the ways in which political considerations shaped the court's creation, structure, jurisdiction and procedures.

Notes

1 K. McEvoy and K. McConnachie, 'Victims and transitional Justice: Voice, Agency and Blame' 22 *Social and Legal Studies* (2013) 489.

2 D.C. Spencer and S. Walklate, 'Themes and Issues in Critical Victimology' in D.C. Spencer and S. Walklate (eds.), *Reconceptualizing Critical Victimology: Interventions and Possibilities* (Lexington Books, 2016) xv–xvi.
3 R. Aldana-Pindell, 'An Emerging Universality of Justiciable Victims' Rights in the Criminal Process to Curtail Impunity for State-Sponsored Crimes' 26(3) *Human Rights Quarterly* (2004) 605.
4 That is genocide, war crimes and crimes against humanity.
5 M.S. Groenhuijsen and A. Pemberton, 'Genocide, Crimes against Humanity and War Crimes: A Victimological Perspective on International Criminal Justice' in R. Letschert et al. (eds.), *Victimological Approaches to International Crimes: Africa* (Intersentia, 2011) 9–34.
6 J. Doak, 'Enriching Trial Justice for Crime Victims in Common Law Systems: Lessons from Transitional Environments' 21(2) *International Review of Victimology* (2015) 139.
7 E. Posner and A. Vermeule, 'Transitional Justice as Ordinary Justice' 117(3) *Harvard Law Review* (2004) 761. See also D. Gray, 'An Excuse-Centered Approach to Transitional Justice' 74 *Fordham Law Review* (2005) 2621.
8 L.E. Fletcher and H.M. Weinstein, 'Transitional Justice and the "plight" of Victimhood' in C. Lawther et al. (eds.) *Research Handbook on Transitional Justice* (Elgar, 2017) 244–266 at 247.
9 N. Krtiz (ed.), *Transitional Justice: How Emerging Democracies Reckon with Former Regimes* (US Institute of Peace, 1995).
10 P. Arthur, 'How "Transitions" Reshaped Human Rights: A Conceptual History of Transitional Justice' 31 *Human Rights Quarterly* (2009) 321.
11 Fletcher and Weinstein, n.8 at 244.
12 B. Spalek, *Crime Victims: Theory, Policy and Practice* (Palgrave Macmillan, 2006) 1.
13 D.L. Rothe and D. Kauzlarich, 'A Victimology of State Crime' in D.L. Rothe and D. Kauzlarich (eds.), *Towards a Victimology of state Crime* (Routledge, 2014) 3. See for example H. Von Hentig, *The Criminal and His Victim* (Yale University Press, 1948); B. Mendelsohn, 'Rape in Criminology' *Giustizia Penale* (1940).
14 S. Walklate, *Imagining the Victim of Crime* (McGraw-Hill, 2006) 31.
15 R. Elias, *The Politics of Victimization – Victims, Victimology and Human Rights* (Oxford University Press, 1986) 17. See Von Hentig, n. 13 and B. Mendelsohn, 'Une nouvelle branche de la science bio-psycho-sociale, la victimologie' *Etudes Internationales de Psycho-Sociologie Criminelle* (1956).
16 Ibid.
17 R. Mawby and S. Walklate, *Critical Victimology* (Sage, 1994) 10.
18 D. Miers, 'Positivist Victimology: A Critique Part 1' 1 *International Review of Victimology* (1989) 1 at 3; M. Hindelang et al., *Victims of Personal Crime: An Empirical Foundation for a Theory of Personal Victimization* (MA Ballinger, 1978).
19 P. Rock, *Helping Victims of Crime: The Home Office and the Rise of the Victim in England and Wales* (Clarendon Press, 1990); P. Rock, *A View from the Shadows: The Ministry of the Solicitor General of Canada and the Justice for Victims of Crime Initiative* (Clarendon Press, 1986); M. Lipsky and D. Olson, *Commission Politics: The Processing of Racial Crisis in America* (Transaction, 1977).
20 H. Genn, 'Multiple Victimization' in M. Maguire and J. Pointing (eds.), *Victims of Crime* (Open University Press, 1988) 90–100; D. Smith and J. Gray, *Police and People in London: the PSI Report, Vol 1* (Gower, 1985).
21 L. Wolhuter, N. Olley and D. Denham, *Victimology: Victimization and Victims' Rights* (Routledge, 2009) 17; S. Green, 'Crime, Victimization and Vulnerability' in S. Walklate (ed.), *Handbook of Victims and Victimology* (Routledge, 2007) 91–119.
22 Wolhuter, Olley and Denham, ibid., at 16.

23 D. Matza, *Delinquency and Drift* (Wiley, 1964).
24 K. McEvoy and B Gormally, '"Seeing" Is Believing: Positivist Terrorology, Peacemaking Criminology, and the Northern Ireland Peace Process' 8(1) *Critical Criminology* (1997) 9 at 11.
25 E.A. Fattah, 'Victims and Victimology: The Facts and the Rhetoric' 1(1) *International Review of Victimology* (1989) 43.
26 W. G. Doerner and S. P. Lab, *Victimology* (3rd edn) (Anderson, 2002); M. Freeman (ed.), *Overcoming Child Abuse: A Window on a World Problem* (Aldershort, 2000); A. Sarat, 'Vengeance, Victims and the Identities of Law' 6(2) *Social and Legal Studies* (1997) 163; M. Maguire, 'The Needs and Rights of Victims of Crime' 14 *Crime and Justice* (1991) 363.
27 Mawby and Walklate, n.17 at 10.
28 J. Doak, *Victims' Rights, Human Rights and Criminal Justice: Reconceiving the Role of Third Parties* (Hart Publishing, 2008) 8.
29 R. Barbaret, 'Feminist Victimology' in B.S. Fisher and S.P. Lab (eds.), *Encyclopaedia of Victimology and Crime Prevention* (SAGE Publications, 2010) 407–409; C. Renzetti, 'Feminist Perspectives on Victimization' in J.K. Wilson (ed.), *The Praeger Handbook of Victimology* (Greenwood Press, 2009) 96.
30 Renzetti, ibid., at 96.
31 Wolhuter, Olley and Denham, n.21 at 20–23; Spalek, n.12 at 40–42.
32 Walklate, n.14.
33 S. Schafer, *Victimology: The Victim and His Criminal* (Reston Publishing Company, 1977).
34 W. Nagel, 'Structural Victimization' 2 *International Journal of Criminology* (1975) 99.
35 D. Kauzlarich, R.A. Matthews and W.J. Miller, 'Towards a Victimology of State Crime' 10 *Critical Criminology* (2001) 173 at 176.
36 *Legalism* can be defined as a process which separates legal analysis from politics and from other social science disciplines, resulting in an attachment to legal standards. See J. Shklar, *Legalism: Law, Morals, and Political Trials* (Harvard University Press, 1964); K. McEvoy, 'Beyond Legalism: Towards a Thicker Understanding of Transitional Justice' 24 *Journal of Law and Society* (2007) 411.
37 R.A. Matthews and D. Kauzlarich, 'State Crimes and State Harms: A Tale of Two Definitions Frameworks' 48 *Cime, Law and Social Change* (2007) 43; A. Chouliaras, 'The Victimological Concern as the Driving Force in the Quest for Justice for State-Sponsored International Crimes' in R. Letschert et al. (eds.), *Victimological Approaches to International Crimes: Africa* (Intersentia, 2011) 35–64 at 44–45.
38 Kauzlarich, Matthews, and Miller, n.35 at 176.
39 R. Jamieson and K. McEvoy, 'State Crime by Proxy and Juridical Othering' 45 *British Journal of Criminology* (2005) 504, 505.
40 L. Moffett, *Justice for Victims at the International Criminal Court* (Routledge, 2014); R. Letschert et al. (eds.), *Victimological Approaches to International Crimes: Africa* (Intersentia, 2011); G. Musila, *Rethinking International Criminal Law: Restorative Justice and the Rights of Victims in the International Criminal Court* (Lambert Academic Publishing, 2010); K. Tibori-Szabó and M. Hirst, *Victim Participation in International Criminal Justice* (T.M.C. Asser Press, 2017).
41 P.J. Green and T. Ward, 'State Crime, Human Rights, and the Limits of Criminology' 27 *Social Justice* (2000) 101; P. Green and T. Ward, *Governments, Violence and Corruption* (Pluto Press, 2004) 7–8.
42 Ibid.
43 Ibid.; Chouliaras, n.37 at 42–43.
44 P. Hillyard et al. (eds.), *Beyond Criminology: Taking Harm Seriously* (Pluto Press, 2004).

45 Chouliaras, n. 37 at 40–41.
46 N. Christie, 'The Ideal Victim' in E Fattah (ed.), *From Crime Policy to Victim Policy* (St. Martin's Press, 1986) 17–30.
47 Mawby and Walklate, n.17
48 D. Miers, 'Positivist Victimology: A Critique Part 2' 1(3) *International Review of Victimology* (1990) 219; J.A. Holstein and G. Miller, 'Rethinking Victimization: An Interactionist Approach to Victimology' 3 *Symbolic Interaction* (1990).
49 E. Carrabine et al., *Criminology: A Sociological Introduction* (Routledge, 2004).
50 K. McEvoy and K. McConnachie, 'Victimology in Transitional Justice: Victimhood, Innocence and Hierarchy' 9(5) *European Journal of Criminology* (2012) 527, 531–532.
51 T. Madlingozi, 'Good Victims, Bad Victims: Apartheid's Beneficiaries, Victims and the Struggle for Social Justice', in W. Le Roux and L. Van Maerle (eds.), *Memory and the Legacy of Apartheid* (Pretoria University Press, 2004).
52 C. Tilly, *Credit and Blame* (Princeton University Press, 2008), 94.
53 P. Rock, 'On Becoming a Victim', in C. Hoyle and R. Young (eds.), *New Visions of Crime Victims* (Hart, 2002); A.M. McAlinden, 'Deconstructing Victim and Offender Identities in Discourses on Child Sexual Abuse: Hierarchies, Blame and the Good/Evil Dialectic' 54(2) *British Journal of Criminology* (2014) 180;
54 Miers, n.1
55 J. Dignan, *Understanding Victims and Restorative Justice* (Oxford University Press, 2005).
56 Kauzlarich, Matthews, and Miller, n.35.
57 Letschert, n.40.
58 For example J. Van Wijk, 'Who Is the Little Old Lady of International Crimes? Nils Christie's Concept of the Ideal Victim Reinterpreted' 19(2) *International Review of Victimology* (2013).
59 H.P. Glenn, *Comparative Legal Families and Comparative Legal Traditions, The Oxford Handbook of Comparative Law* (Oxford University Press, 2006) 421–440.
60 Moffett, n.40.
61 Dignan, n.55 at 65.
62 N. Christie, 'Conflict as Property' 17(1) *British Journal of Criminology* (1977) 1 at 3.
63 D. Miers, 'Looking beyond Great Britain: The Development of Criminal Injuries Compensation' in S. Walklate (ed.), *Handbook of Victims and Victimology* (Routledge, 2007) 337–362; I. Waller, 'International Standards, National Trail Blazing and the Next Steps' in M. Maguire and J. Pointing (eds.), *Victims of Crime: A New Deal?* (Open University Press, 1988); M Fry, *Arms of the Law* (1st edn) (Gollancz, 1951).
64 J. Shapland and D. Cohen, 'Facilities for Victims: The Role of the Police and the Courts' 28 *Criminal Law Review* (1987); J. Shapland, J. Willmore and P. Duff, *Victims in the Criminal Justice System* (Gower, 1985); M. Maguire, 'Victims' Needs and Victim Services: Indications from Research' 10 *Victimology* (1985) 539; G. Chambers and A. Millar, *Investigating Sexual Assault* (HMSO, 1983); M. Maguire and T. Bennett, *Burglary in a Dwelling* (Heinemann, 1982); R. Sparks et al., *Surveying Witnesses* (John Wiley, 1977).
65 B. Williams and H. Goodman, 'The Role of the Voluntary Sector' in S. Walklate (ed.), *Handbook of Victims and Victimology* (Routledge, 2007) 240.
66 Spalek, n.12 at 20–21.
67 T. Booth and K. Carrington, 'A Comparative Analysis of the Victim Policies Across the Anglo-speaking World' in S. Walklate (ed.), *Handbook of Victims and Victimology* (Routledge, 2007) 380–417.
68 Miers, n.63 at 355–356.
69 R. Mawby, 'Public Sector Services and the Victim of Crime' in S. Walklate (ed.), *Handbook of Victims and Victimology* (Routledge, 2007) 209–240.

70 S. Walklate, 'Victims, Policy and Delivery' in S. Walklate (ed.), *Handbook of Victims and Victimology* (2007) 204.
71 C. Hoyle, R. Morgan and A. Sanders, *The Victim's Charter – An Evaluation of Pilot Projects' Home Office Research, Development and Statistics Directorate, Research Findings 107* (UK Home Office, 1999).
72 J. Doak, *Victims' Rights, Human Rights and Criminal Justice: Reconceiving the Role of Third Parties* (Hart Publishing, 2008) 16. That said, some have expressed concern as to the impact on the rights of the accused; see Spalek, n.12 at 124.
73 J. Dignan, 'The Victim in Restorative Justice' in S. Walklate (ed.), *Handbook of Victims and Victimology* (Routledge, 2007) 310; D.W. Van Ness and K.H. Strong, *Restorative Justice: An Introduction to Restorative Justice* (3rd edn) (LexisNexis/Anderson Publishing, 2006) 48–50; I. Bueno, 'The Colombian Conflict and Restorative Justice' in D. L. Rothe and D. Kauzlarich (eds.), *Towards a Victimology of State Crime* (Routledge, 2014) 206; L. Walgrave, 'Restorative Justice: An Alternative for Responding to Crime?' in O.B. Shoham and M. Kett (eds.), *International Handbook of Penology and Criminal Justice* (CRC Press, 2008) 613–691.
74 Dignan, ibid.
75 L. Kurki, 'Restorative and Community Justice in the United States' 27 *Crime and Justice* (2000) 235, 239.
76 Fletcher and Weinstein, n. 8.
77 A. Morris and L. Gelsthorpe, 'Re-visioning Men's Violence against Female Partners' 39(3) *Howard Journal of Criminal Justice* (2000) 412.
78 J. Hodgson, *French Criminal Justice: A Comparative Account of the Investigation and Prosecution of Crime in France* (Hart Publishing, 2005); M. Brienen and E. Hoegen, *Victims of Crime in 22 European Criminal Justice Systems* (Wolf Legal Productions, 2000).
79 H. Kury and M. Kaiser, 'The Victim's Position within the Criminal Proceedings – An Empirical Study' in G. Kaiser, H. Kury and H.J. Albrecht (eds.), *Victims and Criminal Justice: Legal Protection, Restitution and Support* (Max-Planck Institute for Foreign and International Law, 1991) 579–628.
80 J. Doak, 'Victims' Rights in Criminal Trials: Prospects for Participation' 32(2) *Journal of Law and Society* (2005) 294; I. Bacik, C. Maunsell and S. Grogan, *The Legal Process and Victims of Rape* (Dublin Rape Crisis Centre, 1998) for similar findings in common law jurisdictions.
81 Brienen and Hoegen, n.78; Bacik, Maunsell and Grogan, ibid.; E. Erez and E. Bienkowska, 'Victim Participation in Proceedings and Satisfaction with Justice in the Continental Systems: The Case of Poland' 21 *Journal of Criminal Justice* (1993) 47 at 50.
82 J. Doak, 'The Victim and the Criminal Process: An Analysis of Recent Trends in Regional and International Tribunals' 23(1) *Legal Studies* (2003) 1.
83 Doak, n.72 at 32–33.
84 See for example *Council Framework Decision 2001/220/JHA*, European Union, 15 March 2001; *Council Directive 2004/80/EC*, European Union, 29 April 2003.
85 This has been reflected in judicial decision making and through policy making, where human rights are no longer seen as solely concerned with the vertical relationship between states and individuals. Doak, n.72, n.83.
86 J. Doak, 'Participatory Rights for Victims of Crime: In Search of International Consensus' 15(1) *Canadian Criminal Law Review* (2011) 43.
87 F. Klug, 'Human Rights and Victims' in E. Cape, *Reconcilable Rights? Analysing the Tension between Victims and Defendants* (Legal Action Group, 2004) 111–124.
88 Doak, n.72 at 24.

89 *UN Declaration of Basic Principles of Justice for Victims of Crime and Abuse of Power*, UNGA Res. 40/34, 29 November 1985.
90 UNOHCHR, *Updated Set of Principles for the Protection and Promotion of Human Rights through Action to Combat Impunity*, UN Doc. E/CN.4/2005/102/Add.1, 18 February 2005; *UN Basic Principles and Guidelines on the Right to a Remedy and Reparation for Victims of Gross Violations of International Human Rights Law and Serious Violations of International Humanitarian Law*, UNGA Res. 60/147, 16 December 2005.
91 For example the *UN Basic Principles for the Treatment of Prisoners*, UNGA Res. 45/111, 14 December 1990; *UN Standard Minimum Rules for Non-Custodial Measures*, UNGA Res 45/110, 14 December 1990; *Resolution on Children as Victims and Perpetrators*, Ninth UN Congress on the Prevention of Crime and the Treatment of Offenders, UN Doc. A/CONF.169/16, 29 April–8 May 1995; *UN Principles on the Effective Investigation and Documentation of Torture and Other Cruel, Inhuman or Degrading Treatment or Punishment*, UNGA Res. 55/89, 4 December 2000; *Vienna Declaration on Crime and Justice: Meeting the Challenges of the 21st Century* A/CONF.187/4, 15 April 2000.
92 UN Office on Drugs and Crime, *Handbook on Justice for Victims*, 1999 at 62 and 74.
93 *Convention against Transnational Organised Crime*, UNGA 55/25, 15 November 2000.
94 Doak, n.82.
95 Aldana-Pindell, n.3.
96 *Velasquez-Rodriguez v. Honduras,* Judgment, IACtHR, (Ser. C) No. 4, 29 July 1988 at 174.
97 See for example *Blake v. Guatemala*, Judgment (Merits), IACtHR, 24 January 1998, paras 96–97; *Aydin v. Turkey*, Judgment, ECtHR, App. No. 23178/94, 25 September 1997; *Aksoy v. Turkey*, Judgment, ECtHR, App. No. 21987/93, 18 December 1996.
98 Moffett, n.40 at 44.
99 Impunity Principles, n.90.
100 *Moiwana Community v. Suriname*, Preliminary Objections, Merits, Reparations and Costs, IACtHR, Series C, No. 124, 15 June 2005; *Plan de Sánchez Massacre v. Guatemala*, Merits, Reparations and Costs, IACtHR, Series C, No. 116, 19 November 2004; *Salman v. Turkey*, Judgment, ECtHR, App. No. 21986/93, 27 June 2000; *Timurtus v. Turkey*, Judgment, ECtHR, App. No. 23531/94, 13 June 2000.
101 *Bazorkina v. Russia*, ECtHR, App. No. 69481/01, 27 June 2006; *Jordan v. United Kingdom*, ECtHR, App. No. 24746/94, 4 May 2001.
102 *Perez v. France*, ECtHR, App. No. 47287/99, 12 February 2004 at 67; *Villagran Morales et al. v. Guatemala*, IACtHR, Judgment, 19 November 1999 at 227.
103 B. McGonigle Leyh, *Procedural Justice? Victim Participation in International Criminal Proceedings* (Intersentia, 2011).
104 Doak, n.73
105 Walklate, n.14.
106 P. Rock, 'On Becoming a Victim' in C. Hoyle and R. Young (eds.), *New Visions of Crime and Victims* (Hart Publishing, 2002) 1–22.
107 R. Elias, *Victims Still: The Political Manipulation of Crime Victims* (Sage, 1993).
108 R.L. Heilbroner, *The Nature and Logic of Capitalism* (WW Norton, 1985).
109 P. Ramsay, 'Overcriminalization as Vulnerable Citizenship' 13(2) *New Criminal Law Review* (2010) 262; L. Zedner, 'Victims' in M. Maguire, R. Morgan and R. Reiner (eds.), *The Oxford Handbook of Criminology* (3rd edn) (Oxford University Press, 2002) 428–448; A. Ashworth, 'Victims' Rights, Defendants'

Rights and Criminal Procedure' in A. Crawford and J. Goodey (eds.), *Integrating a Victim Perspective within Criminal Justice* (Ashgate, 2000) 185–204.

110 Christie, n. 46.

111 J. Tulloch, *One Day in July: Experiencing 7/7* (Little Brown, 2006); C. Valier, *Crime and Punishment in Contemporary Culture* (Routledge, 2004).

112 Carrabine, et al., n.49 at 117.

113 Shapland, Willmore and Duff, n.64 at 2.

114 J. Shapland, 'Monitoring Victim Needs and Victim Programmes' in A. Alvazzi del Frate, U. Zvekic and J. Van Dijk (eds.), *Understanding Crime: Experiences of Crime and Crime Control*, Acts of the International Conference, Rome, 18–20 November 1992 (UNICRI, 1992) 241–250.

115 A. Sanders et al., 'Victim Impact statements: Don't Work, Can't Work' *Criminal Law Review* (June 2001) 447.

116 P. Dunn, 'Matching Service Delivery to Need' in S. Walklate (ed.), *Handbook of Victims and Victimology* (Routledge, 2007) 255–282.

117 M. Burton, R. Evans and A. Sanders, 'Vulnerable and Intimidation Witnesses and the Adversarial Process in England and Wales' 11(1) *The International Journal of Evidence and Proof* (2007) 1; P. Dunn and E. Shepherd, 'Oral Testimony from the Witness's Perspective – Psychology and Forensic Considerations' in A. Heaton-Armstrong et al., *Witness Testimony: Psychological, Investigative and Evidential Perspectives* (Oxford University Press, 2006); B. Hamlyn et al., 'Are Special Measures Working? Evidence from Surveys of Vulnerable and Intimidated Witnesses' *Home Office Research Study 283* (UK Home Office, 2004); E. Newton 'A Study of the Policies and Procedures Implemented by the Probation Service with Respect to Victims of Serious Crime' 2(1) *British Journal of Community Justice* (2003) 25; G. Rogers, 'Provision of Post-sentence Advice to Victims of Serious Crime: Perceptions in One British Probation Service' 1(4) *Crime Prevention and Community Safety: An International Journal* (1999); A. Crawford and J. Enterkin, 'Victim Contact Work in the Probation Service: Paradigm Shift or Pandora's Box?' 41 *British Journal of Criminology* (2001) 707.

118 Christie, n.62.

119 McEvoy and McConnachie, n.50.

120 S. Robins, 'Transitional Justice as an Elite Discourse' 44(1) *Critical Asian Studies* (2012) 3; C. Etcheson, *Retribution and Reconciliation: Healing What Ails Cambodia* (Project Report to the US Institute of Peace, October 2002); R. Lee (ed.), *The International Criminal Court: The Making of the Rome Statute-Issues, Negotiations, Results* (Kluwer Law International, 1999).

121 C. Picker, 'International Law's Mixed Heritage: A Common/Civil Law Jurisdiction' 41 *Vanderbilt Journal of Transnational Law* (2008); R. Christensen 'Getting to Peace by Reconciling Notions of Justice: The Importance of Considering Discrepancies Between Civil and Common Legal Systems in the Formation of the International Criminal Court' 6 *UCLA Journal of International Law and Foreign Affairs* (2004) 391.

122 C. McCarthy, 'Victim Redress and International Criminal Justice: Competing Paradigms, or Compatible Forms of Justice?' 10 *Journal of International Criminal Justice* (2012) 351.

123 R.E. Barnett, 'Restitution: A New Paradigm of Criminal Justice' 87 *Ethics* (1977) 279.

124 *Agreement for the Prosecution and Punishment of the Major War Criminals of the European Axis, and Charter of the International Military Tribunal*, London, 8 August 1945.

125 *Special Proclamation, Establishment of an International Military Tribunal for the Far East*, TIAS No. 1589, 19 January 1946.

126 T. Taylor, *The Anatomy of the Nuremberg Trials: A Personal Memoir* (Alfred A Knopf, 1992).
127 M. Mohan, 'The Paradox of Victim-Centrism: Victim Participation at the Khmer Rouge Tribunal' 9 *International Criminal Law Review* (2009) 733 at 742.
128 E. Stover, *The Witnesses: War Crimes and the Promise of Justice in The Hague* (University of Pennsylvania Press, 2005) 19.
129 L. Moffett, 'The Role of Victims in the International Criminal Tribunals of the Second World War' 12(2) *International Criminal Law Review* (2012) 245.
130 C. Kohl, *The Witness House,* translated by A. Bell (Other Press, 2010).
131 Taylor, n.126 at 190.
132 S. Garkawe, 'The Role and Rights of Victims at the Nuremberg International Military Tribunal' in H. Reginbogin, C. Safferling and W. Hippel (eds.), *The Nuremberg Trials: International Criminal Law since 1945* (Kluwer, 2006) 86–94.
133 Y. Danieli, 'Reappraising the Nuremberg Trials and their Legacy: The Role of Victims in International Law' 27(4) *Cardozo Law Review* (2006) 1633.
134 Ibid.
135 Ibid., at 1632
136 See Y. Beigbeder, *Judging War Crimes and Torture: French Justice and International Criminal Tribunals and Commissions (1940–2005)* (Martinus Nijhoff, 2006).
137 See H. Arendt, *Eichmann in Jerusalem: A Report on the Banality of Evil* (Penguin, 1963); S. Chakravarti, 'More than "Cheap Sentimentality": Victim Testimony at Nuremberg, the Eichmann Trial, and Truth Commissions' 15(2) *Constellations* (2008) 223.
138 See C.M. Chinkin, 'Women's International Tribunal on Japanese Military Sexual Slavery' 95 *American Journal of International Law* (2001) 335.
139 IMT Transcripts, Vol. XIX at 569.
140 Ibid., at 434.
141 Garkawe, n.58.
142 M. Elander, 'The Victim's Address: Expressivism and the Victim at the Extraordinary Chambers in the Courts of Cambodia' 7(1) *International Journal of Transitional Justice* (2013) 91.
143 *Statute of the International Tribunal for the Prosecution of Persons Responsible for Serious Violations of International Humanitarian Law Committed in the Territory of the Former Yugoslavia since 1991* (hereafter 'ICTY Statute'), UNSC Res. 827, S/Res/827, 25 May 1993.
144 *Statute of the International Criminal Tribunal for Rwanda* (herafter 'ICTR Statute'), UNSC Res. 955, S/Res/955, 8 November 1994.
145 M.C. Bassiouni, 'International Recognition of Victims' Rights' 6 *Human Rights Law Review* (2006) 203.
146 R.G. Teitel 'Transitional Justice Genealogy' 16 *Harvard Human Rights Journal* (2003) 69; T. Bonacker, A. Oettler and C. Safferling, 'Valorising Victims' Ambivalences in Contemporary Trends in Transitional Justice' in T. Bonacker and C. Safferling (eds.), *Victims of International Crimes: An Interdisciplinary Discourse* (Asser Press, 2013) 280.
147 D.E. Anders, 'The Therapeutic Turn in International Humanitarian Law: War Crimes Tribunals as Sites of "Healing"?' *UC Berkeley Electronic Theses and Dissertations* (2012) 58–59.
148 Moffett, n.40 at 66–67.
149 C. Jorda and J. de Hemptinne, 'The Status and Role of the Victim' in A. Cassese, P. Gaeta and R.W. Jones (eds.), *The Rome Statute of the International Criminal Court: A Commentary* (Oxford University Press, 2002) 1387–1419 at 1391.

150 ICTY Statute, n. 143, Articles 22 and 24(3); ICTR Statute, n. 144, Articles 21 and 23(3).
151 B. Nowrojee, '"Your Justice is Too Slow": Will the ICTR Fail Rwanda's Rape Victims?' *Occasional Paper No. 10, UN Research Institute for Social Development* (2005).
152 C. Mahoney, *The Justice Sector Afterthought: Witness Protection in Africa* (Institute for Security Studies, 2001).
153 Stover, n.128.
154 M. Dembour and E. Haslam, 'Silencing Hearings? Victim-Witnesses at War Crimes Trials' 15(1) *European Journal of International Law* (2004).
155 K. Johansen, *The Actual Impact of the International Criminal Tribunal for the former Yugoslavia on the Reconciliation Process in Bosnia-Herzegovina,* Master Thesis for the Master of Philosophy in Peace and Conflict Studies, Department of Political Sciences, University of Oslo, 15 July 2011 at 69; A. Des Forges and T. Longman, 'Legal Response to Genocide in Rwanda' in H. Weinstein and E. Stover (eds.), *My Neighbor, My Enemy: Justice and Social Reconstruction in Rwanda and the Former Yugoslavia* (Cambridge University Press, 2004) 49–68.
156 Des Forges and Longman, ibid.
157 ICTY Statute, n. 143, Article 24(3), ICTR Statute, n. 144, Article 23(3).
158 ICTY, Rules of Procedure and Evidence, Revision 50, 8 July 2015, Rule 105; ICTR, Rules of Procedure and Evidence, 29 June 1995, as amended 13 May 2015, Rule 105.
159 S. Malmström, 'Restitution of Property and Compensation to Victims' in R. May (ed.), *Essays on ICTY Procedure and Evidence* (Kulwer Law International, 2001) 373–384.
160 J. Meernik, 'Justice and Peace? How the International Criminal Tribunal Affects Societal Peace in Bosnia' 42 *Journal of Peace Research* 30 (2005); E. Stover and H. Weinstein, 'Conclusion: A Common Objective, a Universe of Alternatives' in H. Weinstein and E. Stover (eds.), *My Neighbor, My Enemy: Justice and Social Reconstruction in Rwanda and the Former Yugoslavia* (Cambridge University Press, 2004) 334.
161 D.E. Arzt, 'Views on the Ground: The Local Perception of International Criminal Tribunals in the Former Yugoslavia and Sierra Leone' 603 *Annals of the American Academy of Political and Social Science, Law, Society, and Democracy: Comparative Perspectives* (2006) 226.
162 S. Kutnjak Ivković and J. Hagan, *Reclaiming Justice: The International Tribunal for the Former Yugoslavia and Local Courts* (Oxford University Press, 2011).
163 P. Clark and N. Palmer, *Testifying to Genocide: Victim and Witness Protection in Rwanda* (REDRESS, 2013).
164 J. Kamatali, 'From the ICTR to ICC: Learning from the ICTR Experience in Bringing Justice to Rwandans' 12 *New England Journal of International and Comparative Law* (2005) 89.
165 UNSC, *Madeleine Albright Statement to the UN Security Council, Provisional Verbatim Record to the 3217th Meeting*, UN Doc. S/PV 3217, 25 May 1993.
166 *Prosecutor v. Nikolić*, Judgment, IT-02–60/1, 2 December 2003.
167 'Statement by Justice Hassan B Jallow, Chief Prosecutor, ICTR & MICT on the Commemoration of the 20th Anniversary of the Rwandan Genocide' *ICTR Website*, 10 April 2014, unictr.unmict.org/en/news/statement-justice-hassan-b-jallow-chief-prosecutor-ictr-mict-commemmoration-20th-anniversary (accessed 09/02/2018).
168 ICTY, Annual Report to the UNGA, A/49/342, S/1994/1007, 29 August 1994, paras. 50–51.
169 Jorda and de Hemptinne, n.149 at 1389.

170 W.A. Schabas, 'Victor's Justice: Selecting "Situations" at the International Criminal Court' 42 *The John Marshall Law Review* (2009–2010) 535 at 42.
171 E. Haslam, 'Victim Participation at the International Criminal Court: A Triumph of Hope over Experience' in D. McGoldrick et al. (eds.), *The Permanent International Criminal Court: Legal and Policy Issues* (Hart Publishing, 2004) 320.
172 Bassiouni, n.145 at 257.
173 M. Osiel, *Making Sense of Mass Atrocity* (Cambridge University Press, 2009).
174 Y. Danieli, 'Victims: Essential Voices at the Court' *Victims' Rights Working Group Bulletin*, Issue 1, September 2004 at 6.
175 E. Luna, 'Punishment, Holism, and the Procedural Conception of Restorative Justice' 1 *Utah Law Review* (2003) 205 at 228.
176 *Rome Statute of the International Criminal Court*, 2149 UNTS 256, 17 July 1998.
177 Haslam, n.171 at 325.
178 M. Pena, 'Victim Participation at the International Criminal Court: Achievements Made and Challenges Lying Ahead' 16 *ILSA Journal of International and Comparative Law* (2009–2010) 497 at 499.
179 C. Kress, 'The Procedural Law of the International Criminal Court in Outline: Anatomy of Unique Compromises' 1 *Journal of International Criminal Justice* (2003) 603.
180 S. Garkawe, 'Victims and the International Criminal Court: Three Major Issues' 3 *International Criminal Law Review* (2003) 345.
181 T.M. Funk, *Victims' Rights and Advocacy at the International Criminal* Court (Oxford University Press, 2010) 4; A.H. Guhr 'Victim Participation during the Pre-Trial Stage at the International Criminal Court' 8 *International Criminal Law Review* (2008) 109 at 110.
182 ICC, *Report of the Court on the Strategy in Relation to Victims*, ICC-ASP/8/45, 10 November 2009.
183 ICC, Rules of Procedure and Evidence, ICC-ASP/1/3, 9 September 2002, Rules 89–99.
184 Rome Statute, n.176, Article 82(4).
185 'Natural persons who have suffered harm as a result of the commission of any crime within the jurisdiction of the Court' and organisations and institutions that are similarly affected, ICC RPE, Rule 85.
186 Rome Statute, n.176, Article 68(3).
187 REDRESS, *The Participation of Victims in International Criminal Court Proceedings: A Review of the Practice and Consideration of Options for the Future*, October 2012.
188 *Prosecutor v. Lubanga Dyilo*, Judgment on the Appeals of The Prosecutor and The Defence against Trial Chamber I's Decision on Victims' Participation of 18 January 2008, ICC-01/04–01/06–1119, 11 July 2008.
189 J. Wemmers, 'Victims' Rights and the International Criminal Court: Perceptions within the Court Regarding the Victims' Right to Participate' 23 *Leiden Journal of International Law* (2010) 629.
190 S. Zappalà, 'The Rights of Victims v. the Rights of the Accused' 8 *Journal of International Criminal Justice* (2010) 137.
191 S. SáCouto and K. Cleary, 'Victims' Participation in the Investigations of the International Criminal Court' 17 *Transnational Law and Contemporary Problems* (2008) 73; M. Jouet, 'Reconciling the Conflicting Rights of Victims and Defendants at the International Criminal Court' 26 *Saint Louis University Public Law Review* (2007) 249; *Prosecutor v. Bemba*, Fourth Decision on Victims' Participation, TC, No. ICC-01/05/08, 12 December 2008, paras. 15–19; *Prosecutor v. Lubanga Dyilo*, Decision on the Manner of Questioning Witnesses by

the Legal Representatives of Victims, TC, No. ICC-01/04–01/06, 16 September 2009, para 24.

192 *Prosecutor v. Gbagbo*, Organisation of the Participation of Victims, ICC-02/11–01/11–29-Red, 6 February 2012; E. Haslam and R. Edmunds, 'Common Legal Representation at the International Criminal Court: More Symbolic than Real?' 12 *International Criminal Law Review* (2012) 871.

193 Haslam, n.171 at 326.

194 Chouliaras, n.37.

195 J. Doak, 'Participatory Rights for Victims of Crime: In Search of International Consensus' 15(1) *Canadian Criminal Law Review* (2011) 43 at 54.

196 C. Chung, 'Victims' Participation at the International Criminal Court: Are Concessions of the Court Clouding the Promise?' 6(3) *Northwestern Journal of International Human Rights* (2008) 459.

197 Ibid.

198 P. Dixon and C. Tenove, 'International Criminal Justice as a Transnational Field: Rules, Authority and Victims' 7 *International Journal of Transitional Justice* (2013) 393, 398.

199 Chung, n.196 at 516.

200 P. Massidda and S. Pellet, 'Role and Practice of the Office of Public Counsel for Victims' in C. Stahn and G. Sluiter (eds.), *The Emerging Practice of the International Criminal Court* (Brill, 2009) 692.

201 G. Mettraux et al., *Expert Initiative on Promoting Effectiveness at the International Criminal Court* (University of Amsterdam, 2014); C. Van den Wyngaert, 'Victims before International Criminal Courts: Some Views and Concerns of an ICC Trial Judge' 44 *Case Western Reserve Journal of International Law* (2011) 47.

202 *Prosecutor v. Lubanga Dyilo*, Decision Establishing the Principles and Procedures to be Applied to Reparations, ICC-01/04–01/06–2904, 7 August 2012; *Prosecutor v. Lubanga*, Judgment on the Appeals against the 'Decision Establishing the Principles and Procedures to be Applied to Reparations' of 7 August 2012 with AMENDED Order for Reparations (Annex A) and Public Annexes 1 and 2, ICC-01/04–01/06–3129, 3 March 2015; *Prosecutor v. Katanga*, Ordonnance de réparation en vertu de l'article 75 du Statut', ICC-01/04–01/07–3728, 24 March 2017; *Prosecutor v. Ahmad Al Faqi Al Mahdi*, Reparations Order, ICC-01/12–01/15–236, 17 August 2017.

203 L. Moffett, 'Reparations for Victims at the International Criminal Court: A New Way Forward?' 21(9) *The International Journal of Human Rights* (2017) 1204.

204 C. Stahn, 'Reparative Justice after the Lubanga Appeal Judgment' 13 *Journal of International Criminal Justice* (2015) 801–13, 806.

205 L. Chappell, 'The Gender Injustice Cascade: "transformative" Reparations for Victims of Sexual and Gender-based Crimes in the Lubanga Case at the International Criminal Court' 21(9) *The International Journal of Human Rights* (2017) 1223.

206 Moffett, n.202.

207 Chappell, n.204.

208 *Prosecutor v Ruto and Sang*, Common Legal Representative for Victims' Comprehensive Report on the Withdrawal of Victims from the Turbo Area by Letter Dated 5 June 2013, ICC-01/09–01/11–896-Corr-Red, 5 September 2013, para. 12.

209 L. Hovil, *A Poisioned Chalice? Local Civil Society and the International Criminal Court's Engagement in Uganda* (International Refugee Rights Initiative 2011).

210 ICC, 'Statement to the Press by the Prosecutor of the International Criminal Court' (Abidjan, Côte d'Ivoire, 20 July 2013).

211 Rome Statute, n.176, Preamble.
212 F. McKay, *REDRESS Statement on behalf of the Victims Rights Working Group*, Rome Conference, 16 June 1998; K. Annan, 'UN Secretary-General Declares Overriding Interest of International Criminal Court Conference Must be that of Victims and World Community as a Whole' *UN Press Centre*, 15 June 1998, www.un.org/press/en/1998/19980615.sgsm6597.html (accessed 09/02/18).
213 P. Clottey, 'ICC Prosecutor Hails US International Justice Role' *Voice of America*, 4th April 2013, www.voanews.com/content/icc-prosecutor-hails-us-international-justice-role/1635160.html (accessed 09/02/18).
214 A. Sagan, 'African Criminals/African Victims: The Institutionalised Production of Cultural Narratives in International Criminal Law' 39(3) *Millennium Journal of International Studies* (2010) 12.
215 S. Kendall and S. Nouwen, 'Representational Practices at the International Criminal Court: The Gap between Juridified and Abstract Victimhood' 76 *Law and Contemporary Problems* (2013) 235.
216 *Idem.*
217 L. Moffett, 'Meaningful and Effective? Considering Victims' Interests through Participation at the International Criminal Court' 26 *Criminal Law Forum* (2015) 255.
218 L. Raub, 'Positioning Hybrid Tribunals in International Criminal Justice' 41 *New York University Journal of International Law and Politics* (2008–2009) 1013.
219 *Statute for the Special Tribunal for Lebanon*, UNSC Res. 1757, S/RES/1757, 31 January 2007, Article 17.
220 STL, 'Victims' Case in the Ayyash et al. Trial Begins' Special Tribunal for Lebanon, 28 August 2017, www.stl-tsl.org/en/media/press-releases/5922-victims-case-in-the-ayyash-et-al-trial-begins (accessed 09/02/18).
221 *Statute of the Extraordinary African Chambers within the Courts of Senegal Created to Prosecute International Crimes Committed in Chad between 7 June 1982 and 1 December 1990*, February 2013, Article 14.
222 J. Elone, 'The Extraordinary Chambers: A New Approach to Victim Participation in International Criminal Tribunals' *International Justice Monitor*, www.ijmonitor.org/2015/10/the-extraordinary-african-chambers-a-new-approach-to-victim-participation-in-international-criminal-tribunals/ (accessed 09/02/18).
223 Christie, n.62.
224 C. Geertz, 'Thick Descriptions: Toward an Interpretive Theory of Culture' in C. Geertz (ed.), *The Interpretation of Cultures: Selected Essays* (Fontana Press, 1993) 3–30.

3 Compromised justice

The road to the ECCC

1. Introduction

> In the end, the victims of the Khmer Rouge got the tribunal that Hun Sen and his allies, including other former Khmer Rouge throughout the regime, wanted.[1]

This chapter explores how historical contexts and diverse political actors have influenced the selective use of the ECCC as a response to atrocity, and thus 'the crimes and victims that we see as opposed to what we do not see' at the ECCC.[2] It begins by providing a brief overview of Cambodia's history since its independence. In doing so, it highlights a range of victimisations that have remained largely unrecognised by Cambodia's transitional justice process. This chapter offers a number of possible explanations for this selective recognition of harm. It notes the Cold War politics that for so long prevented any attempt to deal with Cambodia's violent past and the factors which contributed to the eventual beginning of negotiations between the UN and the RGC. By analysing the negotiation history, the chapter argues that the court is based on a reluctant compromise between the UN and the RGC, a fact that has had a significant impact on the court's structure, functioning, and ability to credibly pursue justice for the victims of the Khmer Rouge regime. By locating the court in its political reality, this chapter seeks to provide a 'thicker'[3] basis from which to evaluate the court's relationship with the victims of the Khmer Rouge, which is explored in greater detail in subsequent chapters.

2. A violent history

A comprehensive account of Cambodia's recent violent history is far beyond the scope of this book.[4] However, it is important to highlight that the Khmer Rouge era was not an isolated regime of violence but was deeply imbedded in domestic, regional and international politics. Following the fall of the Angkorean Empire, centuries of threat of Vietnamese and Siamese annexation, and almost a century more of French control, Cambodia obtained its independence in 1954.[5] Cambodia was at first governed by a royalist regime headed by Norodom Sihanouk.[6]

Although Sihanouk enjoyed initial popularity,[7] his reign was tainted with allegations of corruption, inequality, repression and violence.[8] The 1960s saw a rise in discontent,[9] and the Khmer Rouge emerged as a radical branch of a broader Indochinese communist movement.[10] Led by Ieng Sary and Saloth Sar (latterly and notoriously known as 'Pol Pot') this group encouraged armed struggle against Sihanouk in the name of socialist revolution.[11]

The Cold War brought more violence to Cambodia, as Sihanouk's apparent collusion with Vietnamese communists[12] prompted a four-year bombing campaign by the US.[13] The resulting deaths of over half a million civilians[14] led to a spike in Khmer Rouge membership,[15] as the group capitalised on the feelings of betrayal, hurt and anger at this attack by a foreign power.[16] A US-backed right-wing military coup finally toppled Sihanouk in March 1970.[17] Power was seized by General Lon Nol,[18] who implemented an authoritarian regime characterised by repression of dissidents and dragged Cambodia further into the Vietnam conflict.[19] Sihanouk fled to China where he aligned himself with the Khmer Rouge,[20] forming a government in exile which, allied with the Chinese and North Vietnamese, fought back against Lon Nol's forces.[21] By 1973 both Vietnam's and Sihanouk's support for the Khmer Rouge had diminished.[22] However, the group had gained both legitimacy and military control within Cambodia and on the 17 April seized Phnom Penh.[23]

This marked the beginning of the DK era, during which the Khmer Rouge attempted to create a 'New Cambodia' based on a particular understanding of agrarian communism.[24] Towns and cities were emptied as the population was forced to brave violence and inhumane conditions to march to their new homes in the countryside.[25] They were then organised into cooperatives and set to forced labour in worksites.[26] Phnom Penh's former inhabitants were identified as 'new people' and were frequent targets of abuse.[27] Family ties were discouraged;[28] parents were separated from their children and spouses from each other,[29] while forced marriages and sexually violent crimes occurred throughout the country.[30] Money, free markets, normal schooling, private property, public transportation, foreign clothing styles, religious practices and traditional cultural practices were abolished.[31] The legal system was dismantled, and although new state institutions were announced, there is no evidence of any functioning legal system during the regime.[32] Communication with the outside world was severed; journalists and reporters were expelled, commercial flights ceased and borders were sealed.[33] The population lived in fear of being sent for 're-education' (torture) or being 'smashed' (murder), two principal methods employed by the Khmer Rouge to root out 'traitors'.[34] While this originally constituted members of the former regime, it quickly expanded to encompass intellectuals; city residents; Buddhist monks; minority people such as the Cham, Vietnamese and Khmer Krom; 'treacherous' members of the Khmer Rouge; and anyone else considered an enemy.[35] Over the course of three years, eight months and twenty days at least 1.7 million people are believed to have died, either through murder or through the starvation, exhaustion and disease that resulted from the Khmer Rouge's policies.[36] As details began to seep out of the country, what was revealed were the remains of one of the most violent regimes in modern history.[37] However, the impact of the Vietnam and Cold War meant that not only did the regime initially go unpunished by the international community; it was also, in fact, supported for many years to come.[38]

From 1977 onwards the Khmer Rouge had begun to perpetrate cross-border raids into Vietnam in furtherance of Pol Pot's plan to reclaim former Cambodian territories.[39] This proved to be its undoing; the Vietnamese – tired of the violent excursions onto their territory – allied with a number of Cambodian resistance fighters to finally oust the Khmer Rouge from Phnom Penh in 1979.[40] The Vietnamese installed a regime known as the People's Republic of Kampuchea (PRK) and filled the intellectual and professional vacuum left by the Khmer Rouge with Vietnamese experts.[41] This regime, aware that revenge killings and retaliation risked exacerbating the ongoing civil war, took a number of steps to address Khmer Rouge atrocities.[42] While many of the main Khmer Rouge leaders were able to flee to Thailand,[43] a number of lower-level Khmer Rouge were tried in domestic courts, while others were encouraged to join rehabilitation programmes.[44] Perhaps the most widely known transitional justice measure was the creation of a People's Revolutionary Tribunal,[45] which charged Pol Pot and former deputy prime minister Ieng Sary *in absentia* with genocide against the Cambodian people, found both guilty and sentenced them to death.[46] Despite its numerous legal shortcomings,[47] and although perhaps motivated primarily by a desire to legitimise the new government and distance the Khmer Rouge leaders from the thousands of lower-level cadres,[48] the trial appeared to initially bring some comfort to victims.[49] However, its sentences were never imposed and, by 1996, had been revoked, accompanied by an amnesty issued as a condition for the mass defection of Ieng Sary and other Khmer Rouge members.[50] The approach within Cambodian politics had developed from one seeking remembrance to one wishing to forget,[51] and despite the consensus that emerged in later years that the 1979 tribunal had not been a sufficient legal response,[52] it was to be many years before another attempt at prosecution was made.

The international community initially adopted classic Cold War approaches to the Vietnamese intervention.[53] Vietnam had acted with Soviet backing, and its adversaries were determined not to allow the USSR a strategic advantage, regardless of any humanitarian concerns.[54] The PRK was labelled by many as a puppet regime, although the reality was considerably more complex, and calls for self-determination abounded despite the lack of capacity within Cambodia.[55] Aid flowed in from China, the US and other states fearing a Vietnamese expansion,[56] allowing the Khmer Rouge to continue the violent conflict with the new government for years to come.[57] Opposition to the PRK was so pronounced that the Khmer Rouge regime was awarded the Cambodian seat at the UNGA in September 1979 and was to hold on to this seat for over a decade, despite increased information emerging about its violent past.[58]

The late 1980s brought changes in international and domestic politics, with Cold War policies being replaced with a more market-orientated, cooperative attitude. The Vietnamese troops finished their unilateral withdrawal in 1989,[59] and the same year France and Indonesia co-hosted the Paris Peace Conference, geared towards finding an end to the Cambodian conflict.[60] However, issues surrounding how to deal with the Khmer Rouge and build a regime that pleased the various domestic and international conference attendees hampered the process.[61] The first real constructive change did not come until 1991, with the conclusion of the Paris accords.[62] This complex multilateral peace treaty contained no sanctions for the Khmer Rouge but, rather, allowed the Khmer Rouge to establish a political presence in Phnom Penh for the first time since 1979. However, it acknowledged the need for measures to ensure the 'non-return to the policies and practices of the past' and contained a ceasefire and general demobilisation.[63] Under the accords, the UN created a Transitional Authority in Cambodia (UNTAC), composed of civilian and military components, and committed the various factions in Cambodia to a free election.[64]

Although the Khmer Rouge benefitted from the Paris accords, they refused to cooperate with its terms or implement any ceasefire or demobilisation and attempted to sabotage subsequent elections.[65] Despite their resistance and continued civil war,[66] in 1993 a coalition government was formed composed of royalists, led by Prince Norodom Ranariddh, and former communists, led by Hun Sen, himself a former Khmer Rouge member who had defected from the organisation.[67] In 1994 the era of Khmer Rouge legitimacy came to an end when the National Assembly passed a law declaring them outlaws and insurgents.[68] The law contained provisions for amnesties, which were extended indefinitely in 1995, leading to mass defections and the implosion of the Khmer Rouge leadership.[69] While calls for the leaders to be prosecuted continued through 1995 and 1996, a draft law requesting the international community to establish a tribunal was shelved in 1996 to allow an amnesty to be granted to Ieng Sary, the former deputy prime minister.[70] In 1997 Hun Sen seized power from his coalition partners in a bloody military coup,[71] returning in 1998 as prime minister of a second coalition government (the RGC), with his ruling party being the Cambodian People's Party (CPP). Over the next few years Hun Sen continued to cement his control over the country (which he holds to this day) and Cambodia slowly began to stabilise. However, structural violence and inequality persisted,[72] and although the Paris Peace Agreements had envisioned a human rights–based constitution and independent judiciary for Cambodia, human rights observers continued to report the absence of an independent judiciary, an absence of legal infrastructure and the politicisation of the legal process.[73]

While Cold War battles were being fought amongst politicians and UN delegates, the survivors of the Khmer Rouge regime mourned their lost family members,[74] dealt with the physical and psychological effects of living through extreme trauma and lived side by side with former Khmer Rouge cadres.[75] Further risks of victimisation were rife. The end of the Khmer Rouge had by no means signalled the end of the conflict, and mines littered the country.[76] The arrival of UNTAC brought some semblance of order,[77] but the high wages of UNTAC staff contributed to escalating costs of living, while incidences of prostitution and HIV/AIDS multiplied, and reports circulated of sexual harassment and mistreatment of locals.[78] While the conflict slowly ceased, state violence continued throughout the 1990s as the new government strengthened its hold on the country through the repression of dissidents and extrajudicial killings.[79] By 1998, the strategy of encouraging defection had resulted in the surrender of most remaining low-level Khmer Rouge, and in 1998 Nuon Chea and Khieu Samphan were welcomed into Cambodian society by Hun Sen.[80] While the prime minister did not rule out holding trials, a culture of silence emerged as Cambodia began to 'bury the past' for the sake of reconciliation.[81]

This section has focused predominantly on the actions of political elites, in order to highlight the international politics and domestic instability that contributed to the prevalence of violence for so many years before, during and after DK. It can be seen that far from representing the sole period of violence within Cambodia, the Khmer Rouge's time in power constituted a particularly deadly period in a long history of conflict and repression. Indeed, the civil parties and civil party lawyers interviewed for this project spoke of continuations of harm that stretched out both before and after the Khmer Rouge era, demonstrating that DK was not the only period of hardship in their lives.[82] This continuation of harm cannot be attributed to the DK leaders alone as Cold War politics undoubtedly contributed to the rise of the Khmer Rouge and bolstered resistance to the new government after their defeat. However, as is explored in the following, the limited jurisdiction of the ECCC, and its status as the only official response to atrocity within Cambodia, has meant that the victimisations perpetrated between 1975 and 1979 by the Khmer Rouge regime remain the only harms which have constituted the subject of transitional justice measures. This selective response to atrocity is, as is often the case in transitional justice, reflective of the agenda of political elites.[83] This is pertinently demonstrated by an examination of the negotiations which led to the ECCC's creation.

3. Negotiating justice

Due in large part to the Cold War considerations detailed earlier, the international community was divided for some time on whether and how to address Cambodia's violent past.[84] However, with the thawing of the Cold War came new political agendas,[85] while the growth of transitional justice theory and practice around the world contributed to an increased international wish to hold the Khmer Rouge regime accountable in some way.[86] The idea of a truth commission, as floated by the UN Special Representative for Human Rights in Cambodia in 1997, received little support either domestically or internationally. It is arguable that too many countries had dirtied their hands in Cambodia to wish for too broad a fact-finding mission.[87] The creation of the tribunals for the former Yugoslavia and Rwanda had re-introduced ICL as a means of dealing with atrocity, and a limited number of prosecutions thus suggested a means of both delimiting accountability and creating a politically acceptable narrative, while furthering the agenda of 'international justice'.[88] Negotiations for an international(ised) criminal court therefore commenced in 1997. Officials from within the UN Office for Human Rights, working alongside the secretary-general's special representative for human rights in Cambodia, obtained Cambodia's co-prime ministers' signatures on a letter requesting UN assistance in 'bringing to justice those persons responsible for the genocide and crimes against humanity during the rule of the Khmer Rouge from 1975 to 1979'.[89] The issue was brought before the UNGA, which requested that the secretary-general establish a group of experts to investigate.[90] Domestic political instability caused by Hun Sen's coup a month later and Pol Pot's mysterious death in 1998[91] resulted in delays in the negotiations.[92] However, a group was eventually established,[93] and issued its report in 1999, adopting similar victim-centric language to that previously used during the UN's establishment of the ad hoc tribunals[94] and citing the victims of the Khmer Rouge as requiring and deserving justice.[95]

As for who should be responsible for delivering this justice, the group expressed fears that the Cambodian judicial system was corrupt, that Cambodia lacked adequate legal infrastructure and that there was no qualified legal profession.[96] In fact, the group advised against the very model of hybrid court that would eventually be created. Its members submitted that negotiations with the RGC might 'drag on' and that the RGC may push for provisions that risked the independence of the court.[97] An internationally driven tribunal of the type utilised for Rwanda and the former Yugoslavia was therefore recommended,[98] with a jurisdiction which excluded both crimes committed before or after the 1975–1979 period and those committed by other states between 1975 and 1979, purportedly so as not to 'detract from the unique and extraordinary nature of the crimes committed by the leaders of Democratic Kampuchea'.[99]

Their recommendations were flatly rejected by the RGC, which bristled at the criticisms. The government insisted that there be a significant domestic presence in the court, noted its obligation under the Genocide Convention to try international crimes domestically[100] and questioned the moral authority of the UN to lecture on 'justice', considering the organisation's historical support for the Khmer Rouge.[101] These opposing stances sparked years of negotiation[102] as both parties fought for greater control over the deliverance of justice.[103] With the ICC out of the question because of its non-retroactive jurisdiction, and with China and Russia likely to use their veto to block any Security Council ad hoc tribunal,[104] the international community was unable to pursue alternative accountability mechanisms or compel Cambodia to take action.[105]

As a means of resolving this deadlock, US and UN officials began to consider the possibility of a 'mixed' tribunal.[106] This suggestion brought a breakthrough and, following some more slightly acrimonious negotiations, spurred on by domestic and international NGOs,[107] a precarious agreement was reached in July 2000. Trials for international and domestic crimes committed between 1975 and 1979 would take place in the 'Extraordinary Chambers' of the existing Cambodian criminal courts. Cambodian procedures and staff would be used, but the UN would provide assistance, and while the majority of judges would be Cambodian, decisions would require a 'super-majority', thus necessitating the consent of at least one international judge.[108] UN support was conditional on the relevant law being in accordance with a draft memorandum of understanding, which set out the blueprint for the tribunal and the modalities for cooperation between the UN and Cambodia.[109] However, at this point the RGC chose to take unilateral action, passing a law that granted it greater control over the proceedings.[110] This amounted to a *fait accompli*, determining all matters that remained in dispute between the RGC and the UN in favour of the RGC and differing in a number of material aspects from the draft memorandum.[111] With control effectively wrestled from the UN's hands, an impasse resulted,[112] and the UN terminated negotiations, stating that the RGC had acted without agreement and that the court as envisaged would not guarantee the required independence, impartiality and objectivity.[113]

This renewed deadlock continued until 2002,[114] when the UNGA fell under pressure from a 'Group of Interested States'[115] with a political interest in the success of the court.[116] As a result, the UNGA passed a resolution forcing its negotiators back to the table.[117] As the UNGA resolution recognised 'the substantial progress made by the Secretary-General and the Government of Cambodia towards the establishment of Extraordinary Chambers within the existing court structure of Cambodia',[118] the tone was set for further negotiations, leaning towards the tribunal envisioned by the RGC, rather than one based on the precedent of the ad hoc tribunals. Despite the diametrically opposed views of the Cambodian and UN negotiators, an agreement was finally reached in March 2003, largely in favour of the Cambodian approach[119] but on the grounds that the agreement, as a bilateral treaty, would have priority over the law and that should the RGC change the structure or function of the ECCC in a way contrary to the agreement, the UN would reserve the right to withdraw support.[120] Despite the secretary-general's ongoing concerns over a lack of judicial independence and fair trial rights in Cambodia's judicial system,[121] the UNGA approved the agreement in May 2003,[122] and the Cambodian National Assembly ratified the agreement on the 4 October 2004.[123] Further setbacks occurred, as it became obvious that the RGC were unable or unwilling to pay its share of the costs, which were intended to cover domestic staff and court premises.[124] However, by March 2005 the international community had pledged sufficient voluntary financial support,[125] and in July 2006 the court began the pursuit of its agreement-stated mandate of addressing 'the legitimate concern of the government and the people of Cambodia in the pursuit of justice and national reconciliation, stability, peace and security'.[126]

The court is thus the result of compromise, as two powers sought to assert their beliefs as to who should have the power to control the official response to Khmer Rouge atrocity.[127] The fact that much of the compromise was the result of UN concessions can be attributed to the simple fact that the UN, or certainly a number of its powerful members, wanted a court more than the RGC did.[128] It seems highly likely that the pursuit of prosecutions was initially deployed by Hun Sen as a method of diverting attention away from his coup while gaining international credibility[129] and threatening the Khmer Rouge into defecting.[130] As his control of Cambodia grew and the remaining Khmer Rouge either defected,[131] were captured[132] or died,[133] international criminal justice became less of a priority.[134] Indeed, Hun Sen had reacted to former Khmer Rouge leaders Khieu Samphan and Nuon Chea's defection with amicability and calls for forgiveness.[135] Furthermore, while the RGC had faced demands for accountability from the victim population,[136] and although two members of the negotiating team had lost relatives during the regime and were invested in ending impunity,[137] there were also a number of powerful Cambodians who had no wish to see themselves or their colleagues placed in the dock, leading to the prioritisation of control.[138] Thus, Hun Sen appears to have been more interested in prosecuting enemies and protecting friends, than in pursuing an independent investigation.[139] However, from the perspective of his regime, if a hybrid court *could* be controlled, then seeking accountability could provide a relatively cheap and internationally legitimised means of distancing the current regime from the Khmer Rouge.[140]

Meanwhile, the UN was under considerable pressure from its member states, particularly the US, Japan, France and Australia, to negotiate.[141] Just as had been the case with Rwanda and the former Yugoslavia,[142] the failure to prevent atrocity (and indeed the prolonged support for the Khmer Rouge) had constituted a dark stain on the UN's history, with ICL providing a means to address this past failure without accepting any official responsibility for the atrocities committed.[143] The US, in particular, had faced pressure from NGOs and Cambodian diaspora to change its policies[144] and was keen to reassert its international moral legitimacy.[145] It therefore played a key role in moving negotiations forward several times.[146] Even among states with less specific interest in Cambodia, the ICTY and the ICTR had demonstrated the use of ICL as a response to atrocity, and there was a desire to further the agenda of international criminal justice.[147] While suspicion of Cambodia's judiciary appeared to motivate a desire for international control, Cambodia's independence from Western aid and the blocking of Security Council action left the UN without the means of coercion.[148] The result was the acceptance of a court structure which had already been decried as unable to assure international justice standards.[149] As is shown in the following, both the hybrid structure and the desire of the RGC to retain control over proceedings have continued to impact on the work of the court.

4. A court with two kings

The negotiations and compromises which led to the ECCC's creation have had significant implications for the court's structure, procedures and budget. The court is one of a number of 'hybrid' institutions created over the last 20 years, characterised by their combining of international and domestic laws, procedures and staff.[150] The ECCC's geographical and legal positioning within Cambodia gives a greater sense of national ownership.[151] At the same time, international staff, laws and procedures have been incorporated into the court at every level. Thus, there are two co-prosecutors, one national and one international, who have joint competence to initiate prosecutions and prosecute the accused at trial.[152] Following Cambodia's (French-based) criminal justice procedures,[153] the CIJ, again one national and one international, are responsible for the bulk of the investigations and the creation of indictments, known as closing orders.[154] There are three chambers, composed of the PTC, which serves as an internal dispute mechanism as well as a pre-trial appeal chamber,[155] the TC and the SCC. These are made up of a majority of national and a minority of international judges, who are selected based on their knowledge of international humanitarian law, human rights law and ICL, rather than their knowledge of Cambodian law.[156] In an attempt to assuage international fears over political interference, all chambers are required to obtain a supermajority (majority plus one) before they are able to pass decisions.[157]

The court's procedures are a mix of Cambodia's own civil law inquisitorial procedures[158] and adversarial procedures introduced into the court's Internal Rules.[159] This has manifested itself in prolonged investigations by the CIJs, followed by full-length adversarial trials.[160] The costs of the court are also divided between the RGC and the UN; the RGC is responsible for the national side but may also receive additional voluntary contributions from foreign governments, international institutions, NGOs or others.[161] The UN is responsible for a trust fund, from which funds are to be found for the international personnel, the defence counsel and 'assistance as may be necessary to ensure the smooth functioning of the investigation, the prosecution and the Extraordinary Chambers'.[162] Both sides rely heavily on voluntary donations, with major donors including Japan, Australia, the UN Trust Fund and the European Union.[163] This method of funding has been problematic in practice;[164] the ECCC has faced continual fiscal crises and budget shortfalls, making it increasingly reliant on emergency funds from donors.[165] It has also had to deal with repeated allegations of managerial inefficiency and corruption,[166] while domestic staff have often been unsure as to whether they would be paid.[167] The situation has caused wide dissatisfaction amongst the court's practitioners, as summarised by a judge interviewed for this study:

> It's been said they've gone on strike, well they haven't gone on strike at all, they've just accepted the breach of contract by their employer, who's failed to pay them, in fact they worked for months without any salary, that shows a great deal of dedication. So I'm very concerned about the funding modality and that comes down to a political decision, by the UN, and by the voluntary donor countries. This must never be repeated, ever, it's a failed model.[168]

The implications of hybridisation are multifaceted, and a full analysis of the court's processes and progress is beyond the scope of this book.[169] The most significant implication for the purpose of this book is the combining of Cambodian and ICL procedures, a combination that has resulted in the development of the ECCC's civil party participation mechanism. The impact this has had on victims' ability to access both procedural and substantive justice has been profound and is considered in greater detail in subsequent chapters. However, before moving to consider this system, it is worth noting that the political wrangling between the UN and the RGC explored within this chapter did not end with the cessation of the court's negotiations. Due in large part to the hybridisation of the court's staff, the distinct political agendas of the two negotiating parties have played out within the court, most visibly in the exercising of the court's personal jurisdiction. This continued political influence deserves a brief analysis, as it has had a significant impact on the ECCC's deliverance of both procedural and substantive justice to victims.

The politicisation of personal jurisdiction

As negotiated, the ECCC has a very specific temporal and personal jurisdiction, covering Khmer Rouge senior leaders and 'those most responsible' for crimes committed between 17 April 1975 and 6 January 1979.[170] The practice of limiting the jurisdiction of a court is common in international criminal law and is explicable at least, in part, by a desire to avoid overburdening courts with an unmanageable number of cases.[171] However, some have expressed disquiet over this limited jurisdiction,[172] arguing that it excludes consideration of the violence that occurred both before and after the regime,[173] allows international actors to avoid accountability and fails to take into account the thousands of lower-ranking Khmer Rouge who may have also committed crimes.[174] Indeed, the use of a criminal trial necessarily introduces an individualised account of history, placing blame on a small number of individuals while failing to account for the systemic and collective nature of the violence.[175] The ECCC has certainly been an example of this; the court has completed only two trials, featuring three defendants.

Case 001 concerned Kaing Guek Eav, alias Duch.[176] Initially investigated alongside four other individuals (see the following discussion), his case was subsequently split from the others because of the specific nature of the allegations against him, which concerned his role as head of the notorious S-21 Security Centre,[177] as opposed to being national in scope.[178] On 26 July 2010 Duch was convicted for crimes against humanity and grave breaches of the Geneva Conventions,[179] a conviction which was upheld on 3 February 2012.[180] Case 002 originally involved four accused, covering crimes that ranged across Cambodia and comprising investigations of 20 specific crime sites. The original four accused were Nuon Chea, Khieu Samphan, Ieng Sary and Ieng Thirith. However, Ieng Thirith was found unfit to stand trial because of her progressive mental illness in November 2011,[181] and the case against her was subsequently dropped altogether following her death in 2015.[182] The case against her husband Ieng Sary was similarly dropped on 14 March 2013, following his death the same day.[183] Because of concerns about trial management, the advanced ages of the accused and the need to procure a judgement before all the defendants passed away, Case 002 has been split into a series of sub-trials; the implications of this split for civil parties are considered in Chapter 5. A guilty verdict and a life sentence were delivered in the first sub-trial (Case 002/01), relating to forced transfers and the killing of the former regime's soldiers, on 7 August 2014; this sentence was upheld (although some findings were overturned) on the 23 November 2016.[184] Case 002/02 concluded in June 2017, and a judgement is due at the time of writing. With only three people on trial for a limited selection of the widespread and systematic crimes perpetrated during the Khmer Rouge regime, it can be seen that the ECCC offers incomplete substantive justice through truth and accountability to the Khmer Rouge's victims. The rest of this section analyses the reasons for this limited number of prosecutions and the unique features of the ECCC that have enabled some progress towards pursuing additional cases.

While it does not seem that the negotiators reached a specific agreement on who would be prosecuted at the ECCC,[185] the court's limited jurisdiction constituted one thing the RGC and the UN negotiators agreed on; neither was keen to see the scope of accountability extend too close to home.[186] As has been explored earlier, few states have been so subjected to the machinations of Cold War politics as Cambodia, and many of the world's most powerful states, including the Soviet Union, the US and China, have undoubtedly contributed in some way to the atrocities experienced by Cambodian citizens.[187] Similarly, the RGC is composed of many former Khmer Rouge, who would have little interest in seeing themselves or their colleagues on trial.[188] While it seems that international concerns had been soothed by the demarcating of the court's temporal and personal jurisdiction, the court's practice has demonstrated that for the RGC, it may not have been limited enough. Certainly, broadening the court's work beyond Case 002 has been steadily resisted by the RGC, which has consistently claimed that prosecuting too many suspects could reignite civil war.[189] As part of the government's 'reconciliation' process had involved offering former cadres informal amnesties, the negotiators may have initially had legitimate concerns about a re-ignition of conflict.[190] However, this position has also been described by interviewees as 'designed to protect the present people in power',[191] a perspective that has arguably gained credence over time; while little evidence has emerged that this remains a risk in practice,[192] Hun Sen has repeatedly stated that Case 002 shall be the last.[193] As a result of these public pronouncements, there has been widespread speculation that the RGC is actively working to prevent any future cases from coming to trial and that this opposition has been reflected in the attitudes of the Cambodian lawyers, judges and staff at the ECCC.[194]

In contrast, it has become evident that the international element of the ECCC is willing to pursue two additional cases, Cases 003 and 004. Case 003 originally concerned two suspects: former Navy Commander Meas Muth[195] and Sou Met, while Case 004 concerns three former mid-level Khmer Rouge members, Ao An, Ta Tith and Im Chaem.[196] Sou Met has since passed away, providing another poignant reminder of the time constraints within which the ECCC works.[197] Both cases languished in the investigatory stages for years while the national staff consistently resisted their progression.[198] That the cases have been able to proceed to the extent that they have is entirely attributable to a number of unique features of the ECCC's hybrid structure, which is explored in the following.

The controversy surrounding these cases began in 2008 following a dispute between the co-prosecutors as to the appropriateness of commencing new investigations.[199] In line with the ECCC's procedures, the international co-prosecutor filed a notice of disagreement and asked the court's PTC to address the issue. The PTC, despite deliberating for nearly a year, was unable to reach the required supermajority agreement on the issue.[200] As noted previously, this supermajority feature had been one of the compromises of the ECCC's negotiations[201] and meant that neither national nor international judges could push a decision through without some degree of support from the other side.[202] In this instance, four of the pre-trial judges were required to agree, but instead, the three Cambodian judges voted against the investigation while the international judges voted in favour.[203] Because of another negotiated clause in the agreement that provides that when a chamber is split, the proposed action may go ahead,[204] the international co-prosecutor's submissions were able to proceed to the CIJ, initiating Cases 003 and 004.[205]

However, the Office of the CIJ has continued to struggle with the obviously opposing aims of its national and international judges. Different international CIJs have responded to the national reluctance to move forward in different ways. Prior to his departure in 2010, Judge Lemonde gathered witness statements alone.[206] In contrast, his successor, Siegfried Blunk, faced a steady stream of criticism from rights activists and jurists for what was seen to be an attempt to bury the cases at the behest of the RGC.[207] In 2011 an announcement that no further investigations would be undertaken in respect of Case 003[208] caused widespread outcry, leading to several of the CIJ's UN legal team resigning in protest while human rights organisations decried the decision.[209] A dispute immediately followed between the CIJ and the international co-prosecutor, who filed a public statement in which he declared that he would be seeking additional investigative action.[210] In response, the CIJ demanded a retraction, which was upheld because of the inability of the PTC to reach consensus.[211]

The same month, Blunk announced his resignation, citing political interference of RGC officials in Case 003 and Case 004.[212] Investigations were then further delayed by the national CIJ's refusal to work with the reserve international CIJ, Laurent Kasper-Ansermet,[213] and the Supreme Council of Magistracy's refusal to appoint him as the new CIJ.[214] Although the official statement from the national CIJ was that he would not work with the judge because of his reserve status, it has been reported that the actual reason was related to posts made on the internet by the reserve judge, in which he demonstrated an interest in the allegations of political interference and the court and a wish to pursue Cases 003 and 004.[215] The issue was brought before the PTC, which once again found itself split along national and international lines.[216] While Judge Kasper-Answemet attempted to officially reopen Case 003, he eventually tendered his resignation, citing the 'dysfunctional' climate within the office and claiming that his national counterpart demanded that he cease his 'unlawful activity'.[217]

Consistent efforts from international CIJs led to official charges eventually being made.[218] However, arrest warrants have not been honoured or executed by the judicial police,[219] leading to the charges being made *in absentia*. This has resulted in criticism being levied not only against the judicial police for making a mockery of the court but also against the court for its failure to openly address this apparent lack of cooperation.[220] The case against Im Chaem was dismissed in February 2017 because of a finding that she was neither 'a senior leader or one of those most responsible officials' of the Khmer Rouge regime.[221] Commentators have continued to critique the court for its failure to acknowledge the role of politics, describing the dismissal as a 'farce and pretence of justice'.[222]

It is worth noting that pressure from the RGC does not appear to constitute the only constraint on the progress of Cases 003 and 004. Concerns that the remaining cases will never make it to trial were raised in May 2017 when a leaked document revealed that the CIJs were considering a 'permanent stay on proceedings' because of a 'lack of funding'.[223] As highlighted earlier, funding has consistently posed a challenge for the court; many interviewees highlighted how the reliance on voluntary contributions has left it particularly susceptible to influence from its donors.[224] Indeed, as donors have grown weary of the court's admittedly lengthy proceedings, the court has faced cutbacks and resource restrictions, arguably creating an additional barrier to its ability to fulfil its mandate.[225] As argued by an interviewee,

> Justice cannot be done like that, justice has very crucial principles that have to be kept at the highest levels, principles like independence, impartiality, and if the judges are dependent, if their work is frustrated by just lack of funding, there is no independence, there is no continuity, it impacts on many principles.[226]

While funding constraints constitute a less direct influence into judicial discretion, the risk that Cases 003 and 004 may not proceed because of a lack of resources demonstrates how such constraints may directly hinder the court's ability to deliver a sense of justice to victims. However, it must be noted that some commentators have expressed scepticism that funding provides a full explanation for the CIJs' position.[227]

Combatting a lack of political will is not a challenge unique to the ECCC. As one interviewee noted,

> If there is political interference, domestically, it's the same as you would get in any country where you have a Ministry of Justice that controls people's promotions within a professional judiciary. And maybe they're not prepared to speak out in a particular way because that may affect their promotions, it's common to many countries.[228]

Nor is the issue unknown within the international criminal context. As has been demonstrated by the ICTR's failure to arrest Felicien Kabuga[229] and the ICC's dropping of the Kenyatta case,[230] a lack of domestic political will can significantly hamper international(ised) criminal courts' ability to pursue accountability. In

Cambodia, continued resistance to Cases 003 and 004 means that it may only ever be three individuals who face charges for their role during the Khmer Rouge regime. Indeed, there has never been any suggestion that additional prosecutions will be pursued domestically, meaning that if Cases 003 and 004 fail, their suspects will avoid all criminal liability.[231] Human rights advocates have argued that the ECCC's scapegoating of a small number of former leaders prevents a more nuanced understanding of the crimes committed during the regime[232] and have claimed that the failure to pursue additional prosecutions would deny justice to victims[233] and threaten the legitimacy of the court.[234] This has been echoed by members of the court's defence teams:

> The prosecution chose only four accused, now two, and of course in doing this it is highly symbolical and also similarly designed to protect the present people in power.[235]

For those who suffered as a direct result of the suspects' crimes, the implications are significant, as they risk having their ability to pursue truth, accountability and reparations denied.[236] The outspoken resistance from the RGC creates a court legacy whereby political will may be seen as being able to stand in the way of pursuing accountability, with implications for the deliverance of procedural justice to victims.[237] Perceived ethicality and neutrality are important components of procedural justice[238] and are likely to factor into the overall legitimacy assessments of the court made by victims and other observers.[239] Indeed, as will be explored in greater depth in Chapter 8, many of the civil parties interviewed spoke of the importance of ethicality and neutrality, as well as their belief that the national side could not be trusted. Thus, political interference hinders not only the deliverance of substantive justice but also the perception of procedural justice amongst victim participants and the overall perceived legitimacy of the court.

5. Conclusion

This chapter has sought to place the creation of the ECCC in its political and historical context, exposing 'the crime and victims that we see as opposed to what we do not see' at the ECCC.[240] I have argued that from the very first days of Cambodian independence, there were more forces at work than those within Cambodia alone. The Khmer Rouge did not manage their rise to power unaided. The push and pull of communist and anti-communist states had an impact on domestic politics, and the international preoccupation with containing communism dramatically influenced the course of Cambodian history. I sought to outline some of the atrocities committed during the Khmer Rouge regime before demonstrating how ongoing Cold War concerns and the changing political climate within Cambodia resulted in limited attempts to pursue accountability for the crimes committed during the regime. An analysis of the negotiations that led to the court's creation has demonstrated the extent to which its structure and jurisdiction has been delimited by those same political concerns. As a result, those who have suffered from crimes that occurred prior to or after the 1975–1979 period or from crimes other than those committed by the Khmer Rouge, no matter how grave, will not see their harms reflected in the practice of the ECCC.

The ECCC can be described as a court of compromise, both in its reflection of the different agendas of the UN and RGC and the hybridisation of its structure, staff, laws, procedures and budget. Several unique features have emerged from the negotiations, from the need for a supermajority within the chambers, to the presence of the two co-prosecutors and CIJs. The court constitutes one of the most 'hybridised' in the world, and as has been explored in this chapter, this has on occasion allowed for external interests to influence the work of the court in a way that has been widely criticised by human rights advocates and scholars. The claim that international(ised) criminal courts are political tools is not one that is unique to the ECCC. The post–World War II tribunals, ad hoc tribunals and the ICC have all been subjected to accusations of political influence. Indeed, recurring attacks on international criminal trials as political show trials are reproduced throughout international criminal courtrooms and within the international legal literature.[241] Whether through the imposition of impunity or through the attaching of conditions to accountability, responses to victimisation are inevitably shaped by politics. What this chapter has sought to demonstrate is that the agendas of political elites have real and significant implications for those most impacted by international crime. In the Cambodian context, this has been demonstrated through the many years of international and national impunity, through the eventual choice of a fiercely negotiated hybrid institution, through the limitations placed on the court's jurisdiction and through the continued limitations placed on the court's ability to pursue prosecutions. The following chapter moves to consider the role of victims within the ECCC in more detail through an exploration of the creation and performance of the court's civil party mechanism.

Notes

1 Former prosecutor R. Petit, 'Lawfare and International Tribunals: A Question of Definition? A Reflection on the Creation of the 'Khmer Rouge Tribunal' 43 *Case Western Reserve Journal of International Law* (2010–2011) 189.

2 R. Mawby and S. Walklate, *Critical Victimology* (Sage, 1994) 9.

3 C. Geertz, 'Thick Descriptions: Toward an Interpretive Theory of Culture' in C. Geertz (ed.), *The Interpretation of Cultures: Selected Essays* (Fontana Press, 1993) 3–30. See also K. McEvoy, 'Beyond Legalism: Towards a Thicker Understanding of Transitional Justice' 24 *Journal of Law and Society* (2007) 411; M. Coppedge, 'Thickening Thin Concepts and Theories: Combining Large-N and Small-N in Comparative Politics' 31 *Comparative Politics* (1999) 465.

4 See for example A. Westad and S. Quinn-Judge (eds.), *The Third Indochina War: Conflict between China, Vietnam and Cambodia, 1972–79* (Routledge, 2006); T. Fawthrop and H. Jarvis, *Getting Away with Genocide?* (University of South Wales, 2005); B. Kiernan, *The Pol Pot Regime* (Yale University Press, 1996); J.F. Metzl, *Western Responses to Human Rights Abuses in Cambodia, 1975–80* (Palgrave McMillan, 1996); F. Ponchaud, *Cambodia Year Zero* (Henry Holt & Co, 1978); K.D. Jackson, *Cambodia 1975–1978: Rendezvous With Death* (Princeton

University Press, 1992); D.P. Chandler, *The Tragedy of Cambodian History* (Yale University Press, 1991). For survivor accounts of the Khmer Rouge regime, see for example L. Ung, *First They Killed My Father* (Mainstream Publishing, 2001); V. Nath, *A Cambodian Prison Portrait* (White Lotus Co., 1999); P. Yathay, *Stay Alive My Son* (Cornell University Press, 2000); C. Mey, *Survivor* (DC-Cam, 2012); H. Vannak, *Bou Meng* (DC-Cam, 2010).

5 C. Kunst, *The Protection of Victims and Witnesses at International and Internationalized Criminal Courts – the Example of the ECCC* (Wolf Legal Publishers, 2013) 7.

6 D. Nohlen et al., *Elections in Asia: A Data Handbook, Volume II* (Oxford University Press, 2001) 74.

7 E. Gottesman, *Cambodia after the Khmer Rouge: Inside the Politics of Nation Building* (Yale University Press, 2003) 18.

8 Chandler, n.4 at 89.

9 C. White, *Bridging Divides in Transitional Justice* (Intersentia, 2017) 100.

10 J.D. Ciorciari and A. Heindel, *Hybrid Justice* (University of Michigan Press, 2014) 15; Case 002, Closing Order, 002/19–09–2007-ECCC-OCIJ, 15 September 2010, para. 18.

11 W. Form, 'Justice 30 Years Later? The Cambodian Special Tribunal for the Punishment of Crimes against Humanity by the Khmer Rouge' 37(6) *Nationalities Papers* (2009) 889.

12 Ibid., at 890.

13 H. Kissinger, *White House Years* (Little, Brown, 1979).

14 T. Owen and B. Kiernan, 'Bombs over Cambodia' *The Walrus Magazine*, October 2006.

15 Interview of Chhit Do by Bruce Palling, cited in Kiernan, n.4 at 23.

16 Owen and Kiernan, n.14.

17 B. Kiernan, 'Background to the Conflict in Cambodia' in K. Ambos and M. Othman (eds.), *New Approaches in International Criminal Justice* (Max-Planck Institute, 2003) 176.

18 Metzl, n.4 at 2–3.

19 Chandler, n.4.

20 Ibid., at 199–200.

21 A. Buckley, 'The Conflict in Cambodia and Post-Conflict Justice' in M. Cherif Bassiouni (ed.), *Post-Conflict Justice* (Transnational Publishers, 2002) 637.

22 Chandler, n.4 at 216–220.

23 *Idem.*

24 Kunst, n.5 at 9; Ponchaud, n.4 at 214–15.

25 Case 002, Closing Order, n. 10 at 240; Report of the Group of Experts for Cambodia established pursuant to General Assembly Resolution 52/135, UN Doc. A/53/850, 15 March 1999.

26 Kiernan, n.4 at 177.

27 Case 002, Closing Order, n. 10 at 227.

28 A.L. Hinton, 'Why Did You Kill?: The Cambodian Genocide and the Dark Side of Face and Honor' 57(1) *The Journal of Asian Studies* (1998) 93.

29 Kiernan, n.17 at 37.

30 Case 002, Closing Order, n. 10 at 1442–1446.

31 R.S. Taylor, 'Better Late Than Never' in J.E. Stromseth (ed.), *International and Comparative Criminal Law Series, Accountability for Atrocities: National and International Responses* (Transnational Publishers, 2003) 240.

32 White, n.9, at 105.

33 S. Luftglass, 'Crossroads in Cambodia: The United Nation's Responsibility to Withdraw Involvement from the Establishment of a Cambodian Tribunal to Prosecute the Khmer Rouge' 90 *Virginia Law Review* (2004) 893 at 899.

34 Case 002, Closing Order, n. 10 at 21, 179.
35 K.M. Klein, 'Bringing the Khmer Rouge to Justice: The Challenges and Risks Facing the Joint Tribunal in Cambodia' 4(3) *Northwestern Journal of International Human Rights* (2006).
36 B. Kiernan, 'The Demography of Genocide in Southeast Asia' 35(4) *Critical Asian Studies* (2003).
37 C. Etcheson, 'The Politics of Genocide in Cambodia' in C.P.R. Romano et al. (eds.), *Internationalized Criminal Courts: Sierra Leone, East Timor, Kosovo, and Cambodia* (Oxford University Press, 2004) 182.
38 Ciorciari and Heindel, n.10 at 15–16.
39 White, n.9 at 106–107.
40 Kiernan, n.4 at 178–179.
41 *Idem;* White, n.9 at 107–108.
42 Ciorciari and Heindel, n.10 at 17.
43 Kunst, n.5 at 10.
44 Ciorciari and Heindel, n.10 at 17.
45 *Decree Law No. 1: Establishment of People's Revolutionary Tribunal at Phnom Penh to Try the Pol Pot-Ieng Sary Clique for the Crime of Genocide*, Phnom Penh, 15 July 1979; R. Killean, 'Pursuing Retributive and Reparative Justice within Cambodia' in C. Lawther, L. Moffett and D. Jacobs, *Research Handbook on Transitional Justice* (Elgar, 2017) 466–488; F. Selbmann, 'The 1979 Trial of the People's Revolutionary Tribunal and Implications for ECCC' in S. Meisenberg and I Stegmiller, *The Extraordinary Chambers in the Courts of Cambodia* (Asser Press, 2016) 77–103.
46 Ibid., Article 1; both of the accused had taken refuge in Thailand at this point; see Fawthrop and Jarvis, n.4 at 44.
47 H.J. De Nike et al. (eds.), *Genocide in Cambodia: Documents from the Trial of Pol Pot and Ieng Sary* (University of Pennsylvania, 2000).
48 White, n.9, at 110.
49 R.C. Boulet, 'The World's First Genocide Trial, 30 Years on' *Phnom Penh Post*, 19 August 2009.
50 S. Scully, 'Judging the Successes and Failures of the Extraordinary Chambers of the Courts of Cambodia' 13 *Asian-Pacific Law and Policy Journal* (2011–2012) 300; Fawthrop and Jarvis, n.4 at 137.
51 S. Strangio, *Hun Sen's Cambodia* (Yale University Press, 2014) 238.
52 T. Hammarberg, 'How the Khmer Rouge Tribunal was Agreed: Discussions Between the Cambodian Government and the UN, Part 1: March 1997 – March 1999' *Searching for the Truth* (DC-Cam, 2011).
53 Fawthrop and Jarvis, n.4 at 24–25.
54 Ibid., at 31.
55 Ibid., at 18–19.
56 Kiernan, n.4 at 179–181.
57 E. Mysliweic, *Punishing the Poor: The International Isolation of Kampuchea* (Oxfam Professional, 1988).
58 Kunst, n.5 at 11; Fawthrop and Jarvis, n.4 at 37.
59 T. Findlay, *The Legacy and Lessons of UNTAC* (Oxford University Press, 1995) 5.
60 Ciorciari and Heindel, n.10 at 19–20.
61 Ibid., at 20.
62 *Agreements on a Comprehensive Political Settlement of the Cambodia Conflict,* Paris Peace Accords, 23 October 1991.
63 White, n.9 at 114.
64 UNSC Resolution 745, S/RES/745, 28 February 1992.
65 Kiernan, n.4 at 184.
66 J. Zasloff and M. Brown, *Cambodia Confounds the Peacemakers 1979–1998* (Cornell University Press, 1998) 297.

67 Ciorciari and Heindel, n.10 at 20.
68 *Law on Outlawing the Group of 'Democratic Kampuchea'*, KHM/30, 15 July 1994.
69 White, n.9 at 118.
70 Ibid at 114–115.
71 S. Mydans, 'Cambodia Purge Said to Claim 40 Victims' *New York Times*, 16 July 1997.
72 J. Galtung, 'Violence, Peace and Peace Research' 6(3) *Journal of Peace Research* (1969) 167.
73 White, n.9 at 116.
74 An estimated 89.42 per cent of respondents to a DC-Cam study reported losing relatives. See S. Linton, *Reconciliation in Cambodia* (DC-Cam, 2004) 57.
75 J.D. Veneciano and A. Hinton (eds.), *Night of the Khmer Rouge: Genocide and Justice in Cambodia* (Paul Robeson Gallery, 2007) 16.
76 E. Stover et al., 'The Medical and Social Consequences of Land Mines in Cambodia' 272(5) *Journal of the American Medical Association* (1994) 331.
77 Strangio, n.51 at 60.
78 Ibid., at 52.
79 Ibid., at 62–88.
80 White, n.9 at 121.
81 Hun Sen famously opined that Cambodians should 'dig a hole and bury the past'; see Linton, n.74.
82 Interview with Former Civil Party Lawyer, 11 September 2015; Interview with Civil Parties 1–4, and 7–8, December 2013, discussing their continued lack of Cambodian citizenship.
83 T.L.H. McCormack, 'Selective Reaction to Atrocity: War Crimes and the Development of International Criminal Law' 60 *Albany Law Review* (1996–1997) 681; R. Cryer, *Prosecuting international crimes: Selectivity and the international criminal law regime* (Cambridge University Press, 2005); A. Kramer and R. Killean 'Security Council Referrals to the ICC: A Politicised System' *The Irish Yearbook of International Law* (2012) 117.
84 J.D. Ciorciari (ed.), *The Khmer Rouge Tribunal* (DC-Cam, 2006) 15–16
85 K. Ainley, 'Transitional Justice in Cambodia: The Coincidence of Power and Principle' in R. Jeffery (ed.), *Transitional Justice in the Asia-Pacific* (Cambridge University Press, 2014) 125–156.
86 J.D. Ciorciari, 'History and Politics Behind the Khmer Rouge Trials' in J.D. Ciorciari and A. Heindel (eds.), *On Trial: the Khmer Rouge Accountability Process* (DC-Cam, 2009) 33–85.
87 T. Klosterman, 'The Feasibility and Propriety of a Truth Commission in Cambodia: Too Little? Too Late?' 15(3) *Arizona Journal of International and Comparative Law* (1998) 833.
88 Ciorciari and Heindel, n.10 at 20–21 and 25.
89 Letter from Norodom Ranariddh, Cambodian First Prime Minister, and Hun Sen, Cambodian Second Prime Minister, to Secretary General Annan, 21 June 1997; Identical letters dated 23 June 1997 from the Secretary-General addressed to the President of the General Assembly and to the President of the Security Council, A/51/930, S/1997/488, 24 June 1997.
90 UNGA Resolution A/RES/52/135, 27 February 1998.
91 S. Mydans, 'Cambodia Is Swept by Reports Saying that Pol Pot Has Died' *New York Times*, 16 April 1998.
92 D. Scheffer, 'The Extraordinary Chambers in the Courts of Cambodia', in MC Bassiouni, (ed.), *International Criminal Law* (3rd edn) (Martinus Nijhoff Publishers, 2008) 219–256.
93 S.R. Ratner, 'The United Nations Group of Experts for Cambodia' 93 *American Journal of International Law* (1999) 948.

94 UNSC, *Madeleine Albright Statement to the UN Security Council, Provisional Verbatim Record to the 3217th Meeting*, UN Doc. S/PV 3217, 25 May 1993.
95 Group of Experts, n. 25.
96 Ibid., at 126–129.
97 Ibid., at 190.
98 Ibid., at 148.
99 Fawthrop and Jarvis, n.4, at 127.
100 White, n.9, at 123.
101 Strangio, n.51 at 244; Ciorciari and Heindel, n.10 at 25.
102 C. Etcheson, *Retribution and Reconciliation: Healing What Ails Cambodia* (Project Report to the US Institute of Peace, October 2002).
103 Luftglass, n.33 at 910.
104 See D. Scheffer, *All the Missing Souls: A Personal History of the War Crimes Tribunals* (Princeton University Press, 2012) 382–383.
105 White, n.9, at 125.
106 Ciorciari and Heindel, n.10 at 27.
107 Ainley, n.85.
108 S. de Bertodano, 'Current Developments in Internationalized Courts' 1(1) *Journal of International Criminal Justice* (2003) 226 at 227.
109 'Tribunal Memorandum of Understanding between the UN and the Royal Government of Cambodia' *Phnom Penh Post*, Issue 9/22, 27 October–9 November 2000, gsp.yale.edu/tribunal-memorandum-understanding-between-united-nations-and-royal-government-cambodia (accessed 09/02/18).
110 *Law on the Establishment of Extraordinary Chambers in the Courts of Cambodia for the Prosecution of Crimes Committed during the Period of Democratic Kampuchea*, Law NS/RKM/0801/12, 10 August 2001; M. Buyanunda, 'The Khmer Rouge on Trial: Whither the Defense?' 74 *Southern California Law Review* (2001) 1581.
111 S. Linton, 'New Approaches to International Justice in Cambodia and East Timor' 84 *International Review of the Red Cross* (2002) 845.
112 *Letter from Prime Minister Hun Sen to the UN Legal Counsel*, 23 November 2001, cited in Bertodano, n.108 at 227.
113 'UN Ends Negotiations with Cambodia for Proposed Court to Try Former Khmer Rouge' *UN News Centre*, www.un.org/apps/news/story.asp?NewsID=2829#.Wn2x0macZTY (accessed 09/02/18).
114 UN High Commissioner for Human Rights, 'Secretary-General Replies to Cambodian Prime Minister's Letter on Trial of Khmer Rouge Leaders' *UN News Centre,* 20 August 2002, www.un.org/press/en/2002/SGSM8341.doc.htm (accessed 09/02/18).
115 Led by Japan, France, Australia and the US; Kunst, n.5 at 18.
116 Strangio, n.51 at 245.
117 UNGA A/RES/57/228, 27 February 2003.
118 Ibid.
119 *Report of the Secretary-General on Khmer Rouge Trials*, UN Doc A/57/769, 31 March 2003.
120 *Agreement between the UN and the Royal Government of Cambodia Concerning the Prosecution under Cambodian Law of Crimes Committed during the Period of Democratic Kampuchea*, 6 June 2003.
121 Secretary General, n.127.
122 UN Press Office, *General Assembly Approves Draft Agreement Between UN, Cambodia on Khmer Rouge Trials*, UN Doc. GA/10135, 13 May 2003.
123 *Letter from Prime Minister Hun Sen to Mr. Kofi Annan, UN Secretary-General, on the Adoption by the National Assembly of Cambodia of the Draft Law Approving the Agreement between the UN and the Royal Government of Cambodia*

Concerning the Prosecution under the Cambodian Law of Crimes Committed during the Period of Democratic Kampuchea, 4 October 2004.

124 Y. Chhang, 'The Thief of History – Cambodia and the Special Court' 1(1) *The International Journal of Transitional Justice* (2007) 157; ECCC Agreement, n.120, Articles 14–15.

125 'United Nations Mission Led by Mr. Mohammed Said, Coordinator for UN Assistance to the Khmer Rouge Tribunal (UNAKRT) to Phnom Penh Finalize the Budget for the EC. The Budget Is Set at USD 56.3 Million' ECCC Website, 12 August 2004 www.eccc.gov.kh/en/United%20Nations%20Mission%20led%20by%20Mr.%20Mohammed%20Said%2C%20Coordinator%20for%20UN%20Assistance%20to%20the%20Khmer%20Rouge%20Tribunal%20%28UNAKRT%29%20%2C%20to%20Phnom%20P (accessed 09/02/18).

126 ECCC Agreement, n.120, Preamble.

127 Hammarberg, n.52.

128 Ciorciari and Heindel, n.10 at 39.

129 S. Ratner, 'Justice for the Khmer Rouge? Sir Ninian Stephen and the United Nations Group of Experts for Cambodia' in T. McCormack and C. Saunders (eds.), *Sir Ninian Stephen: A Tribute* (Melbourne University Publishing, 2007) 216.

130 Strangio, n.51 at 241.

131 C. Fontaine, 'Cambodia Premier Says No to Trial' *Associated Press*, 28 December 1998.

132 Two key figures, Ta Mok and Duch were captured in 1999, charged with crimes against humanity by a military court and placed in provisional detention: 'Khmer Rouge "Butcher" captured' *BBC News*, 6 March 1999, news.bbc.co.uk/1/hi/world/asia-pacific/291566.stm (accessed 09/02/18); 'UN Official to Meet Khmer Rouge Killer' *BBC News*, 10 May 1999, news.bbc.co.uk/1/hi/world/asia-pacific/340151.stm (accessed 09/02/18).

133 Mydans, n.91; J. Aglioby, 'Khmer Rouge 'Butcher' Dies Waiting to Be Tried' *The Guardian*, 22 July 2006, www.theguardian.com/world/2006/jul/22/cambodia (accessed 09/02/18).

134 Petit, n.1 at 193–194.

135 Kunst, n.5 at 19.

136 Scheffer, n.100; Chhang, n.124.

137 White, n.9, at 127.

138 Strangio, n.51 at 241.

139 Kunst, n.5 at 19.

140 Ciorciari and Heindel, n.10 at 27.

141 Ibid., at 33.

142 C. Cisse, 'The International Tribunals for the Former Yugoslavia and Rwanda: Some Elements of Comparison' 7 *Transnational Law and Contemporary Problems* (1997) 103.

143 Ainley, n.85.

144 White, n.9, at 117.

145 Ainley, n.85.

146 Strangio, n.51 at 244; Scheffer, n.106.

147 Strangio, n.51 at 242.

148 Ciorciari and Heindel, n.10 at 38–39; Scheffer, n. 106.

149 Strangio, n.51 at 245.

150 L. Raub, 'Positioning Hybrid Tribunals in International Criminal Justice' 41 *New York University Journal of International Law and Politics* (2008–2009) 1013.

151 Ainley, n.85.

152 ECCC Internal Rules, passed 12 June 2007, last amended 16 January 2015, Rule 49.

153 See the *Code de Procédure Pénale du Royaume du Cambodie* (hereafter 'CPC') passed on 7 June 2007. See also G. Acquaviva, 'New Paths in International Criminal Justice? The Internal Rules of the Cambodian Extraordinary Chambers' 6 *Journal of International Criminal Justice* (2008) 129.
154 Internal Rules 53(1) and (2).
155 Internal Rules 71–73.
156 Case 001, Decision on Appeal against Detention Order of Kaing Guek Eav, 001/18–07–2007-ECCC-OCIJ, 3 December 2007.
157 ECCC Agreement, n.120, Article 4.
158 It should be noted that the civil/common or adversarial/inquisitorial dichotomy is a simplification, as very few legal systems could be considered a 'pure' example of either. As will be seen, the ECCC is no exception.
159 S. Vasiliev, 'Trial Process at the ECCC: The Rise and Fall of the Inquisitorial Paradigm in International Criminal Law?' in S. Meisenberg and I. Stegmiller (eds.), *The Extraordinary Chambers in the Courts of Cambodia* (T.M.C. Asser Press, 2016) 389–435.
160 Ciorciari and Heindel, n.10 at 48.
161 ECCC Law, n. 110, Article 44.
162 ECCC Agreement, n.120, Article 17.
163 'How Is the Court Financed?' ECCC Website, 8 August 2017, www.eccc.gov.kh/en/faq/how-court-financed (accessed 09/02/18).
164 H. Jarvis, 'Trials and Tribulations: The Long Quest for Justice for the Cambodian Genocide' in S. Meisenberg and I. Stegmiller (eds.), *The Extraordinary Chambers in the Courts of Cambodia* (T.M.C. Asser Press, 2016) 35–38.
165 J.A. Hall, 'Court Administration at the ECCC' in J.D. Ciorciari and A. Heindel (eds.), *On Trial: The Khmer Rouge Accountability Process* (DC-Cam, 2009) 198–200.
166 S.M. Torrens, 'Allegations of Political Interference, Bias and Corruption at the ECCC' in S. Meisenberg and I. Stegmiller (eds.), *The Extraordinary Chambers in the Courts of Cambodia* (Asser Press, 2016) 45–75.
167 Ibid.
168 Interview with Judge 1, 7 November 2013.
169 See Ciorciari and Heindel, n.10 for a comprehensive overview.
170 Its subject-matter jurisdiction includes genocide, crimes against humanity, grave breaches of the 1949 Geneva Conventions, torture, religious persecution, destruction of cultural property during armed conflict and crimes against internationally protected persons. ECCC Law, n. 118, Article 1.
171 White, n.9, at 138.
172 R. Skilbeck, 'Defending the Khmer Rouge' 8 *International Criminal Law Review* (2008) 423.
173 Closing Statement of Co-Defence Counsel, Koppe, Trial Transcript, 31 October 2014, at 45.
174 A. Bates, 'Cambodia's Extraordinary Chamber: Is it the Most Effective and Appropriate Means of Addressing the Crimes of the Khmer Rouge?' in R. Henham and P. Behrens (eds.), *The Criminal Law of Genocide: International, Comparative, and Contextual Aspects* (Ashgate, 2007) 185–197.
175 M. Osiel, *Making Sense of Mass Atrocity* (Cambridge University Press, 2009).
176 Former chairman of notorious Khmer Rouge detention centre S-21.
177 A prison in Phnom Penh where thousands of individuals were tortured and killed during the DK era.
178 Case 001, Separation Order, 002/14–08–2006, 19 September 2007.
179 Case 001, Trial Judgement, 001/18–07–2007-ECCC/TC, 26 July 2010
180 Case 001, Appeal Judgement, 001/18–07–2007-ECCC/SC, 3 February 2012.

181 Decision on IENG Thirith's Fitness to Stand Trial, 002/19–09–2007/ECCC/TC, 17 November 2011.
182 Termination of the Proceedings against the Accused IENG Thirith, 002/19–09–2007/ECCC/TC, 27 August 2015.
183 Termination of the Proceedings against the Accused IENG Sary, ECCC Trial Chamber, 002/19–09–2007/ECCC/TC, 14 March 2013.
184 Case 002/01, Trial Judgement, 002/19–09–2007/ECCC/TC, 7 August 2014; Case 002/01, Appeals Judgement, 002/19–09–2007/ECCC/SC, 23 November 2016.
185 S. Heder, 'A Review of the Negotiations Leading to the Establishment of the Personal Jurisdiction of the Extraordinary Chambers in the Courts of Cambodia' *Cambodia Tribunal Monitor*, 2 August 2011; D. Scheffer, 'The Negotiating History of the ECCC's Personal Jurisdiction' *Cambodia Tribunal Monitor*, 22 May 2011.
186 Strangio, n.51 at 243.
187 Ainley, n.85.
188 Strangio, n.51, at 241.
189 N. Vannarin and D. Gillison, 'Hun Sen Again Warns ECCC of Civil War' *The Cambodia Daily*, 8 September 2009, www.cambodiadaily.com/archives/hun-sen-again-warns-eccc-of-civil-war-1451/ (accessed 09/02/18); K. Naren, 'Hun Sen Warns of Civil War if ECCC Goes Beyond Limit' *The Cambodia Daily*, 27 February 2015, www.cambodiadaily.com/archives/hun-sen-warns-of-civil-war-if-eccc-goes-beyond-limit-78757/ (accessed 09/02/18).
190 Ciorciari, n.86, at 72.
191 Interview with Lawyer (Defence) 8 November 2013. See also Human Rights Watch, 'Cambodia: Government Obstructs Khmer Rouge Court' 5 September 2013, www.hrw.org/news/2013/09/05/cambodia-government-obstructs-khmer-rouge-court (accessed 09/02/18).
192 Ciorciari and Heindel, n.10 at 174.
193 S. Se, 'Cambodian PM Says No Third Khmer Rouge Trial' *Agence France-Presse*, 27 October 2010; I. MacKinnon, 'Prosecutor Wants to Indict Five More Khmer Rouge' *Financial Times*, 7 September 2009.
194 R.C. DeFalco, 'Cases 003 and 004 at the Khmer Rouge Tribunal: The Definition of "Most Responsible" Individuals According to International Criminal Law' 8(2) *Genocide Studies and Prevention: An International Journal* (2014) 45.
195 Case 003, Decision to Charge Meas Muth In Abstentia, 003/07–09–2009-ECCC-OCIJ, 3 March 2015.
196 'Case 004', ECCC Website, www.eccc.gov.kh/en/case/topic/120 (accessed 14/02/18).
197 S. White and C. Sokha, 'Death of Sou Met Highlights Concerns over Court: Monitors' *Phnom Penh Post*, 28 June 2013, www.civilparties.org/?p=1259 (accessed 14/02/18).
198 D. Crowe, *War Crimes, Genocide and Justice: A Global History* (Palgrave Macmillan, 2014) 366.
199 'Statement of the Co-Prosecutors' ECCC Website 5 January 2009, www.eccc.gov.kh/sites/default/files/media/Statement_OCP_05-01-09_EN.pdf (accessed 14/02/18).
200 Considerations of the Pre-Trial Chamber Regarding the Disagreement between the Co-Prosecutors Pursuant to Internal Rule 71, 001/18–11–2008-ECCC/PTC, 18 August 2009.
201 Kunst, n.5 at 17.
202 Ainley, n.85.
203 Ibid.

204 ECCC Agreement, n.120, Article 7(4); Kunst, n.5 at 17.
205 See A. Bates, 'Transitional Justice in Cambodia: Analytical Report' Atlas Project, October 2010 at 42.
206 Ciorciari and Heindel, n.10.
207 D. Gillison, 'Justice Denied' *Foreign Affairs*, 23 November 2011, foreignpolicy.com/2011/11/23/justice-denied/ (accessed 14/02/18); Human Rights Watch, 'Cambodia: Judges Investigating Khmer Rouge Crimes Should Resign', 3 October 2011, www.hrw.org/news/2011/10/03/cambodia-judges-investigating-khmer-rouge-crimes-should-resign (accessed 14/02/18).
208 Notice of Conclusion of Judicial Investigation, 002/19–09–2007-ECCC-OCIJ, 29 April 2011.
209 Scully, n.50 at 328
210 Case 003, Considerations of the Pre-Trial Chamber Regarding the International Co-Prosecutor's Appeal against the Co- Investigating Judges' Order on International Co-Prosecutor's Public Statement Regarding Case 003, 003/07–09–2009-ECCC/OCIJ, 24 October 2011, para. 5.
211 Ibid.
212 'Statement by the International Co-Investigating Judge' ECCC Website, 10 October 2011, www.eccc.gov.kh/en/articles/statement-international-co-investigating-judge (accessed 14/02/18).
213 'Press Release of the National Co-Investigating Judge' ECCC Website, 6 December 2011, www.eccc.gov.kh/sites/default/files/media/ECCC%20IntRCIJ%206%20Dec%202011%20En.pdf (accessed 14/02/18).
214 Judges must be appointed by Cambodia's Supreme Council of Magistracy. This was a controversial decision as articles 5(5) and 5(6) of the agreement state that the council is required to replace a resigning international co-investigating judge with the reserve.
215 M. Ellis, *The ECCC-A Failure of Credibility* (International Bar Association, February 2012).
216 Case 003, Opinion of the Pre-Trial Chamber Judges Downing and Chung on the Disagreement between the Co-Investigating Judges Pursuant to Internal Rule 72, 003/16–12–2011-ECCC/PTC, 10 February 2012.
217 'Press Release by the International Reserve Co-Investigating Judge' ECCC Website, 19 March 2012, www.eccc.gov.kh/en/articles/press-release-international-reserve-co-investigating-judge (accessed 14/02/18). See also 'Note of the International Reserve Co-Investigating Judge to the Parties on the Egregious Dysfunction within the ECCC Impeding the Proper Conduct of Investigations in Cases 003 and 004' 003/05–09–2009/ECCC-D114 and 004/07–09–2009/ECCC-D114, 21 March 2012.
218 'Mr Meas Muth charged in Case 003' ECCC Website, 14 December 2015, www.eccc.gov.kh/en/articles/mr-meas-muth-charged-case-003; 'The International Co-Investigating Judge charges Ao An in Case 004' ECCC Website, 27 March 2015, www.eccc.gov.kh/en/document/public-affair/international-co-investigating-judge-charges-ao-case-004; 'The International Co-Investigating Judge charges Im Chaem in absentia in Case 004' ECCC Website, 3 March 2015, www.eccc.gov.kh/en/document/public-affair/international-co-investigating-judge-charges-im-chaem-absentia-case-004–0 (all accessed 14/02/18).
219 The judicial police and/or gendarmerie officers of the Kingdom of Cambodia assigned to the ECCC; see Glossary annexed to ECCC Internal Rules.
220 Open Society Justice Initiative, *Political Interference at the Extraordinary Chambers in the Courts of Cambodia* (July 2010).
221 Closing Order on Case 004/01, 004/1/07–09–2009-ECCC-OCIJ, 22 February 2017.

222 J. Wallace, 'The Bucolic Life of a Cambodian Grandmother Accused of Mass Killings', *New York Times*, 24 February 2017.
223 'Staying Khmer Rouge Tribunal Cases Mulled' *Phnom Penh Post*, 8 May 2017, www.phnompenhpost.com/national/staying-khmer-rouge-tribunal-cases-mulled (accessed 16/02/18).
224 Interview with Judge 4, 13 January 2014; Interview with Judge 1, 7 November 2013; Interview with Lawyer 1 (Chambers) 11 November 2013; Interview with Lawyer 2 (Chambers) 11 November 2013; Interview with Lawyer 2 (Co-Prosecutors' Office) 8 November 2013; Interview with Judge 3, 11 November 2013; Interview with Lawyer 4 (Defence), 13 December 2013.
225 Interview with Judge 1, 7 November 2013.
226 Interview with Lawyer 1 (Chambers) 11 November 2013.
227 J. Birchall, 'Concerns over Bid to Wrap up Outstanding Investigations at Cambodia's ECCC' *International Justice Monitor*, 16 June 2017.
228 Interview with Judge 1, 7 November 2013.
229 UNSC Res 1932, S/RES/1932, 29 June 2010.
230 See for example *The Prosecutor v. Kenyatta*, Decision on Prosecution's Application for a Finding of Non-Compliance under Article 87(7) of the Statute, ICC-01/09–02/11–982, 3 December 2014.
231 DeFalco, n.194 at 55.
232 Skilbeck, n.172; Scully, n.50.
233 Open Society Justice Initiative, 'Recent Developments at the Extraordinary Chambers in the Courts of Cambodia' (May 2008).
234 'Civil Society Calls for Investigation of Further Suspects by the ECCC' *CHRAC*, 14 January 2009, ki-media.blogspot.co.uk/2009/01/civil-society-calls-for-investigation.html (accessed 16/02/18).
235 Interview with Lawyer (Defence) 8 November 2013.
236 White and Sokha, n.197.
237 E.E. Stensrud, 'New Dilemmas in Transitional Justice: Lessons from the Mixed Courts in Sierra Leone and Cambodia' 46(1) *Journal of Peace Research* (2009) 5; J. Glaspy, 'Justice Delayed? Recent Developments at the Extraordinary Chambers in the Courts of Cambodia' 21 *Harvard Human Rights Journal* (2008) 143.
238 J. Shapland, 'Victims, the Criminal Justice System and Compensation' 24(2) *British Journal of Criminology* (1984) 136.
239 T. Tyler, 'Procedural Justice, Legitimacy, and the Effective Rule of Law' 30 *Crime and Justice* (2003) 283.
240 Mawby and Walklate, n.2 at 9.
241 See n.83.

4 Crafting victim participation through judicial policy making

1. Introduction

The ECCC's civil party system constitutes one of the most extensive forms of victim participation in an international(ised) criminal court. Yet, while the ECCC's agreement acknowledges the legitimate concern of the Cambodian people in pursuing 'justice and national reconciliation, stability, peace and security',[1] neither the agreement nor the ECCC law provides substantial provisions for victim participation. The agreement refers to the protection of victims,[2] while the ECCC law allows for victims' questioning by the co-prosecutor[3] and for their right to appeal decisions of the TC.[4] While this might be considered as implying victims constitute parties with appellant rights, David Scheffer, one of the negotiators of the agreement, has opined that the ECCC 'was never conceived by those who negotiated its creation as an instrument of direct relief for the victims'.[5] That victims are able to participate as civil parties is instead attributable to the actions of the court's judiciary, which constitute the focus of this chapter. By exploring why and how the ECCC judges first created a civil party system of victim participation, this chapter seeks to provide a 'thicker' description of judicial conduct[6] while critically examining the actions, motivations, consequences, philosophical assumptions and power relations which may inform and shape judicial actions.[7] As noted by Wilson, in placing judicial actors at the centre of analysis, we 'get the sense of law as a dynamic and in some ways, even contingent process, shaped by rules . . . but also refashioned by the changing strategies of the legal actors'.[8] To aid this analysis, the chapter draws on theories of judicial behaviour, which is explored in the first subsequent section. The chapter then turns to its analysis of the various factors which influenced the creation of the civil party system

2. Theories of judicial behaviour

Theories of judicial behaviour within the context of domestic jurisdictions have been the subject of much scholarly analysis.[9] In contrast, the judiciary's role within the context of international(ised) criminal justice systems continue to receive relatively little attention.[10] Yet, just as within domestic systems,[11] international judges have the ability to use their discretion to further a variety of political and legal agendas.[12] Judges may engage in judicial policy making, encompassing the two related phenomena of gap-filling (whereby gaps in laws and procedure are judicially addressed) and activism (whereby judges act as lawmakers).[13] Indeed, the space given to judicial opinion, discretion and innovation is perhaps greater within international courts because of the developing nature of the law.[14] Such a phenomenon has already been briefly highlighted in Chapter 2 in the context of the ICC, when the uncertain nature of international criminal procedure and the issues surrounding the combination of different legal traditions resulted in significant judicial discretion being given to the ICC's judges.[15]

Judicial behaviours are inevitably influenced by a myriad of external and internal factors.[16] Dominant approaches within the political science literature on judicial behaviour have included the attitudinal model, whereby the ideas, attitudes and values of judges are considered the key variables determining behaviour,[17] and the strategic model, whereby judges are seen to be pursuing specific political and legal goals.[18] Others have explored the relationship between judges and their audiences, noting that concern for reputation and approval among certain audiences may influence judicial behaviour.[19] Such models contribute to an understanding of *why* judges pursue certain goals. Others have considered the various factors which will influence *how* judges exercise judicial discretion and policy making. As noted by Baum in his hierarchal model, 'judges are constrained by the legal rules they are called on to apply, by other participants in the courts, and by their political environments'.[20]

This chapter draws on these theories, without adopting one specific approach. Utilising Wessel's adaption of Baum's hierarchical model, this chapter explores the *creational*, *external* and *internal* factors that have influenced the ECCC judges in their establishment of civil party participation.[21] In this context, creational factors are defined as the textual constructs and legal language used to limit judicial discretion;[22] external factors are defined as the abilities of external forces and other parties to influence the judges' actions;[23] and internal factors are considered those that relate to the judges' own professional norms.[24] Although Wessel does not consider judges' own domestic legal tradition as a relevant internal factor, it is included within the present analysis, as the data suggest that legal cultures do influence judicial behaviour within the ECCC. The extent to which the judges appear to be acting in the furtherance of certain strategies, or as a result of their own attitudes and feelings, is also given attention. By combining data from my interviews with judges and other court staff with examples of the judges' public actions and decisions, the attitudes and strategies of the judges can be considered.

3. Drafting the internal rules

The court's legal framework initially comprised the agreement between the RGC and the UN, the Law on the Establishment of the ECCC and existing Cambodian procedural codes. The agreement and law comprise the RGC and UN's explicit creational restrains on the exercising of judicial discretion, providing the mandate for the court's composition, jurisdiction, procedures and powers.[25] With regards to the court's procedures, both the agreement and the law stipulated that ECCC proceedings should be primarily based on Cambodian law, conceding that

> [w]here Cambodian law does not deal with a particular matter, or where there is uncertainty regarding the interpretation or application of a relevant rule of Cambodian law, or where there is a question regarding the consistency of such a rule with international standards, guidance may be also sought in procedural rules established at the international level.[26]

It is therefore apparent that the negotiators and RGC legislatures wished for Cambodian procedural law to have primacy, with some limited reference to international standards and procedure in order to address any gaps or inconsistencies. Nevertheless, one of the first acts of the newly sworn-in judges of the ECCC was to draft a comprehensive set of Internal Rules, which differed not only from Cambodian procedures[27] but also from other procedural rules established at the international level.[28] This was done over the course of plenary sessions in 2006 and 2007, the details of which have been declared confidential, despite calls for transparency from a number of civil society actors.[29]

Neither of the founding documents explicitly provided for such rule-making behaviour.[30] However, the judges relied on the exceptions outlined earlier, adopting a broad interpretation of their right to seek guidance from international procedure[31] and citing the uncertainties surrounding Cambodian procedure as justification.[32] As a result of Cambodia's tumultuous past,[33] a certain amount of confusion surrounding what constituted Cambodian criminal procedure and whether laws drafted by UNTAC should be included within it was perhaps understandable.[34] The courts which were created following the Khmer Rouge's downfall were shaped around a Vietnamese socialist model of justice largely based on one-party autocratic rule, raising concerns over fair-trial rights.[35] Despite the introduction of new criminal procedure codes and improvements within Cambodia's legal system,[36] problems continued, particularly in relation to the rights of the defence, the independence of judges and prosecutors, adequate protection of witnesses and the right to counsel.[37] As a result, the judges justified the rules as an attempt to 'consolidate' the court's procedures,[38] relying on external factors to legitimise a broadening of their creational constraints and thus implicitly defining the rules as constituting judicial policy making through gap-filling.[39]

The judges' assumption of such far-reaching powers in the absence of an explicit statutory right is legally problematic;[40] judges generally do not have such rule-making authority, not least because of the separation of powers issues at stake.[41] Many of the rules undeniably go beyond 'consolidating' existing Cambodian procedure, amounting to judicial activism through the creation of new procedural rules.[42] This has led some to argue that the judges acted incorrectly or *ultra vires*.[43] Others have noted that international(ised) tribunals such as the ICTY, the ICTR and the SCSL have also allowed their judges to adopt and amend procedural rules, and argued that such empowerment is a necessary response to the new and evolving nature of ICL.[44] Kunst has argued that such justifications apply to the ECCC due to its status as the first international(ised) criminal tribunal to utilise inquisitorial methods.[45] Certainly, it is possible that the uniform application of domestic procedures may have struggled with the large-scale nature of the crimes charged, as two judges interviewed for the present study explained:

> You just cannot give a blanket authorisation for national law to apply. Considering that there are so many particularities, idiosyncrasies, of first of all mass atrocity proceedings . . . and secondly, proceedings of a hybrid nature with international and national elements. So we need to depart from it because our cases are simply too big to be fitted within this detailed framework of national law. We need specific solutions for big cases and these solutions are absent in the national law.[46]

> Mass atrocity crimes have different dynamics and they have to be dealt with differently from domestic crimes, and it wouldn't matter if it was a common law domestic system or a French based domestic system, domestic systems are not designed for mass atrocity crimes, they're not designed for international crimes by and large, you can adapt them but that's very very difficult.[47]

It is arguable that a certain amount of judicial policy making was justified by the need to create a functioning court system, and the ECCC judges were facing a system without precedent.[48] Nevertheless, a crucial difference between the ECCC and other international(ised) criminal courts is that the ICTY, the ICTR and the SCSL judges were explicitly empowered by statutes, which is not the case in the ECCC.[49] Furthermore, despite the ECCC law and the agreement stating that Cambodian law should be *primarily* applied, the judges have since found that 'the Internal Rules form a self-contained regime of procedural law', meaning that it constitutes 'the *primary* instrument to which reference should be made in determining procedures before the ECCC'.[50] Such a decision deviates significantly from the court's founding documents and allows the judges to adopt and amend procedurally binding rules without control and with little scrutiny in relation to being consistent with international standards and/or Cambodia law.[51] Indeed, at the time of writing the rules had been amended a total of nine times.[52] This judicial activism has attracted significant criticism from academics and court practitioners alike,[53] as vividly illustrated by one frustrated defence lawyer:

> Who gives a shit what the Internal Rules say? They're certainly not fixed; the Internal Rules weren't passed by anybody. They said that you judges can look elsewhere in international procedure if there's a conflict between domestic law and international procedure, and then the judges just got together in a room and made up a bunch of rules . . . that would be legitimate if the Internal Rules merely consolidate Cambodian criminal procedure with reference to international standards . . . but that's so patently not true.[54]

While this interviewee was primarily focused on the impact of this practice on the rights of the accused, the flexibility of the rules has had implications for victims too, most notably through the initial creation and subsequent limiting of the civil party system.

4. Crafting the civil party system

The crafting of the civil party system within the Internal Rules can be attributed to a number of creational, external and internal factors.[55] First, the judges utilised the agreement and the law's prioritisation of Cambodian procedure to draw on Cambodia's civil, French-based system of victim participation,[56] as explained by the Rules Committee:

> [A] complex issue has been how to ensure the rights and involvement of victims. While a familiar element of Cambodian law, this was not spelled out in detail in the ECCC Law and Agreement . . . We note that the ECCC is a court within the existing court structure of Cambodia. We interpreted this to mean that victims have the right to join as civil parties.[57]

Thus, the creational limitations placed on the judges through the use of 'textual constructs and legal language' were broadly interpreted,[58] allowing for the adaption of a system that had not been specifically contained within the court's founding documents or appeared to have been envisioned by the court's architects.[59] Second, the Internal Rules' drafting was accompanied by intense lobbying from victims' advocates, as well as several studies by experts and NGOs, who examined what scope the Internal Rules could give to victim participation.[60] The result was a number of comments submitted to the judges which urged for an expansive approach towards victim participation,[61] for example:

> Victim participation will help bridge the gap between the court and the people and will give victims a voice in this important process . . . The trial process should be responsive to their needs to the greatest extent possible.[62]
>
> The ECCC has an important role to play in setting a positive example of a criminal justice process for past human rights crimes that both protect the fundamental rights of suspects and accused persons, while balancing this with the interests of victims.[63]

External actors thereby exerted their influence to remind the judges both of the advances that had been made internationally and nationally with regards to victims' rights, and of the international civil community that would be observing their approach.[64] As the rules were being drafted post-2002, the judges would also have likely been aware of the ICC's victim participation mechanism and of the general impetus behind more victim-responsive approaches to ICL. Such a submission is supported by the rules governing the selection of ECCC judges, which require them to have experience in 'criminal law, international law, including international humanitarian law and human rights law'.[65] Wessel has noted the role of a 'humanitarian technocrat' is often placed on international judges, who are expected to legalise and develop humanitarian norms.[66] International judges are therefore encouraged to adopt professional customs and ethics which further humanitarian goals, leading to progressive approaches to their work which encourage and accept judicial policy making.[67] Thus, the ECCC judges' status as 'humanitarian technocrats' potentially further influenced the development of the civil party status.

This desire to develop the role of victims was certainly expressed by one judge involved in the rules' drafting:

> The way in which victim participation was organised here was an experiment, because we didn't have a model, we had the ICC but we were not overly happy with that model, it's incomplete and it doesn't work.[68]

Indeed, as the same judge also noted, 'legally it's stimulating to try and be creative', and it is possible that the intellectual desire to create a new victim participation system provided another motivation. It is also likely that the domestic legal system of the specific judges played a role. Reportedly, most international judges originating from common law systems favoured a lesser form of participation than that of a civil party because of concerns over the number of individuals who could qualify and the lack of resources to fund reparations.[69] However, the French judge Marcel Lemonde, along with his legal officer, pressed for a system based on the French/Cambodian model, while the national judges came to favour the scheme as a way of incorporating Cambodian law.[70] A variety of external influences and internal attitudes and strategies therefore combined, resulting in a strategy of victim inclusion and the creation of rules which originally provided for some of the most extensive procedural and substantive rights ever granted to victims in an international or hybrid criminal court.[71]

By way of example, Internal Rule 21, which outlines the basic principles that guide the ECCC, places the safeguarding of the interests of victims at the heart of its mandate, holding that their rights be respected throughout the proceedings.[72] A 'victim' is defined as any natural person or legal entity who has suffered harm caused by a crime within the jurisdiction of the ECCC; the person or entity need not be a resident or a national of Cambodia.[73] Victims are able to participate in the ECCC's work through a number of methods: they are entitled to file complaints with the court,[74] participate as witnesses if approached to do so by one of the parties and apply to participate as civil parties.[75] Those victims who are accepted as civil parties constitute a party to the proceedings and exercise legal action, one purpose of which is to support the prosecution.[76] This stated purpose is an example of the judicial activism that permeates the unique civil party system: neither Cambodian law nor other international(ised) criminal courts have placed such a duty on participating victims.[77] Critics have noted that such a requirement risks undermining the rights of the accused through the creation of an additional prosecutor[78] and decried the requirement as an example of the judges acting with outside their powers.[79] The requirement has certainly been difficult to implement in practice, as is explored in the next chapter.

The Internal Rules provide civil parties with a variety of participatory rights related to the procedural justice elements of voice and representation.[80] Although they cannot initiate investigative action themselves (again, unlike Cambodian law), during the pre-trial phase they can request hearings, interviews, confrontations, site investigations and expert reports.[81] Civil parties may also participate in provisional detention appeal hearings[82] and have certain rights in common with the other parties, such as the right to access the case file,[83] the right to service of decisions of the CIJs and the chambers,[84] the right to be interviewed by the CIJs,[85] the right to have their lawyers ask questions during confrontations organised by the CIJs,[86] the right to appeal most orders by the CIJs,[87] the right to raise procedural defects[88] and the right to be notified at the end of an investigation and to make observations thereon.[89] At trial, they testify without being under oath, in a similar fashion to the accused, and are entitled to a range of protective measures, including anonymity and in camera proceedings.[90] Civil parties also exercise the right to make limited appeals,[91] to make submissions on fact and law,[92] to be present at hearings,[93] to request and question witnesses,[94] to question the accused,[95] to make closing arguments and rebut the closing arguments of the accused.[96] When participating, they receive support from the VSS (formerly known as the Victims' Unit) a faction of the Office of Administration which became fully operational in 2010.[97] The court also has a Witness/Experts Support Unit which is mandated with the protection of witnesses.

In relation to substantive justice, the Internal Rules define the other purpose of civil party participation as being to seek collective and moral reparations.[98] Reparations based on state responsibility have developed within national, international and human rights law as a fundamental component of addressing human rights abuses.[99] Encompassing compensation, rehabilitation, guarantees of non-repetition and satisfaction, reparations seek to repair the damage or harm done and, at their ideal, re-establish the situation prior to the illegal act.[100] While ICL is based on individual rather than state responsibility, the inclusion of reparations in the ICC's Rome Statute demonstrates the growing awareness of the potential role for reparations within ICL.[101] Such developments are reflected in the inclusion of a reparations regime within the ECCC's Internal Rules.[102] Neither the ECCC law nor the agreement provided for any such substantive rights, but reparations are provided for within Cambodian law, providing a legal basis for their inclusion within the judges' policy making.[103] However, what is interesting about the judges' approach is that it follows neither Cambodian procedure nor international.[104] Under Cambodian criminal law, civil parties have the right to seek reparations for harm suffered because of the crimes being prosecuted, with reparations being understood as direct compensation and damages borne by the individual(s) liable.[105] No distinctions are made based on either the gravity of the offence or the number of civil parties entitled to reparations.[106] Meanwhile, other international(ised) criminal courts, while struggling to implement meaningful reparations in practice, have generally allowed for individual reparations at least to be included within the possibilities.[107] In contrast, the ECCC judges decided to provide for only 'collective and moral reparations'.[108] While the rules do not give a comprehensive definition of 'collective and moral',[109] they have been amended to state that such reparations are to 'acknowledge the harm' suffered by civil parties and 'provide benefits' which address this harm.[110] The intention appears to be to respond to moral harms, such as emotional distress, or damage inflicted on social structures, values and human comforts,[111] as distinguished from material reparations for lost property and other quantifiable losses.[112] The focus on such reparations was described by the judges as being 'due to the specific character of the ECCC', a reference to the widespread nature of the Khmer Rouge's crimes and the difficulties associated with granting individual reparations to potentially thousands of applicants.[113]

It is likely that predicted difficulties surrounding who would pay for reparations were also a motivating factor in precluding individual claims. Following Cambodian law, the rules initially stipulated that reparations were to be borne by the convicted person.[114] Sole reliance on such an approach was opposed by the VSS, civil party lawyers and NGOs from the beginning, because of their knowledge of the accused's indigence, and indeed Case 001 swiftly demonstrated the limits of such an approach.[115] Subsequent amendments have therefore allowed for externally funded reparative measures to be recognised by the court,[116] constituting another example of judicial policy making through gap-filling. This was acknowledged by one judge:

> This was an attempt by us to provide some sort of meaningful recognition, because we have no money . . . So it was more about tinkering on the edge.[117]

Certainly, the issue of who should fund reparations is one that remains problematic; no space was made in the court's budget for victim-centric measures of any kind, let alone for the awarding of reparations.[118] While human rights instruments have repeatedly established reparations for international crimes as a state obligation,[119] some commentators have argued persuasively that it is likely that the judges were wary of introducing any measures which risked upsetting the relationship between the court and the RGC.[120] Furthermore, as noted by one judge, the ECCC is a criminal court, rather than a human rights court, thus limiting its jurisdiction:

> The government is the successor of the Khmer Rouge, and the government has this obligation [to provide reparations] under national and international standards. And it was not our role to pronounce on it as a court . . . we cannot impose or ascertain the obligation of the government, as it is not party to our proceedings . . . We do not have such jurisdiction.[121]

This awareness of the government is reflective of a trend noted within the literature on judicial behaviour, which notes that judges will be wary of antagonising the 'political' branches of government.[122] Potential outcomes of such antagonism could include non-compliance, the overriding of the decision, or even retaliation through the freezing of salaries or punishing of individual judges.[123] Considering the precarious nature of the relationship between the RGC and the international side of the court, not to mention the level of control the RGC exercises over its national judiciary,[124] it would be natural for the judges to be wary of provoking retaliation for unwelcome reparation orders, leading them to make decisions aimed at avoiding such conflicts.[125] Such an approach is reflective of the strategic model of judicial behaviour, in which judges make decisions in line with their political and legal goals.[126] It is also illustrative of Baum's hierarchal model as explored earlier, in which he notes that judges are constrained by their political environments.[127]

One judge expressed a hope that the ECCC's judgements would assist victims in their pursuit of more substantial reparations from their government in the future:

> By reading our judgment, and by reading the names of the victims, the civil parties, they can do something in the future, for the more concrete, more substantial reparations. So what we can do now is just give guidance, so I think moral and collective is best thing we can do at the moment. And the final, more concrete substantial reparations should be done by Cambodian people themselves.[128]

Thus, one can discern that a desire to deliver something of substance was met by an awareness of the creational limits imposed by the court's jurisdiction, as well as the political and practical external limitations within which the court operates. The rules on reparation can therefore be interpreted as an attempt to pursue a strategy of victim-orientated judicial policy making through activism[129] while catering to the external factors of a sensitive political climate and a lack of financial resources.[130] Such a finding already demonstrates the multitude of factors that have influenced the role given to victims within the ECCC. The implications of these limitations for the victims is explored in greater detail in the next chapter.

5. Conclusion

This chapter has argued that the civil party system's initial drafting can be attributed to a variety of creational, external and internal factors.[131] The international growth in victims' rights and advocacy, the creation of the ICC's victim participation system and the pressure applied by civil society actors, all provided motivation for the judges to adopt their role as 'humanitarian technocrats',[132] expanding the norm of victim-centric justice within international(ised) criminal courts. Specific approaches varied amongst the judges, demonstrating the influence of their own legal cultures and personal attitudes towards victim-centric international justice. The unique nature of the ECCC, and indeed the evolving nature of ICL, arguably contributed to a context which enabled judicial activism, leading to an expansive interpretation of their legislative powers under the founding documents. With Cambodian civil law providing the means, a unique system was created, one that attempted to balance a role for victims with the external realities within which the court operated, particularly the vast scale of victimisation, limited court funding and a government unlikely to allow the court to step on its toes.

Despite the initial activism of the judges in granting extensive rights to civil parties, the practicalities of running an international criminal trial and dealing with mass crimes, multiple accused and numerous civil parties have taken their toll. It is unlikely that the judges fully grasped the magnitude of what they had created or the impact civil party participation was likely to have on a court dealing with such widespread victimisations. As observed by other court staff,

> I don't think there was anyone from this court who really thought from the beginning what victim participation should look like. I just think there was never really a clear idea of how it would work.[133]

> They came up with this idea . . . that they wanted to do this great thing, they were going to tell the story of Democratic Kampuchea and punish Nuon Chea and include the victims . . . They didn't have the first clue about what the role of these people was going to be . . . And as a consequence, again it's a whole bunch of well-intentioned disasters, the Chamber didn't know how to deal with them either.[134]

The result is that the civil party system has been one of continuous change and uncertainty, as the judges have struggled to balance the right to a fair trial, the rights of victims to participate and the real practical challenges posed by the two often competing principles.[135] The Internal Rules have been repeatedly revised, leading to a compilation of rules relating to civil parties (12, 12 *bis*, 12 *ter*, 23, 23 *bis*, 23 *ter*, 23 *quater* and 23 *quinquies*)[136] and continued criticism of the judges tendency to go far beyond their originally purported purpose of merely 'consolidating' applicable Cambodian procedures.[137] The rights of civil parties have also been limited through the court's jurisprudence, as the judges' attitudes have developed from a spirit of victim-centricity, to one focused on trial efficiency.[138] In light of these factors, their strategy appears to have moved away from one of judicial activism and has become more about containment. A number of changes to the civil party system have been introduced, some of which have already been highlighted earlier. The following chapter analyses these changes in more detail and assesses the ability of victims to access procedural and substantive justice during Case 001 and Case 002/01.

Notes

1 *Agreement between the UN and the Royal Government of Cambodia Concerning the Prosecution under Cambodian Law of Crimes Committed during the Period of Democratic Kampuchea*, 6 June 2003, Preamble.
2 Ibid., Article 23.
3 *Law on the Establishment of Extraordinary Chambers in the Courts of Cambodia for the Prosecution of Crimes Committed during the Period of Democratic Kampuchea*, Law NS/RKM/0801/12, 10 August 2001, Article 23.

4 Ibid., Article 36
5 D. Scheffer, 'The Extraordinary Chambers in the Courts of Cambodia', in M.C. Bassiouni, (ed.), *International Criminal Law* (3rd edn) (Martinus Nijhoff Publishers, 2008) 253.
6 C. Geertz, 'Thick Descriptions: Toward an Interpretive Theory of Culture' in C. Geertz (ed.), *The Interpretation of Cultures: Selected Essays* (Fontana Press, 1993) 3–30.
7 K. McEvoy, 'Beyond Legalism: Towards a Thicker Understanding of Transitional Justice' 24 *Journal of Law and Society* (2007) 411.
8 R.A. Wilson, *Writing History in International Criminal Trials* (Cambridge University Press, 2011) 109.
9 For example R.A. Posner, *How Judges Think* (Harvard University Press, 2008); L. Baum, *Judges and Their Audiences: A Perspective on Judicial Behaviour* (Princeton University Press, 2007); L. Epstein and J. Knight, *The Choices Judges Make* (CQ Press, 1998); L. Baum, *The Puzzle of Judicial Behaviour* (University of Michigan, 1997).
10 Exceptions include S. Jodoin, 'Understanding the Behaviour of International Courts: An Examination of Decision-Making at the ad hoc International Criminal Tribunals' 6(1) *Journal of International Law and International Relations* (2010) 1; J. Wessel, 'Judicial Policy-Making at the International Criminal Court: An Institutional Guide to Analyzing International Adjudication' 44 *Columbia Journal of Transnational Law* (2006) 377.
11 N. Arajärvi, 'The Role of the International Criminal Judge in the Formation of the Customary International Law' 1(2) *European Journal of Legal Studies* (2007); M.A. Graber, 'Legal, Strategic, or Legal Strategy: Deciding to Decide during the Civil War and Reconstruction' in R. Kahn and K. Kersch (eds.), *The Supreme Court and American Political Development* (University Press of Kansas, 2006) 33–66.
12 M.R. Brubacher, 'Prosecutorial Discretion Within the International Criminal Court' 2 *Journal of International Criminal Justice* (2004) 71; S.W. Tiefenbrun, 'The Paradox of International Adjudication: Developments in the International Criminal Tribunals for the Former Yugoslavia and Rwanda, The World Court and the International Criminal Court' 25 *North Carolina Journal of International Law and Commercial Regulation* (2000).
13 H. Rasmussen, *On Law and Policy in the European Court of Justice: A Comparative Study in Judicial Policymaking* (Martinus Nijhoff, 1986).
14 Jodoin, n.10 at 4.
15 C. Kress, 'The Procedural Law of the International Criminal Court in Outline: Anatomy of Unique Compromises' 1 *Journal of International Criminal Justice* (2003) 603.
16 Wessel, n.10.
17 G.A. Tarr, *Judicial Process and Judicial Policy Making* (Wadsworth, 2003); J.A. Segal and H.J. Spaeth, *The Supreme Court and the Attitudinal Model Revisited* (Cambridge University Press, 2002).
18 L. Epstein and J. Knight, 'Towards a Strategic Revolution in Judicial Politics: A Look Back, A Look Head' 53(3) *Political Research Quarterly* (2000) 625.
19 T. Garoupa and T. Ginsburg, 'Judicial Audiences and Reputation: Perspectives from Comparative Law' 47 *Columbia Journal of Transnational Law* (2008) 451; F. Schauer 'Incentives, Reputation, and the Inglorious Determinants of Judicial Behavior' 68 *University of Cincinnati Law Review* (1999) 615; T.J. Miceli and M.M. Cogel 'Reputation and Judicial Decision-Making' 23 *Journal of Economic Behavior and Organisation* (1994) 31.
20 L. Baum, 'Electing Judges' in L. Epstein (ed.), *Contemplating Courts* (SAGE, 1995) 18.

21 Wessel, n.10.
22 Ibid., at 384.
23 Ibid., at 285.
24 Amended slightly from Wessel, n.10 at 385.
25 L. R. Helfer and G. B. Dinwoodie, 'Designing Non-National Systems: The Case of the Uniform Domain Name Dispute Resolution Policy' 43 *William and Mary Law Review* (2001) 141 at 224.
26 ECCC Agreement, Article 12; See also ECCC Law, Arts. 20 new, 23 new, 33 new.
27 *Code de Procédure Pénale du Royaume du Cambodie* ('CPC'), passed on 7 June 2007.
28 Taken to mean the procedures adopted in other international(ised) criminal courts, see S. Starygin, 'Internal Rules of the Extraordinary Chambers in the Courts of Cambodia (ECCC): Setting an Example of the Rule of Law by Breaking the Law?' 2(2) *Journal of Law and Conflict Resolution* (2011) 20.
29 'Civil Society Deeply Concerned about the ECCC Draft Internal Rules' *CHRAC*, 24 January 2007, www.licadho-cambodia.org/pressrelease.php?perm=138 (accessed 24/02/18).
30 S. Vasiliev, 'Trial Process at the ECCC: The Rise and Fall of the Inquisitorial Paradigm in International Criminal Law?' in S. Meisenberg and I. Stegmiller (eds.), *The Extraordinary Chambers in the Courts of Cambodia: Hybrid Contributions to International Criminal Law* (Asser Press, 2016) 389–435; G. Acquaviva, 'New Paths in International Criminal Justice? The Internal Rules of the Cambodian Extraordinary Chambers' 6 *Journal of International Criminal Justice* (2008) 129 at 132.
31 ECCC Agreement, Article 12(1).
32 Acquaviva, at 129.
33 K. D. Magliveras, 'Difficulties and Status of Efforts to Create an International Criminal Court in Cambodia' 3(2) *Asia-Pacific Journal on Human Rights and the Law* (2002) 105.
34 C. Kunst, *The Protection of Victims and Witnesses at International and Internationalized Criminal Courts – the Example of the ECCC* (Wolf Legal Publishers, 2013) 62–63.
35 J. P. Bair, 'From the Numbers Who Died to Those Who Survived: Victim Participation in the Extraordinary Chambers in the Court of Cambodia' 31 *University of Hawaii Law Review* (2008–2009) 508.
36 CPC, n.27.
37 H. Friman, 'Procedural Law of Internationalized Criminal Courts' in C. P. R. Romano (ed.), *Internationalized Criminal Courts: Sierra Leone, East Timor, Kosovo, and Cambodia* (Oxford University Press, 2004) 327–328.
38 ECCC Internal Rules, Preamble.
39 Rasmussen, n.13.
40 Vasiliev, n.30
41 Kunst, n.34. The separation of powers doctrine would hold that one body should not hold legislative, executive and judicial powers.
42 Explored in the following discussion.
43 Starygin, n.28.
44 Kunst, n.34.
45 Ibid., at 64–65.
46 Interview with Judge 4, 13 January 2014.
47 Interview with Judge 1, 7 November 2013.
48 E. Benvenisti, 'Customary International law as a Judicial Tool for Promoting Efficiency' in E. Benvenisti and M. Hirsh (eds.), *The Impact of International Law on International Cooperation* (Cambridge University Press, 2004) 85.
49 S. Studzinsky, 'Participation Rights of Victims as Civil Parties and the Challenges of Their Implementation before the Extraordinary Chambers in the Courts of

Cambodia' in T. Bonacker and C. Safferling (eds.), *Victims of International Crimes: An Interdisciplinary Discourse (*Asser Press, 2013) 175–189.

50 Case 002, Decision on Nuon Chea's Appeal against Order Refusing Request for Annulment, 002/19-09-2007-ECCC/OCIJ, 26 August 2008. Emphasis added.

51 Studzinsky, n.49 at 179. While the co-prosecutors, the director and the deputy director of the Office of Administration, the head of the Defence Support Section and the head of Victims Support Section can attend the sessions, only the judges can vote.

52 The latest revision is dated 16 January 2015.

53 Vasiliev, n.20; Studzinsky n.49; Starygin, n.28; Case 002, Civil Party Co-Lawyers' Joint Request for Reconsideration of the Pre-Trial Chamber's Assessment of the Internal Rules in the Decision on Nuon Chea's Appeal Against Refusing Request for Annulment, 002/19–09–2007/ECCC/OCIJ, 13 October 2008.

54 Interview with Lawyer 3 (Defence), 29 October 2014.

55 Wessel, n.10.

56 D. Boyle, 'The Rights of Victims: Participation, Representation, Protection, Reparation' 4 *Journal of International Criminal Justice* (2006) 307 at 310; M. Guiraud, *Victims' Rights before the Extraordinary Chambers in the Courts of Cambodia (ECCC): A Mixed Record for Civil Parties* (FIDH, November 2012) 17.

57 ECCC, 'Joint Statement by Judicial Officers: ECCC Plenary Session Unanimously Adopts Internal Rules' ECCC Website, 13 June 2007, www.eccc.gov.kh/sites/default/files/media/Joint_Press_Statement__on_internal_rules_eng_fr_13_june_2007.pdf (accessed 16/02/18).

58 Wessel, n.10 at 384.

59 Scheffer, n.5.

60 International Center for Transitional Justice, 'Comments on Draft Internal Rules for the ECCC', 17 November 2006; Human Rights Watch, 'Comments on ECCC Internal Rules', 17 November 2006, www.hrw.org/news/2006/11/17/extraordinary-chambers-courts-cambodia (accessed 16/02/18); Cambodian Human Rights Action Committee, 'Comments on ECCC Draft Internal Rules', 17 November 2006, www.licadho-cambodia.org/reports.php?perm=97 (accessed 16/02/18); FIDH, ADHOC, LICADHO and the Collective for Khmer Rouge Victims, 'Key Comments and Proposals on ECCC Draft Internal Rules' 17 November 2006, www.fidh.org/IMG/pdf/Key_Comments_FIDH-ADHOC-LICADHO-ADHOC.pdf (accessed 16/02/18); DC-Cam, 'Comments on ECCC Internal Rules', 16 November 2006, www.d.dccam.org/Tribunal/Documents/index1.htm (accessed 16/02/18).

61 Ibid.

62 LICADO et al., ibid.

63 International Center for Transitional Justice, n.60.

64 See Chapter 2.

65 ECCC Agreement, Article 3(1).

66 Wessel, n.10 at 440–442.

67 Ibid., at 443.

68 Interview with Judge 1, 7 November 2013.

69 J.D. Ciorciari and A. Heindel, *Hybrid Justice: The Extraordinary Chambers in the Courts of Cambodia* (University of Michigan Press, 2014) 204, citing an anonymous interview.

70 Ibid., at 205.

71 M. Mohan, 'The Paradox of Victim-Centrism: Victim Participation at the Khmer Rouge Tribunal' 9 *International Criminal Law Review* (2009) 733.

72 Internal Rule 21(c).

73 Internal Rule 23*bis*(2).

74 Internal Rule 12(2)(c) and 49(2); ECCC, Practice Direction on Victim Participation, Revision 1, 27 October 2008.
75 Similar to the CPC, a victim may not simultaneously act as both a civil party and a witness. Neither can a person act first as a witness before applying to be a civil party as the deadlines for submitting civil party applications are set for before the commencement of trial. Thus, if victims are approached by one of the parties seeking to use them as a witness, they must decide whether they wish to testify or whether they wish to apply for civil party status.
76 Internal Rule 23.
77 Starygin, n.28 at 25.
78 S. Zappalà, 'The Rights of Victims v. the Rights of the Accused' 8 *Journal of International Criminal Justice* (2010) 137 at 162; G. Mettraux, 'Victims' Participation in International Criminal Law, Symposium Forward' 8 *Journal of International Criminal Justice* (2010) 75.
79 Starygin, n.28 at 25–26.
80 Provisions for the implementation of rights in practice can also be found in the ECCC's Practice Direction on Victim Participation, n.74.
81 Internal Rule 59(5).
82 See the following discussion.
83 Internal Rule 55(6).
84 Internal Rule 46(1).
85 Internal Rule 59(1).
86 Internal Rule 58(5).
87 Internal Rule 74(4).
88 Internal Rule 76(2).
89 Internal Rule 66.
90 Internal Rule 29; Case 001, Decision on Protective Measures for Civil Parties, 001/18-07-2007/ECCC/TC, 2 June 2009.
91 Internal Rules 23(a) and 74(f).
92 Internal Rule 139.
93 Ibid.
94 Internal Rules 139 and 91.
95 Internal Rule 90.
96 Internal Rule 94.
97 B. McGonigle Leyh, *Procedural Justice? Victim Participation in International Criminal Proceedings* (Intersentia, 2011) 216–217.
98 Internal Rule 23.
99 L. Moffett, *Justice for Victims at the International Criminal Court* (Routledge, 2014) 143.
100 *UN Basic Principles and Guidelines on the Right to a Remedy and Reparation for Victims of Gross Violations of International Human Rights Law and Serious Violations of International Humanitarian Law*, UNGA Res. 60/147, 16 December 2005; J.M. Pasqualucci, 'Victim Reparations in the Inter-American Human Rights System: A Critical Assessment of Current Practice and Procedure' 32 *Michigan Journal of International Law* (1996–1997) 1.
101 Moffett, n.99 at 143.
102 Internal Rule 23.
103 Cambodia is also a party to treaties which recognise the right to reparations for serious human rights violations, including UNGA, *International Covenant of Civil and Political Rights*, UNGA Resolution 2200A (XXI), 16 December 1966; *Rome Statute of the International Criminal Court*, 2149 UNTS 256, 17 July 1998; *Convention against Torture and Other Cruel Inhuman or Degrading Treatment or Punishment*, UNGA Resolution 39/46, 10 December 1984.

104 Starygin, n.28 at 23.
105 CPC, n.27, Articles 355, 356, 523 and 533.
106 Starygin, n.28 at 23–24.
107 ICC, Rules of Procedure and Evidence, ICC-ASP/1/3, 9 September 2002, Rule 97; ICTY, Rules of Procedure and Evidence, Revision 50, 8 July 2015, Rule 106; ICTR, Rules of Procedure and Evidence, 29 June 1995, as amended 13 May 2015, Rule 106; *Statute for the Special Tribunal for Lebanon*, UNSC Res. 1757, S/RES/1757, 31 January 2007, Article 25; SCSL Rules of Procedure and Evidence, adopted on 16 January 2002, Rule 105.
108 Internal Rules, Rule 23 and Rule 23 *quinquies.*
109 Indeed, no globally recognised definition exists. F Rosenfeld, 'Collective Reparations for Victims of Armed Conflict' 92 *International Review of the Red Cross* (2010) 731.
110 Internal Rule 23 *quinquies.*
111 R. Jeffery, 'Beyond Repair?: Collective and Moral Reparations at the Khmer Rouge Tribunal' 13 *Journal of Human Rights* (2014) 103; C. Sperfeldt, 'Collective Reparations at the Extraordinary Chambers in the Courts of Cambodia' 12 *International Criminal Law Review* (2012) 457.
112 Jeffery, ibid., at 104.
113 Joint Statement, n.57; Case 001, Trial Judgement, 001/18–07–2007-ECCC/TC, 26 July 2010 at 667–75.
114 Internal Rule 23(11).
115 Sperfeldt, n.111; CHRAC and ECCC Victims Unit, *Reparations for Victims of the Khmer Rouge Regime, Report of a Conference Held in Phnom Penh from 26–27 November 2008* (Phnom Penh, 2009); CHRAC, 'Open Letter to the Members of the ECCC Plenary and the Rules Committee', 3 June 2009, khmernews.wordpress.com/2009/06/05/open-letter-to-the-members-of-the-eccc-plenary-and-the-rules-committee/ (accessed 16/02/18).
116 Internal Rule 23 *quinquies.*
117 Interview with Judge 1, 7 November 2013.
118 See Chapter 7.
119 For example International Law Commission, *Draft Articles on Responsibility of States for Internationally Wrongful Acts*, Supplement No. 10 (A/56/10), chp. IV.E.1, November 2001.
120 Jeffery, n.111.
121 Interview with Judge 4, 13 January 2014.
122 T. Ginsburg, *Judicial Review in New Democracies; Constitutional Courts in Asian Cases* (Cambridge University Press, 2003).
123 Ibid.
124 'Cambodia: Withdraw Fundamentally Flawed Judiciary Laws' *Human Rights Watch*, 3 May 2014, www.hrw.org/news/2014/05/03/cambodia-withdraw-fundamentally-flawed-judiciary-laws (accessed 16/02/18).
125 Epstein and Knight, n.9.
126 Posner, n.9; Epstein and Knight, n.18.
127 Baum, Puzzle of Judicial Behaviour, n.9 at 18.
128 Interview with Judge 2, 11 November 2013.
129 Posner, n.69 Epstein and Knight, n.18.
130 Ginsburg, n.122; Baum, n.20.
131 Wessel, n.10.
132 Ibid.
133 Interview with Lawyer 2 (LCL Office), 21 November 2013.
134 Interview with Lawyer 3 (Defence), 8 November 2013.
135 Case 001, Decision on Civil Party Co-lawyers' Joint Request for a Ruling on the Standing of Civil Party Lawyers to Make Submissions on Sentencing and

Directions Concerning the Questioning of the Accused, Experts and Witnesses Testifying on Character, Dissenting Opinion of Judge Lavergne, 001/18-07-2007/ECCC/TC, 9 October 2009.

136 Internal Rules.

137 I. Stegmiller, 'Legal Developments in Civil Party Participation at the Extraordinary Chambers in the Courts of Cambodia' 27 *Leiden Journal of International Law* (2014) 465.

138 Ibid.

5 Judicial implementation of civil party participation

1. Introduction

The chapter details the experiences of civil parties within the courtroom of the ECCC over the course of Case 001 and Case 002/01. In doing so, it examines the crucial role of the judiciary in delivering procedural and substantive justice to victims. As those primarily responsible for governing courtroom proceedings, judges are critical actors in the implementation and protection of procedural rights for all parties to the trial.[1] Similarly, their remit over the production of judgements, sentences and reparations renders them largely responsible for the deliverance of substantive justice to victim populations. The judges at the ECCC have been particularly and uniquely involved in the provision of procedural and substantive justice to victims; indeed, as explored within the previous chapter, judicial policy making is primarily responsible for the creation of the ECCC's civil party system. By continuing to draw on the theories of judicial behaviour highlighted in Chapter 4, this chapter highlights the role of judicial policy making[2] in shaping procedural and substantive justice. [3] In summary, it considers the attitudes and strategies adopted by the judiciary[4] and the creational,[5] external[6] and internal[7] factors that influenced those attitudes and strategies. The implications of judicial behaviour for victims' ability to *access justice*, their experience of *procedural justice* and their ability to obtain *substantive justice*[8] are each explored in the following sections.

2. Case 001: from judicial activism to restraint

Accessing justice

Judicial attitudes with regards to who should be accepted as a civil party have varied over the course of the court's first two cases. During Case 001, applicants were required to show that they were 'victims of a crime coming within the jurisdiction' of the ECCC, and that their injury was 'physical, material or psychological' and 'the direct consequence of the offence, personal and have actually come into being'.[9] Thus, the judges accepted applications in relation to any crimes that fell under the subject-matter and temporal jurisdiction of the court.[10] Although the Internal Rules implied that only direct victims would have standing, they allowed applications from indirect victims too, as well the successors of a deceased applicant in certain cases.[11] Applying these criteria, the judges[12] accepted 93 victims as civil parties throughout the course of Case 001.[13] However, this initially inclusive approach was subsequently restricted. The first restriction occurred at the case's initial hearing, where the TC determined that applicants would be required to prove their identity.[14] Such a requirement constituted judicial policy making, as no such requirement was contained within the rules and was arguably insensitive to the difficulties many victims might have with proving their identity. The chamber acknowledged that this could be problematic, stating that a flexible approach could be adopted.[15] Yet, their focus on documentation such as electoral cards and voter registration forms arguably failed to respond to the reality within Cambodia, where the nature of registration procedures means it can be impossible in some cases for an applicant to provide documentary proof.[16]

The next restriction occurred in 2010, through an amendment to the Internal Rules requiring applicants to demonstrate a direct link between their injury and the *crimes alleged against the defendants* rather than the previously required link to a crime coming within the court's jurisdiction.[17] This amendment followed the publication of Case 002's significantly broader scope, and judges would have been aware of the challenges associated with involving large numbers of civil parties in a trial of its size and complexity.[18] It is therefore arguable that this restriction reflected a strategy of trial expediency, through an attempt to limit the number of victims who could successfully apply. However, these amendments were also retrospectively applied at the Case 001 judgement stage.[19] In cases of indirect victimhood, immediate relatives of direct victims could be presumed to have suffered harm, while others were required to prove 'a close kinship or bond of affection or dependency'.[20] Indirect victims were required to prove that their relatives had been detained at one of the security centres with which the case was concerned.[21] These requirements resulted in 19 civil parties who had claimed to have lost a loved one having their status revoked,[22] as well as a further four who could not supply sufficient evidence that they had been victims of crimes perpetrated by Duch.[23]

The revocation of civil party status at such a late stage in the proceedings resulted in a widespread sense of secondary victimisation and was criticised by the rejected applicants, civil party advocates and the wider victim population.[24] Nor was it uniformly supported within the court. One judge attributed the decision to the attitudes of their colleagues:

> I think it was entirely insensitive of the particular Judges, and I don't think it was the national judges who were responsible for it. I think that they have a degree of compassion. I think as a judge, in circumstances such as this, there is no reason why you can't be compassionate, if the accused are not adversely affected, because victims need compassion. They don't need trauma as a result of being involved in a process, they need understanding, and I don't think that enough judges fully understand that.[25]

Another attributed the decision to the language used within the Internal Rules:

> It seems to be that both the legal framework was obscure and perhaps the information was too technical to be accessible to many of the victims, this could have been resolved earlier without dragging them through the process and then rejecting them in the end.[26]

The latter perspective, that the decision was the result of the obscurity of the legal framework, was also expressed by the SCC in their appeal judgement. Although the chamber held that the TC had lawfully assessed civil party applications, the chamber acknowledged that the apparent misunderstanding about the application process had caused anguish to many applicants.[27] Indeed, with the civil party system's unique and 'experimental' nature limiting the external guidance available to judges,[28] it seems likely that the last-minute revocations may also have been attributable to the TC adapting to the new procedures as they went along.

Regardless of the reasoning, the revocation of their status undoubtedly severely impacted the applicants' sense of procedural justice, as well as their ability to access substantive justice.[29] The distress was mitigated for some at the appeal stage.[30] The chamber found that indirect victims could encompass 'a wide range of persons', who might suffer material harm, physical harm or psychological harm as a result of the injury of a loved one or a caregiver, or resulting from 'uncertainty and fear about the direct victims' fate or knowledge of their suffering, or the loss of the sense of safety and moral integrity'.[31] The SCC proceeded to grant the appeals of ten applicants on the basis of further information submitted.[32] While this addressed the secondary victimisation of some civil parties, allowing persons who ultimately did not qualify as civil parties to participate throughout a trial raises additional issues, including the resources spent on their participation and the impact on the rights of the accused.[33]

Procedural justice

This section considers the quality of civil parties' experience during the trial by analysing a number of aspects of procedural justice, including the civil parties' ability to participate through their representatives,[34] their ability to exercise their voice in the proceedings and the extent to which they were treated with dignity and respect. The role of the judges in delivering (or restricting) those aspects of procedural justice is particularly examined.

Each of the 93 civil parties in Case 001 chose their own legal representation,[35] resulting in four legal teams.[36] As each legal team comprised at least an international and a national lawyer, this meant that as many as eight different lawyers might question a witness.[37] The likelihood of multiple rounds of questioning was enhanced by the fact that the civil party legal teams were not necessarily collaborating or cooperating with each other.[38] Indeed, a number of disagreements occurred throughout trial proceedings,[39] as the different civil party legal teams adopted differing trial strategies.[40] While the rules had not required the civil party lawyers to work together,[41] the implications of these additional representatives had perhaps not been fully anticipated by the chamber,[42] and judges quickly became irritated, reminding the lawyers to stick to relevant questions,[43] to avoid 'personal' or 'hypothetical questions', to stick to the facts before the chamber[44] and to properly prepare their clients prior to questioning [45] The addition of these new representatives also irritated the two traditional adversarial parties. While one of the goals of civil party participation is defined as being 'to support the prosecution', it became evident that little coordination had occurred between the co-prosecutors and the civil party lawyers.[46] While on some occasions the civil party lawyers contributed to the prosecution's case, there were also incidents where their line of questioning damaged the prosecution's case.[47] Nevertheless, the defence objected to what it perceived to be an auxiliary prosecutor, even openly critiquing the activism of the judges:

> Looking at the letter of the law, the law is on your side. But the law is a living organism and more specifically, we all know here that we are in a tribunal that creates law.[48]

Thus, the judges were faced with civil parties' additional filings and oral interventions, as well as debates about the proper scope of participation.[49] Although Case 001 was concerned with narrow factual allegations against one defendant, who had admitted large parts of the case against him, the proceedings lasted about ten months. This can, in part, be attributed to the fact that Duch contested his individual responsibility, and as there was no mechanism to plead guilty, a full trial was held.[50] Still, the inclusion of civil parties undoubtedly contributed.

It is likely that these delays caused concern within the court; as with other courts, the ECCC is tasked with conducting trials in a fair and expeditious manner.[51] However, the advanced age of the accused and victims, and the risk of donor fatigue, made delays a dangerous threat to the court's ability to deliver justice.[52] Indeed, the subsequent death of two accused during Case 002 was to become 'emblematic of the saying that justice delayed is justice denied'.[53] With Case 002 looming, and the prosecution and the defence expressing frustration, it is clear that the judges were being subjected to pressure from within the courtroom, as well as the constant external pressures of donors wishing for expedient proceedings.[54] As noted by Wessel, judges will respond to other actors, particularly those who have the power to 'punish' unwelcome judicial decision making.[55] Attempts to curtail the delays therefore soon revealed themselves in their attitudes towards the civil party lawyers. Although initially supportive of broad participatory rights,[56] the TC soon began to adopt a more restrictive approach, holding that while the purpose of civil party participation was to support the prosecution, this did not mean that the civil parties should have a 'general right of equal participation with the Co-Prosecutors'.[57] They therefore took steps to limit the situations in which civil party lawyers could question witnesses and the accused, barring them from making submissions relating to sentencing and from questioning character witnesses on the grounds that character evidence was a matter related to sentencing rather than guilt.[58] Such restrictions caused dismay amongst the civil parties, some of whom boycotted subsequent proceedings, arguing that truth and justice were illusionary if they were not given the opportunity to understand the motivations of the accused.[59] Attempts to appeal these decisions were declared inadmissible by the SCC, who found decisions on sentencing or on limits of examinations to be outside the scope of the Internal Rules.[60] Given the Internal Rules' judge-made nature, such a decision can be interpreted as being more reflective of judicial attitudes than of any creational restraints placed on them.

The restrictions created a distinction between the ECCC and other international courts; both the ICC and the STL allow victims a role in the sentencing stage.[61] Nor were the restrictions unanimous. The French judge Lavergne notably dissented, wondering, 'How far can one go without breaching the spirit of the law, or fundamentally distorting the meaning of the involvement of Civil Parties?'[62] Such dissent highlights the differing attitudes within the judiciary as to the goals of the trial and the role of civil parties, as well as the influence of domestic legal jurisdictions. [63] Indeed, as opined by one judge,

> I think the Trial Chamber's attitude was informed by largely one judge who knew nothing about the French system and didn't want to know anything about the French system . . . .[64]

Highlighting further the strategy of trial expediency, the chamber also introduced strict restrictions on the time parties had to question witnesses, a move that has been criticised as reducing the right of civil party lawyers to question witnesses to 'often impracticable brevity'.[65]

With regards to the ability of the civil parties themselves to exercise their voice in the proceedings, the judges exerted significant control over access to this form of procedural justice. Although civil parties could be called by any of the three parties, it remained at the discretion of the TC who would be allowed to take the stand.[66] Although civil parties could not testify under oath, as they do not constitute 'witnesses',[67] their testimony was treated as evidence,[68] and they were therefore selected on the basis of having something relevant to contribute to the trial,[69] whether as evidence of the crimes alleged or the harm suffered.[70] Thus, their participation was shaped by the needs of the trial, in contrast to the ICC for example, where victim participants express personal 'views and concerns'.[71] In Case 001, 22 civil parties addressed the court, providing unsworn testimony and 'statements of suffering',[72] a creation of the TC which allowed civil parties to express their harm in broader terms than permitted while testifying.

The testimony of the civil parties was described as being highly emotional and as providing a poignant reminder of what victims had suffered.[73] They would frequently run over their allotted time, which the chamber would often allow.[74] While such measures appear to reflect a strategy of victim inclusiveness, the constraints of the retributive trial proved ill suited to hearing individuals' stories,[75] as judges occasionally requested that they limit themselves to facts relevant to the trial.[76] Displays of emotion were also discouraged;[77] for example when a survivor of S-21 grew angry towards Duch, he was rebuffed by the president for being abusive and insulting in a courtroom setting.[78] Indeed, individual judicial attitudes played an important role in the dignity and respect afforded to the civil parties, with the president, in particular, receiving criticism for his lack of sensitivity.[79] During the closing statements of the trial, civil party lawyers drew attention to the expectations their clients had held and the suffering that had occasionally resulted from their testimony.[80] Civil party lawyers described their clients as being upset that the chamber did not acknowledge their suffering nor thank them for their testimony, with some expressing fear after witnessing other civil parties being reprimanded by the president for showing distress.[81] As noted by one lawyer, many of her clients were so nervous that they were unable to remember what they wanted to say.[82] In addition to encountering lack of sensitivity, some civil parties found themselves preoccupied with the need to comply with the rules, hindering their ability to testify fully.[83]

It is worth briefly noting a form of participation that has not been the subject of jurisprudence, or identified as a procedural right, but which has developed as a significant practice within the ECCC. Throughout Case 001, NGOs and the VSS pooled their resources to ensure that the ten seats designated for civil parties within the courtroom were filled every day of the trial.[84] The ECCC was the first court to establish a system for supporting victims' observational attendance, and there is a consensus that civil parties' presence in the courtroom should be limited only by space and logistics.[85] The court has since established a system whereby the victims present within the courtroom rotate on a daily basis.[86] Although this constitutes a more passive form of participation, it has been described as an important feature of the ECCC's hearings.[87] Indeed, trial observation can be linked to the procedural justice element of information provision, as well as the substantive justice element of truth, as it arguably facilitates victims' understandings of the proceedings, and contributes to the 'experience of justice'.[88]

Overall, it appears that judicial attitudes during Case 001 reflected a tension between the strategies of allowing victims space to exercise voice and maintaining the legal structure of the trial.[89] This had an inevitable impact on civil parties' experience of procedural justice through voice, dignity and respect as participation was characterised by initially broad procedural rights, followed by subsequent restrictions. It is possible that if trial management techniques had been implemented from the beginning, many of the challenges could have been alleviated.[90] However, the TC preferred to blame civil party lawyers for a lack of preparation rather than accept responsibility for a lack of trial management. It is likely that this can, in part, be attributed to the lack of ICL experience amongst the judges, as opined by one lawyer:

> The problem is that it seems that the three national Judges don't really have any idea about how to do a trial like this, which is understandable as they will never have done such a thing. So then the two international Judges should come up and assist them and manage the trial properly, but they haven't,

which, if you consider their backgrounds is also not very strange, because they've never done an international criminal trial like this.[91]

With little experience to draw on, judges drew on their domestic legal understandings and attempted to engage with trial management issues as they arose. Yet, many of the limitations imposed had no basis in either the Internal Rules or Cambodian law, demonstrating a continued tendency towards judicial policy making within the chambers.[92]

Substantive justice

This section analyses the extent to which the court delivered substantive justice in Case 001, through accountability, truth and reparations.[93] With regards to accountability, on 26 July 2010, the TC sentenced Duch to 35 years in prison. This was then reduced to about 19 years left to serve in order to take into account the time he had already served and the violations of his rights resulting from his pre-trial detention from May 1999 until July 2007 by Cambodia's military court.[94] Such a reduction was deemed unacceptably lenient by a number of civil parties, as well as by members of the public.[95] Several appeals were filed,[96] leading to the judgement being partially confirmed and partially amended by the SCC on 3 February 2012.[97] Duch's sentence was changed to life imprisonment, with the SCC majority finding that the TC had placed too much weight on the mitigating factors and not enough on the severity of the crimes.[98] While this change in the sentence was undoubtedly a welcome decision to many, the decision to overlook the violation of Duch's rights brought about by his illegal detention has been criticised by human rights organisations as sending a damaging message to the Cambodian judicial system.[99] On the other hand, a significant number of Cambodians remained unsatisfied and expressed their wish for a return of the death sentence for former Khmer Rouge perpetrators, demonstrating the challenges in delivering a sense of substantive justice following incidences of mass atrocity.[100]

Opinions as to the correctness of the two judgements differed amongst the judges I spoke with, highlighting the range of attitudes within the chambers:

> People who are charged with mass atrocity crimes are not actually held fully responsible for them, as is demonstrated by the sentence . . . you can kill 5,000 people and get eleven years . . . now why is that?[101]
>
> In the end the whole Chamber was unanimous as to the gravity of the crimes attributed to Duch. But the detention at this tribunal and prior to these proceedings should have been deducted from the sentence given out.[102]
>
> If I had been a judge of Duch's case, I would also have said life time imprisonment, because I am from a civil law system, and just killing one person can mean life in prison.[103]

With regards to the truth, throughout the trial Duch denied any facts that were not proved by documentation and would evade questions that related to his own responsibility.[104] However, he also frequently cooperated with the court, allowing for light to be shed on the atrocities perpetrated during the regime.[105] In furtherance of the court's civil law foundations, there was a strong truth-finding focus within the chambers, and the judges both allowed civil parties to confront Duch with direct questions about their loved ones and made space for Duch to make statements of apology and explanation.[106] Research has shown that for many Cambodians, 'truth' relates to knowing the facts surrounding their own experiences and that of their loved ones, as well as gaining an understanding as to why such abuses occurred.[107] A number of civil parties have suggested that Duch's cooperation and truth telling were of value and praised the court for establishing a historical record and allowing Duch to provide a direct account of what happened.[108] However, only a small number accepted his apologies.[109]

When it came to reparations, the civil party lawyers submitted a joint claim requesting the compilation and dissemination of statements of apology made by Duch throughout the trial; access to free medical care; funding for education programmes about the Khmer Rouge, in general, and S-21, in particular; the erection of memorials and pagoda fences at S-21 as well as in the civil parties' local communities; and inclusion of all civil party names in the final judgement, along with the details of their connection to S-21.[110] They requested that the court find a way around the provision within the Internal Rules that reparation awards can only be borne by the accused, either through a trust fund or through assistance from the state of Cambodia.[111] Some teams additionally requested individual monetary payments. The requests were generally worded and lacking in specific detail, because of the understanding amongst the legal teams that a subsequent hearing would be held to address the more specific issues.[112]

In response, the TC stressed that reparations were intended to be symbolic rather than compensatory. They held that it was not within their power to award individual compensation or avoid the limitations imposed by their Internal Rules.[113] They therefore granted only two reparations, declaring that all admitted civil parties suffered harm as a direct consequence of Duch's crimes and agreeing to compile all statements of apology and acknowledgements of responsibility made by Duch during the course of the trial and to post this compilation on the ECCC's official website within 14 days of the judgement becoming final.[114] All other requests were denied, usually on the grounds of a lack of specificity or unenforceability, and no opportunity was made available to the civil parties to provide more details. Two of the four civil party legal teams appealed this reparations decision,[115] but the SCC support the TC's decision, noting that the court could not grant reparations that required RGC funding, nor could it grant reparations that were unrealistic because of Duch being declared indigent, as to do so would be 'confusing and frustrating for the victims'.[116] However, in addition to the reparations ordered, it also recognised other requests as 'appropriate forms of reparation' and urged national and international donors to help to implement these awards. As noted earlier, the argument that the Internal Rules preclude certain actions is inherently unconvincing, given the proven malleability of the Rules. However, the judgements reveal some of the other constraints and attitudes that were influencing the judges' approach. First, they reveal a concern, common in international(ised) criminal tribunals,[117] over the limited resources available because of indigence and a lack of external funding, combined with a belief that awards should be capable of implementation. Such a belief is contestable; at least some would argue that awarding reparations can constitute important acknowledgement of harm, irrespective of the capacity to enforce them.[118] Second, the judgements reveal a consciousness as to the limits on the judges' mandate and a determination to avoid inferences of state responsibility within the context of an individual criminal trial.[119] In its appeal judgement the SCC claimed that the proceedings should be interpreted as a 'starting point' for reparations, 'not the ultimate remedy', and that the ECCC should not be 'overloaded with utopian expectations that would ultimately exceed the attainable goals of transitional justice'.[120] Such defensive language highlights the court's restrictive interpretation of its mandate,[121] yet whether the civil parties' requests for reparations deserve the critique of being 'utopian' is questionable.

Civil parties and their lawyers expressed serious disappointment with the reparations awarded in Case 001,[122] while trial observers and NGOs criticised the decision as 'sorely lacking'[123] and 'unable to meet the majority of victims' requests, due to the inadequacy of the applicable Internal Rules that the Judges had established'.[124] Indeed, the reparations awarded failed to even remotely meet internationally recognised standards of proportionality, adequacy and effectiveness.[125] Furthermore, despite the rules, many civil parties had believed that they were entitled to individual monetary reparations (discussed further in Chapter 7), a belief that no doubt further added to their disappointment with the eventual award.[126] The TC's failure to clearly explain what information the civil parties needed to provide when requesting reparations and a lack of proper arguments explaining the acceptance or rejection of specific remedies can only have added to this sense of confusion and disappointment.[127]

This section has demonstrated the extent to which a variety of external and internal factors have influenced the procedural and substantive justice delivered to civil parties by the judges in Case 001. Despite the challenges explored, it may be concluded that some procedural justice has been delivered to some victims, through the provision of representation and voice. Similarly, some substantive justice was delivered through accountability, truth and reparation, although the provision of this justice has been curtailed by the political, financial and legal realities of the trial. The extent to which civil parties have considered this procedural and substantive justice adequate will be returned to in Chapter 8. For now, this chapter turns to the court's second trial, Case 002/01.

3. Case 002/01: judicial restrictions and innovations

With the frustrations of Case 001 and the increased complexity of Case 002 undoubtedly causing alarm bells to ring in heads throughout the court, the judges introduced a number of amendments to the Internal Rules in 2010, designed to 'balance the rights of all parties, to safeguard the ability of the ECCC to achieve its mandate while maintaining civil party participation, and to enhance the quality of civil party representation'.[128] In sum, their strategy had hardened into one that aimed to 'streamline' victim participation, as acknowledged by the judges themselves.[129] The implications of these changes and their application by the different chambers are considered under the headings of accessing justice, procedural justice and substantive justice.

Accessing justice

A change to the Internal Rules[130] requiring applications to be determined during the judicial investigation stage meant that Case 002 avoided the revocation of civil party status at the judgement stage.[131] However, the issue of who should be accepted as a civil party remained divisive. In the first instance, the CIJs found that injury must be 'personal'[132] and a 'direct consequence' of the material facts for which the judicial investigation had already been opened.[133] These restrictions excluded extended family, as well as applicants who had suffered from identical conduct within Cambodia but at sites that were not subject to a specific investigation. This reflected the approach adopted in Case 001, where victims were required to link their harm to the specific crime sites, either as a direct victim or a close relative of the direct victim.[134] Of the 3,970 applications considered, 2,123 were admitted. Of the rejected applicants, 1,747 appealed.[135]

Demonstrating further differences in approach, the PTC was unable to reach a unanimous appeal decision. The majority disagreed with the CIJs' approach towards 'direct consequence' and 'injury'. They submitted that rather than require a link between injury and *material facts*, the focus should be on the link between the injury and the *crimes alleged*, thereby admitting appellants alleging suffering as a result of the implementation of policies against the population and 'throughout the country', as long as the injury related to any of the crimes alleged against the accused.[136] On the issue of injury, the chamber found that the social and cultural context relevant at the time when the alleged crimes occurred required a broader consideration of victimisation, allowing for injury to be caused not just through the death of a close relative but also through the death of members of the appellant's community, through the witnessing of direct victimisation, through the knowledge of a direct victims fate and through the fear of a similar fate that the policies instilled in groups and the population.[137] The majority therefore applied a presumption of collective injury, based on the nature of the victimisation in the context of mass atrocities.[138] The majority also adopted a more flexible approach to applicants' identification than the CIJs and TC in Case 001. Referring to the practice in domestic courts, the chamber accepted statements from village elders or communal chiefs as proof of identity.[139] As a result, 1,728 applicants were declared admissible, increasing the number of civil parties admitted to 3,866.

In addition to highlighting how victims' access to justice can vary as a result of changing judicial attitudes and strategies,[140] these decisions demonstrate how divisive the issue of civil party participation was within the chambers. Reflecting the attitudinal model of judicial behaviour, interviewees appeared to be influenced by predominantly internal factors, including both their domestic legal traditions and their perspectives on how courts should respond to the needs of victims. Thus, interviewees from civil law jurisdictions, which require a link between victims' harm and the specific crimes charged, were often quite critical of the majority view:

> I have to say I think it is problematic . . . Because you end up accepting the entire country into the criminal process and it's obvious that this is not appropriate. I think it was farfetched and I don't think it should be repeated. Notwithstanding the well-intended approach.[141]

> I think for me it was legally wrong, definitely. The rules are quite clear and the trial had a specific scope which was already quite broad.[142]

In her dissenting judgement, French judge Machi-Uhel argued that the inclusive approach would frustrate those who satisfied the original, narrower criteria while disappointing those who were admitted but did not subsequently see their specific harms reflected in the court's work.[143] Instead, she argued that the broader victim population could be better served using non-judicial measures. Such an approach arguably reflects a desire to protect the traditional focus of a criminal trial, as well as an awareness of the dangers of 'overselling' what a court can achieve.[144] In contrast, those who supported the majority position spoke of the importance of acknowledging the nature of harm under the regime[145] and were, in turn, critical of an overly legalistic approach. One judge discussed the perceived basis for the more restrictive approach, arguing that it was not entirely attributable to being from a civil system:

> I thought the Co-Investigating Judges took a very legalistic, French, domestic approach. One of my colleagues took a very legalistic, French, domestic approach. My other colleague who was Dutch from the continental civil law system took I thought an appropriate approach, a broader approach, worked on with national colleagues . . . the amount of re-victimization of those people by their exclusion was inappropriate.[146]

This decision was made during my own time interning within the PTC, and I witnessed first-hand the approval with which the Cambodian judges spoke of the majority approach. They also spoke of the widespread nature of the harm within Cambodia and their desire to recognise this harm. Thus, in a reflection of the attitudinal model of judicial behaviour, the values and personal experiences of the judges were shown to influence the strategy adopted.[147]

Procedural justice

Had individual representation been set to continue into Case 002, it is possible that the PTC may have been more reluctant to accept such a high number of applicants. However, fears over how to manage victim participation in a case of Case 002's size had led to the establishment of a working group within the ECCC, as well as consultations with lawyers, intermediary organisations and NGOs.[148] The resulting amendments to the Internal Rules introduced significant changes to civil party representation, including a requirement that civil parties obtain legal counsel by the time judicial investigations close,[149] and the introduction of two LCLs.[150] They consist of one national lawyer and one international lawyer who represent the entire group of civil parties during the trial stage and beyond.[151] While civil parties could still choose their representatives in pre-trial proceedings, those representatives would no longer have standing in their own right at the trial stage.[152] The introduction of these representatives illustrates the strategy of enhancing trial expediency. As acknowledged by one judge,

> We couldn't live up to the promise of the national legal framework and we had to invent something new which is not necessarily the best solution, because we couldn't handle it otherwise.[153]

Reflecting underlying attitudes as to the court's main purpose, another judge noted,

> It was the best we could do, I think to have retained individual representation would have meant that the case would never finish and therefore our primary remit wouldn't have been discharged . . . the primary remit is the guilt of the accused.[154]

The desire for expediency was also evident in the TC's attitudes towards the civil party representatives in court. Although civil party lawyers retained the right to address the court, as managed by the LCLs,[155] the TC expressed displeasure when lawyers other than the LCLs spoke.[156] The LCLs also had their own rights restricted, with the TC denying their request to make opening statements[157] and expressing irritation when they intervened separately from the prosecution, stating that as they are on the same side, they should cooperate in order to make proceedings efficient.[158] Such an approach is not entirely correct; the fact that the Internal Rules require civil parties to 'support the prosecution' does not guarantee that their goals will naturally align. Similarly, the LCLs' exclusion from opening statements is questionable. Their exclusion is contrary to international practice; both the ICC and the STL allow victim representatives the opportunity to make opening statements.[159] While the Internal Rules limit this right to the co-prosecutors and accused,[160] no such right is granted to *any* party under Cambodian law.[161] The TC's statement that no right for the LCLs was provided for in the court's procedures is therefore unconvincing, all the more so because of the judge-made nature of the rules.[162]

Overall, it appears a prioritisation of expedient retributive justice was deemed sufficient justification for a significant restriction on the rights of civil parties.[163] Certainly, witnesses and civil parties in Case 002/01 did not face the multiple civil party lawyers that those in Case 001 did, with a positive impact on the efficiency of the court proceedings.[164] The representation of civil parties also arguably became more coherent, removing the duplication or potential for inconsistency that had been an issue during the first trial.[165] Nevertheless, the loss of individual representation was a controversial restriction on civil parties' rights. Indeed, with the minimum rights granted to 'parties' to the trial no longer available to civil parties and their direct representatives, it appears that the concept of the 'group as a party' may be a more accurate description of civil party participation.[166] Such a concept is further supported by the collective nature of reparations and the presumption of collective harm utilised by the PTC. Yet, such an approach fails to reflect the reality of victims' individual experiences, as acknowledged by one judge:

> I think that the collective representation here has had some difficulties, and that's because the victims are not homogenous as a group.[167]

This collectivisation of participation restricts the ability of individuals to access procedural justice, by restricting their ability to select their courtroom representatives and influence courtroom strategy.[168] Civil parties have no say in the hiring of the LCLs[169] and, in contrast to other international courts, have no avenues through which to challenge the selection of their collective representatives.[170] Although the LCLs have a duty to consult and reach a consensus when coordinating representation at trial,[171] their regulations include no way for a dissenting civil party lawyer to make their alternative views known to the court.[172] While the Court has allowed civil parties to obtain separate civil party lawyers in cases of conflicted interests, this has not had an impact on the representation of civil parties as a single consolidated group.[173] This grouping therefore potentially excludes victims whose experiences appear contradictory or outside the LCLs' focus,[174] leaving them little recourse beyond withdrawing from proceedings.[175]

With regards to the provision of voice, Case 002/01 featured a number of different means through which civil parties were able to share their experiences and views.[176] Seventeen testified during the trial proceedings, during which 12 made broader 'statements of suffering'.[177] While this form of participation allowed civil parties greater space to express their harms, the TC again demonstrated a reluctance to allow such statements to interfere with the efficiency of their proceedings, cutting off civil parties with reminders that they be brief.[178] Fifteen civil parties were also chosen by the LCLs to participate in victim-impact hearings, during which they presented evidence on the effect the crimes had had on their lives and took questions from the different legal teams about facts related to the charges. These hearings were not contained within the Internal Rules, instead constituting an example of the TC judges' own innovation. While this allowed almost double the number of civil parties to exercise voice, decisions as to which civil parties would address the court continued to be shaped by the requirements of the trial rather than by the wishes of victims. Civil parties were chosen on their ability to assist the chamber with assessing 'the gravity of the crimes, in their proper context and determining the appropriateness of the reparations claimed'.[179] The choice to split Case 002 into sub-trials also had an impact, as only those victims whose harms fell within the factual scope of Case 002/01 were able to participate.[180] Thus, victims' voices continued to be 'picked out, appropriated and then re-presented to suit' the particular structure and goals of the trial,[181] with less than 2 per cent of civil parties participating in this way.[182] The hearings also flagged the challenges that can arise when attempting to balance victim participation with the rights of the defence,[183] with the defence teams unsuccessfully appealing the use of testimony given during the hearings within the judgement.[184]

The desire to protect the trial's expediency was also evident in judicial attitudes towards victims who attempted to engage directly with the court. Following repeated attempts by one civil party to address the court and question the accused, a decision was made that to ensure 'expeditious proceedings and relevant submissions, and to avoid disruptions', civil parties should only participate through their lawyers.[185] In an attempt to circumvent these restrictions, the civil party dismissed her lawyer during proceedings, arguing that as she was unrepresented she should be able to address the court directly.[186] However, the majority (Judge Downing dissenting) reasserted that 'only lawyers for civil parties have the right' to speak.[187] The reality of a victim with a voice, and a desire to use it so directly, appeared to contrast with how the judges envisioned civil party participation,[188] and the PTC's decisions received support March 2009 when the Internal Rules were changed, stating that 'where civil parties are represented by a lawyer, it is the lawyer and not the civil parties themselves who must make legal submissions before the Court'.[189]

The practice of inviting civil parties to attend the proceedings continued into Case 002/01. Logistical support was provided by the VSS, through funding supplied by the German Ministry of Foreign Affairs, and the UN Trust Fund to End Violence Against Women.[190] The VSS provided travel and accommodation, and also arranged for security and protection, psychosocial support if requested, and financial support if required. This passive form of participation has continued to be uncontroversial, perhaps because it neither disrupts civil party representation within the courtroom, nor conflicts with the strategy of ensuring an expedient trial.[191]

Substantive justice

In relation to delivering substantive justice through accountability, truth and reparations, the first thing to note must be the impact of the death of two accused and the severance of the trial. Highlighting the risks of pursuing trials many decades after crimes were committed, the deaths of Ieng Thirith and Ieng Sary left their responsibility for the crimes of the Khmer Rouge undetermined and victims without insight into their alleged actions. The severance further meant that only a limited amount of the charges levied against the accused were addressed, leaving some of the most serious, such as genocide and nationwide forced marriage, to be adjudicated in Case 002/02 (judgement pending at the time of writing). Thus, both accountability and truth telling were limited by the specific charges of the case, and by the halved number of defendants.

With these limitations in mind, the court has nonetheless offered some accountability for the actions of the remaining defendants. On 7 August 2014, the TC released its judgement in Case 002/01. It found Nuon Chea and Khieu Samphan guilty of the crimes against humanity of murder, extermination, political persecution and other inhumane acts (including forced transfers, enforced disappearances and attacks on human dignity). It therefore sentenced both of the accused to life imprisonment.[192] All parties launched appeals on numerous aspects of the judgement, with Nuon Chea's team citing 223 grounds of appeal on issues of fact and law. Outside the court, a civil society report was released critiquing the judgement as failing to deliver 'systematic application of the elements of crimes to a well-documented body of factual findings'[193] and as drawing 'inferences from a factual narrative that assumes rather than justifies the validity of those inferences'.[194] It appears the SCC shared some of these concerns. While upholding the life sentence and convictions for crimes against humanity, persecution on political grounds and other humane acts, the SCC's appeal judgement on 23 November 2016 also reversed a number of the two accused's convictions.[195] These included extermination in relation to forced transfers and extermination, murder and persecution on political grounds in relation to the execution of former Lon Nol soldiers and officials. The chamber noted 'marked inadequacies in the evaluation of the evidence' and a consistent failure to engage with fundamental issues affecting the strength of the evidence. This appeal judgement is arguably an important contribution to the substantive justice offered by the court. While civil parties may (or may not) be less concerned with the specifics of the judgement than legal teams and trial-monitoring bodies,[196] the critiques of the trial judgement threatened the legitimacy of the court. By choosing to reverse some of the more contentious findings yet maintaining the life sentence because of the gravity of the crimes, the SCC delivered accountability while strengthening the reputation of the ECCC's jurisprudence.

With regards to truth, the court once again allowed civil parties to ask the accused questions during Case 002/01. The accused initially responded[197] but latterly chose their right to remain silent. While their answers rarely offered any new information, such interactions led to a sense of empowerment amongst some civil parties and allowed them to share their own truths, another important aspect of the concept.[198] Many survivors had been unaware of what was happening outside their community during the Khmer Rouge regime and understood even less about why the Khmer Rouge acted as it did.[199] The decades of silence meant that the judgement constituted a particularly valuable documentation of Khmer Rouge crimes.[200] The TC judgement also acknowledged that the US had carried out a 'devastating' bombing campaign,[201] which had radicalised Khmer Rouge forces and caused the deaths of tens of thousands of people.[202] Such findings arguably move beyond the court's jurisdictional limitations to offer a more contextualised form of acknowledgement and truth, despite not being the focus of the judgement itself.[203]

With regards to reparations, the negative responses to Case 001 had spurred a change to the Internal Rules. Amidst calls from civil society to establish a fund or related mechanism to ensure the implementation of reparations, changes were introduced with regards to how reparations might be funded.[204] As both the TC and the SCC had determined that they could not order the RGC or any third party to award reparations, they chose to react to these external limitations by pursuing a course of judicial activism.[205] The 2010 amendments therefore introduced a new process whereby the court would recognise that certain externally funded projects, designed or identified in cooperation with the VSS, could also constitute reparations.[206] While this can perhaps be praised as a pragmatic attempt to pursue a legal strategy of reparation provision in light of the external limitations posed by the lack of an ECCC trust fund,[207] the indigence of the accused and the inability or unwillingness of the court to authorise initiatives requiring government approval, it is not without its problems. For one, it reinforces the enforceability requirement first witnessed in Case 001, as projects without sufficient funding are likely to be rejected.[208] Such a requirement is another example of judicial activism, as it is an issue of relevance within neither Cambodian nor most international legal proceedings.[209] The amendments also amount to an outsourcing of reparations, placing the onus on civil society to provide substantive justice to victims,[210] and reducing the role of the TC to 'rubber-stamping' the proposed projects.[211] This was acknowledged by one of the judges involved in their creation:

> It was the best we could do, to say 'we haven't got any money, if you can find some and you're happy to negotiate then we may be able to accommodate this as part of reparation' . . . I think that it has some problems, it has huge practical problems, it puts it very much on the victims to go off and do things.[212]

The status of reparations as an acknowledgement of harm 'suffered by civil parties as a result of the commission of the crimes for which an Accused is convicted' has undeniably changed as a result of these amendments.[213] The TC has explicitly stated that those reparations which receive external funding may benefit all civil parties in the consolidated group rather than those linked to the specific crimes charged. While this has prevented additional issues arising out of the severance of Case 002, which may have led to only certain civil parties benefiting from Case 002/01's reparations, it moves the reparation system further away from the acts of the accused. Indeed, it is questionable whether such measures can be termed *reparations*, as they have no link to either the accused or the Cambodian government.[214] Indeed, civil party lawyers had sought the PTC's assistance in investigating the location and tracing and implementing measures for the preservation of accused persons' assets. However, in contrast to the activist approach adopted in creating an externally funded system, the court chose to adopt a restrictive interpretation of its mandate, finding that as the accused's assets were not under investigation by the CIJs, civil parties could not request such an investigation. The

PTC acknowledged that such provisions existed before other courts but found that civil parties did not have the right to 'initiate enforcement of reparations at the pre-trial stage' and that to allow it would place the PTC in 'the position of acting beyond our collective jurisdiction'.[215] This phrasing is interesting, given the fact that the judges are the authors of their own provisions.[216] The alternative approach of externally funded projects was criticised by a civil party lawyer:

> This reparations scheme that they have created, I find it very difficult because usually reparation is based on the conviction of the accused and is a reflection of the responsibility and the accountability of the accused. Now what the court is doing is separating the reparations from the accused. You still need a conviction, and you still need a link to the crimes this person was convicted of, but it's not the accused at all who is responsible for paying for the reparations.[217]

With civil parties receiving group benefits, without any link to their specific harms, it can be seen that the ECCC has continued to move away from a system of individual participation as parties and more and more towards a collective victim participation model. This was reflected in the reparations awarded. Some relate to specific crimes of Case 002/01, such as the construction of a memorial for victims of forced transfer, the inclusion of a chapter on forced population movement and executions at Tuol Po Chrey within the Cambodian school curriculum, the publication of a booklet on the facts adjudicated in Case 002/01 and civil party participation in the trial and the publication and distribution of full and summary-length Khmer-language editions of the verdict in Case 002/01. However, many other projects were recognised as reparations, which had little relation to the specific crimes, such as the creation of a national day of remembrance, testimonial therapy and more general history and memorial projects.[218] Furthermore, the court's failure to provide individual reparations has continued to be a source of frustration for civil parties, as demonstrated by a protest held by approximately 200 civil parties at the opening of Case 002/01.[219]

The 2010 amendments also introduced a new potential output of the court, in the form of non-judicial measures. In discussions with NGOs prior to the implementation of the changes, it had been emphasised that the restrictions on the procedural rights of civil parties (through the introduction of the LCLs) would be balanced by an expansion of the VSS's mandate.[220] Thus, the VSS can also collaborate with external agencies in order to work towards 'the development and implementation of non-judicial programs and measures addressing the broader interests of victims'.[221] Also relying on civil society involvement, these projects are separate from the finding of the accused's guilt. The judges hoped that this would become 'a major legacy of the Tribunal',[222] as it would provide some substantive justice to those victims who did not participate in the court's work.[223] However, little of substance has been delivered in this regard, and that which has been done has been mainly attributable to the work of civil society.[224] This is explored in greater depth in Chapter 7.

4. Conclusion

An initial product of judicial policy making through gap-filling and activism,[225] civil party participation has been subjected to a number of changes and restrictions over the course of the ECCC's first two trials. This chapter has sought to explore those changes, while highlighting the judicial attitudes and strategies that shaped participation. It has demonstrated that these attitudes and strategies have exerted significant influence over civil parties' ability to access procedural and substantive justice, with the ability of the judges to amend their own Internal Rules, enabling an ongoing process of judicial policy making.[226] It is clear the civil party participation has constituted a constantly evolving experiment, as ruefully acknowledged by one judge:

> The form of representation and participation, we haven't got it right, it still needs to be tweaked, but as an experiment, that's a terrible thing to say, not as an experiment but as a best try, I think a lot has been learned from it.[227]

In terms of the factors that have influenced judicial attitudes and strategies, it seems probable that the judges failed to fully consider the impact civil party participation was to have on proceedings. This was exacerbated by the different legal cultures of the judges, some of whom did not originate from systems where victims had party rights. The personal attitudes of different judges undoubtedly also influenced the performance of civil party participation, with approaches ranging from the strictly legalistic to a more victim-centric approach. Such differences demonstrated different understandings of what a trial can achieve and what role it should play in responding to victimisation. Within the courtroom, judges were increasingly influenced by the pressure to ensure expedient and efficient proceedings.[228] External pressures included the deaths of two accused and the advancing ages of the remaining two, the pressure from donors to finish quickly and the Cambodian population waiting for justice. Responding to these pressures, a number of restrictions were imposed, with implications for the ability of the court to deliver procedural justice through voice, representation, dignity and respect. Frustration with civil party lawyers, on whom blame for the lack of efficiency was frequently and perhaps unfairly placed, further contributed to a shift in strategy, from one that sought to expand the rights of victims to one that prioritised the expedient and efficient deliverance of judgements.

It has been argued that more effective trial management would have allowed for a more inclusive approach to civil parties and avoid some of the restrictions imposed. Yet, it is worth acknowledging the creational limitations of a criminal institution. The 'theft of the conflict' from victims, the resulting dominance of legal professionals and legalese, the retributive nature of the trial and the accompanying focus on the rights of the accused, all create barriers to a truly victim-centric process.[229] These significant limitations mean that participation in a trial should not be the only 'right' offered to victims of crime but should constitute part of a broader response.[230] Indeed, the ECCC has arguably attempted to develop such a broader response in the creation of its reparations and non-judicial measure mandates. However, the ability of the judges to deliver meaningful and effective reparations in practice has been critiqued by observers and victims alike. The disinclination to award reparations borne by the accused because of the lack of enforceability constitutes an approach with little support in domestic or international law, while the court's unwillingness to pursue any approach that requires RGC involvement or additional funding illustrates an awareness of the creational limits placed on the court's jurisdiction and finances, the individualistic focus of a criminal trial and the political tenterhooks on which the court hangs. While the judges have continued to be creative in this regard, the result is that the reparations mandate has little resemblance to what reparations are internationally considered to be, as they lack any connection to either the perpetrators or the state and place the onus on civil society and the civil parties' lawyers to give what the court cannot.

Notes

1 S. Zappalà, 'The Rights of Victims v. the Rights of the Accused' 8 *Journal of International Criminal Justice* (2010) 137.
2 H. Rasmussen, *On Law and Policy in the European Court of Justice: A Comparative Study in Judicial Policymaking* (Martinus Nijhoff, 1986).
3 See Chapter 4, section 2.
4 S. Jodoin, 'Understanding the Behaviour of International Courts: An Examination of Decision-Making at the ad hoc International Criminal Tribunals' 6(1) *Journal of International Law and International Relations* (2010) 1 at 5–6.
5 *Creational factors* are defined as the textual constructs and legal language used to limit judicial discretion; see J. Wessel, 'Judicial Policy-Making at the International Criminal Court: An Institutional Guide to Analyzing International Adjudication' 44 *Columbia Journal of Transnational Law* (2006) 377.
6 *External factors* are defined as the abilities of external forces and other parties to influence the judges' actions, ibid., at 384.
7 Internal factors are considered those that relate to the judges' own professional norms, ibid. at 385.
8 See Chapter 1.
9 Internal Rule 23(2) Revision 3, 6 March 2009.
10 *Law on the Establishment of Extraordinary Chambers in the Courts of Cambodia for the Prosecution of Crimes Committed during the Period of Democratic Kampuchea*, Law NS/RKM/0801/12, 10 August 2001 Arts. 2, 4, 5, 6, 7 and 8.
11 Case 001, Trial Judgement, 001/18-07-2007-ECCC/TC, 26 July 2010.
12 Applications went to the CIJs until the case file was submitted, after which they were sent to the TC.
13 Internal Rules, Rule 23, until Revision 4.
14 Case 001, Decision of the Trial Chamber Concerning Proof of Identity for Civil Party Applicants, 26 February 2009, 001/18-07-2007-ECCC/TC. par. 6
15 H. Dumont, 'Requirements for Victim Participation' in K. Tibor-Szabó and M. Hirst (eds.), *Victim Participation in International Criminal Justice* (Asser Press, 2017) 72.
16 Case 002, Decision on Appeals against Orders of the Co-Investigating Judges on the Admissibility of Civil Party Applications, Case No. 002/19-09-2007/ECCC/OCIJ, 24 June 2011.
17 Internal Rule 23 *bis*, Revision 5, adopted 9 February 2010.

18 S. Studzinsky, 'Victims Participation before the ECCC' *Zeitschrift für Internationale Strafrechtsdogmatik* (2011) 997.
19 Case 001, Judgement, n.11 at 639.
20 Ibid., at 649.
21 Ibid., at 547–551.
22 Ibid., at 648–649
23 Ibid., at 647
24 Interview with former civil party Lawyer, 11 September 2015; TPO, Report on TPO's After-Verdict Intervention with Case 001 Civil Parties, 27 July 2010, at 2; P. Phuong et al. 'Victim Participation and the Trial of Duch at the Extraordinary Chambers in the Courts of Cambodia' 3(3) *Journal of Human Rights Practice* (2011) 264.
25 Interview with Judge 2, 7 November 2013
26 Interview with Judge 1, 13 January 2014.
27 Case 001, Appeal Judgement, 001/18-07-2007-ECCC/SC, 3 February 2012 at 185–246.
28 Interview with Judge 1, 7 November 2013.
29 J.D. Ciorciari and A. Heindel, *Hybrid Justice: The Extraordinary Chambers in the Courts of Cambodia* (University of Michigan Press, 2014) 62.
30 Appeal Judgement, n.27 at 252–280.
31 Ibid., at 415–418.
32 Ibid., at 252–280.
33 B. McGonigle Leyh, *Procedural Justice? Victim Participation in International Criminal Proceedings* (Intersentia, 2011).
34 J. Wemmers, *Victims in the Criminal Justice System* (Kugler Publications, 1996); L. Musante, M.A. Gilbert and J. Thibaut, 'The Effects of Control on Perceived Fairness of Procedure and Outcome' 19 *Journal of Experimental Social Psychology* (1983) 223.
35 McGonigle Leyh, n.33 at 218. See Chapter 7.
36 Ibid., at 219.
37 Interview with Lawyer 1 (Co-Prosecutors' Office) 8 November 2013; Ciorciari and Heindel, n.29 at 109.
38 Ibid.; Interview with Lawyer 1 (CP Team) 11 November 2013; Interview with Lawyer 1 (Defence) 13 December 2013.
39 McGonigle Leyh, n.33 at 193.
40 Case 001, Trial transcripts, 20 July 2009, at 27–33.
41 Interview with Lawyer 1 (Co-Prosecutors' Office) 8 November 2013; Interview with Lawyer 2 (Co-Prosecutors' Office) 8 November 2013; Interview with Lawyer 3 (Defence) 8 November 2013
42 Interview with Judge 4, 11 November 2013; McGonigle Leyh, n.33 at 204.
43 Case 001, Trial Transcripts, 29 July 2009, at 88–90
44 Case 001, Trial Transcript, 12 August 2009, 41 and 13 July 2009, 47–48.
45 Case 001, Trial Transcript, 6 July 2009, at 56.
46 Interview with Judge 2, 7 November 2013.
47 Case 001, Trial Transcript, 29 July 2009, at 93–94; Case 001, Trial Transcript, 22 July 2009, at 34, 37–39, 71; Interview with Lawyer 1 (Co-Prosecutors' Office) 8 November 2013; Interview with Lawyer 2 (Co-Prosecutors' Office) 8 November 2013.
48 Case 001, Trial Transcript, 27 August 2009, at 70, see also 68–69.
49 Ciorciari and Heindel, n.29 at 111.
50 Ibid., at 108.
51 Internal Rules, Rule 79 (7) refers to the chamber facilitating the 'fair and expeditious conduct of the proceedings'.
52 C. Sperfeldt, 'Cambodian Civil Society and the Khmer Rouge Tribunal' 6(1) *International Journal of Transitional Justice* (2012) 149 at 154.

53 Open Society Justice Initiative, *Recent Developments at the ECCC,* March 2013.
54 Interview with Judge 1, 7 November 2013.
55 Wessel, n.5 at 385.
56 Case 001, Trial Transcript, 22 June 2009, at 92.
57 Case 001, Decision on Civil Party Co-Lawyer' Joint Request for a Ruling on the Standing of Civil Party Lawyers to Make Submissions on Sentencing and Directions Concerning the Questioning of the Accused, Experts and Witnesses Testifying on Character, Trial Chamber, 9 October 2009.
58 Case 001, Trial Transcript, 27 August 2009 at 42–66, 74.
59 M. Saliba, 'Civil Parties Boycott Start of Character Witness Testimony while Experts Offer Psychological Assessment of Duch' *Cambodia Tribunal Monitor,* 31 August 2009.
60 Case 001, Supreme Court Chamber, Decision on the Appeals Filed by Lawyers for Civil Parties (Groups 2 and 4) against the Trial Chamber's Oral Decisions of 27 August 2009, 001/18-07-2007/ECCC/SC, 24 December 2009, at 10–12.
61 P. Haynes, 'Victims' Lawyers in the Courtroom: Opening and Closing Statements, Questioning Witnesses, Challenging and Presenting Evidence' in K. Tibori-Szabó and M. Hirst (eds.), *Victim Participation in International Criminal Justice* (Asser, 2017) 277.
62 Decision on Sentencing, n.57, Dissenting Opinion of Judge Lavergne, at 4.
63 Ibid.
64 Interview with Judge 1, 7 November 2013.
65 Haynes, n.61 at 256.
66 D. Rudy and M. Hirst, 'Victims Appearing in Person before a Chamber' in K. Tibori-Szabó and M. Hirst (eds.), *Victim Participation in International Criminal Justice* (Asser, 2017) 301.
67 Internal Rule 23(4).
68 Case 001, Trial Judgement, n.11, for example paras 42, 52–55.
69 'The Purpose of Hearing Victims' Suffering' ECCC Website, www.ecccc.gov.kh/en/blog/2013/07/07/purpose-hearing-victims-suffering (accessed 16/02/18).
70 Rudy and Hirst, n.66 at 286.
71 ICC Statute, Article 68(3).
72 Case 001, Direction on the Scheduling of the Trial, Trial Chamber, 20 March 2009.
73 Interview with Lawyer 2 (Chambers) 11 November 2013.
74 Saliba, n.59
75 J. Doak, 'Victims' Rights in Criminal Trials: Prospects for Participation' 32(2) *Journal of Law and Society* (2005) 294 at 298.
76 Case 001, Trial Transcript 20 June 2009; 20 August 2009 at 64; 1 July 2009 at 14; 24 August 2009 at 71.
77 McGonigle Leyh, n.33 at 213.
78 Case 001, Trial Transcript, 30 June 2009, at 12.
79 McGonigle Leyh, n.33 at 213.
80 Case 001, Trial Transcript, 23 November 2009, 50–53.
81 Ibid., at 50.
82 Ibid.
83 J.D. Ciorciari and J. Ramji-Nogales, 'Lessons from the Cambodian Experience with Truth and Reconciliation' 19 *Buffalo Human Rights Law Review* (2012–2013) 193 at 208.
84 E.A. Turchi, 'Victims' Attendance in the Courtroom to Observe Proceedings' in K. Tibori-Szabó and M. Hirst (eds.), *Victim Participation in International Criminal Justice* (Asser, 2017) 349, 353.
85 Ibid., at 349.

86 Ibid.
87 Ibid., citing correspondence with Christoph Sperfeldt, former reparations advisor to the VSS.
88 Ibid., at 344. See Chapter 8.
89 M. Dembour and E. Haslam, 'Silencing Hearings? Victim-Witnesses at War Crimes Trials' 15(1) *European Journal of International Law* (2004).
90 Interview with former civil party lawyer, 11 September 2015; Interview with Judge 1, 13 January 2014.
91 Interview with Lawyer 4 (Defence) 8 November 2013.
92 D.S. Sokol, 'Reduced Victim Participation: A Misstep by the Extraordinary Chambers in the Courts of Cambodia' 10 *Washington University Global Studies Law Review* (2011).
93 UN Basic Principles and Guidelines on the Right to a Remedy and Reparation for Victims of Gross Violations of International Human Rights Law and Serious Violations of International Humanitarian Law, UN Doc. A/RES/60/147 (2005).
94 Case 001, Trial Judgement, n.11.
95 R. Dubler, 'Kaing Guek Eav (alias Duch), Judgement, ECCC, Case No 001/18–07–2007/ECCC/TC (26 July 2010)' *Australian International Law Journal* (2010); T. Chy, *When the Criminal Laughs* (DC-Cam, 2014); D McCargo, 'Politics by Other Means? The Virtual Trials of the Khmer Rouge Tribunal' 87(3) *International Affairs* (2011); P Phuong et al., 'Victim Participation and the Trial of Duch at the Extraordinary Chambers in the Courts of Cambodia' 3(3) *Journal of Human Rights Practice (*2011) 264.
96 Appeal Brief by the Co-Lawyers for Kaing Guek Eav alias "Duch" against the Trial Chamber Judgement of 26 July 2010, Supreme Court Chamber, 18 November 2010; Co-Prosecutors' Appeal against the Trial Chamber Judgement of 26 July 2010, Supreme Court Chamber, 13 October 2010; Appeal against Rejection of Civil Party Applicants in the Judgement (Civil Party Group 2), Supreme Court Chamber, 22 October 2010; Appeal against Judgment on Reparations (Civil Party Group 2) Supreme Court Chamber, 2 November 2010; Appeal of the Co-Lawyers from the Group 3 Civil Parties against the Judgment of 26 July 2010, Supreme Court Chamber, 5 October 2010
97 Case 001, Appeal Judgement, n.27.
98 Ibid.
99 Amnesty International, 'Cambodia: Khmer Rouge Judgment Welcome, But Raises Human Rights Concerns', 3 February 2012, www.amnesty.org/en/news/cambodia-khmer-rouge-judgment-welcome-raises-human-rights-concerns-2012-02-03 (accessed 16/02/18).
100 J.P. Bair, 'From the Numbers Who Died to Those Who Survived: Victim Participation in the Extraordinary Chambers in the Courts of Cambodia' 31 *University of Hawaii Law Review* 508 (2008–2009) 536; M. Mohan, 'The Paradox of Victim-Centrism: Victim Participation at the Khmer Rouge Tribunal' 9(5) *International Criminal Law Review* (2009) 733.
101 Interview with Judge 2, 7 November 2013.
102 Interview with Judge 1, 13 November 2014.
103 Interview with Judge 4, 11 November 2013.
104 Case 001, Trial Transcript, 25 November 2009; D Gillison, 'Duch Denies Teaching to Kill; Also Denies Personally Killing' *Cambodia Daily*, 18 June 2009.
105 Ciorciari and Heindel, n.29 at 107.
106 Case 001, Trial Transcript, 31 March 2009, at 67–68.
107 Phuong et al., n.95.
108 Ibid., 281

109 E. Stover, M. Balthazard and K.A. Koenig, 'Confronting Duch: Civil Party Participation in Case 001 at the ECCC' 93(882) *International Review of the Red Cross* (2011).
110 Case 001, Trial Judgement, n.11 at 652.
111 Case 001, Civil Parties' Co-Lawyers' Joint Submission on Reparations, 14 September 2009, at 45–47.
112 McGonigle Leyh, n.33 at 196; Internal Rule 100.
113 Case 001, Trial Judgement, n.11 at 661–664.
114 Ibid., at 682–683.
115 Civil Party Appeals, n.96.
116 Case 001, Appeal Judgement, n.27 at 281–320.
117 C. Ferstman, 'Reparations, Assistance and Support' in K. Tibor-Szabó and M. Hirst (eds.), *Victim Participation in International Criminal* Justice (Asser Press, 2017) 389.
118 Ibid., at 403.
119 Ibid., at 389.
120 Case 001, Appeal Judgment, n.27 at 655.
121 Ferstman, n.117 at 398.
122 J. O'Toole, 'Reparation Remains a Key Issues' *Phnom Penh Post*, 27 July 2010.
123 J.D. Ciorciari, The Duch Verdict, *Cambodia Tribunal Monitor*, 28 July 2010.
124 REDRESS, *Justice for Victims. The ICC's Reparations Mandate* (REDRESS, 2011) 22.
125 Ferstman, n.117.
126 J. Herman, 'Reaching for Justice: The Participation of Victims at the Extraordinary Chambers in the Courts of Cambodia' *Centre on Human Rights in Conflict Policy Paper* No. 5, September 2010.
127 M. Guiraud, *Victims' Rights before the Extraordinary Chambers in the Courts of Cambodia (ECCC): A Mixed Record for Civil Parties* (FIDH, November 2012) 52–53.
128 ECCC, '7th Plenary Session of the ECCC Concludes' ECCC Website, 9 February 2010, www.eccc.gov.kh/sites/default/files/media/Press_Release_Conclusion_7th_Plenary_Session_(ENG).pdf (accessed 16/02/18).
129 I. Stegmiller, 'Legal Developments in Civil Party Participation at the Extraordinary Chambers in the Courts of Cambodia' 27 *Leiden Journal of International Law* (2014) 465 at 470.
130 Internal Rules, Rule 23, Revision 4. See also ECCC Practice Direction on Victim Participation, Article 3.8.
131 Interview with Lawyer (CP Team) 11 November 2013.
132 Order on the Admissibility of Civil Party Applicants from Current Residents of Oddar Meanchey Province, 002/19–09–2007-ECCC-OCIJ, 26 August 2010 at 13.
133 Closing Order, Case 002, 002/19–09–2007-ECCC-OCIJ, at 10–12.
134 Case 001, Trial Judgement, n.11 at 644.
135 Case 002, Pre-Trial Chamber Decision, n.16.
136 Ibid., at 76–78.
137 Ibid., at 83–92.
138 Ibid., at 86.
139 Ibid., at 95.
140 S. Kendall and S. Nouwen, 'Representational Practices at the International Criminal Court: The Gap between Juridified and Abstract Victimhood' 76 *Law and Contemporary Problems* (2013) 235 at 246.
141 Interview with Judge 4, 13 January 2014.
142 Interview with Lawyer 2 (Chambers), 11 November 2013.

143 Case 002, Decision on Appeals Against Orders of the Co-Investigating Judges on the Admissibility of Civil Party Applications, Separate and Partially Dissenting Opinion of Judge Marchi-Uhel, 002/19–09–2007-ECCC/PTC, 24 June 2011.
144 K. McEvoy, 'Beyond Legalism: Towards a Thicker Understanding of Transitional Justice' 24 *Journal of Law and Society* (2007) 411.
145 Interview with Judge 2, 11 November 2013.
146 Interview with Judge 2, 7 November 2013.
147 G.A. Tarr, *Judicial Process and Judicial Policy Making* (Wadsworth, 2003); J.A. Segal and H.J. Spaeth, *The Supreme Court and the Attitudinal Model Revisited* (Cambridge University Press, 2002).
148 H. Jarvis, '"Justice for the Deceased": Victims' Participation in the Extraordinary Chambers in the Courts of Cambodia' 8(2) *Genocide Studies and Prevention: An International Journal* (2014) 19; M. Hirst, 'Legal Representation of Participating Victims' in K. Tibor-Szabó and M. Hirst, *Victim Participation in International Criminal Justice* (Asser Press, 2017) 117.
149 Internal Rule 23 *ter*, introduced in February 2010.
150 Internal Rule 23(3).
151 Internal Rule 12*ter(4)*.
152 Hirst, n.148, at 118.
153 Interview with Judge 1, 13 January 2014.
154 Interview with Judge 2, 7 November 2013.
155 Jarvis, n.148 at 23.
156 Case 002, Trial Transcript, 30 June 2011 at 33.
157 Trial Chamber Response to Lead Co-Lawyers and Civil Party lawyers' request to make brief preliminary remarks on behalf of Civil Parties, 15 November 2011, 002–19–09–2007-ECCC/TC.
158 Case 002, Trial Transcript, 2 February 2012, at 30.
159 ICC RPE, Rule 89(1); STL Rule 143; see Haynes n.61 for a comparison.
160 Internal Rule 89 *bis*.
161 Ciorciari and Heindel, n.29 at 220.
162 Ibid.
163 S. Studzinsky, 'Participation Rights of Victims as Civil Parties and the Challenges of Their Implementation before the Extraordinary Chambers in the Courts of Cambodia' in T. Bonacker and C. Safferling (eds.), *Victims of International Crimes: An Interdisciplinary Discourse* (Asser Press, 2013) 186–187.
164 Jarvis, n.148 at 23.
165 Hirst, n.148 at 124.
166 A.F. Diamond Esq., 'Victims Once Again? Civil Party Participation before the Extraordinary Chambers in the Courts of Cambodia' 38 *The Rutgers Law Record* (2010–2011) 34.
167 Interview with Judge 2, 7 November 2013; Judicial Solutions, 'Some "do's" and "don'ts" of Communicating with Victims' www.justicesolutions.org/art_pub_communicating_with_victims.pdf (accessed 16/02/18).
168 R. Killean and L. Moffett, 'Victim Legal Representations before the ICC and ECCC' 15(4) *Journal of International Criminal Justice* (2017) 713. Similar criticisms have been offered with regards to collective representation at the ICC. See M. Hebert-Dolbec, 'Towards Bureaucratization: An Analysis of Common Legal Representation Practices before the International Criminal Court' 23(3) *Revue québécoise de droit international* (2015) 34; E. Haslam and R. Edmunds, 'Common Legal Representation at the International Criminal Court: More Symbolic than Real?' 12 *International Criminal Law Review* (2012) 871.
169 Ibid at 134.

170 Hirst, n.148 at 145.
171 Lead Co-Lawyers and Civil Party Lawyers Administrative Internal Regulations, August 2011, Article 1(2).
172 Ibid., Article 6(1).
173 Hirst, n.148 at 128–129.
174 Killean and Moffett, n.168.
175 Diamond n.166.
176 J.D. Ciorciari and A. Heindel, 'Victim Testimony in International and Hybrid Criminal Courts: Narrative Opportunities, Challenges and Fair Trial Demands' 56(2) *Virginia Journal of International Law* (2016).
177 Case 002, Trial Transcript, 11 January 2012 at 87.
178 Case 002, Trial Transcript, 29 August 2012 at 28–30.
179 ECCC, n.69.
180 A. Heindel, 'Impact of Severance on Individual Civil Parties' Legal Status and Right to Reparations' *Cambodian Tribunal Monitor*, 23 February 2013, www.cambodiatribunal.org/wp-content/uploads/2013/08/commentary_130223-english.pdf (accessed 16/02/18). For information on the severance more generally see Severance Order Pursuant to Internal Rule 89ter, 002/19–09–2007-ECCC/TC, 22 September 2011; Decision on Severance of Case 002/01 following Supreme Court Chamber Decision of 8 February 2013, 002/19–09–2007/ECCC/TC, 26 April 2013; Decision on Additional Severance of Case 002/02 and Scope of Case 002/02, 002/19–09–2007-ECCC/TC, 4 April 2014.
181 K. McEvoy and K. McConnachie, 'Victims and Transitional Justice: Voice, Agency and Blame' 22 *Social and Legal Studies* (2013) 489 at 495
182 'Highlights of Issues Related to Civil Party Participation' *Khmer Rouge Trial Monitor*, 9 October 2013, krtmonitor.org/2013/10/09/highlights-civil-party-participation/ (accessed 16/02/18); 'KRT Monitor Case 002/02 – Issue 79 (9–11 January 2017), *Khmer Rouge Trial Monitor*, 9 February 2017, krtmonitor.org/2017/02/09/krt-monitor-case-00202-issue-79–9–11-january-2017/ (accessed 16/02/18).
183 Similarly, the statements of suffering given by the civil parties in Case 001 and Case 002/01 have been relied on as a source of evidence by the TC. See Rudy and Hirst, n.66 at 303, fn 86.
184 Case 002/01, Appeal Judgment, 002/19–09–2007-ECCC/SC, paras 314–315.
185 Case 002, Written Version of Oral Decision of 1 July 2008 on the Civil Party's Request to Address the Court in Person, Pre-Trial Chamber, 002/19–09–2007-ECCC/OCIJ, 3 July 2008.
186 Case 002, Decision on Application for Reconsideration of Civil Party's Right to Address Pre-Trial Chamber in Person, 1 July 2008 (Judge Downing dissenting).
187 Case 002, Decision of 1 July on the Civil Party's Request to Address the Court in Person, 1 July 2008.
188 Mohan, n.100.
189 'Fifth Plenary Session of Judicial Officers, Closing Press Statement' ECCC Website, 6 March 2009, www.eccc.gov.kh/sites/default/files/media/closing_plenary_session_EN.pdf (accessed 23/02/18).
190 Turchi, n.85 at 353.
191 Ibid., at 345.
192 Case 002/01, Trial Judgement, 002/19-09-2007/ECCC/TC, 7 August 2014.
193 D. Cohen, M. Hyde and P. van Tuyl, *A Well-Reasoned Opinion? Critical Analysis of the First Case Against the Alleged Senior Leaders of the Khmer Rouge (Case 002/01)* (East West Centre, 2015) 6.
194 Ibid., at 73.

195 Case 002/01, Appeal Judgment, n.184, 23 November 2016.
196 See Chapter 8.
197 See for example Khmer Rouge Tribunal Monitor, 'Case 002, Issue No.62, Hearing on Evidence Week 57', 3–7 June 2013, krtmonitor.org/2013/06/07/krt-trial-monitor-c002-issue-62–3–7-june-2013/ (accessed 16/02/18).
198 Ciorciari and Heindel, n.176
199 K. Yesberg, 'Accessing Justice through Victim Participation at the Khmer Rouge Tribunal' 40 *Victoria University of Wellington Law Review* (2009) 555.
200 'Villagers React to Verdict in Case 002/01' *DC-Cam,* 7 August 2014, www.d.dccam.org/Projects/Living_Doc/pdf/Villagers_React_to_Verdict_in_Case_002-01.pdf (accessed 16/02/18).
201 Case 002/01, Trial Judgement, n.192 at 155, 527.
202 Ibid., at 121, 155.
203 R. Hopkins, 'The Case 002/01 Trial Judgment: A Stepping Stone from Nuremberg to the Present?' in S. Meisenberg and I. Stegmiller (eds.), *The Extraordinary Chambers in the Courts of Cambodia* (Asser Press, 2016) 201.
204 Internal Rule 23 *quinquies.*
205 Baum, n.17; Wessel, n.5.
206 Internal Rule 23 *quinquies* (b).
207 Although it is arguable that the judges could have established a trust fund as part of their revisions, see Ferstman at 407.
208 Case 002/01, Trial Judgement, *supra* n.192.
209 Studzinsky, *supra* Ch.1, n.19 at 182.
210 See Chapter 7.
211 Ferstman, n.117 at 407.
212 Interview with Judge 1, 7 November 2013.
213 Internal Rule 23 *quinquies* (a).
214 On the obligation for awards of reparations to be made against the accused, see *Prosecutor v. Lubanga Dyilo*, Judgment on the Appeals against the 'Decision establishing the Principles and Procedures to be applied to Reparations' ICC-01/04–01/06–3129, 7 August 2012. On states' obligation to provide reparations, see the UN Basic Principles, n.93.
215 Case 002, Pre-Trial Chamber, Decision on Appeal of Co-Lawyers for Civil Parties against Order on Civil Parties' Request for Investigative Actions Concerning all Properties Owned by the Charged Persons, Case No. 002/19–09–2007-ECCC/OCIJ, 4 August 201 at 23.
216 Ferstman, n.117at 392.
217 Interview with Lawyer 1 (CP Team) 11 November 2013.
218 Case 002/01, Trial Judgement, n.192 at 1161–1164.
219 K. Naren and H. Robertson, 'Victims Call for Money from ECCC' *The Cambodia Daily*, 17 October 2014; K. Naren, 'Victims Stage Protest Outside Tribunal' *The Cambodia Daily*, 18 October 2014, www.cambodiadaily.com/news/victims-call-for-compensation-from-eccc-70135/ (accessed 22/02/18). Discussed further in Chapter 8.
220 Ciorciari and Heindel, n.29 at 227.
221 Internal Rule 12 *bis.*
222 Judge Sylvia Cartwright, 'Opening Speech to the ECCC 7th Plenary Session' ECCC Website, 2 February 2010, www.eccc.gov.kh/sites/default/files/media/02Feb2010Plenary-VicePresident-speech(Eng)_.pdf (accessed 16/02/18).
223 Open Society Justice Initiative, 'Recent Initiatives at the Extraordinary Chambers in the Courts of Cambodia' (March 2010).
224 Fertman, n.117 at 409.
225 Rasmussen, n.2.

226 Interview with Lawyer 3 (Defence), 29 October 2014.
227 Interview with Judge 1, 7 November 2013.
228 Diamond, n.166.
229 R. Killean, 'Constructing Victimhood at the Khmer Rouge Tribunal: Visibility, Selectivity and Participation' *International Review of Victimology* (2018).
230 R. Mawby and S. Walklate, *Critical Victimology* (Sage, 1994) 189–198.

6 Practitioner perspectives on working for and with victims

1. Introduction

Chapter 2 explored the ways in which 'justice for victims' rhetoric is used to bolster support for the establishment of international criminal courts.[1] It argued that despite this pro-victim rhetoric, the 'theft of the conflict' identified by Christie within domestic systems has been mirrored on the international stage.[2] The literature offers a range of explanations for this gap between the theory and practice of 'justice for victims'. Some have offered a practical perspective which focuses on the difficulties associated with incorporating the high number of victims that result from international crimes.[3] Others have offered more critical perspectives, noting that the 'abstract' victim is a far less political, more compliant and ultimately useful entity for the purposes of justifying ICL than actual individual victims.[4]

This chapter seeks to build on these theoretical analyses of the 'imagined' and 'actual' victim dichotomy by investigating the ways in which justice for victims has been 'produced, perceived and interpreted' by those actively engaged in the work of the ECCC.[5] Institutions are shaped, interpreted and re-configured by the approaches and attitudes of those working within them, who are, in turn, influenced by their location within the institution.[6] As victims have received enhanced roles within international criminal justice processes, it has fallen on lawyers, court officials, outreach workers and others to implement these policies in practice.[7] In the context of the ECCC, the large volume of victims, the evolving nature of its legal framework, and the multitude of legal traditions represented by its practitioners, all potentially exemplify the impact of such attitudes and behaviour. In contrast to national jurisdictions, the founding legal statutes of international(ised) courts such as the ECCC vest in the judges and lawyers working within it a symbolic and legal authority to speak on behalf of the institutions. Furthermore, the mobility of professionals between ICL institutions, as well as their shifting between roles as scholars, advocates and practitioners, potentially expands their sphere of influence.[8] Therefore, the way in which practitioners speak about their work within the institution, their self-understanding and their image of victims is crucial for understanding the role of victims within the ECCC, the development of victim participation so far and its potential future in ICL.

During the fieldwork it soon became apparent that the interviewees were utilising the term *victim* in three main ways – the *'imagined victim'*, the *'victims' legal representative'* and the *'actual' victim* – and that these mapped onto three main themes: *legitimation work*, *ownership of trials* and *voice*, which will each be analysed in turn.[9] Drawing on Barker's theory of self-legitimation[10] section 2 explores the ways in which professionals engage in 'legitimation work'[11] and, more specifically, the way they utilise a broad and symbolic notion of the 'imagined victims' to legitimise their own work, the work of the ECCC and the work of ICL institutions more generally. Section 3 draws on Christie's notion of conflicts as property, in order to examine the divergent attitudes towards 'actual' victims amongst practitioners.[12] In this context, it is shown that for many interviewees, the 'actual' victims participating as civil parties were often considered synonymously with their legal representatives and that tension existed between these representatives and other practitioners, as different groups each sought to pursue their own, by no means aligned, agendas. Section 4 considers attitudes towards individual civil parties, as distinct from their representatives. While it is shown that the majority of interviewees were open to hearing the victims' voice during trials, this was frequently tempered by a belief that this voice should be framed to suit the other goals of the trial. This dichotomy between the reverence of the 'imagined victim' and the sidelining of the actual victims can arguably be explained as a desire to do justice *for* victims but not necessarily *with* them.

2. Legitimation work and the 'imagined victim'

The architects and supporters of ICL have long been engaging in 'legitimation work',[13] by which is meant the rituals and claims used to justify the activities and purposes of an industry. Although victims and their interests were not initially cited as the rationale for ICL, they have increasingly featured in its legitimation work,[14] with such language appearing in the context of the ECCC since its conception:

> For accountability first and foremost is a statement to the millions of Cambodian victims and their relatives and friends that their cries have at last been heard, providing the survivors with a sense of justice and some closure on the past.[15]

Similar language has since been used in the public pronouncements of the UNGA,[16] the court's judges[17] and lawyers,[18] by donor state representatives[19] and by the court's various observers and commentators.[20] It appears that the notion of bringing justice to the symbolic 'victim' is valuable currency, utilised not only to legitimise the court but also to justify its expenses and encourage continued financial support, as evidenced by former co-prosecutor Andrew Cayley's statement:

> I remain optimistic because I have found senior government officials sincerely interested in and committed to seeing this endeavour through to its end, and we at the United Nations as well as, if I may speak on their behalf, Cambodia's victim population are deeply grateful for their support.[21]

It seems that the invocation of 'the victims' has been routinised in the context of international(ised) criminal institutions, in general, and the ECCC, in particular, with their suffering being used to both legitimise the creation of such institutions, and to drum up continued financial and moral support for the institutions once they are created.[22] Yet, following Barker's theory of self-legitimation, it can be argued that often, these legitimising practices are also for the benefit of the profession themselves.[23] Barker has identified self-legitimation as the activities utilised by individuals to demonstrate, as much to themselves as to others, that they are justified in the pattern of actions that they follow. Barker has explored the process of self-legitimation in the context of governance and rulers, but similar processes of self-legitimation can be found within legal systems.[24] As an elite profession, lawyers have long been identified as seeking to justify their enhanced social status and monopoly over certain spaces and services.[25] The creation of educational mechanisms and autonomous monitoring bodies have traditionally been utilised to demarcate and protect the jurisdiction within which lawyers alone can operate, while 'a particular sense of self regard'[26] is developed through 'professional myths imposed on a gullible public'.[27] Self-legitimising is therefore likely to include justifications relating not only to the individual's own actions but also to the common goals of the system to which the actions relate.[28]

In order to understand the different ways in which the interviewees understood and legitimised their work, they were asked to reflect on a variety of questions related to their motivations and theoretical understanding of their work, including why they had chosen their profession, why they had wanted to work at the ECCC specifically, what they thought the goals of international criminal institutions were and ought to be and what success for the ECCC would look like. Their responses revealed that the 'imagined victim' was seen as different and sometimes overlapping 'ideal' types:[29] as *symbols of personal or collective suffering*, as the *beneficiary of justice* and as a *constituent* whose support contributed to the success and legitimacy of the court. These are considered in turn.

Victims as symbols of personal or collective suffering

A particular kind of legitimation practice has been noted amongst lawyers engaged in humanitarian work or other 'worthy' causes. Such individuals are often defined as 'cause lawyers',[30] those that seek 'to use law-related means . . . to achieve greater social justice – both for particular individuals . . . and for disadvantaged groups'.[31] Research into the motivations and goals of lawyers has shown that 'cause lawyers' may not only draw from the usual legitimising practices of the elite professional but may combine such justifications with a personal identification with the particular causes of their clients, or with broader notions of utilising their skills for the 'greater good'.[32] Previous studies amongst lawyers and legal students have revealed that a desire to help persons or groups with whom there is a personal sense of identification or sympathy can influence career choices.[33] Lawyers have spoken of being moved from an experiential base to 'do something' for 'their' people because of having faced discrimination themselves.[34] Motivation may also come from a personal connection to people who have suffered in the past, leading to a desire to represent others who have suffered in similar ways.[35] Such motivations may lead to lawyers undertaking work that is 'less well compensated than traditional private legal work and that may involve some personal, physical, economic, and social status risks'.[36] In such contexts, the work of legal professionals can become personalised and humanised, through a sense of identification with those whose interests they represent.[37] While much of the cause lawyer literature focuses on lawyers who 'represent social movements or activists',[38] similar sympathies and feelings of identification were apparent amongst some of my interviewees. Rather than seeking to make an objective determination on the status of ICL as 'cause lawyering',[39] what is interesting for the purpose of this chapter's analysis is the personal motivations of the practitioners interviewed, and the extent to which they self-legitimised and identified with certain 'causes'.[40]

Reflecting the literature explored above, some practitioners voiced their sense of personal affinity with the victims and their experiences. This was expressed not only by national interviewees,[41] amongst whom such an identification might be expected, but also by a number of international staff. Practitioners spoke of personally identifying with the victims[42] or of having survived periods of conflict and violence themselves. When asked their motivation for choosing to work at the ECCC, one judge explained:

> The tragedy of the people of the Cambodia, that sort of brought to mind, all the atrocities that [my] people went through . . . So this was this identification with a tragedy of mass atrocity on political grounds.[43]

Similarly, another lawyer working within the court's chambers noted,

> I come from a country where human rights were continuously violated, especially at the time when I grew up . . . I was really very curious about what is the best way to find a solution to what had been done and then I found out that we were not the only ones to suffer from communism, there were other places, Cambodia one of them.[44]

In this context, the Khmer Rouge's victims were classed as symbols of personal suffering and as part of a broader community of victims who had suffered as a result of conflict around the world. As Cohen has noted, awareness of atrocities and suffering has multiplied and internationalised over the past 50 years, with globalisation and media allowing for images of suffering to be spread around the world, providing illustrations for calls to action.[45] Such images can raise awareness of the 'universality of suffering' and prompt a feeling of 'wanting to do something'.[46] Indeed, as highlighted by one of the interviewees cited earlier,

> I have to say that I was very impressed, a long time ago, when I watched the movie The Killing Fields in the 80s,[47] this was the film that made an imprint in my mind.[48]

Thus, the imagery of the victims of the Khmer Rouge within this film (based on the true story of an American journalist and Khmer photographer) brought the victims into the interviewee's 'moral universe' invoking empathy and a desire to act.[49] This visual stimulus, leading to a sense of shared victimisation and collective suffering is resonant of Levinas's discussion of 'moral obligations', whereby the presence of the 'other' creates a moral obligation to act.[50]

Victims as beneficiaries of justice

Although only some interviewees personally identified with the victims, many more shared the belief that the court could or should bring justice to victims. Such a belief is not exclusive to ECCC practitioners; while the potential for such deliverance of justice has been subjected to critiques, many scholars have continued to express a belief that through modification and development, international(ised) criminal tribunals can be rendered capable of delivering such a goal.[51] At the same time, debates as to what constitutes 'justice' in this context continue, with definitions ranging from retributive notions of determining guilt[52] to a focus on reparative justice[53] to transformative justice ideals of promoting greater equality[54] to 'bottom up' notions of local ownership and participation.[55] As explored by Hoyle and Ullrich, the 'opening up of the conventional retributive justice discourse' has led to widespread discussions and contestations as to the meaning of justice within ICL.[56] Despite these different understandings of justice, it seems that victims often continue to be placed at the heart of such debates.[57]

Amongst the interviewees were several who identified the desire to do something towards bringing justice to victims as a personal motivation:[58]

> I was trying to do something for the victims, so that's why I decided, really because I wanted to work with victims.[59]
>
> [T]his desire to somehow help victims of these mass atrocity crimes by making a little contribution to the criminal proceedings.[60]

Others, although not explicitly identifying victims as factoring into their own personal motivations, cited 'justice for victims' as a goal of the ECCC:

> International justice is for their country, for those people, for Cambodian people.[61]
>
> This is a country with a lot of souls missing, and there needs to be justice, justice on an international level, justice for victims.[62]
>
> Ultimately, for me, these trials are about setting as accurate a record as possible, ascribing responsibility, providing some measure of justice to the victims and really enabling a society to move forward.[63]

Others spoke in more general terms of justice for victims being a goal of ICL, which the work of the ECCC could contribute to:

> Another goal is to bring some measure of justice to the victims of these different atrocities that are committed around the world.[64]

> Justice is not for the lawyers, and not for the judges. Justice is done for people, for the victims, the accused, and society, people.[65]

From such a perspective, victims were viewed as the key beneficiaries of international criminal justice, with practitioners drawing their legitimacy from a sense of doing something meaningful for people who had suffered.[66] Yet, just as the literature reveals a multitude of conceptions as to how justice should be delivered, the responses from interviewees also highlighted a variety of interpretations of what constituted 'justice'. This included 'restoring the moral equilibrium',[67] 'the consideration of compliance with the international norms of behaviour'[68] and 'the application of due process and rule of law'.[69] Some definitions included specific victim-orientated considerations, such as 'that those who got wrongfully hurt are compensated fairly'[70] and that '[victims] have the opportunity to address a court at some point concerning their victimization'.[71] One particularly optimistic judge claimed that by 'being admitted as a civil party, I think from that moment, they are cured'.[72] However, others seemed rooted in more traditional retributive notions of justice, such as 'ending impunity'[73] and 'to determine someone's individual criminal responsibility'.[74] Thus, while many interviewees cited victims as beneficiaries, understandings around the nature of that benefit varied significantly.

Victims as constituents

The legitimacy of international(ised) criminal courts is often tied to the positive perceptions of victim populations.[75] The term *legitimacy* in this context can be generally understood to refer to the justification of authority, in the case of a court, the authority to decide cases and impose sentences and reparation orders. There are a variety of theories which seek to identify what factors might constitute this justification.[76] The concept incorporates both sociological and normative elements, with the sociological elements pertaining to the *perceived* legitimacy of the institution and the normative relating to a more objective analysis of whether the institution *should* be accepted.[77] The two elements are closely related, with some theories of legitimacy making perceived legitimacy an important or even necessary part of a regime's normative justification.[78] Indeed, in his seminal study, Beetham has found that in order to be legitimate, the exercise of power must (1) conform to established rules, (2) the rules must be justified by reference to beliefs shared by both dominant and subordinate parties in the power relation and (3) there must be evidence of consent by the subordinate to that particular relationship.[79]

Beetham's third criterion finds particular resonance in the context of international institutions, who do not have the same options of coercion as those open to nation states.[80] Certainly, practitioners within the ECCC appeared conscious of a need to garner the support of the victim collective, in order to enhance the legitimacy and impact of their work. Just as Fletcher has highlighted the concept of victims as a 'constituency to which the [ICC] must answer',[81] victims were referred to as the court's constituents or, in the words of one interviewee, 'those whom we serve'.[82] In this context, practitioners were drawing their legitimacy from notions that they were in a sense appointed to do justice not just *for* victims but also on their behalf. The perceptions held by the victims were therefore seen as important, if not crucial, to the success of the court:

> I think [victim support] is quite important because we do that for them. So for me this is something that is really important.[83]
>
> I have to say that even if only the victims were happy it would be enough for me.[84]

As such, victims were defined as being not only the beneficiaries deserving of justice but also those demanding it. Thus, the 'imagined victim' and 'justice for victims' rhetoric repeatedly appeared in the self-legitimation practices of interviewees, appearing in the discussions of the majority of interviewees, who cited 'the victims' in their explanations of their own motivations, the goals of the institution in which they were employed, and/or the body of law to which their work was contributing.

It is worth noting that the 'imagined victims' were not the only element within the self-legitimising practices of court practitioners. Naturally, many motivations and goals were identified in the interviews, with capacity building,[85] establishing a historic narrative,[86] protecting fair trial rights[87] and establishing liability[88] being some of the goals most frequently mentioned. Often, these were mentioned in addition to 'justice for victims', suggesting that the 'imagined victim' was being utilised to bolster these other goals.[89] That a variety of motivations and goals can be identified is particularly understandable in the context of ICL, which has been critiqued as having an almost 'overabundance' of goals.[90] These goals are often cited concurrently by its supporters, perhaps because of the lack of empirical support for any individual justification.[91] Tallgren has explored this concept theoretically, noting the 'sensibility and sense' of ICL and describing its use as having an almost religious element of hope.[92] Koller has similarly spoken of the 'faith of international criminal lawyers' and the processes by which practitioners will utilise a variety of justifications to justify responding to mass atrocities with the creation of judicial processes.[93] Elsewhere, Palmer's exploration of the self-perceptions held by ICTR practitioners revealed that a number of understandings were present as to the ICTR's purpose, which was frequently cited concurrently but without universal endorsement from practitioners.[94]

Thus, as with other courts, there exists within the ECCC a number of individuals with varying, not always concordant, ideas as to the purpose of the court, what their own role was within it and to what extent 'justice for victims' should factor into these considerations. The 'imagined victim' identified in the literature certainly appeared in the legitimation work of many interviewees, whether as a symbol of personal or collective suffering, a beneficiary of justice or the constituent who must be served. Despite the personal connection expressed by some interviewees, these 'victims' were often de-personalised, symbolising human suffering and justifying action done for them or on their behalf.[95] Such language has remnants of Christie's notion of the ideal victim,[96] a depiction which is further problematised by the power relations inherent within the ECCC's work. Practitioners, influenced by genuine sympathy and moral outrage on behalf of victims, may reproduce disempowered depictions of victimised populations.[97] As Kapur has noted, advocates for human rights can reinforce notions of the 'real or authentic victim subject' as 'helpless and vulnerable', particularly in the context of Western interventions into the 'Third World'.[98] Indeed, one theme that emerged within each 'ideal type'[99] was that victims were seen predominantly as a group on whose behalf ICL should be done rather than those who should be actively involved in that process. This approach was reflected in the attitudes of interviewees towards the civil party participation, as will now be explored.

3. Who owns the case?

The second way in which interviewees spoke of victims was again not as the specific individuals participating in the ECCC's work; for the majority of interviewees, civil parties were seen as synonymous with their legal representatives in the courtroom. In the beginning of the interview process, requests that the interviewee reflect on the role of civil parties were likely to provoke a response actually relating to the interviewee's attitudes towards the civil party lawyers and LCLs. Specific questions therefore had to be asked in order to prompt a distinction between the civil parties and their legal representatives. Responses to such questions soon revealed that the predominantly negative attitudes towards civil parties were not arising from a wish to deny victims a voice but from objections to the specific approach adopted by the ECCC with regards to victim representation.

In his seminal work on conflicts as property, Christie argued that the 'owners' of conflicts, and thus those who should be involved in any response to that conflict, should be those most affected, namely the victims and perpetrators.[100] He maintained that current systems of justice exclude these parties and delegate the process to lawyers, who he describes as 'professional thieves'.[101] Victims are therefore represented so thoroughly that they find themselves 'pushed completely out of the arena, reduced to the triggerer-off of the whole thing'.[102] Although Christie was writing about common law domestic systems, similar criticisms can be made of many international(ised) criminal courts.[103] The ECCC has nominally incorporated victims as parties to the trial, a move that appears to concede some level of ownership to those most affected by the crimes, offering a 'potential for activity, for participation'.[104] However, these rights are exercised either through their own lawyers during the pre-trial phase, who may be representing up to 1,000 other victims,[105] or by the LCLs at the trial phase, who represent all participating victims as a collective. Thus, the civil party system brings with it another brand of 'professional thieves', shifting what Alcoff has defined as 'the problem of speaking for others' from one legal team to another.[106] Attempts by civil parties to circumvent this rule of speaking through legal representatives have been rebuffed by the chambers: civil parties must participate through their lawyers.[107]

While the issue of victim 'ownership' of the justice process is explored in Chapter 8 what is relevant for the present discussion is the competing claims of ownership that exist amongst the civil party lawyers, LCLs and other legal actors within the court. In this context, it became clear that disputes over to what extent different legal teams could legitimately claim ownership over the conflict were occurring. The main issues raised by interviewees when questioned about the role of civil parties were primarily related to the role and conduct of civil party legal teams and tended to focus on the interviewee's opinions on (a) the necessity of civil party representation, (b) what the civil parties' lawyers' role should be and (c) the level of professionalism displayed by individual lawyers. Demonstrating the extent to which these conflicts were removed from the victims themselves, one interviewee identified them as 'a legal battle, it's not any more a battle on a human level'.[108]

The necessity of civil party representation

Historically there has been a tendency, prevalent within both common law domestic systems and international(ised) criminal courts, to see the needs and wishes of victims as synonymous with that of the prosecution.[109] Within the common law legal tradition, the interests of victims are represented within criminal trials by the prosecutor, who seeks vindication for crimes as a breach of community norms.[110] This focus on dichotomous proceedings offers little space for victims to participate through their own representatives; victims who wish for direct compensation must file a separate, private action.[111] In contrast, the civil law tradition allows victims to access their own legal representation, in order to seek reparation for the harm caused by a wrongdoer in the same proceedings as the prosecution.[112] However, studies conducted with practitioners have revealed that even within such systems, victims are often viewed as predominantly a witness or 'assistant' to the prosecutor.[113] Such opinions were evident amongst court practitioners, with both the legal culture of the interviewees and their position within the court proving to be strong influences on their perspectives.

The interviewees from the co-prosecutors' office were the most vocal critics of the civil party system and had a number of critical reflections to offer. The first was that the civil party lawyers (to be taken as including civil party lawyers and the LCLs) were not necessary, as the prosecution were more than able to reflect the interest of the victims, alongside the interest of society more broadly:

> I think it's manifestly absurd to elevate civil party lawyers to fully fledged participants in a criminal trial . . . I think the interests of the victims could have been properly and professionally presented before the Court by the prosecution without civil party lawyers being involved.[114]
>
> I don't believe civil party legal participation has added very much at all to the evidential scope of this trial . . . if a civil party had come into Court, been asked questions by I hope fully qualified prosecutors, their evidence would have got to the Court quicker. And that could have led to more crime sites being added to this case.[115]

This feeling was not limited to the co-prosecutors' office but was most notably shared by members of the defence teams:

> The prosecutor could try the case on behalf of the victims and society as a whole, because these crimes affect everybody.[116]
>
> From a systematic perspective, the contribution of civil parties to the trial was virtually zero . . . Legally, there's no place for them.[117]

It seemed that the interviewee's legal tradition influenced their perception of the necessity of victim legal representatives; the opinion that civil party lawyers were unnecessary was predominantly voiced by lawyers coming from a common law tradition.[118] However, it is likely that the position of those making the criticism within the ECCC itself was also relevant: members of the prosecution team wished to have sole control over the case against the accused, while the defence was reluctant to accept an additional prosecutorial voice within the courtroom.[119] Such views also speak to broader understandings of the criminal trial as a competition between the two parties, an approach that is found predominantly within common law trials[120] but which has developed at the ECCC despite its civil law basis.[121] In contrast, several of those working within civil party legal teams were adamant that there was a need for specific civil party legal representation[122] and spoke of the difficulties in convincing other parties that this was so:

> I think the main challenge was to make a place for civil parties in this trial, because a lot of persons from many places, the prosecutors, the Trial Chamber, the defence, they did not really accept the civil parties, or they did accept them but as a different party, not with all the rights of a party. It's their trial, it's their story, so they have the right to be present, they have the right to ownership of the trial, as the accused are and the prosecutors are.[123]

This interviewee's legal work experiences were rooted in a civil law tradition, where legal representation for victims would be more commonplace, and it is likely that their view was influenced by both their role, and their perceptions on how criminal trials should be structured.[124] The ECCC's merging of common law procedures into its trial proceedings likely contributed to the challenge spoken of by the interviewee; adversarial proceedings undoubtedly create an obstacle to effective victim participation.[125] Thus, a struggle is apparent between the civil party lawyers and the other parties, with each seeking to defend their own place within the judicial process, further their own goals and resist attempts to infringe on their perceived role within the courtroom.

Defining the role of civil party lawyers

A further and related criticism, voiced by interviewees from every section of the court, also concerns issues of ownership. This was that if civil party lawyers were to be included, then their role should be more clearly defined and limited.[126] The court's Internal Rule 23 defines the purpose of civil party action as being to participate in criminal proceedings 'by supporting the prosecution'. However, this leaves room for interpretation and led to significant confusion as to the role of the civil party lawyers and LCLs,[127] as well as extra litigation as parties requested chamber rulings to clarify the role.[128] As noted by one defence lawyer,

> Nobody knew what their role was, including and most especially them, including the judges.[129]

In particular, it was argued by interviewees that civil party lawyers should not engage with the process in ways which might influence the determination of guilt of the accused or adopt a role akin to a secondary prosecutor.[130] The vague definition of the civil party's role certainly led to some civil party's lawyers occasionally involving themselves in evidence pertaining to the guilt of the accused. While this was mentioned by some defence interviewees,[131] it appeared to cause the greatest frustration amongst the co-prosecutors' team, who lamented the lack of understanding amongst civil party lawyers as to the prosecutorial strategy:

> They have not been party to the common criminal plan is, what the prosecution's case theory is, what the detailed evidence on modes of liability is, and on numerous occasions . . . I have seen the evidence significantly undermined by an ill equipped civil party lawyer asking liability questions, bringing out inconsistencies, asking long convoluted, ill prepared questions that end up lessening the strength of the prosecution's evidence, and thereby not assisting the ultimate aim of bringing some justice to the victims.[132]

Again, the influence of the individual's role within the court and legal background is evident here. Strong criticisms came from lawyers originating from systems where adversarial procedures are utilised; it often seemed that their focus was on 'winning', rather than determining the truth.[133] As explained by Landsmann, adversarial trials centre on the 'sharp clash of proofs presented by litigants in a highly structured forensic setting'.[134] A heavy onus is therefore placed on the parties to prove their own case and refute the arguments of the other, leaving little space to address the needs of those actually affected by the crimes.[135] Coming from such legal cultures, the focus on winning is understandable. Thus, the involvement of civil party lawyers was decried as infringing on their ability to pursue this aim, an aim which was assumed to be synonymous with what victims would want – the successful prosecution of the accused. Such views also provide an interesting contrast to the more usual concerns of commentators with regards to victim participation: that it would be to the detriment of the rights of the accused and interfere with an objective pursuit of justice.[136]

Amongst those working with the civil parties, views were mixed; some conceded the issues identified by the prosecution:

> You might go into areas where you elicit answers that are not very helpful to the prosecution, and not very helpful to proving the case beyond reasonable doubt. So you get into this conflict with the prosecutors when you're supposed to be on the same side.[137]

However, others were defiant:

> It would be reducing the position of the civil parties to say they only speak about their suffering, they are not here for that, they are here to bring evidence and for giving their impact on the trial.[138]
>
> Sometimes we didn't agree with the prosecutor also, which doesn't make them happy because they would just like us to follow what they say and it's not like that.[139]

It appears that what was being revealed were the parties' underlying opinions on who should have the ability to claim 'ownership' of trials,[140] with ownership being interpreted as the ability to influence court's proceedings and exercise power relations within the court setting.[141] This protectiveness was evidenced by the view expressed that civil party lawyers should limit themselves to expressing the views of victims, leaving the substantive case to the prosecution.[142] It was also evidenced by the lack of coordination and cooperation between the prosecution and the civil party lawyer teams, a situation that was blamed by the prosecution on the civil party lawyers' unwillingness to cooperate[143] but blamed by others on the prosecution's unwillingness to share their case strategy.[144]

This lack of cooperation and need to protect one's own role was explained by one practitioner as being a matter of lawyer egos:

> I think that's a problem with this court in that there's too many egos, there's too many people who want to do something, they want to have their name, they want to be the ones doing this and not the other ones.[145]

McEvoy's critique of the legal profession has resonance here. As he notes, the intellectual and technical demands of law, the elevated social status granted to their profession, the importance of their work's subject matter, the relatively closed nature of their social and professional world, the specific legal education required and the modes of self-governance utilised by the profession can all contribute to a sense of elitism and occasional arrogance amongst lawyers.[146] Whether an issue of professional ego or commitment to the case at hand, it seemed that practitioners' own role and wish to further the aims associated with that role were highly influential on their attitudes towards the civil party system. However, the perspectives of those interviewees who were not working in one of the parties' teams reveal the extent to which legal traditions also influenced perspectives on civil party representation. Overall, those from a common law tradition were more resistant to victims having legal representation with party rights. This did not mean that they were resistant to a role for victims (as explored later) but that they failed to see the need for civil parties to be introduced into the judicial process.[147] In contrast, those from a civil law tradition, while often still critical of the way in which the system had been implemented, tended to be more accepting of the presence of victim representatives and thus supportive of the ECCC's attempt to involve civil parties.[148] Therefore, while different legal traditions were not the only factor in the divergent views and criticisms expressed, they played a critical role in determining the level to which victims as parties with lawyers were accepted by practitioners working within the ECCC.[149]

The professionalism of civil party lawyers

The final criticism raised with regards to the civil party lawyers pertained less to issues of ownership but was likely an exacerbating factor to the frustrations expressed. This was the perceived lack of professional advocacy skills displayed by some civil party lawyers and the impact their repetitive questioning had on the efficiency of the trial. In this case, a distinction was drawn between civil party lawyers and the LCLs, who, it was conceded, had significantly improved the performance of victim representation in the courtroom. However, the civil party lawyers were decried as

> not well equipped for standard criminal courtroom advocacy . . . I have seen a train of French lawyers coming into this court for two days, who have not prepared their briefs properly, who have not asked relevant questions and on occasions . . . because of their lack of knowledge of the case, their lack of any discussion with the OCP, their lack of any inquiry into the facts, have conducted questioning in court which has, in my view, significantly damaged the interests of victims.[150]

This was a fairly commonly held belief, with the impact of the civil party lawyers' conduct on the expediency of the proceedings being particularly criticised and, indeed, leading the TC to introduce time limits and request that civil party lawyers limit their questions to those that were not repetitious, long-winded or irrelevant:[151]

> [A]nyone who has listened to the proceedings will have heard the President on countless occasions say to civil party lawyers, not exclusively but mainly, 'Where are you going with this question, you are repeating what the prosecution asked ten minutes ago, please move on to a relevant subject, please confine yourself to the scope of this trial'.[152]

While for some, the conduct was seen as damaging to the victims' interests, it seemed that for many, their frustrations were primarily linked to issues of legal professionalism and trial management. The criticism that international criminal trials take too long is not one that is unique to the ECCC[153] but certainly one that has been exacerbated by the death of two accused and the knowledge that the remaining defendants, and indeed the victims, are of advanced age.[154] With such fears over expediency being prevalent, it was unsurprising that the introduction of the LCLs was almost uniformly praised by the interviewees. However, it was not as happily accepted by the civil party lawyers themselves, who fought for the continued right of audience,[155] again illustrating the wishes of lawyers to be able to exert their own agendas and that of their clients within the courtroom. This was acknowledged by a former civil party lawyer:

> [I]t was the reason why I left, because I could not appear in Court anymore without their agreement or endorsement for legal submissions. So what can I do, I am like a legal assistant, providing information from my clients to them but without consideration.[156]

This desire for individual rights of audience was the subject of derision from other interviewees and was interpreted as being motivated by selfish desires for court time, rather than as a wish to continue being able to individually represent their clients' interests.[157] Indeed, there was a prevalent view that civil party lawyers lacked integrity and were out to further their own careers rather than genuinely work in the victims' interests:

> It boosts their own profile, it's a bit of self-promotion for sure.[158]
>
> Even amongst themselves they were fighting, who's gonna sit where, who's gonna say what, how much time they're going to have.[159]
>
> I have the feeling sometimes that it is just to put on your CV that you are a civil party lawyer, and it's something that is good than to be really involved with them. So I think it's also a problem because I think that victims is something that everyone also thinks is very glamorous to work with, but then you really have to work for them and not just pretend, and we have a lot of that, of just pretending to.[160]

If credence is to be given to this perspective – and as I encountered many dedicated civil party lawyers, I would dispute at least the uniform application of such criticisms – then it highlights the need to hold lawyers to appropriate standards of conduct. Civil party lawyers are bound by the Code of Ethics for Lawyers Licensed with the Bar Association of the Kingdom of Cambodia and should be held to account if they breach the obligations of their oath and the code's principles on conscience, humanity and tact. It also highlights the need to ensure victims have access to professional, capable lawyers in order to ensure that their interests are being correctly and well represented. If such representation is to be guaranteed, then victims must be given full access to legal aid, something that was initially lacking at the ECCC.[161] It is possible that many of the frustrations voiced, particularly with regards to civil party lawyers being underprepared, could have been avoided had many of the international civil party lawyers not been working pro bono and therefore balancing their work at the ECCC with their practices at home.[162] Balancing pro bono work with full-time legal work may naturally inhibit civil party lawyers from ensuring a level of preparation similar to that of co-prosecutors working full-time at the ECCC. This lack of sufficient funding becomes particularly troubling because of the obligatory nature of representation, as summarised by a former civil party lawyer:

> You have it as an obligation, a must, but you don't have any legal aid for those lawyers. This is completely absurd.[163]

These critiques also reflect a broader tendency noted within legal systems, of lawyers pushing back against changes and developments which do not suit them, or which they believe will inhibit their ability to carry out their role.[164] This pushback, when combined with the common assumptions that victims' wishes are synonymous with that of the prosecution, is problematic; it risks contributing to a normative way of assuming what is good for the 'imagined victims' while reducing real empathy for the lived reality of victims and what they may wish for in judicial proceedings.[165]

4. Hearing the victims' voice

One criticism that is frequently made about international criminal courts is their instrumentalising of the victims' voice: victims may appear as witnesses but, as such, will have their stories shaped by the needs and wishes of the parties.[166] As noted by McEvoy and McConnachie, the transitional justice context makes such processes all the more politically and emotionally charged because of the scale and nature of suffering amongst victim participants. They argue that such processes have not always been handled with adequate sensitivity.[167] One response to this has been the growth of more restorative or truth telling based transitional justice practices, such as truth commissions.[168] Another has been moves within international(ised) criminal courts to allow for victims to speak with greater autonomy. The ECCC has followed this path through its introduction of victim impact hearings and statements of suffering, both of which allow victims to speak more expansively to their harms.[169] This last section explores the attitudes amongst ECCC staff as to the amount of voice that should be granted to victims into court proceedings.

Despite the predominantly negative views held about the civil party system, there were few interviewees who did not consider it important and valuable to have some form of victim participation. Perspectives ranged from those who, while acknowledging that the ECCC's approach had been problematic, continued to support a more limited type of party status for victims[170] to those who felt there should have been no place for victims as parties at all.[171] The majority were critical of any role that infringed on the lawyers' ownership of the trial, instead favouring models of participation that limited the victims' role to an expressive one.[172] The specific approach taken tended to reflect the interviewee's position within the trial and their perception of how victim participation could help or hinder them in their goals. For example, the co-prosecutor interviewees expressed their appreciation of and preference for victim-witness testimony:

> I'd have rather seen thirty civil parties give meaningful evidence . . . And you would have had then, really meaningful participation on a limited scale. And probably, in my view, would have done more to empower victims generally, than by giving them this global right to have lawyers representing them.[173]

A preference was expressed for an approach closer to that adopted by the ICTY and ICTR, where victims' testimonial opportunities were limited to being called as a victim.[174] Once again, the prosecution team voiced their belief that theirs and the civil parties' interests would, or at least should, be in alignment. This opinion, voiced despite the negative reactions that have been expressed amongst victim populations with regards to the role of the victim within the ICTR and ICTY,[175] demonstrates a preference for the traditional adversarial model of criminal prosecutions, and a preoccupation with the needs of that trial, rather than the needs of victim populations. As Pizzi has remarked, such a focus 'turns witnesses into weapons to be used against the other side',[176] reducing them to 'evidentiary cannon fodder'.[177]

The defence interviewees, on the other hand, who had witnessed unsworn civil party testimony being used as evidence,[178] tended to favour an approach which limited victim involvement until after the judgement:

> I think everyone thinks having lots of civil party participation on a reparation level is a great thing. Having a second set of lawyers who are leading evidence which is used substantively and not given under oath . . . we have a HUGE problem with that.[179]
>
> I think civil parties should say something about the suffering and the loss they have experienced, but ideally they would do that after the judgment in which somebody has been convicted.[180]

This preference appears similar to the victim impact statements used within a number of common law systems, which allows victims voice once the guilt of the accused is determined,[181] thereby continuing to respect the traditional adversarial focus of the trial.[182] One cannot but understand such a position, the TC's reliance on civil party testimony had highlighted the challenges that exist when incorporating victims within proceedings while ensuring the rights of the accused.[183] Yet concerns have also been raised over the impact of victim statements on fair trial rights, while studies have shown that victims themselves can be disappointed by the experience of giving a statement,[184] signifying the difficulties inherent in resolving the conflict between the rights of the victim and the accused.

Amongst those working in the judiciary, there was a tendency to support some form of victim participation. However, all seemed to be aware that victim autonomy within the courtroom must be limited by the demands of the legal process, including the need for a fair trial and expeditious proceedings.[185] Several spoke of the power of victim testimony as adding a human element to the proceedings but did not translate this to justifying legal representation:

> I think the best moment in Case 002 was when the civil parties asked questions of the accused, this was for me the best moment of the whole trial, the moment that was the most real and really meaningful of what was happening.[186]

Similar opinions were voiced by both ECCC practitioners and trial observer,[187] with one trial observer lauding the involvement of victims because of their provision of 'depth'.[188] It seemed that for many of the interviewees, the ideal role for victims would go beyond the former positioning of victims as 'passive objects' within international justice, with no rights to take part in the proceedings or to obtain compensation.[189] This suggests a normative progression from the Nuremberg trials and the desire to keep the victims out of the courtroom.[190] However, it was clear that the interviewees expected 'ownership' of the trial to remain in the hands of the lawyers and that the preferred model was far from Christie's victim-oriented process.[191] The failure of other parties to recognise the legal value of victim participation was bemoaned by a lawyer in the LCLs section:

> I think they are an essential component of it, the only problem I have is that they should see us as a component that has a legal value, and not only that we have this 'human face' I mean I really cannot hear that anymore, because it's not only that.[192]

Dembour and Haslam have spoken of the tension inherent in international trials between adhering to the strictures of the legal process while attending to the suffering of individual victims.[193] It seemed that in the view of the majority of the interviewees, it should be the demands of a legal process that receive priority in dealing with such tensions, and the victims' voice should be limited to allow for the furthering of the other goals of the institution.[194] Christie's notion of the ideal victim resonates here, particularly in relation to the sixth and final attribute of the ideal victim: that they are powerful enough to make their case known but without threatening strong countervailing vested interests.[195] Similarly, victims should be able to come to the court and share their experiences and views, as long as those views did not conflict with or disrupt the court.[196]

5. Conclusion

Just as international criminal institutions are at least, in part, premised on, and draw legitimacy from, pursuing justice for victims,[197] ECCC practitioners utilised 'justice for victims' rhetoric in their self-legitimising practices. The 'imagined victim' in this context was seen as a homogenous vulnerable entity on whose behalf and in whose name justice should be delivered. However, this goal was complicated by the fact that different individuals expressed different interpretations as to what constitutes justice and the extent to which 'justice for victims' rhetoric should guide the work of the ECCC. Similarly, opinions as to the extent to which actual victims should be involved varied significantly between individuals and were often influenced by their legal tradition and role within the court.

Perceptions of the civil party system tended to be negative, but that appeared to be because victims were regarded as synonymous with their legal representatives. The inclusion of civil party lawyers was subjected to substantial criticisms, yet the majority of interviewees were open to granting victims some voice within trial processes. However, this was not being interpreted as requiring a conceding of ownership of the conflict to the actual victim population; instead, there was a general desire to limit the victims' role to one that, while going beyond that of a witness, did not reach the level of a party to the trial. The perception remained that lawyers, and preferably prosecutors, were best positioned to pursue justice for victims.

This is not a purely theoretical discussion but has practical implications for victim participation, both within the ECCC and in any future international criminal courts. Practitioners working within ICL are often able to exert real influence over the procedures adopted within institutions. Their professional mobility, combined with the new and evolving nature of ICL as a legal system, grants them an influence that would not often be found within domestic jurisdictions. A resistance to an enhanced role for victims within trial proceedings may therefore lead to a curtailing of that role, as indeed has been the case at the ECCC, for example through the role practitioners have played in influencing the form of representation given to civil parties.[198] Thus, while 'justice for victims' rhetoric grows ever more valuable to the legitimation practices of the proponents of ICL, the reluctance of practitioners to concede ownership of the conflict to those most affected may lead to victims continuing to find themselves instrumentalised rather than empowered by international criminal proceedings. The attitudes of civil parties themselves towards the level of participation granted are considered in Chapter 8, after consideration is given to another group of actors who have exerted considerable influence over the court's deliverance of justice to victims: professional civil society.

Notes

1 See for example ICTY, Annual Report to the UNGA, A/49/342, S/1994/1007, 29 August 1994, paras. 1 and 198–199; ICTR, Annual Report to the UNGA, A/53/429-S/1998/857, 23 September 1998 para. 160.

2 N. Christie, 'Conflict as Property' 17(1) *British Journal of Criminology* (1977) 1.

3 For example H. Hobbs, 'Victim Participation in International Criminal Proceedings: Problems and Potential Solutions in Implementing an Effective and Vital Component of Justice' 49 *Texas International Law Journal* (2014); E. Hoven, M. Feiler and S. Scheibel, 'Victims in Trials of Mass Crimes: A Multi-Perspective Study of Civil Party Participation at the Extraordinary Chambers in the Courts of Cambodia' 3 *Cologne Occasional Papers on International Peace and Security Law* (2013); C. Aptel, 'Prosecutorial Discretion at the ICC and Victims' Right to Remedy: Narrowing the Impunity Gap' 10 *Journal of International Criminal Justice* (2012) 1357; C. Jorda and J. de Hemptinne, 'The Status and Role of the Victim' in A. Cassese, P. Gaeta and R.W. Jones (eds.), *The Rome Statute of the International Criminal Court: A Commentary* (Oxford University Press, 2002) 1387–1419.

4 For example S. Kendall and S. Nouwen, 'Representational Practices at the International Criminal Court: The Gap between Juridified and Abstract Victimhood' 76 *Law and Contemporary Problems* (2013) 235; K. McEvoy and K. McConnachie, 'Victims and Transitional Justice: Voice, Agency and Blame' 22 *Social and Legal Studies* (2013) 489; E. Haslam and R. Edmunds, 'Victim Participation, Politics and the Construction of Victims at the International Criminal Court: Reflections on Proceedings in Banda and Jerbo' 14 *Melbourne Journal of International Law* (2013) 727; S. Marks and A. Clapham, *International Human Rights Lexicon* (Oxford University Press, 2005).

5 C. Geertz, 'Thick Descriptions: Toward an Interpretive Theory of Culture' in C. Geertz (ed.), *The Interpretation of Cultures: Selected Essays* (Fontana Press, 1973) 7.
6 M. Douglas, *How Institutions Think* (Routledge and Kegan Paul Ltd., 1987).
7 J. Eisenstein and H. Jacob, *Felony justice: An Organizational Analysis of Criminal Courts* (Little, Brown and Company, 1977).
8 L. Vinjamuri and J. Snyder, 'Advocacy and Scholarship in the Study of International War Crime Tribunals and Transitional Justice' 7 *Annual Review of Political Science* (2004) 345 at 359.
9 See also J. Wemmers, 'Victims and the International Criminal Court: Evaluating the Success of the ICC with Respect to Victims' 16 *International Review of Victimology* (2009) 221 at 218.
10 R. Barker, *Legitimating Identities: The Self-Presentation of Rulers and Subjects* (Cambridge University Press, 2001).
11 A. Thumula, B. Goold and I. Loader, 'A Tainted Trade? Moral Ambivalence and Legitimation Work in the Private Security Industry' 62 *British Journal of Sociology* (2011) 283.
12 Christie, n.2.
13 Barker, n.10; Thumula, Goold and Loader, n.11.
14 Kendall and Nouwen, n.4 at 6.
15 *Report of the Group of Experts for Cambodia Established Pursuant to General Assembly Resolution 52/135*, UN Doc. A/53/850, 15 March 1999.
16 For example UNGA Resolution, A/RES/57/228, 27 February 2003.
17 For example Opening Speech by the Plenary's President Judge KONG Srim, ECCC Website, 13 September 2010, www.eccc.gov.kh/sites/default/files/media/8th_plenary_president_speech_EN.pdf (accessed 16/02/18).
18 For example Co-Prosecutor William Smith, cited in 'Hearing Debates Delay, Scope, of Case 002/02' *Cambodia Tribunal Monitor*, 11 November 2014, www.cambodiatribunal.org/2014/02/11/hearing-debates-delay-scope-for-case-00202/ (accessed 16/02/18).
19 For example 'Statement by the Principal Donors Group for the Extraordinary Chambers in the Courts of Cambodia' ECCC Website, 27 June 2014, www.eccc.gov.kh/en/articles/statement-principal-donors-group-extraordinary-chambers-courts-cambodia (accessed 16/02/18).
20 For example M. Guiraud, *Victims' Rights before the Extraordinary Chambers in the Courts of Cambodia (ECCC): A Mixed Record for Civil Parties* (FIDH, November 2012); K. Yesberg, 'Accessing Justice Through Victim Participation at the Khmer Rouge Tribunal' 40 *Victoria University of Wellington Law Review* (2009) 555.
21 M. Wolfe-Robinson, 'Cambodia Court Hearing Khmer Rouge Trials Close to Bankruptcy' *The Guardian*, 4 December 2012, www.theguardian.com/law/2012/dec/04/cambodia-khmer-rouge-court-bankruptcy (accessed 16/02/18).
22 See also L.E. Fletcher, 'Refracted Justice: The Imagined Victim and the International Criminal Court' in C. De Vos, S. Kendall and C. Stahn (eds.), *Contested Justice: the Politics and Practice of International Criminal Court Interventions* (Cambridge University Press, 2015) 302–326 at 304; C. Lawther, 'The Construction and Politicisation of Victimhood' in O. Lynch and J. Argomaniz, *Victims of Terrorism: A Comparative and Interdisciplinary Study* (Routledge, 2015) 10–31.
23 Barker, n.10.
24 See also N. Palmer, *Courts in Conflict* (Oxford University Press, 2015).
25 F. Kay, 'Professionalism And Exclusionary Practices: Shifting the Terrain of Privilege And Professional Monopoly' 11 *International Journal of the Legal Profession* (2004) 11; G. Hanlon, 'Lawyers, the Market and Significant Others' 60 *Modern Law Review* (1997) 798; H. Sommerlad, 'Managerialism and the Legal Profession:

A New Professional Paradigm' 2 *International Journal of the Legal Profession* (1995) 159; T. Halliday, *Beyond Monopoly: Lawyers, State Crises and Professional Empowerment* (University of Chicago Press, 1987); M. Burrage, 'Revolution and the Collective Action of the French, American, and English Legal Professions' 13 *Law and Social Inquiry* (1988) 225; D. Duman, 'The Creation and Diffusion of a Professional Ideology in Nineteenth Century England' 27 *Sociological Review* (1979) 113.

26 K. McEvoy and R. Rebouche, 'Mobilising the Professions?: Lawyers, Politics and the Collective Legal Conscience' in J. Morison, K. McEvoy and G. Anthony (eds.), *Judges, Human Rights and Transition* (Oxford University Press, 2007) 280.

27 J. McKinlay 'On the Professional Regulation of Change' in P. Halmos (ed.), *Professionalisation and Social Change* (The Sociological Review, 1973) 77.

28 Ibid.

29 W. J. Cahnman, 'Ideal Type Theory: Max Weber's Concept and Some of Its Derivations' 6(3) *The Sociology Quarterly* (1965) 268.

30 A. Sarat and S. Scheingold (eds.), *Cause Lawyering and Social Movements* (Stanford University Press, 2006).

31 C. Menkel-Meadow, 'The Causes of Cause Lawyering: Toward and Understanding of the Motivation and Commitment of Social Justice Lawyers' in A. Sarat and S Scheigold (eds.), *Cause Lawyering: Political Commitments and Professional Responsibilities* (Oxford University Press, 1998) 31–68.

32 Ibid., at 45–47.

33 R. Meadow and C. Menkel-Meadow, 'The Origins of Political Commitment: Social Background and Ideology Among Legal Services Attorneys' *Paper Presented at the Annual Meeting of the Law and Society Association*, Toronto, Canada, June 1982, cited in Menkel-Meadow, n.31 at 46; N. D. Polikoff, 'Am I My Client?: The Role Confusion of a Lawyer Activist' 31 *Harvard Civil Rights-Civil Liberties Law Review* (1996) 443; R. Stover and H.S. Erlanger, *Making It and Breaking It: The Fate of Public Interest Commitment during Law School* (University of Illinois Press, 1989).

34 D. B. Wilkins, 'Two Paths to the Mountain Top? The Role of Legal Education in Shaping the Values of Black Corporate Lawyers' 45 *Stanford Law Review* (1993) 1981.

35 S. Lawrence-Lightfood, *I've Known Rivers: Lives of Loss and Liberation* (Basic Books, 1994).

36 Menkel-Meadow, n.31 at 34.

37 Ibid.

38 R. Michalowski, 'All or Nothing: An Inquiry into the (Im)possibility of Cause Lawyering under Cuban Socialism' in A. Sarat and S Scheigold (eds.), *Cause Lawyering: Political Commitments and Professional Responsibilities* (Oxford University Press, 1998) 523.

39 See Menkel-Meadow, n.31 at 33–34 for a discussion on the challenges associated with such a determination.

40 E. Fogelman, *Conscience and Courage: Rescuers of Jews during the Holocaust* (Anchor Books, 1995).

41 Interview with VSS Staff 2, 13 January 2014; Interview with Legal Assistant (CP Team), 10 December 2013.

42 Interview with Lawyer 2 (CP Team), 26 September 2015.

43 Interview with Judge 4, 13 January 2014.

44 Interview with Lawyer 1 (Chambers), 11 November 2013.

45 S. Cohen, *States of Denial: Knowing about Atrocities and Suffering* (Polity Press, 2001).

46 Ibid., at 185 and 195.

47 Based on the book C. Hudson, *The Killing Fields* (Dell Publishing Co. 1984).

48 Interview with Judge 4, 13 January 2014.
49 Cohen, n.45 at 216.
50 R.P. Blum, 'Emmanuel Levinas' Theory of Commitment' 44(2) *Philosophy and Phenomenological Research* (1983) 145.
51 For example L. Moffett, *Justice for Victims at the International Criminal Court* (Routledge, 2014); B. McGonigle Leyh, *Procedural Justice? Victim Participation in International Criminal Proceedings* (Intersentia, 2011).
52 M. Rauschenbach and D. Scalia, 'Victims and International Criminal Justice: A Vexed Question?' 870 *International Review of the Red Cross* (2008).
53 F. Rosenfeld, 'Collective Reparations for Victims of Armed Conflict' 92 *International Review of the Red Cross* (2010) 731.
54 W. Lambourne 'Transitional Justice and Peacebuilding after Mass Violence' 3(1) *International Journal of Transitional Justice* (2009) 28.
55 P. Lundy and M. McGovern, 'Whose Justice? Rethinking Transitional Justice from the Bottom Up' 35(2) *Journal of Law and Society* (2008) 265; K. McEvoy, 'Beyond Legalism: Towards a Thicker Understanding of Transitional Justice' 24 *Journal of Law and Society* (2007) 411.
56 C. Hoyle and L. Ullrich, 'New Court, New Justice? The Evolution of 'Justice for Victims' at Domestic Courts and at the International Criminal Court' 12 *Journal of International Criminal Justice* (2014) 681 at 702.
57 McEvoy and McConnachie, n.4.
58 Interview with Lawyer 2 (LCL Office), 21 November 2013; Interview with Lawyer 2 (Chambers), 11 November 2013; Interview with Judge 3, 11 November 2013; Interview with Judge 1, 7 November 2013.
59 Interview with Lawyer 1 (CP Co-Lawyer Team), 21 November 2013.
60 Interview with Lawyer 2 (Chambers), 11 November 2013.
61 Interview with Judge 2, 11 November 2013.
62 Interview with Judge 1, 7 November 2013.
63 Interview with Lawyer 2 (Co-Prosecutors' Team) 8 November 2011.
64 Interview with Lawyer 1 (Defence), 8 November 2013.
65 Interview with Lawyer 1 (LCL Office), 8 November 2013.
66 S. Nouwen 'Justifying Justice' in J. Crawford and M. Koskennieme (eds.), *The Cambridge Companion to International Law* (Cambridge University Press, 2012) 327–352.
67 Interview with Judge 4, 13 January 2014.
68 Interview with Judge 1, 7 November 2013.
69 Interview with Judge 2, 11 November 2013.
70 Interview with Lawyer 1 (Chambers), 11 November 2013.
71 Interview with Judge 1, 7 November 2013.
72 Interview with Judge 2, 11 November 2013.
73 Interview with Lawyer 1 (CP Team), 11 November 2013.
74 Interview with Lawyer 3 (Defence), 8 November 2013.
75 J. Ramji-Nogales, 'Designing Bespoke Transitional Justice: A Pluralist Process Approach' 32(1) *Michigan Journal of International Law* (2010) 1; J.E. Stromseth, 'Pursuing Accountability for Atrocities after Conflict: What Impact on Building the Rule of Law?' 38 *Georgetown Journal of International Law* (2007) 251.
76 J. Tankebe and A. Liebling (eds.), *Legitimacy and Criminal Justice* (Oxford University Press, 2015); R.A. Dahl and B. Stinebrickner, *Modern Political Analysis* (6th edn) (Pearson, 2002); D. Beetham, *The Legitimation of Power*, P. Jones and A. Weale (eds.) (MacMillan, 1991); J. Habermas, *Communication and the Evolution of Society, Unitarian Universalist Association* (Beacon Press, 1979).
77 H. Pitkin, 'Obligation and Consent – II' 60(1) *American Political Science Review* (1996) 39.

78 D. Bodansky, 'The Legitimacy of International Governance: A Coming Challenge for International Environmental Law?' 93(3) *The American Journal of International Law* (1999) 596 at 601.
79 Beetham, n.76 at 15–16. See also D. Beetham, 'Revisiting Legitimacy, Twenty Years On' in J. Tankebe and A. Liebling (eds.), *Legitimacy and Criminal Justice* (Oxford University Press, 2015) 19–37.
80 I. Hurd, *After Anarchy: Legitimacy and Power in the United Nations Security Council* (Princeton University Press, 2007).
81 Fletcher, n.22 at 315.
82 Interview with Lawyer 1 (Chambers), 11 November 2013.
83 Interview with Lawyer 2 (Chamber), 11 November 2013.
84 Interview with Lawyer 1 (LCL Office), 8 November 2013.
85 Interviews with Lawyer 1(Co-Prosecutors' Team), 8 November 2013; Lawyer 1 (Defence), 8 November 2013; Lawyer 2 (Defence), 8 November 2013; Lawyer 1(CP Team), 11 November 2013; Judge 2, 11 November 2013; Lawyer 1 (Chambers), 11 November 2013; Lawyer 2 (LCL Office), 21 November 2013; Lawyer 4 (Defence), 13 December 2013; VSS Staff 2, 13 January 2014.
86 Interviews with Judge 1, 7 November 2013; Lawyer 1 (Chambers), 11 November 2013; Lawyer 2 (LCL Office), 21 November 2013; Lawyer 2 (Co-Prosecutors' Team), 8 November 2013; Lawyer 1 (Defence), 8 November 2013; VSS Staff 2, 13 January 2014.
87 Interview with Lawyer 4 (Defence), 13 December 2013; Lawyer 3 (Defence), 8 November 2013.
88 Interviews with Judge 4, 13 January 2014; Judge 2, 7 January 2013; Lawyer 2 (LCL Office), 21 November 2013; Lawyer 1(CP Team), 11 November 2013; Lawyer 4 (Defence), 13 December 2013; Lawyer 2 (Co-Prosecutors' Team), 8 November 2013; Lawyer 1 (Defence), 8 November 2013; Lawyer 2 (Defence), 8 November 2013.
89 McEvoy and McConnachie, n.4 at 490.
90 M. Damaska, 'What Is the Point of International Criminal Justice?' 83 *Chicago Kent Law Review* (2008) 329 at 331.
91 See E. Stover, *The Witnesses: War Crimes and the Promise of Justice in The Hague* (University of Pennsylvania Press, 2005) on the lack of connection between trials and reconciliation; M. Koskenniemi, 'Between Impunity and Show Trials' 6 *Max Planck Yearbook of United Nations Law* (2002) on the lack of proof for deterrence.
92 I. Tallgren, 'The Sensibility and Sense of International Criminal Law' 13(3) *European Journal of International Law* (2002) 561.
93 D.S. Koller, 'The Faith of the International Criminal Lawyer' 40 *New York University Journal of International law and Politics* (2008) 1019.
94 Palmer, n.24 at 60–69.
95 Cohen, n.45 at 178–179.
96 N. Christie, 'The Ideal Victim' in E Fattah (ed.), *From Crime Policy to Victim Policy* (St. Martin's Press, 1986) 17–30.
97 Ibid.; McEvoy and McConnnachie, n.4 at 498.
98 R. Kapur, 'The Tragedy of Victimization Rhetoric: Resurrecting the "Native" Subject in International/Post-Colonial Feminist Legal Politics' 15 *Harvard Human Rights Journal* (2002) 1.
99 Cahnman, n.56.
100 Christie, n.2.
101 Ibid., at 3.
102 *Idem.*
103 McEvoy and McConnachie, n.4 at 495.
104 Christie, n.2 at 7.

105 Interview with Lawyer 1 (CP Team), 11 November 2013.
106 L. Alcoff, 'The Problem of Speaking for Others' 20 *Cultural Critique* (1991–1992).
107 Case 002, Written Version of Oral Decision of 1 July 2008 on the Civil Party's Request to Address the Court in Person, Pre-Trial Chamber, 002/19–09–2007-ECCC/OCIJ, 3 July 2008.
108 Interview with Lawyer 1 (Chambers), 11 November 2013.
109 McEvoy and McConnachie, n.4 at494; McEvoy, n.55 at 437–438.
110 G. Samuel, *A Short Introduction to the Common Law* (Edward Elgar, 2014).
111 J. Doak, 'Victims' Rights in Criminal Trials: Prospects for Participation' 32(2) *Journal of Law and Society* (2005) 294 at 297.
112 Fletcher, n.22 at 319.
113 E. Erez and E. Bienkowska, 'Victim Participation in Proceedings and Satisfaction with Justice in the Continental Systems: The Case of Poland' 21 *Journal of Criminal Justice* (1993) 47 at 50; I. Bacik, C. Maunsell and S. Grogan, *The Legal Process and Victims of Rape* (Dublin Rape Crisis Centre, 1998); M. Brienen and E. Hoegen, *Victims of Crime in 22 European Criminal Justice Systems* (Wolf Legal Productions, 2000).
114 Interview with Lawyer 1(Co-Prosecutors' Team), 8th November 2013.
115 Lawyer 1(Co-Prosecutors' Team), 8 November 2013.
116 Interview with Lawyer 4 (Defence), 13 December 2013.
117 Interview with Lawyer 1 (Defence), 8 November 2013.
118 Doak, n.111 at 297.
119 Interview with Lawyer 1 (Defence), 8 November 2013.
120 Doak, n.111 at 297.
121 J.D. Ciorciari and A. Heindel, *Hybrid Justice: The Extraordinary Chambers in the Courts of Cambodia* (University of Michigan Press, 2014) 48.
122 Interview with Lawyer 1 (LCL Office), 8 November 2013; Interview with Lawyer 2 (LCL Office), 21 November 2013; Interview with Lawyer (Former CP Team member), 11 September 2015; Interview with Lawyer 2 (CP Team), 26 September 2015.
123 Interview with Lawyer 1 (LCL Office), 8 November 2013.
124 M.C. Bassiouni, *Introduction to International Criminal Law* (Martinus Nijhoff Publishers, 2012) 120.
125 Jorda and de Hemptinne, n.3.
126 Similar frustrations have been noted by Hoven, Feiler and Scheibel, n.3.
127 E. Hoven, 'Civil Party Participation in Trials of Mass Crimes: A Qualitative Study at the Extraordinary Chambers in the Courts of Cambodia' 12(1) *Journal of International Criminal Justice* (2014) 81.
128 For example Decision on Civil Party Co-lawyers' joint request for a ruling on the standing of Civil Party lawyers to make submissions on sentencing and directions concerning the questioning of the accused, experts and witnesses testifying on character, 001/18–07–2007/ECCC/TC, 9 October 2009.
129 Interview with Lawyer 3(Defence) 8 November 2013.
130 Lawyer 1 (Defence), 8 November 2013; Lawyer 2 (Defence), 8 November 2013; Lawyer 3 (Defence), 8 November 2013; Interview with Lawyer 2 (Co-Prosecutors' Office); Interview with Judge 3, 11 November 2013; Interview with Lawyer 1 (CP Team) 11 November 2013.
131 Lawyer 1 (Defence), 8 November 2013; Lawyer 3 (Defence), 8 November 2013.
132 Interview with Lawyer 1 (Co-Prosecutors' Team), 8 November 2013. Similar critiques were offered by Lawyer 2 (Co-Prosecutors' Team), 8 November 2013.
133 Doak, n.111.
134 S. Landsman, *Readings on Adversarial Justice* (West Publishing Company, 1988) 2.
135 Doak, n.111 at 297.

136 J. Doak, *Victims' Rights, Human Rights and Criminal Justice: Reconceiving the Role of Third Parties* (Hart Publishing, 2008) 118–119.
137 Interview with Lawyer 1 (CP Team), 11 November 2013.
138 Interview with Lawyer 1 (LCL Office), 8 November 2013.
139 Interview with Lawyer 2 (LCL Office), 21 November 2013.
140 C. M. Englebrecht, 'The Struggle for "Ownership of the Conflict": An Exploration of Victim Participation and Voice in the Criminal Justice System' 36 *Criminal Justice Review* (2011) 129; McEvoy, n.55 at 411.
141 M. Foucault, *Power/Knowledge: Selected Interviews and Other Writings 1972–1977* (Harvester Press, 1980); M.G.E. Kelly, *The Political Philosophy of Michel Foucault* (Routledge, 2009).
142 Interview with Lawyer 2 (Defence) 8 November 2013.
143 Interview with Lawyer 1 (Co-Prosecutors' Team), 8 November 2013.
144 Interview with Judge 1, 7 November 2013.
145 Interview with Lawyer 2 (LCL Office), 21 November 2013.
146 McEvoy, n.55 at 425.
147 For example interviews with Judge 3, 11 November 2013; Judge 1, 7 November 2013.
148 For example interviews with Lawyer 3 (Chambers), 11 November 2013; Judge 1, 3 January 2014; Judge 2, 11 November 2013; VSS Staff 2, 13 January 2014.
149 See also Hoven, Feiler and Scheibel, n.3.
150 Interview with Lawyer 1 (Co-Prosecutors Office), 8 November 2013.
151 Case 001, Trial Transcript, 22 June 2009, at 92–95.
152 Interview with Lawyer 1 (Co-Prosecutors' Office), 8 November 2013.
153 B. Nowrojee, '"Your Justice is Too Slow": Will the ICTR Fail Rwanda's Rape Victims?' *Occasional Paper No. 10, UN Research Institute for Social Development* (2005).
154 J. Brinkley, 'Justice Squandered: Cambodia's Khmer Rouge Tribunal' *World Affairs*, September/October 2013, www.worldaffairsjournal.org/article/justice-squandered-cambodia%E2%80%99s-khmer-rouge-tribunal (accessed 16/02/18).
155 Interview with Lawyer 2(Co-Prosecutors' Team), 8 November 2013.
156 Interview with Lawyer (Former CP Team member), 11 September 2015.
157 Interview with Lawyer 4 (Defence), 13 December 2013.
158 Interview with Lawyer 2 (Co-Prosecutors' Team), 8 November 2013.
159 Interview with Lawyer 4 (Defence), 13 December 2013.
160 Interview with Lawyer 2 (LCL Office), 21 November 2013.
161 I explore this issue in greater depth in R. Killean and L. Moffett, 'Representation, Agency and Voice: Victim Legal Representation before the ICC and ECCC' 15(4) *Journal of International Criminal Justice* (2017) 713–740.
162 Interview with Lawyer 2 (CP Team), 26 September 2015.
163 Interview with Lawyer (Former CP Team member), 11 September 2015.
164 *Supra* n.113.
165 McEvoy, n.55 at 411; D. Kennedy, *Dark Sides of Virtue: Reassessing International Humanitarianism* (Princeton University Press, 2004) 15.
166 D. Orentlicher, *That Someone Guilty Be Punished: Impact of the ICTY in Bosnia* (Open Society Justice Initiative and International Center for Transitional Justice, 2010); Z. Pearson, 'Non-Governmental Organisations and the International Criminal Court: Changing Landscapes of International Law' 39 *Cornell International Law Journal* (2006) 243.
167 McEvoy and McConnachie, n.4 at 495.
168 G. Johnstone and D. Van Ness, *Handbook of Restorative Justice* (Taylor and Francis, 2007).
169 J. Ciorciari and A. Heindel, 'Experiments in International Criminal Justice: Lessons from the Khmer Rouge Tribunal' 35(2) *Michigan Journal of International Law* (2014) 369.

170 Interview with Judge 4, 13 January 2014.
171 Interview with Lawyer 2 (Defence), 8 November 2013.
172 M. Elander, 'The Victim's Address: Expressivism and the Victim at the Extraordinary Chambers in the Courts of Cambodia' 7(1) *International Journal of Transitional Justice* (2013) 91.
173 Interview with Lawyer 1 (Co-Prosecutors' Team), 8 November 2013.
174 W. Lobwein, 'Experiences of the Victims and Witnesses at the ICTY' in U. Ewald and K. Turkovic (eds.), *Large-scale Victimization as a Potential Source of Terrorist Activities: Importance of Regaining Security in Post-Conflict Societies* (IOS Press 2006) 197–207.
175 Stover, n.91; A. Des Forges and T. Longman, 'Legal Response to Genocide in Rwanda' in H. Weinstein and E. Stover (eds.), *My Neighbor, My Enemy: Justice and Social Reconstruction in Rwanda and the Former Yugoslavia* (Cambridge University Press, 2004) 49–68.
176 W. Pizzi, *Trials Without Truth: Why Our System of Criminal Trials Has Become an Expensive Failure and What We Need to Do to Rebuild It* (New York University Press, 1999) 197.
177 J. Doak, 'The Therapeutic Dimension of Transitional Justice: Emotional Repair and Victim Satisfaction in International Trials and Truth Commissions' 11 *International Criminal Law Review* (2011) 263 at 264.
178 Case 002/01, 001/18-07-2007-ECCC/TC, 26 July 2010.
179 Interview with Lawyer 2 (Defence), 8 November 2013.
180 Interview with Lawyer 3 (Defence), 8 November 2013.
181 C. Hoyle, R. Morgan and A. Sanders, *The Victim's Charter – An Evaluation of Pilot Projects' Home Office Research, Development and Statistics Directorate, Research Findings 107* (UK Home Office, 1999); R. Mawby, 'Public Sector Services and the Victim of Crime' in S. Walklate (ed.), *Handbook of Victims and Victimology* (Routledge, 2007) 209–240.
182 Doak, n.136 at 16.
183 S. Zappalà, 'The Rights of Victims v. the Rights of the Accused' 8 *Journal of International Criminal Justice* (2010) 137.
184 R. Morgan and A. Sanders, *The Uses of Victim Statements* (UK Home Office, 1999); C. Hoyle, *An Evaluation of the One-Stop Shop and Victim Statement Pilot Projects* (UK Home Office, 1998).
185 Haslam and Edmunds, n.4 at 745.
186 Interview with Lawyer 2(Chambers), 11 November 2013.
187 Hoven, Feiler and Scheibel, n.3.
188 Open Society Justice Initiative, *Recent Developments at the Extraordinary Chambers in the Courts of Cambodia* (November 2009).
189 Jorda and de Hemptinne, n.3 at 1389.
190 M.R. Maurrus, 'A Jewish Lobby at Nuremberg: Jacob Robinson and the Institute for Jewish Affairs 1945–1946' 27 *Cardozo Law Review* (2006) 1651.
191 Christie, n.2 at 10.
192 Interview with Lawyer 2 (LCL Office), 21 November 2013.
193 M. Dembour and E. Haslam, 'Silencing Hearings? Victim-Witnesses at War Crimes Trials' 15(1) *European Journal of International Law* (2004).
194 Haslam and Edmunds, n.4 at 745.
195 J. van Wijk, 'Who is the "Little Old Lady" of International Crimes? Nils Christie's Concept of the Ideal Victim Reinterpreted' 19 *International Review of Victimology* (2013) 159.
196 Elander, n.172.
197 Haslam and Edmunds, n.4 at 743.
198 See Chapter 5.

7 Professionalised civil society and the civil party system

1. Introduction

This chapter turns to another key stakeholder within international criminal justice: civil society.[1] Historically, civil society actors have often played a role in the development of victims' rights within domestic criminal systems, whether through the provision of services or through advocacy and policy work.[2] This has continued to be the case within transitional justice, with civil society lobbying states to create transitional justice mechanisms, advocating for victim participatory rights, cooperating with institutions to deliver support and other services to victims[3] and challenging the overlooking of traditionally marginalised victim groups.[4] These examples underline one of the main benefits a strong civil society can bring to the development of transitional justice: an ability to contest the terms of justice, highlighting what have been elsewhere termed 'elitist blind spots' in official responses to atrocity.[5] In the context of ICL, since the end of the Cold War there has been a surge in literature relating to international civil society, with the general argument being that civil society has significantly contributed to the development and implementation of ICL.[6] While this contribution was for a long time given little official recognition within international(ised) criminal courts,[7] the undeniable value of civil society participation has led to an increased willingness to engage with such actors.[8] The presence of over 200 non-state actors at the Rome Statute negotiations, and the ICC's subsequent creation of 'Guidelines Governing the Relations between the Court and Intermediaries'[9] seemed to cement the role of these actors in the field of ICL.[10]

These developments are reflective of the broader 'professionalisation' of ICL,[11] a process which has seen not only the growth of laws and procedures but also increasing numbers of ICL professionals, not all of whom work within the courts themselves. This chapter explores this professionalisation within the context of the ECCC and its civil party regime. After providing a brief overview of civil society's development within Cambodia and an introduction to the relationship between that civil society and the ECCC, it analyses the means through which civil society actors have contributed to the ECCC's provision of both procedural and substantive justice to victims.[12] Broadly I argue that these interactions can be grouped into two sometimes overlapping categories. The first involves civil society adopting a cooperative role, assisting the court in its implementation of victim-orientated measures, including civil party participation, outreach and the provision of reparations and non-judicial measures. Second, civil society actors have adopted a more confrontational role, for example through trial monitoring and by their lobbying for increased recognition of victims of SGBV and minority groups. The chapter then considers some of the challenges associated with professionalised civil society's involvement, focusing on the implications of a reliance of donors on the deliverance of services to victims and on the issues that may arise in relation to the privileging of professional voices over those of the victims themselves.

2. The unwelcome third sector

Historically, Cambodia has not been characterised by a strong tradition of professionalised civil society, with the social culture being based on informal pagoda communities, kinship and patronage networks.[13] However, the peacebuilding process, the presence of UNTAC and the subsequent influx of development aid led to the creation of multiple Cambodian NGOs in the 1990s.[14] Donors were quick to channel funding through these organisations,[15] many preferring to cooperate with NGOs rather than provide direct assistance to what was widely viewed as a corrupt government.[16] In contrast to this international support, the RGC has been generally unfriendly towards civil society organisations, drawing little distinction between them, opposition political parties and opposition press.[17] This has led to several attempts to limit civil society's freedom of assembly and speech, most notably through the introduction of a 'Law on Associations and Non-Governmental Organisations'.[18] This law has been consistently opposed by civil society actors, who fear registration for NGOs may be denied or revoked on arbitrary or political grounds.[19]

Notwithstanding this opposition, civil society has grown to include several hundred international and several thousand national organisations.[20] Many of these are deeply involved in work related to the ECCC,[21] a fact that was not initially legislated for by the court. NGOs are listed as one of the institutions that may provide information prompting investigations by the CIJs,[22] again as one of those to whom the trials shall be public and open[23] and once more as a potential source of voluntary financial contributions towards the court's expenses.[24] However, the Internal Rules developed the potential for civil society involvement further, with provisions made for *amicus curiae* briefs,[25] for NGOs to have access to the investigations[26] and, perhaps most significantly, for NGOs to cooperate with the court's VSS and LCLs in the provision of reparations and non-judicial measures.[27] It is apparent from these provisions that while both the architects of the court and its judges viewed civil society actors as useful outside actors, they foresaw engagement occurring within a limited consensual framework, an approach that follows the typical approach of international law towards civil society.[28] Indeed, attitudes towards civil society within the court have not always been supportive of a closer relationship than that identified in the law and rules. Some commentators suggest that the tendency of the RGC to view NGOs with suspicion has influenced the attitudes of national staff, who tend to be hired from within governmental and judicial offices.[29] The fact that many NGOs have engaged in trial monitoring has also possibly aggravated this friction.[30] Suspicion around their motives was also expressed by one international interviewee:

> I'm a little bit concerned about NGOs generally . . . they're not my favourite people because they're primarily interested in funding for themselves, and if someone gets some knowledge along the way well then that's I suspect incidental, because we have this big NGO industry around the court and lots of people getting a salary as a consequence.[31]

It is interesting to note the distinction made by the interviewee between the 'NGO industry', whose search for funding and salaries is condemnable, and the ECCC, which is itself dependent on donors,[32] engages in fundraising activities,[33] allows many people to obtain substantial salaries, and indeed could be classed as part of an ICL 'industry' itself'.[34] This perspective is arguably reflective of tendencies amongst international criminal justice professionals to develop a self-image of 'serving higher goals', to see justice delivery as the business of legalistic 'state-like' institutions,[35] and to prize 'formal legal judgement', all of which can contribute to the dismissal of civil society actors.[36] It appears that such views were initially reflected in practice; Sperfeldt, a former advisor to VSS, has noted that in the beginning there was very little coordination in the relationship between the ECCC and civil society. He attributed this to reluctance on the part of the court[37] and highlighted the difficulties associated with combining 'the Court's legal discourses and the requirements of a judicial process with the NGOs' imperative of social reconstruction and reconciliation'.[38] Such reluctance was also noted by interviewees:

> At the beginning I think it was more difficult the coordination between NGOs and the Court because the Court was not very interested in a close cooperation with NGOs because they had their mandate and whatever the NGOs do let them do it.[39]

Despite the court's initial reluctance, financial restrictions quickly necessitated a more collaborative relationship with civil society,[40] which has evolved to include the provision of evidence,[41] outreach activities and court monitoring.[42] Perhaps the most significant involvement has related to the court's victim-orientated measures, which this chapter now examines further. The following section first provides a more detailed explanation of the resource shortages that required greater civil society cooperation and then explores the various ways in which civil society has been involved in the victim-orientated aspects of the court's work.

As will be seen, this involvement has included enhancing both procedural and substantive elements of justice.[43]

3. Cooperating with the court

Allowing victims to participate in ICL trials is increasingly seen as a way of delivering justice to victims, with one of the arguments in favour of in-country tribunals being their greater ability to facilitate victim participation, thus enhancing procedural justice.[44] Certainly, the ECCC has expressed pride in its civil party regime, with the acting director of administration describing the system as 'breaking new ground and setting new standards for courts'.[45] However, a report released during the early phases of the ECCC's work notes that

> [a] number of interviewees felt that the [Victims] unit was never properly supported by the ECCC's administration, one of whom suggested that this may have been because of a fear of escalating costs and difficulties in securing sufficient funding for the structure of the court as it then stood without the added complication of a fully-staffed and fully-operational Victims' Unit.[46]

In fact, the Victims' Unit (now the Victim Support Services) was not originally included within the court's structure. Following lobbying from civil society,[47] the unit was created in 2007, with a limited mandate focused on administrative tasks related to processing civil party applications and victim complaints and facilitating representation and participation.[48] Financing the unit was not included in the court's budget, and as a result very limited support was available until 2009 when specific funding from GIZ[49] allowed it to begin more extensive operations.[50] As a result, the separation between the ECCC's offices and the VSS is quite pronounced, from the separate funding to the almost entirely national staff[51] to the location of the office buildings:

> I mean that's what made us in the beginning, our offices and everything that's why our offices are on the other side because it was made with GIZ money, not with the UN.[52]

Continued external support has been crucial to the work of VSS because of an ongoing reluctance within the Office of Administration to earmark funding for its functioning. Reportedly only 10 per cent of its personnel and expenditures go towards VSS functions.[53] Such disinclination suggests that while the ECCC wishes to bring in more reparative victim-orientated measures in principle,[54] it prioritises the retributive focus of its mandate. This perception has not been helped by the practice of the VSS. A high turnover of staff, frequent changes in leadership, a lack of international involvement and overall limited engagement in the court's processes have led to frequent criticisms being levied at the VSS.[55]

Indeed, a number of interviewees were highly critical of the professionalism of the unit and its staff:

> I'm sorry but this is just laughing at the victim when you see the composition of the Victims Unit who are supposed to help them . . . this is not serious business honestly.[56]
>
> I know . . . they recruit only their nephew, their niece, their relative. Some question their professionalism. I blame GIZ as well, not only for lack of funding, but for lack of control over fund using and effective work.[57]

With struggles to ensure appropriate financing and personnel plaguing the VSS, it is likely that if left unsupported by civil society, the ECCC would have struggled to ensure procedural justice for civil parties. However, a number of donor organisations, particularly from Europe and the US, expressed an interest in promoting and funding victim participation.[58] This led to many civil society organisations involving themselves in the civil party system,[59] and a cooperative relationship developed between civil society and the VSS.[60] The following subsections highlight some of the most significant contributions of civil society in delivering (1) access and representation, (2) service provision and (3) information dissemination.[61]

Access and representation

Allowing victims' interests to be heard and represented within criminal proceedings has become an important goal within domestic and ICL alike,[62] while psychologists have identified both voice and representation as key aspects of procedural justice.[63] The ECCC's civil party regime promises to provide such opportunities to victims.[64] Yet, for victims to access these rights, they must be aware that they can apply to become civil parties, be willing and able to fill in the necessary application forms and have access to lawyers qualified to represent their interests. Indeed, the UN Victims' Declaration notes that the promotion of victims' access to justice must be accompanied by the provision of the necessary tools to allow the exercise of that right.[65]

At the ECCC, no provision was made for potential applicants obtaining legal assistance with their application forms.[66] With the majority of the population living in the provinces without easy access to information about the court,[67] and many survivors of the Khmer Rouge also lacking literacy skills,[68] it is unlikely that many of those who could qualify as civil parties would be aware, willing and able to apply without assistance.[69] As noted by a VSS staff member,

> [i]t's not like a victim who wants to be a civil party can go to the internet and download the form. Many of them have to be assisted by someone.[70]

In practice, while the VSS is tasked with assisting in facilitating civil party applications and arranging representation,[71] a lack of budget and resources has meant it has been unable to hold sole responsibility for reaching out to potential civil party applications. Indeed, in the beginning it was actively discouraged from doing so because of fears as to how it would cope with large numbers of victim applications.[72] As a result, much of this initial work was carried out by civil society actors.[73] As explained by a VSS staff member,

> VSS cannot work alone, VSS, CDP, ADHOC, DC-Cam, all the intermediary organisations like the NGO partners, they have some budget also, they go to communities and explain to the people there, and then if they are interested we can fill in a victim information form.[74]

Overall, about 84 per cent of applications in Cases 001 and 002 were submitted through intermediary NGOs,[75] while 71 per cent of the Case 001 civil parties living in Cambodia stated that NGOs were the first to inform them of their rights to participate in the court's work.[76] Such statistics underline the significant role these organisations play in ensuring victims are able to participate in the court's work.[77] Even with their assistance, it is possible that only a small fraction of those victims who may have wished to participate in the court's proceedings were made aware of their right to do so.[78] Nor was the reliance on civil society without challenges; as little was known of the scope of the cases, particularly in relation to Case 002, civil society actors were limited in the advice they could give on what information victims should provide.[79] This resulted in extra resources being required to obtain further information and, in some cases, the initial or ultimate rejection of applications.[80]

With regards to legal representation, the initial lack of legal aid meant that civil parties in Case 001 were represented entirely by lawyers backed by civil society organisations.[81] This resulted in four legal teams, comprising a combination of international and national lawyers either working pro bono or funded by various organisations.[82] While this civil society involvement allowed victims' interests to be represented in the courtroom, which would not have been possible otherwise, it was not without drawbacks. Victims were grouped according to which organisation had assisted in their application,[83] leading to groups incorporating victims with quite disparate views and experiences.[84] Grouping on the basis of class of victim or type of injury may have allowed for a more logical and consistent representation and fewer delays to the proceedings.[85] The reliance on NGO funding also brought tensions amongst the Case 001 legal teams as each pursued their own agenda and sought to defend their own civil society 'territory'.[86] Indeed, in the opinion of some judges, there was a tendency amongst certain NGO lawyers to follow the political agenda of their organisation, without considering the limits of a legal trial.[87]

A series of amendments to the Internal Rules in 2010 led to some financial assistance being allocated for the employment of a limited number of court-funded lawyers.[88] Nevertheless, two thirds of the civil parties in Case 002 remain represented by externally funded lawyers.[89] The potential conflict of different agendas has been mitigated somewhat, at least within the courtroom, by the introduction of the LCLs. However, NGOs continue to have influence over several legal teams most directly linked with civil parties. Despite disputes between legal teams remaining a possibility, no provision has been made within the rules to deal with such conflicts.[90] While the LCLs have adopted regulations intended to facilitate coordination,[91] there remains little recourse for civil party lawyers who feel the views of their clients are being overlooked.[92]

Service provision

Victims can often suffer 'secondary victimisation' as a result of their interactions with official institutions and individuals,[93] and the act of addressing a courtroom has been shown to be potentially traumatic.[94] Criminal trials can produce unexpected evidence or arguments during proceedings, while the traumas that may have been experienced by victims of international crimes heighten the emotional risks of testifying.[95] This was painfully highlighted by the traumatic experiences of witnesses at the ICTY and the ICTR,[96] with the result that the provision of counselling services has been increasingly recognised as an essential aspect of victim assistance.[97] This has been demonstrated by the ICC, where the Victims and Witness Unit is specifically required to hire individuals with expertise in trauma and provide psychological support.[98]

Despite this recognition, a lack of financial support continues to restrict the ECCC's ability to deliver such assistance.[99] Demonstrating a failure to fully assess what the experience of civil party participation might entail for the victims, the court itself had not established any such in-house counselling capacity,[100] a fact bemoaned by one judge:

> I don't know that the international community has thought about the psychological wellbeing of victims of mass atrocity crimes . . . there's very little assistance for the psychological wellbeing of the victims. There's one NGO and 38 psychologists and 3 registered psychiatrists for the whole country. It just hasn't been that adequate and I think that part of justice is taking care of the victims. We can't do it financially because there's no money but why can't the court provide services to those people?[101]

As a result, it fell to a civil society organisation known as the Transcultural Psychosocial Organisation (TPO), to deliver psychological support to the civil parties and witnesses who took part in the trials. The TPO has a memorandum of understanding with the ECCC which allows it to work closely with the court's Witness and Expert Support Unit and VSS, offering psychological services to survivors attending and participating in the ECCC's proceedings.[102] Their services include psychological preparation before participating, on-site support and follow-up care.[103] The TPO has also provided telephone counselling due to the practical difficulties of arranging face-to-face therapy for civil parties living throughout the Cambodian provinces.[104] In a country where professional mental health services are woefully inadequate, such assistance is significant.[105] Yet, the ECCC's legal texts include reference to protecting the well-being of vulnerable victims and witnesses,[106] and it is arguable that resources should have been made available to allow for the internal provision and supervision of psychological support.

Information dissemination

The provision of information has been highlighted as a particularly important component of procedural justice in both domestic and international criminal contexts.[107] However, I would argue that the worlds of international(ised) courts and survivors are often very distant from one another. The legalistic jargon and procedures of the court can be difficult for non-lawyers to understand, potentially inhibiting meaningful engagement and participation. As a way of combatting this, outreach has increasingly been cited as a crucial task of those institutions seeking to address human rights abuses.[108] In the words of the UNOHCHR, 'a hybrid court may be seen as largely irrelevant unless there is a robust outreach program than informs the public about its activities'.[109] Cambodian NGOs have expressed a hope that the ECCC's civil party participation mechanism will help provide greater information to the public and enhance the ECCC's impact on reconciliation.[110] However, they have also highlighted the need for continued outreach and information provision, both to civil parties and the population more generally.[111]

At the ECCC the Public Affairs Section provides outreach to the public at large,[112] while the VSS is in charge of providing information and support to victims and, particularly, civil parties.[113] The ECCC's location within Cambodia offers a significant advantage with regards to outreach. However, it seems that only limited funding has been earmarked for such activities, a fact court staff attributed to the lack of importance placed on such activities by donors:

> I would say that as long as there is some capacity, there should be outreach activities, our lawyers and judges were ready to go out. I know that the trial chamber judges, when they were in between cases they would go to meetings, they spoke to the general public . . . But this activity was blocked by donors, it's not that we refused, we would have found the time.[114]

Former public affairs officer Peter Foster has asserted that this reluctance came from 'all sides, the UN, the donors and the Cambodian officials',[115] while Ciorciari and Heindel have submitted that the donors' awareness of a well-developed NGO sector was seen as justifying a small budget for outreach activities.[116] Indeed, both Cambodian and international NGOS have been involved at different stages in the commission of outreach activities throughout Cambodia;[117] activities have included the distribution of materials, radio shows, websites, films, public forums and community meetings.[118] As noted in Chapter 5, organisations have also assisted in bringing civil parties to visit the court, a project which was described by one interviewee as having particular importance:

> The civil parties have to see the court, not just hear the case on the radio. They want to know what the accused says, so coming to the court is very important, that the civil party can see the court, and meet with their lawyers.[119]

Certain NGOs have also implemented civil party representative schemes, whereby 'focal persons' receive training and information about the court and are then trusted to spread information to other civil parties.[120] Several large NGOs have also played a central role in disseminating information on the tribunal's process to a wider audience.[121] This has led to a broad range of Cambodians having access to information about the ECCC.[122]

While demonstrating the benefits of having an active civil society,[123] the reliance on NGO outreach also underlines the risks involved. Civil society actors did not have a clear idea of what to expect from the ECCC's work in the beginning, and it seems that the expectations of victims were not well managed, particularly with regards to the ability of the court to grant individual reparations.[124] Certain information, particularly with regards to the limits of participation and constraints on what the court can achieve, perhaps should have been delivered by the court itself.[125] The ECCC has attempted to address such misconceptions through an increase in its own outreach activities. However, this only really began to develop in 2009, by which time NGOs had been engaged in their own outreach to victims and civil parties for some time.[126] This has been acknowledged within the court:

> I think there was a lot of blind outreach and a lot of expectation, I'm not blaming it on them I'm not, I blame it more on the court, and the UN and the government who hadn't thought about it from the outset, what needed to be done for victims.[127]

It appears that the spreading of misinformation has continued despite the emergence of court-organised outreach, as explained by one civil party lawyer:

> There was a school built in their community which was funded by the Vietnamese association in Australia. And it was simply charity work . . . But some NGOs had been informing the civil parties who lived there that that's the reparations from the Court. And of course the civil parties think that the Court's done wonderful things for them . . . and that's a bit of a worry, because you want to manage clients' expectations.[128]

Such misinformation, as highlighted by the lawyer, risks raising false expectations as to what the court is able to deliver, heightening the possibility of subsequent disappointment and feelings of injustice.[129]

Despite such challenges, it is apparent that civil society has done much to assist the court in the pursuit of its victim-orientated mandates. While procedural justice has been found to be of importance in its own right,[130] it is also inextricably linked to the pursuit of substantive justice (encompassing truth, accountability and reparations).[131] It is evident that civil society has significantly assisted in victims' pursuit of substantive justice from the ECCC. However, civil society has also been intrinsically involved in the actual delivery of substantive justice, through its role in the provision of reparations and non-judicial measures.

Reparations and non-judicial measures

In 2010, an amendment was made to the court's Internal Rules allowing for externally funded projects, designed or identified in cooperation with the VSS, to also be acknowledged as reparations.[132] While such an arrangement can perhaps be praised as a pragmatic reaction to a lack of other financial options,[133] it means that funding must be secured before the judgement and amounts to an outsourcing of reparations. Both pragmatic and problematic aspects featured in interviews with civil party lawyers:

> I understand the change in the rules, however in terms of international standards, international law, it's very critical. Because in that way you shift all the responsibility for this project and for the compensation that you provide, the redress you provide, away from the accused, away from the government, away from anybody who is actually responsible for what happened, and put it on NGOs. But in terms of benefits for the victims, then of course it is better to have something than to have nothing.[134]

The lack of resources and know-how within the VSS is also problematic, given their primary responsibility for locating financial sponsors and suitable projects. In an interview with Ciorciari and Heindel, one NGO worker highlighted some of the difficulties:

> There are no staff who are actually experienced enough to deal with project management . . . proposal writing, dealing with donors and all that . . . Also, [there is] probably a lack of motivation to really go forward and systematically and effectively address it with potential donors.[135]

Similar suspicions were evident amongst my interviewees, with one lawyer opining that the VSS was 'not interested in that, they just want to get computers for themselves'.[136] As a result, civil society actors have been deeply involved in the funding and strategising of reparation mechanisms.[137] With regards to those awarded in Case 002/01 and requested in Case 002/02, NGOs have assisted in the sourcing of funding for and the delivery of, amongst others: the establishment of memorials, the provision of psychological services and the creation of several exhibition, media and education projects.[138] It is worth noting that NGOs could have funded and conducted similar projects without requiring a link to the Court, indeed projects were frequently already being implemented. As noted by one civil party lawyer,

> [w]here it's building a museum or something, the Court endorsement is significant at the end of the day, but if there was no conviction and there was no endorsement, the fact that civil society has come together, found funding, designed and implemented a project that has meaning for the Cambodian population and is able to proceed and go ahead, it's from one perspective like the Court is a bit superfluous.[139]

In an attempt to balance the various restrictions being placed on civil party participation with an expansion of the VSS's mandate to assist victims more generally,[140] the 2010 changes to the Internal Rules provided that the VSS could collaborate with external agencies in order to work towards 'the development and implementation of non-judicial programs and measures addressing the broader interests of victims'.[141] Relying on civil society involvement, these are separate from reparations related to findings on the accused's guilt. It was hoped by the judges that such measures would be a major legacy of the court, but in practice, it seems that initiatives have been relatively limited, and largely driven by civil society actors rather than the VSS itself.[142] As explained by VSS staff, the problem once again relates to resources: 'the reparations project and non-judicial measures gets bigger and bigger . . . we don't have enough resources so we don't have enough staff'.[143]

Despite these difficulties, the VSS has successfully collaborated with civil society to design and propose some projects, including a national reconciliation event, Community Peace Learning Centers, a Victims Foundation, the construction of a stupa at Tuol Sleng (see the following discussion on the controversy surrounding this project), and a UN-funded project titled 'Promoting Gender Equality and Improving Access to Justice for Female Survivors and Victims of Gender-Based Violence under the Khmer Rouge Regime'.[144] The latter project has been significant, because of the relative absence of SGBV prosecutions at the ECCC. Working with the TPO and the Cambodian Defenders Project, the VSS developed a number of different initiatives within the project,[145] including attempts to increase the number of female civil parties attending hearings, providing psychological services for survivors and attempting to enhance awareness of gender and SGBV amongst Cambodian lawyers.[146] This project has also incorporated work outside the context of the ECCC, such as women's hearings, self-help groups, one-to-one therapy sessions and forum theatre.[147] Such mechanisms have also attempted to address broader issues of gender inequality within Cambodia and are valuable both in light of the relative absence of SGBV prosecutions at the ECCC and the ongoing gender discrimination that exists within Cambodia.[148]

Such projects demonstrate one of the initially unforeseen outcomes of the court. The attraction of donor funding and interest in Cambodia's past has allowed for projects to develop which seek to address the Khmer Rouge legacy in a way that is potentially beneficial to the wider Cambodian society. As one interviewee noted, the work of the court is important, but 'outside the court is more important, because it is more space, more participants . . . non-judicial [measures] might be a more open space'.[149] A similar view was expressed by a civil party lawyer:

> There are victims everywhere, but the admissions process is in a sense arbitrary, because the civil parties are those who were informed of victim participation. You know, how far did the outreach go? Who had access to justice? Who had access to assistance with filling in the forms? So it was important in this setting that the Internal Rules were formulated also to cater to the mass victims in Cambodia instead of the select few who could participate.[150]

The preceding subsections have sought to demonstrate the many ways in which civil society has formed a cooperative relationship with the ECCC, seeking to enhance both the procedural and substantive aspects of the court's victim-orientated measures. Stepping in to bolster a resource-weak and inexperienced VSS, there is no doubt that NGOs have contributed significantly to the procedural challenges posed by the court's attempt to involve victims in its work. Certain challenges were highlighted, such as the court's initial reluctance to involve civil society in its work, the misinformation spread through civil society outreach and the introduction of NGO agendas into the courtroom through civil party representation. However, without civil society involvement, thousands of victims may have remained uninformed about the work of the court and their right to participate within it, while representation in Case 001 may have remained unavailable. Benefitting in some cases from an established local presence and network, civil society played an important role in 'bridging the gap between courts and local communities'.[151] Furthermore, through their involvement in the provision of reparations and non-judicial measures, a number of additional forums and means through which victims can discuss and address their past experiences and harms have been introduced, some of which may outlive the court itself. As put by one interviewee, 'civil society is kind of filling the gap by trying to address justice needs that the court cannot fulfil'.[152]

However, it is not only through cooperation that civil society can contribute to the justice delivered by international criminal courts. As will now be argued, by adopting a more confrontational attitude and highlighting the ways in which international criminal courts may be failing their victim constituents, civil society can also assist in the addressing of 'elitist blind spots'.

4. Confronting the court

As discussed earlier, civil society has long had a role to play in the development of ICL, not only through its cooperation but also through its ability to adopt a confrontational stance and contest the terms of 'justice'.[153] Such a stance includes a variety of approaches, including campaigning for victims' participatory rights, court monitoring and advocacy on behalf of marginalised victim groups.[154] This has also been the case at the ECCC, where many civil society groups have engaged in critical court monitoring[155] and have worked to highlight harms initially overlooked by the ECCC.[156]

NGOs have been involved in court monitoring since 2006. Although international NGOs were predominantly responsible for this in the beginning, a number of Cambodian NGOs became involved once the ECCC began its operations, setting up specialised websites and issuing reports and commentary. This independent critical voice has not always been welcomed by ECCC staff. For example, former chief of the Public Affairs Section and head of the VSS Helen Jarvis decried what she termed 'the crusade against the ECCC', arguing that critical reports and press releases undermined and destabilised the court, weakened support from the UN and the RGC and unsettled donors.[157] However, she offers little evidence for this claim, and her critique appears to stem from a belief that external organisations should offer unquestioning 'support for this long-overdue' institution.[158] Yet, such a critique overlooks the valuable role trial monitoring can have in ensuring transparency, identifying weaknesses and strengths, holding courts to international standards and generating recommendations for improved practices.[159] Monitoring may also allow subsequent institutions to learn lessons in best practice. This can be particularly valuable in the context of ICL, where laws and procedures are constantly evolving. In the context of the ECCC, trial monitors have provided critical analysis of the court's judgements,[160] highlighted suspected political interference[161] and developed 'lessons learned' reports after the conclusion of trials.[162] While such reports may create a more negative public image of the court in the short term, it is arguable that this is outweighed by the benefits of ensuring a transparent process and enhancing the knowledge of the court's stakeholders.[163]

NGOs have also gone beyond reporting to engage in advocacy and activism, both outside the court and through their involvement in the civil party system. Examples include the advocacy conducted around victims of SGBV and victims from minority ethnic groups.[164] As I have discussed elsewhere, following the initial lack of SGBV crimes in Cases 001 and 002's indictments, a number of civil society organisations began to advocate to see SGBV included in the crimes charged at the ECCC.[165] Those who represented civil parties used this status to file petitions and request further investigations,[166] failing to expand the scope of Case 001 but successfully ensuring the inclusion of forced marriage within the Case 002 Closing Order.[167] The charge of forced marriage, covered in the Case 002/02 trial, is second only to forced transfer in the number of civil parties who have identified themselves as victims of the policy, demonstrating the prevalence of this initially overlooked crime.[168] Investigations into SGBV have also been undertaken in Cases 003 and 004, with civil parties' evidence cited as a motivating factor.[169]

In the context of minority groups, the Khmer Kampuchea Krom Human Rights Association (KKKHRA) has been crucial in its assistance to ethnic Vietnamese wishing to participate as civil parties, who may not otherwise have been unable to apply, because of high illiteracy.[170] Civil party lawyers hired by the KKKHRA also contributed evidence to the co-prosecutors' Final Submission,[171] leading to Case 002's inclusion of allegations of genocide, deportation and other crimes specific to the treatment of the Vietnamese.[172] Similarly, the advocacy of the Khmer Krom ethnic minority group and their representatives has successfully drawn attention to the crimes perpetrated against that group under the Khmer Rouge.[173] Such crimes were for a long time overlooked within the court's judicial investigations, purportedly because of the difficulties associated with distinguishing this minority from the broader Khmer population.[174]

Uncertainty surrounding Cases 003 and 004 risks preventing the further prosecution of SGBV and the full prosecution of the crimes perpetrated against the Khmer Krom, whose victimisations are most prominent within Case 004.[175] Yet the work of civil society has at the very least shone light on some of the court's blind spots. It is arguable that by acknowledging the provision of 'justice' as a contested space, courts may benefit from the confrontations of civil society actors, becoming aware of interests which they may otherwise have overlooked[176] and allowing more victims the chance to access procedural and substantive justice through civil party participation and the recognition of their harm.

5. The challenges of civil society involvement

Both civil society confrontation and collaboration with the ECCC have been shown to contribute to the advancement of victims' interests within the system. The architects and proponents of international criminal institutions could therefore gain much from acknowledging and furthering communication and collaboration with such organisations working outside the courtroom. However, there are challenges associated with such involvement. Some of the specific challenges posed over the course of the court's two cases have been highlighted already. However, the following sections explore some of the more general challenges associated with incorporating civil society into the work of international(ised) criminal courts in greater detail, focusing on the risks associated with donor funding, and the dangers associated with the prioritising of professional civil society voices.

Donor justice

It is no secret that both civil society and the ECCC depend significantly on contributions made by international donors. Over the years since the court's establishment, a number of international donors have complemented their contributions to the court with additional funding to NGOs.[177] This is illustrative of a broad trend within international relations.[178] Since the 1990s, 'justice' has constituted a key feature of foreign policy and cooperation, with the international community engaging in peace-building, reconciliation, development, democratisation, governance, Nation-building and rule-of-law initiatives.[179] Indeed, as Ignatieff has noted, human rights and rights-based action have become one of the prime manifestations of globalisation.[180]

Such globalisation does not remain unchallenged. Foreign-funded NGOs who adopt policies that are seen as anti-government have found themselves denounced for example as 'foreign agents' in Israel,[181] 'anti-national' in India[182] and 'undesirable' in Russia.[183] Often, this government resistance manifests itself in the passing of laws restricting international NGOs' ability to work, whether through anti-protest laws, gagging laws or restrictions on registration.[184] There appears to be growing evidence that states increasingly view foreign-funded NGOs as potential adversaries,[185] leading to a 'seismic shift and closing down of human rights space'.[186] Cambodia has been no exception to this, the introduction of the Law on Associations and Non-Governmental Organisations was the latest in a series of attempts to control and restrict the movements of both domestic and international NGOs. Related debates also exist as to the effectiveness of international aid in bringing about real change within developing states.[187] Again, such concerns are relevant to Cambodia; despite the influx of international aid, poverty and infant mortality remain at high levels, while corruption and repression of political dissidents continue to hinder the development of good governance.[188]

Nevertheless, Cambodian NGOs are generally welcoming of foreign donors and advisors, considering them a necessary presence to assist in Cambodia's development.[189] As highlighted within this chapter, such funding has allowed for a wide variety of projects relating to the court or dealing with the past more generally to be carried out. However, this leads to questions as to who is steering the work; while Cambodian civil society activists are predominant amongst the staff of the majority of NGOs, there is no doubt that donors are central to both the agenda setting and implementation of their projects.[190] This 'donor justice' has been critiqued by numerous commentators,[191] particularly for its tendency to introduce broader social, political and economic interests into what are often represented as politically and economically neutral transitional justice processes.[192] With investors driving the agenda of such processes, rather than the needs and wishes of the victims,[193] particular narratives that suit those agendas are likely to acquire dominance, leading to the potential silencing of those whose narratives do not fit with the official line.[194]

The reliance on donors has other implications for the services being provided to victim populations. Donor support is generally directed at specific projects, only contributing a limited amount to general operating costs.[195] This can place a great deal of stress on NGOs, creating a lack of job security and inability to plan long term.[196] Reliance on donors also has long-term implications for the ability of NGOs to contribute to the work of the ECCC, as donor fatigue has begun to show itself with regards to the court's work. Issues such as outreach, victim participation and reparations have traditionally received little funding when compared to running the criminal process, and this has diminished as the court has moved towards the end of its mandate.[197] For example, funding for outreach has been dropping consistently since 2010, reportedly, in part, because of the increase in public affairs outreach but also because of a reluctance amongst donors to support outreach relating to Cases 003 and 004.[198] As expressed by a representative of GIZ,

> The discussion was the ECCC will probably stop working soon so we changed our strategy and we said we're going away from outreach and civil party participation.[199]

Cuts in funding inevitably result in NGOs changing focus, with implications for the ability of victims to participate in the proceedings. Interviewees working within NGOs with a focus on civil party participation frequently expressed their concerns in this regard:

> NGOs right now are not focusing on the ECCC work anymore, especially to support the victims in the ECCC . . . Because they think that Cases 003 and 004 will not move forward.[200]

> A lot of NGOs have dropped their programme related to the past or transitional justice, so there is less and less players.[201]

The decreasing of donor support over time has been observed in other post-conflict situations around the world,[202] with donors being critiqued for lacking the commitment required to ensure that those processes are able to complete their mandate, risking their ability to bring real benefit to post-conflict communities.[203] Dosch has found that NGOs in Cambodia struggle to continue their work without international donor support and that there is a lack of an institutionalised approach to achieving sustainable interventions in post-conflict states.[204] With the RGC demonstrably unwilling to provide the funding instead, and the court's Office of Administration similarly unwilling to allocate resources to the VSS, many services currently offered to civil parties and other survivors of the Khmer Rouge could be restricted or even brought to a halt by a lack of funds. Such challenges raise questions as to the extent to which courts should delegate aspects of their mandate to civil society[205] and highlight the need for sustainability when pursuing post-conflict justice.

The privileging of voice

While this chapter has noted the value of both cooperative and confrontational roles for civil society, it should note that such organisations are not free from power dynamics,[206] which may exist within the organisations themselves or between different organisations. Within Cambodia, NGOs range from small domestically run organisations to large, internationally backed institutions. The relative power and standing granted to different civil society organisations may influence the narratives being conveyed and the interests being protected. It has been noted in other post-conflict settings that donors often bypass grass-roots organisations in favour of more 'professionalised' NGOs.[207] However, these 'elite' organisations may not be genuinely engaged on the ground, leading to a fictitious view of local engagement, detached from social reality.[208] As Pena notes, such risks highlight the importance of 'uncovering the motivations' of local organisations, many of whom will have reasonable motivations but some of whom may be pursuing less legitimate goals, such as financial gain without due regard to the needs of the victims for whom they purport to speak.[209] One must also be wary of underestimating the divergences that can occur between victims and those purporting to represent them.[210] Victims and their advocates may share objectives, but the need for funding or the mission of the NGO may lead to compromises which impact on the message being delivered and the objectives pursued.[211] Indeed, victims' interests may be misinterpreted or misrepresented by the most well-meaning representatives, while community power relations may influence whose voices are heard in the first place.[212] Thus, even grass-roots organisations may play a role in the 'theft of the conflict',[213] demonstrating the importance of scrutinising and critiquing the extent to which victim populations are genuinely able to exercise voice and agency through such organisations.

In cases where there is a conflict between the voice of professional civil society and the voice of the victims, there is a danger that there will be a prioritisation of the voice of the professionals.[214] As explored by Haslam, international criminal institutions often ascertain the interests of affected populations through international criminal 'experts', thereby framing the discourse and potentially silencing other, more critical perspectives.[215] A desire to consult experts on issues of victim participation was certainly expressed by one judge interviewee:

> I think the involvement of academics in this area is really important. I've spoken with a number of victimologists . . . I don't think that the academics who are involved in it realise just how important their input could be to courts, or to judges of courts. We use academics a great deal and I have the greatest admiration for the academics . . . I personally would appreciate their involvement still in relation to victims.[216]

Similarly, while the court has been reluctant to accept *amicus curiae*, those that have been accepted have generally come from professionalised civil society actors or academics.[217] This prizing of professionalised expert voices indicates a preference for 'civil society as a subject' over 'civil society as an object'[218] and has been observed in other areas of international law, for example in the context of international human rights law. Martens has described it as favouring of participation by 'relevant subject-specific knowledge, experience and training' rather than by 'political activism'.[219] NGOs may have been critical of the ECCC, but their criticisms still tend to be framed within a general world view that supports international criminal legal processes. Thus, even while critiquing court practice, NGOs continue to assert the dominance of legalistic responses to atrocity, and the 'institutionalisation' of transitional justice.[220] This leads to questions as to whether victims interests can be genuinely represented by organisations entrenched in the dominant narrative of dealing with the past.[221] Indeed, it is arguable that such organisations may contribute to the further instrumentalisation of victims in the pursuit of other goals, such as the growth and development of ICL.[222]

There have occasionally been stark illustrations of some of the issues highlighted in this section at the ECCC. These have included civil parties' consistent demands for individual compensation, despite no such request being put forward by their representatives.[223] Indeed, the start of Case 002/02 saw 200 civil parties gather on the steps of the ECCC to protest what they termed 'worthless' collective reparations and demanding individual compensation.[224] This group claimed to represent 1,780 civil parties, a claim that if true, suggests a real disconnect between civil parties and their representatives. Their representatives may well be aware of the victims' attitudes towards reparations; certainly, those I spoke with were very conscious of what their clients desired:

> I think still some of them would want individual monetary compensation, they know that it's not, cannot be granted, I think to that extent everyone

is aware of that, but if you ask them directly without any limitation 'what do you want' I think it's still important to them.[225]

Lawyers may be aware that such claims will fail and feel they have no choice but to try and get what they can for their clients. Yet their complicity in accepting the limitations of the court's reparation mandate reaffirms its legitimacy and plays down the strong dissatisfaction that led to civil parties taking to the streets in protest.

Another example of the privileging of elite voices can be found in the controversy which followed the VSS's decision to inscribe the names of those killed at S-21 on a stupa constructed on the site. As many of the victims at S-21 were Khmer Rouge cadres themselves, other victims expressed upset at their relatives' names being included alongside them.[226] Despite this resistance, and despite the fact that the inscribing of names is not a traditional Cambodian practice, the names of the 12,320 prisoners who died in S-21 were included on the stupa.[227] The stupa was designed by the Ministry of Culture and Fine Arts and funded by the German government, suggesting a privileging of elite organisations over those of the survivors themselves. Such examples highlight the need for institutions seeking to deliver meaningful justice to consider ways to 'listen and respond to the voices of the subalterns',[228] increasing 'victims' agency in defining their own interests and preferences'.[229]

6. Conclusion

The value of the relationship between civil society and international(ised) criminal courts has been starkly highlighted by the ECCC. Responding to the gap left by an initially absent, then under-resourced VSS, civil society actors have developed a strong cooperative relationship with the VSS, ensuring civil parties are able to access, participate in and receive information about the court's proceedings. Their engagement has extended beyond the courtroom, and many NGOs are also involved in the planning, funding and implementation of reparations and non-judicial measures, further enhancing the potential benefit the ECCC may bring to victim communities. These findings have broader implications in relation to ownership and delivery of the 'justice for victims' mandate adopted by international(ised) criminal courts.[230] While courts have often been reluctant to see civil society as equal partners in their quest to bring justice to victims, the Cambodian example provides strong support for a more multiparty approach, where courts are not seen as the sole owner and distributer of justice, but rather as one party doing justice in partnership with a range of other actors.[231] However, the development of such a collaborative approach is not without challenges. The failure to fund the ECCC's victim-orientated measures remains problematic. As interest in the court wanes, and donors move on to new projects, those victims wishing to participate and remain involved in the work of the ECCC risk having their access to resources and ability to meaningfully participate restricted or tailored to suit the interests of donors.

Civil society actors have further contributed to the delivery of both procedural and substantive justice, through their ability to confront the court's 'elitist blind spots' and increase the visibility of harms which may have gone overlooked. This is to be welcomed; victims may be unable to advocate for themselves for a variety of reasons, including trauma, lack of skills or capacity or lack of social standing and power. Professional voices purporting to represent victim groups may be given credence and allowed to exert significant influence over proceedings. However, the prioritisation given to professional voices risks limiting the ability of other, less elite, members of civil society to make themselves heard.[232] This points to another challenge linked to the involvement of civil society actors and their donors: the risked exclusion of certain voices,[233] whose victimisation may not be considered the cause *de rigueur* by donors.

Thus, while civil society's involvement in the ECCC's work has been constructive, it has brought its own share of challenges. These challenges do not mean civil society involvement in international criminal justice should be curtailed. By acknowledging and developing relationships with actors outside the courtroom, the ECCC, and other international(ised) criminal courts, might do much to enhance their impact on victim communities. However, those who speak for others, whether inside or outside the courtroom must be subjected to sufficient scrutiny.[234] The voices of professionals must not be taken in place of the voices of the victims themselves, and therefore attempts to meaningfully engage with civil society beyond the confines of professional organisations should be both sufficiently budgeted for and pursued in order to ensure the voices of those most affected by the court's work are heard.

Notes

1 A distinction is made here between what Haslam terms 'civil society as object', encompassing the communities at which ICL is directed, and 'civil law as subject', denoting professionalised third-party actors who engage with ICL. This chapter focuses on the latter and extends its analysis to include many civil party legal representatives, who exist for the most part outside of the court's structure, usually receive external funding and are sometimes affiliated with an NGO engaged in other work outside the courtroom. See E. Haslam, 'Subjects and Objects: International Criminal Law and the Institutionalization of Civil Society' 5(2) *International Journal of Transitional Justice* (2011) 221.

2 A. Muleefu, 'The Role of Civil Society in Addressing Problems Faced by Victims in Post-Genocide Rwanda' in R. Letschert et al. (eds.), *Victimological Approaches to International Crimes: Africa* (Intersentia, 2011) 411–436; M. Kaldor, *Global Society: An Answer to War* (Polity Press, 2003); J. Kean, *Global Civil Society?* (Cambridge University Press, 2003).

3 J. Shapland (ed.), *Justice, Community and Civil Society: A Contested Terrain* (Willan Publishing, 2008); A. Cornwall and C. Nyamu-Musembi, 'Putting the "Rights-Based Approach" to Development into Perspective' 25 *Third World Quarterly* (2004) 1415.

4 R. Copelon, 'Gender Crimes as War Crimes: Integrating Crimes against Women into International Criminal Law' 46 *McGill Law Journal* (2000) 217.

5 B. Rajagopal, 'International Law and Social Movements: Challenges of Theorizing Resistance' 41 *Colombia Journal of Transnational Law* (2003) 397 at 406.

6 M. Glasius, *The International Criminal Court: A Global Civil Society Achievement* (Routledge, 2006); S. Charnovitz, 'Nongovernmental Organisations and International Law' 100 *American Journal of International Law* (2006) 348; T. Treves et al. (eds.), *Civil Society, International Courts and Compliance Bodies* (Asser Press, 2005); A. Van Rooy, *The Global Legitimacy Game: Civil Society, Globalization and Protest* (Palgrave Macmillan, 2004).
7 M. Pena, 'The Role of Intermediaries and Third Parties in Victim Participation' in K. Tibori-Szabó and M. Hirst (eds.), *Victim Participation in International Criminal Justice* (Asser Press, 2017) 83.
8 L. McGregor, 'International Law as a "Tiered Process"' in K. McEvoy and L. McGregor (eds.), *Transitional Justice from Below: Grassroots Activism and the Struggle for Change* (Hart Publishing, 2008) 50–51.
9 ICC, Guidelines Governing the Relations between the Court and Intermediaries: for the Organs and Units of the Court and Counsel working with intermediaries, March 2014. For a discussion on the creation of these guidelines see E. Haslam and R. Edmunds, 'Managing a New "Partnership": "Professionalisation", Intermediaries and the International Criminal Court' 24 *Criminal Law Forum* (2013) 49 at 61.
10 A. Boyle and C. Chinkin, *The Making of International Law* (Oxford University Press, 2006); F. Trombetta-Panigadi, 'NGOs and the Activities of the International Criminal Court' in T. Treves et al. (eds.), *Civil Society, International Courts and Compliance Bodies* (Asser Press, 2005) 121–129.
11 J. Iontcheva Turner, 'Transnational Networks and International Criminal Justice' 105(5) *Michigan Law Review* (2007) 985; K. Martens, 'Professionalised Representation of Human Rights NGOs to the United Nations' 10(1) The *International Journal of Human Rights* (2006) 19. Also referred to as 'vertical expansion' in T. O. Hansen, 'The Vertical and Horizontal Expansion of Transitional Justice' in S. Buckley-Zistel et al. (eds.), *Transitional Justice Theories* (Routledge, 2014) 105–124.
12 See Chapter 1.
13 J. Dosch, 'The Role of Civil Society in Cambodia's Peace-building Process: Have Foreign Donors Made a Difference?' 52 *Asian Survey* (2012) 1067 at 1072.
14 S. Peou, *International Democracy Assistance for Peacebuilding: The Cambodian Experience* (Palgrave Macmillan, 2007); C. Hughes, *The Political Economy of the Cambodian Transition, 1991–2001* (Routledge Curzon, 2003).
15 C. Sperfeldt, 'Cambodian Civil Society and the Khmer Rouge Tribunal' 6(1) *International Journal of Transitional Justice* (2012) 149.
16 Dosch, n.13 at 1068.
17 S. Strangio, *Hun Sen's Cambodia* (Yale University Press, 2014) 198.
18 Signed and promulgated by Hun Sen on 12 August 2015.
19 J. Retka, 'Two Years on, NGO Law Remains "Ambiguous"' *The Cambodia Daily*, 13 July 2017, www.cambodiadaily.com/news/two-years-on-ngo-law-remains-ambiguous-132456/ (accessed 16/02/18).
20 Sperfeldt, n.15 at 2.
21 *Idem.*
22 *Law on the Establishment of Extraordinary Chambers in the Courts of Cambodia for the Prosecution of Crimes Committed during the Period of Democratic Kampuchea*, Law NS/RKM/0801/12, 10 August 2001, Article 23 new.
23 Ibid., Article 34 new.
24 Ibid., Article 44 new.
25 Internal Rule, Revision 9, Rule 33.
26 Internal Rule 56.
27 Internal Rule 12 *bis.*
28 E. Haslam, 'Law, Civil Society and Contested Justice' in M. Dembour and T. Kelly (eds.), *Paths to International Justice: Social and Legal Perspectives* (Cambridge University Press, 2007) 57–82.

29 Sperfeldt, n.15 at 6.
30 See for example H. Jarvis, 'Trials and Tribulations: The Long Quest for Justice for the Cambodian Genocide' in S.M. Meisenberg and I. Stegmiller (eds.), *The Extraordinary Chambers in the Courts of Cambodia* (Springer, 2016) 40–41.
31 Interview with Judge 1, 7 November 2013.
32 UNGA Resolution A/RES/57/228B 22 May 2003; 'How is the Court Financed?' ECCC Website, www.eccc.gov.kh/en/faq/how-court-financed (accessed 16/02/18).
33 J. O'Toole, 'ECCC Officials to Seek Funds in US' *The Phnom Penh Post*, 20 May 2010
34 S. Kendall, 'Donors' Justice: Recasting International Criminal Accountability' 24 *Leiden Journal of International Law* (2011) 585; S. Kendall, 'Commodifying Global Justice: Economies of Accountability at the International Criminal Court' 13(1) *Journal of International Criminal Justice* (2015) 113.
35 K. McEvoy, 'Letting Go of Legalism: Developing a 'Thicker' Version of Transitional Justice' in K. McEvoy and L. McGregor (eds.), *Transitional Justice from Below: Grassroots Activism and the Struggle for Change* (Hart Publishing, 2008) 28.
36 Haslam, n.28.
37 Sperfeldt, n.15.
38 Ibid., at 153.
39 Interview with Lawyer 1 (CP Team), 11 November 2013.
40 J.D. Ciorciari and A. Heindel, *Hybrid Justice: The Extraordinary Chambers in the Courts of Cambodia* (University of Michigan Press, 2014) 237.
41 C. Etcheson, *After the Killing Fields: Lessons from the Cambodian Genocide* (Praeger, 2005); 'A Response Team for the Khmer Rouge Tribunal', DC-CAM Website, www.d.dccam.org/Projects/Tribunal_Response_Team/Tribunal_response.htm (accessed 16/02/18).
42 For example Asian International Justice Initiative's Khmer Rouge Tribunal Monitor, the Cambodian Tribunal Monitor and International Justice Monitor.
43 See Chapter 1.
44 Ciorciari and Heindel, n.40 at 202.
45 ECCC, 'Germany Pledges More Financial Support to Maximise Victims' Participation in KR Trials', 17 June 2010, www.eccc.gov.kh/en/articles/germany-pledges-more-financial-support-maximise-victims-participation-kr-trials (accessed 16/02/18).
46 A. Bates, *Transitional Justice in Cambodia: Analytical Report* (Atlas Project, October 2010) n.340.
47 J. Herman, 'Realities of Victim Participation: The Civil Party System in Practice at the Extraordinary Chambers in the Courts of Cambodia (ECCC)' 16(4) *Contemporary Justice Review: Issues in Criminal, Social, and Restorative Justice* (2013) 461 at 469.
48 Internal Rule 12.
49 The Deutsche Gesellschaft für Internationale Zusammenarbeit or 'German Corporation for International Cooperation'.
50 Dosch, n.13 at 1079.
51 Herman, n.47 at 469.
52 Interview with Lawyer 2 (LCL Office), 21 November 2013.
53 Ciorciari and Heindel, n.40 at 207.
54 B. McGonigle, 'Two for the Price of One: Attempts by the Extraordinary Chambers in the Courts of Cambodia to Combine Retributive and Restorative Justice Principles' 2(1) *Leiden Journal of International Law* (2009) 127.
55 Ciorciari and Heindel, n.40 at 205–211; Herman, n.47 at 470; Open Society Justice Initiative, 'Recent Developments at the Extraordinary Chamber in the Courts of Cambodia' (September 2010).
56 Interview with Lawyer 2 (Chambers), 11 November 2013.

57 Interview with Legal Assistant (CP Team), 10 December 2013.
58 Pena, n.7 at 94.
59 Including the Cambodian Human Rights and Development Association, the Documentation Center of Cambodia, the Khmer Institute of Democracy and the Cambodian Defender Project.
60 Dosch, n.13 at 1076.
61 Ciorciari and Heindel, n.40 at 206–207, 210, 237.
62 K. McEvoy and K. McConnachie, 'Victims and Transitional Justice: Voice, Agency and Blame' 22 *Social and Legal Studies* (2013) 489.
63 T. Tyler, 'What is Procedural Justice?: Criteria Used by Citizens to Assess the Fairness of Legal Procedures' 22(1) *Law and Society Review* (1988).
64 See Chapter 5.
65 *UN Declaration of Basic Principles of Justice for Victims of Crime and Abuse of Power*, UNGA Res. 40/34, 29 November 1985; Y. Alvarez, 'The Protection of Victims Participating in International Criminal Justice' in K Tibori-Szabó and M. Hirst, *Victim Participation in International Criminal Justice* (Asser Press, 2017) 72.
66 M. Hirst, 'Legal Representation of Participating Victims' in K. Tibori-Szabó and M. Hirst, *Victim Participation in International Criminal Justice* (Asser Press, 2017) 119.
67 'Cambodia Statistics', *World Bank Website*, data.worldbank.org/country/Cambodia (accessed 16/02/18).
68 Ibid.
69 P. Kroker, 'Transitional Justice Policy in Practice: Victim Participation in the Khmer Rouge Tribunal' 53 *German Yearbook of International Law* (2010) 753.
70 Interview with VSS Staff 2, 13 January 2014.
71 Internal Rule 12*bis*.
72 Ciorciari and Heindel, n.40 at 206.
73 H. Jarvis, '"Justice for the Deceased": Victims' Participation in the Extraordinary Chambers in the Courts of Cambodia' 8(2) *Genocide Studies and Prevention: An International Journal* (2014) 19 at 22.
74 Interview with VSS Staff 1, 27 November 2013.
75 M. Guiraud, *Victims' Rights before the Extraordinary Chambers in the Courts of Cambodia (ECCC): A Mixed Record for Civil Parties* (FIDH, November 2012) 23.
76 P. Pham et al., 'Victim Participation and the Trial of Duch at the Extraordinary Chambers in the Courts of Cambodia' 3(3) *Journal of Human Rights Practice* (2011) 264 at 273.
77 Pena, n.7 at 91.
78 In fact, nearly all Cambodians who lived through the Khmer Rouge consider themselves victims; see P. Pham et al., *So We Will Never Forget: A Population-Based Survey on Attitudes About Social Reconstruction and the Extraordinary Chambers in the Courts of Cambodia* (Human Rights Center, Berkeley, 2009) 2.
79 M. Fardel and N. Vehils Olarra, 'The Application Process: Procedure and Players' in K. Tibori-Szabó and M. Hirst (eds.), *Victim Participation in International Criminal Justice* (Asser Press, 2017) 20.
80 See Chapter 5.
81 B. McGonigle Leyh, *Procedural Justice? Victim Participation in International Criminal Proceedings* (Intersentia, 2011) 218.
82 Including the British Embassy, the German Development Corporation, Advocats Sans Frontiers, the Paris Bar Association and the Cambodian Defenders' Project.
83 E. Hoven, M. Feiler and S. Scheibel, 'Victims in Trials of Mass Crimes: A Multi-Perspective Study of Civil Party Participation at the Extraordinary Chambers in the Courts of Cambodia' 3 *Cologne Occasional Papers on International Peace and Security Law* (2013) 15.

84 M. Saliba, 'Civil Party Participation at ECCC: Overview' *Cambodia Tribunal Monitor*, 6 November 2009.
85 Ibid.
86 E. Hoven, 'Civil Party Participation in Trials of Mass Crimes: A Qualitative Study at the Extraordinary Chambers in the Courts of Cambodia' 12(1) *Journal of International Criminal Justice* (2014) 81 at 96.
87 Hoven, Feiler and Scheibel, n.83 at 51.
88 Hirst, n.66 at 151.
89 S. Studzinsky, 'Victim Participation before the Extraordinary Chambers in the Courts of Cambodia' 6 *Zeitschrift fur Internationale Strafrechtdogmati* (2011).
90 A. Werner and D. Rudy, 'Civil Party Representation at the ECCC: Sounding the Retreat in International Criminal Law?' 8(3) *Northwestern Journal of International Human Rights* (2010) 301 at 306.
91 Lead Co-Lawyers and Civil Party Lawyers Administrative Internal Regulations, August 2011.
92 Interview with Lawyer (Former CP Team member), 11 September 2015.
93 U. Orth, 'Secondary Victimization of Crime Victims by Criminal Proceedings' 15(4) *Social Justice Research* (2002) 313.
94 UN Office on Drugs and Crime, Ch.1, n.73 at 9–10.
95 E. Smith, 'Victims in the Witness Stand: Socio-Cultural and Psychological Challenges in Eliciting Victim Testimony' in K. Tibori-Szabó and M. Hirst (eds.), *Victim Participation in International Criminal Justice* (Asser Press, 2017) 315–341.
96 M. Dembour and E. Haslam, 'Silencing Hearings? Victim-Witnesses at War Crimes Trials' 15(1) *European Journal of International Law* (2004).
97 L. Moffett, *Justice for Victims at the International Criminal Court* (Routledge, 2014) 34.
98 ICC Rome Statute, Article 43(6).
99 McGonigle Leyh, n.81 at 217.
100 Ibid.
101 Interview with Judge 1, 7 November 2013.
102 K. Tibori-Szabó et al., 'Communication Between Victims' Lawyers and Their Clients' in K. Tibori-Szabó and M. Hirst (eds.), *Victim Participation in International Criminal Justice* (Asser Press, 2017) 461.
103 P. Pham et al., *After the First Trial: A Population-Based Survey on Knowledge and Perception of Justice and the Extraordinary Chambers in the Courts of Cambodia* (Human Rights Center, Berkeley, 2011) 13.
104 Interview with two TPO Staff members, 26 November 2013; TPO, *2014 Annual Report*, tpocambodia.org/annual-reports/ (accessed 16/02/18).
105 Ciorciari and Heindel, n.50 at 259.
106 ECCC Practice Direction on Protective Measures, Article 3.3(b).
107 See Chapter 1.
108 For example UNOHCHR, *Updated Set of Principles for the Protection and Promotion of Human Rights through Action to Combat Impunity,* UN Doc. E/CN.4/2005/102/Add.1, 18 February 2005, Principle 33; *UN Basic Principles and Guidelines on the Right to a Remedy and Reparation for Victims of Gross Violations of International Human Rights Law and Serious Violations of International Humanitarian Law*, UNGA Res. 60/147, 16 December 2005, Principle 12(a).
109 UNOHCHR, *Rule-of-Law Tools for Post-Conflict States: Maximizing the Legacy of Hybrid Courts*, HR/PUB/08/2, 2008 at 19.
110 International Center for Transitional Justice, Victims Unit and Cambodian Human Rights Action Committee, 'Leaving a Lasting Legacy for Victims: Practical

Workshop for ECCC Victims' Representatives' *Workshop Report*, Phnom Penh, 10 March 2009 at 3.
111 International Center for Transitional Justice, 'Outreach Strategies in International and Hybrid Courts' *Workshop Report*, Phnom Penh, 3–5 March 2010 15–18.
112 Internal Rule 9(4).
113 Internal Rule 12*bis* (f) and (i).
114 Interview with Judge 1, January 2014.
115 Ciorciari and Heindel, n.50 at 237.
116 Ibid.
117 M. Elander, 'The Victim's Address: Expressivism and the Victim at the Extraordinary Chambers in the Courts of Cambodia' 7(1) *International Journal of Transitional Justice* (2013) 91 at 112–113.
118 Sperfeldt, n.16.
119 Interview with NGO Staff, 15 November 2013
120 N. Kirchenbauer et al., 'Victims Participation before the Extraordinary Chambers in the Courts of Cambodia' *Baseline Study of the Cambodian Human Rights and Development Association's Civil Party Scheme for Case 002* (ADHOC, 2013); M. Balthazard, *Khmer Rouge Tribunal Justice Project Evaluation Report, 2010–2012* (ADHOC, 2013).
121 Sperfeldt, n.16 at 11.
122 Pham et al., n.103 at 12.
123 International Centre for Transitional Justice, n.111.
124 Ibid.
125 Pena, n.7 at 96.
126 Ciorciari and Heindel, n.50 at 237.
127 Interview with Lawyer 2 (LCL), 21 November 2013.
128 Interview with Lawyer 2 (CP Team), 26 September 2015.
129 See also Herman, n.47.
130 E.A. Lind et al., 'Procedure and Outcome Effects on Reactions to Adjudicated Resolution of Conflicts of Interests' 39 *Journal of Personality and Social Psychology* (1980) 643.
131 Moffett, n97 at 35; E. Kiza, C. Rathgeber and H. Rohne, *Victims of War: An Empirical Study on War Victimization and Victims' Attitudes towards Addressing Atrocities* (Hamburger Edition, 2006).
132 Internal Rule 23 *quinquies* (b).
133 R. Jeffery, 'Beyond Repair?: Collective and Moral Reparations at the Khmer Rouge Tribunal' 13 *Journal of Human Rights* (2014) 103.
134 Interview with Lawyer 1 (CP Team), 11 November 2013.
135 Ciorciari and Heindel, n.50 at 226–227.
136 Interview with Lawyer 2 (Chambers), 11 November 2013.
137 Open Society Justice Initiative, 'Funding Reparations for Victims in Case 002 is Critical to the Legacy of the Extraordinary Chambers in the Courts of Cambodia (ECCC)' *Position Paper* (September 2013).
138 Case 002/01, Trial Judgement, paras. 1126–1140; Case 002/02, Civil Party Lead Co-Lawyers' Final Claim for Reparation in Case 002/02, 002/19-09-2007-ECCC/TC, 30 May 2017.
139 Interview with Lawyer 2 (CP Team), 26 September 2015.
140 Ciorciari and Heindel, n.50 at 227.
141 Internal Rule 12 i (3).
142 Ciorciari and Heindel, n.50 at 227.
143 Interview with VSS Staff 2, 13 January 2014.
144 T. De Langis, *Final Results for ECCC Baseline Study on Gender Sensitivity in Transitional Justice Processes in Cambodia* (ECCC VSS, 2012).

145 Interview with VSS Staff 2, 13 January 2014.
146 'Promoting Gender Equality and Improving Justice for Female Survivors and Victims of Gender-Based Violence under the Khmer Rouge Regime' TPO Website, tpocambodia.org/index.php?id=134 (accessed 16/02/18).
147 'GBV under the Khmer Rouge Information Platform' CDP Website, gbvkr.org (accessed 16/11/18).
148 'The Cambodian NGO Committee on CEDAW (NGO-CEDAW) Shadow Report' NGO-CEDAW, 9 June 2013, tbinternet.ohchr.org/Treaties/CEDAW/Shared%20Documents/KHM/INT_CEDAW_NGO_KHM_15169_E.pdf (accessed 16/02/18); 'Breaking the Silence: Sexual Violence in Cambodia' *Amnesty International*, 8 March 2010, www.amnesty.org/en/documents/ASA23/002/2010/en/ (accessed 16/02/18).
149 Interview with NGO Staff, 15 November 2013.
150 Interview with Lawyer 2 (CP Team), 26 September 2015.
151 Pena, n.7 at 95.
152 Interview with Lawyer (CP Team), 11 November 2013.
153 Haslam, n.23.
154 For example L. Hovil and J. Quinn, *Peace First, Justice Later: Traditional Justice in Northern Uganda* (Refugee Law Project, 2005); E. Evenson, *Unfinished Business: Closing Gaps in the Selection of ICC Cases* (Human Rights Watch, 15 September 2011), P. Clark and N. Palmer, *Testifying to Genocide: Victim and Witness Protection in Rwanda* (REDRESS, 2013).
155 For example Asian International Justice Initiative's Khmer Rouge Tribunal Monitor, the Cambodian Tribunal Monitor and International Justice Monitor.
156 See for example the work of 'Minority Rights Organisation' at www.mirocambodia.org; Cambodian Defenders Project at www.gbvkr.org (accessed 16/02/18).
157 Jarvis, n.30 at 40–41.
158 Ibid.
159 'Trial Monitoring: A Reference Manual for Practitioners' (OSCE, Office for Democratic Institutions and Human Rights, 2012).
160 D. Cohen, M. Hyde and P. van Tuyl, *A Well-Reasoned Opinion? Critical Analysis of the First Case against the Alleged Senior Leaders of the Khmer Rouge (Case 002/01)* (East West Centre, 2015).
161 'Cambodia: Stop Blocking Justice for Khmer Rouge Crimes', *Human Rights Watch*, 22 March 2015, www.hrw.org/news/2015/03/22/cambodia-stop-blocking-justice-khmer-rouge-crimes (accessed 24/0218).
162 M. Kelsall et al., *Lessons Learned from the Duch Trial: A Comprehensive Review of the First Case Before the ECCC* (The Asian International Justice Initiative, 2009).
163 OSCE, n.159.
164 I explore the ECCC's response to SGBV in greater depth in R. Killean, 'An Incomplete Narrative: Prosecuting Sexual Violence Crimes at the ECCC' 13(2) *Journal of International Criminal Justice* (2015) 331–352; R. Killean, 'Exposing Coercive Control in the Commission of Forced Marriage: A Cambodian Case Study' 14(2) *Contemporary Issues in Law* (2017) 95–118.
165 M. Lilja, *Resisting Gendered Norms: Civil Society, the Juridical and Political Space in Cambodia* (Ashgate, 2013) 62.
166 Case 002, Forwarding Order to the Office of the Co-Prosecutors, 002/19-09-2007-ECCC/OCIJ, 13 March 2009.
167 Case 002, Closing Order, 002/19-09-2007-ECCC-OCIJ, 15 September 2010, paras. 216–220.
168 T. De Langis, 'A Missed Opportunity, A Last Hope? Prosecuting Sexual Crimes under the Khmer Rouge Regime' 2 *Cambodia Law and Policy Journal* (2014) 39 at 40.

169 ECCC, 'International Co-Prosecutor Requests Investigation of Alleged Sexual and Gender-based Violence in Case 004', ECCC Website, 24 April 2014, www.eccc.gov.kh/en/articles/international-co-prosecutor-requests-investigation-alleged-sexual-and-gender-based (accessed 16/02/18); 'International Co-Prosecutor Files Supplementary Submission in Case 003' ECCC Website, 4 November 2014, www.eccc.gov.kh/en/articles/international-co-prosecutor-files-supplementary-submission-case-003 (accessed 16/02/18).

170 L. Nguyen and C. Sperfeldt, 'Victim Participation and Minorities in Internationalised Criminal Trials: Ethnic Vietnamese Civil Parties at the Extraordinary Chambers in the Courts of Cambodia' 14 *Macquarie Law Journal* (2014) 97 at 117.

171 Case 002, 'Rule 66 Final Submission' 002/19–09–2007-ECCC-OCIJ (Public Redacted Version) 16 August 2010.

172 Case 002, Closing Order, n.167 paras 778–814.

173 M. Mohan, 'Reconstituting the "Un-Person": The Khmer Krom and the Khmer Rouge Tribunal' 12 *Singapore Yearbook of International Law* (2010) 43.

174 Ibid., at 48–49.

175 'Case 004' ECCC Website, www.eccc.gov.kh/en/case/topic/120 (accessed 16/02/18).

176 Haslam, n.28 at 77.

177 J. Dosch, D. Virorth and K. Sedara, *The German Civil Peace Service: Case Study of Cambodia* (Federal Ministry for Economic Cooperation and Development, 2010).

178 B. Oomen, 'Donor-Driven Justice and its Discontents: The Case of Rwanda' 36(5) *Development and Change* (2005) 887.

179 P. Lundy and M. McGovern, 'The Role of Community in Participatory Transitional Justice' in K. McEvoy and L. McGregor (eds.), *Transitional Justice from Below: Grassroots Activism and the Struggle for Change* (Hart Publishing, 2008) 103.

180 M. Ignatieff, *Whose Universal Values? The Crisis in Human Rights* (Praemium Erasmianum Foundation, 1999) 13.

181 J. Lis, 'Yisrael Beiteinu Renews Bid to Brand Foreign-funded NGOs as Foreign Agents' *Haaretz*, 11 June 2015, www.haaretz.com/israel-news/.premium-1.660648 (accessed 16/02/18).

182 V. Rajalakshmi, 'Targeting NGOs' *Frontline*, 11 July 2014, www.frontline.in/cover-story/targeting-ngos/article6141097.ece (accessed 16/02/18).

183 *Russian Federation Laws on Introducing Amendments to Certain Legislative Acts of the Russian Federation*, 2006; *Introducing Amendments to Certain Legislative Acts of the Russian Federation Regarding the Regulation of Activities of Non-commercial Organisations Performing the Function of Foreign Agents*, 2012.

184 T. Carothers and S. Brechenmacher, *Closing Space: Democracy and Human Rights Support Under Fire* (Carnegie Endowment for International Peace, 2014).

185 O. B. Breen, 'Allies or Adversaries? Foundation Responses to Government Policing of Cross-Border Charity' 17(1) *International Journal of Non-for-Profit Law* (2015) 45.

186 James Savage of Amnesty International quoted in H. Sherwood, 'Human Rights Groups Face Global Crackdown "Not Seen in a Generation"' *The Guardian*, 26 August 2015, www.theguardian.com/law/2015/aug/26/ngos-face-restrictions-laws-human-rights-generation (accessed 16/02/18).

187 W. Easterly, *The Tyranny of Experts: Economists, Dictators, and the Forgotten Rights of the Poor* (Basic Books, 2014); D. Moyo, *Dead Aid: Why Aid Is Not Working and How There Is a Better Way for Africa* (FSG, 2010); W Easterly, *The White Man's Burden: Why the West's Efforts to Aid the Rest Have Done So Much Ill and So Little Good* (Oxford University Press, 2007).

188 S. Ear, 'The Political Economy of Aid and Governance in Cambodia' 15(1) *Asian Journal of Political Science* (2007) 68.
189 Dosch, n.13 at 1074.
190 Ibid., at 1088.
191 G. Knaus and F. Martin, '"Travails of the European Raj" Lessons from Bosnia Herzegovina' 14 *Journal of Democracy* (2003) 60; R. Paris, 'International Peacebuilding and the "Mission Civilisatrice"' 28 *Review of International Studies* (2002) 637; W. Robinson, *Promoting Polyarchy: Globalisation, US Intervention, and Hegemony* (Cambridge University Press, 1996).
192 Kendall, n.45.
193 Lundy and McGovern, n.179 at 104.
194 Hansen, n.11 at 61 and 112; McGregor, n.8 at 103.
195 T. Parks, 'The Rise and Fall of Donor Funding for Advocacy NGOs: Understanding the Impact' 18(2) *Development in Practice* (2008) 213.
196 Dosch, n.13 at 1075.
197 A. Cuddy, 'Victim Lawyers Stung By Cuts' *Phnom Penh Post*, 11 May 2015, www.phnompenhpost.com/national/victim-lawyers-stung-cuts (accessed 16/02/18).
198 Ciorciari and Heindel, n.50 at 238.
199 Cuddy, n.197.
200 Interview with Legal Assistant (CP Team), 10 December 2013.
201 Interview with Lawyer 1 (CP Team), 11 November 2013.
202 Pena, n.7 at 95.
203 I. Samset, S. S. Petersen and V. Wang, 'Maintaining the Process? Aid to Transitional Justice in Rwanda and Guatemala, 1995–2005' *Paper Presented at 'Building a Future on Peace and Justice'* (Nuremberg, 25–27 June 2007); W. Muck and E. Wiebelhaus-Brahm, 'Patterns of Transitional Justice Assistance among the International Community' *Paper Presented at Sixth European Consortium for Political Research General Conference* (Reykjavik, 25–27 August 2011).
204 Dosch, n.13 at 1089.
205 Penan, n.7 at 96–97.
206 H. Veltmeyer, *The Critical Development Studies Handbook: Tools for Change* (Pluto Press, 2011); R. Munck and D. O'Hearn (eds.), *Critical Development Theory: Contributions to a New Paradigm* (Zed Books, 2009).
207 Lundy and McGovern, n.179 at 111.
208 F. Haniffa, *In the Pursuit of Democracy in Post Colonia Sri Lanka: Local Human Rights Approaches to Transitional Justice* (Law and Trust Society, 2006); Z. Papic et al., *International Support Policies to South East European Counties – Lessons (Not) Learned in Bosnia-Herzegovina* (Open Society Fund, 2001).
209 Pena, n.7 at 97.
210 R. Killean and L. Moffett, 'Representation, Agency and Voice: Victim Legal Representation before the ICC and ECCC' 15(4) *Journal of International Criminal Justice* (2017).
211 Sperfeldt, n.16 at 9.
212 G. Mohan, 'Not so Distant, Not so Strange: The Personal and the Political in Participatory Research' 2 *Ethics, Place and the Environment* (1999) 41 at 46.
213 N. Christie, 'Conflict as Property' 17(1) *British Journal of Criminology* (1977) 1.
214 McEvoy and McConnachie, n.62 at 498.
215 Haslam, n.28.
216 Interview with Judge 1, 7 November 2013.
217 'Amicus Curiae Briefs' ECCC Website, www.eccc.gov.kh/en/topic/333 (accessed 16/02/18).
218 Haslam, n.28.
219 Martens, n.11 at 21.

220 McEvoy, n.35.
221 Haslam, n.28 at 75.
222 McEvoy and McConnachie, n.62 at 495.
223 J. Wallace and K. Naren, 'Khmer Rouge Victims Seek Cash Damages to Honour their Dead' *International Justice Tribune,* 14 January 2015.
224 K. Naren and H. Robertson, 'Victims Call for Money from ECCC' *The Cambodia Daily*, 17 October 2014, www.cambodiadaily.com/news/victims-call-for-compensation-from-eccc-70135/ (accessed 23/02/18).
225 Interview with Lawyer 1 (CP Team), 11 November 2013.
226 J. Herman, 'Uncooked Rice: Justice and Victimhood at the Extraordinary Chambers in the Courts of Cambodia and Beyond' in V. Druliolle and R. Brett (eds.), *The Politics of Victimhood in Post-Conflict Societies* (Palgrave MacMillan, 2018) 187–209 at 194.
227 Ibid., at 125.
228 B. Rajagopal, *International Law from Below: Development, Social Movements and Third World Resistance* (Cambridge University Press, 2003).
229 D Orentlicher, 'Settling Accounts' Revisited: Reconciling Global Norms with Local Agency' 1 *International Journal of Transitional Justice* (2007) 10 at 19.
230 P. Akhavan, 'Beyond Impunity: Can International Criminal Justice Prevent Future Atrocities?' 95(7) *American Journal of International Law* (2001) 7.
231 For a discussion on these issues in relation to the state, see D. Garland and R. Sparks, 'Criminology, Social Theory and the Challenge of Our Times' in D. Garland and R. Sparks (eds.), *Criminology and Social Theory* (Oxford University, 2000) 5.
232 Lundy and McGovern, n.179 at 120.
233 McEvoy, n.35 at 40–42.
234 L. Alcoff, 'The Problem of Speaking for Others' 20 *Cultural Critique* (1991–1992).

8 Civil parties, justice and legitimacy at the ECCC

1. Introduction

The preceding chapters have considered the ways in which different professional actors have 'produced, perceived and interpreted' responses to victimisation at the ECCC.[1] In assessing the ways in which various actors and contexts have shaped both the court's structure and the role of the victims within it, they have aimed to provide a 'thicker' description of victim participation within the ECCC.[2] Drawing on notions of procedural and substantive justice, legitimacy and self-legitimation, they have argued that while victims have had their access to both procedural and substantive justice repeatedly modified and restricted, the 'imagined victim' has taken a crucial place in the legitimising practices of both the court as an institution and the practitioners engaged in its work.

Drawing from interviews with civil parties, civil party representatives, VSS staff members and NGO workers,[3] as well as quantitative and qualitative studies conducted by other researchers,[4] this chapter seeks to explore civil parties' assessments of the justice delivered to them by the ECCC and the legitimacy of the ECCC as an institution. Such an analysis provides an important balance to the preceding chapters' focus on professional actors. While international(ised) criminal institutions and practitioners may engage in self-legitimising practices, they also continue to be evaluated against the interests and beliefs of the people subordinate to their authority.[5] It is therefore worth assessing to what extent the victims consider the 'justice for victims' mandate to be fulfilled, and to what extent they express support for the court's work. Such an approach is in keeping with a 'bottom-up' approach,[6] which provides an account of the ECCC's justice process 'from below'[7] by examining the interpretations of those individuals subjected to the authority of the court.[8]

The chapter proceeds by introducing the connections between procedural justice, substantive justice and legitimacy theory before considering the assessments of civil parties with regards to each in turn. It assesses the extent to which the ECCC is considered a legitimate institution in the eyes of civil parties, offering some tentative thoughts on the extent to which procedural justice might enhance perceived legitimacy and cushion negative outcomes within international(ised) criminal courts.

2. Procedural justice, substantive justice and perceived legitimacy

Proponents of procedural justice theory have claimed that when making their overall fairness judgements about a decision-making process, participants will be influenced not only by the perceived fairness of outcomes (substantive justice) but also by the procedures utilised within the process (procedural justice).[9] The specific criteria that inform perceptions of procedural justice may vary depending on the situation[10] and context[11] but will generally include such concepts as neutrality and ethicality, consistency and correctability of decisions (subsumed under 'quality of decision making'),[12] as well as dignity and respect, voice, representation and the provision of information (subsumed under 'quality of interpersonal treatment').[13] In terms of outcomes, substantive justice comprises the three elements of truth, accountability and reparations.[14] In order to assess the overall judgements made about the ECCC by civil parties, this chapter analyses the extent to which civil parties consider these different facets of procedural and substantive justice to be important, as well as whether they consider the court as having delivered them.

Procedural justice theory also provides a useful tool for an analysis of the court's perceived legitimacy in the eyes of civil parties. The term *legitimacy* can be generally understood to refer to the justification of authority[15] and can incorporate sociological elements pertaining to the *perceived* legitimacy of the institution[16] and normative elements relating to whether the institution *should* be accepted.[17] Thus, there is a requirement to demonstrate legitimacy through conformity with legal standards, as well as a more moral or value-driven need to demonstrate that the institution is accepted by those subordinate to its authority.[18] The two elements are strongly interconnected, with some theories considering perceived legitimacy as a crucial aspect of a regime's normative justification.[19] Beetham has found that in order to be legitimate, there must be evidence of consent by the subordinate to that particular relationship.[20] This last aspect has become particularly valuable in the legitimising practices of international(ised) criminal courts, where perceived legitimacy amongst the victim population is often held up as crucial to the court's success.[21] The ECCC has been no exception, the support of the victim population and the ECCC's 'justice for victims' mandate have been used to bolster moral and financial support for the court, as well as forming an important part of ECCC practitioner's self-legitimating practices.[22]

Studies within domestic jurisdictions have suggested that perceptions of procedural justice influence evaluations not only of specific experiences with institutions but also of the perceived legitimacy of the institution overall, particularly in the context of criminal justice.[23] In fact, studies suggest that procedural elements can be of greater value and importance to participants than substantive outcomes[24] and that by enhancing procedural justice, institutions can promote perceptions of legitimacy[25] and cushion negative outcomes.[26] Empirical studies further suggest that when the participant feels unstable, for example because of distressing events or troubled contexts, procedural justice becomes even more important.[27] A lack of fairness can make individuals feel that they are not a valued member of society.[28] Such findings suggest that the application of procedural justice theory to international criminal procedure is a proposition worth exploring further. The aftermath of conflict can create feelings of significant uncertainty and instability amongst victim populations, while the very experience of atrocity can make victims feel unvalued by their society.[29]

The potential for procedural justice to provide 'an opportunity for redress and healing' has been highlighted in the literature,[30] as has its ability to ensure that justice mechanisms are responsive to the actual needs of victims.[31] Moffett has noted the frequent 'secondary victimisation' experienced by victims as a result of their treatment by official institutions and individuals, arguing that ensuring procedural justice is an important part of satisfying the needs of victims without subjecting them to additional trauma.[32] Indeed, survivors of the Khmer Rouge regime have described feelings of helplessness, sadness, disturbed sleep, suicidal thoughts, anxiety and panic.[33] Very few of the survivors have been able to access treatment or support in the decades between the events and the current judicial proceedings, because of the continuation of conflict for many years and the general lack of such services within Cambodia.[34] The need to ensure procedural justice is therefore exacerbated by the particularly traumatic nature of the events civil parties have experienced; it can be seen that the risks of re-traumatisation through participation are high.[35]

Furthermore, international(ised) criminal courts are unable to guarantee victims substantive justice.[36] A criminal court's conception of 'truth' is likely to be narrower than that of a victim,[37] with the facts being 'manipulated, decontextualized and recategorized' to correspond with abstract legal principles.[38] Not every perpetrator can be prosecuted, nor can each case be guaranteed a guilty verdict.[39] The use of plea bargains and the acceptance of guilty pleas may leave victims feeling unsatisfied and marginalised.[40] In the case of a guilty verdict there can be no 'eye for an eye', and sentences are often seen as too lenient by victim populations.[41] Very few international(ised) courts have the ability to grant meaningful reparations,[42] let alone on the scale that victim populations might seek. Thus, a number of scholars have begun to recognise the value of procedural justice in international criminal proceedings,[43] positing that victims are more likely to respond positively to a court if its treatment of victims is fair, even if the court fails to deliver all the outcomes hoped for by the victim population.[44] Comparatively little empirical research has been done to explore the importance of procedural justice theory in international criminal contexts.[45] This chapter therefore seeks to contribute to the growing discussion around the role of procedural justice within international(ised) criminal courts. The following sections begin the analysis by considering aspects of procedural justice that were highlighted as particularly important by civil parties. These are subsumed under the headings of 'Quality of Decision Making' and 'Quality of Interpersonal Treatment'.

3. Quality of the decision making

A number of procedural justice scholars have identified the quality of decision making as an important aspect of participants' perceptions of procedural justice.

Some have found that participants will favour proceedings in which they can control decision making;[46] others, that while participants wish to have a role in the process, this does not extend to exerting control over the decision.[47] Studies have shown that victims are often willing to give decision making power to an external body,[48] as long as certain standards are maintained in relation to the quality, consistency, neutrality, correctability and ethicality of the decision making.[49] In the context of courts, Tyler has argued that participants will trust decision makers who are neutral, principled, honest and open, and who act without bias or prejudice.[50] In ICL proceedings, Wemmers has posited that perceptions of procedural justice are likely to be influenced by the amount of trust the population has in the authority;[51] in a similar vein Moffett has argued that procedural justice will be linked to the impartiality of decisions and judgements.[52] In the case of victim attitudes towards the ICTY, Kutnjak Ivkovich and Hagan's study demonstrated the significant negative impact a lack of trust could have on a population, with victims criticising the court for its perceived lack of impartiality.[53]

In the current study, civil party interviewees appeared to place particular importance on the ethicality of the decision maker, as evidenced by the uniform support expressed for the presence of UN-appointed staff. Several interviewees raised the issue of corruption and their belief that without an international presence, the court would be biased:

> The Court would be biased if it was only a Cambodian court but now it is very good that we have half international and half Cambodian.[54]
>
> I think it is good that it is half Khmer and half international because if all Cambodian it might be biased and corrupt, but it will be better with international involvement.[55]
>
> The international will maybe help to give justice and balance and not bias, because I am afraid that if the Cambodian law 100%, easy [for] corruption and bias.[56]

A similar opinion was voiced by a civil party lawyer, who, when asked why their clients had chosen to participate in the ECCC, replied, 'I think, the whole thing being international, and having an international voice appealed to them'.[57] Overall, in light of the international presence, all respondents expressed a belief that the decision making would be neutral and ethical. This finding has been echoed in other studies conducted with civil parties[58] and demonstrates the influence of cultural, political and social context on perceptions of procedural justice.[59] The support for an international presence contrasts strongly with the experiences of the ICTY and the ICTR, who frequently struggled to garner positive reactions from victim populations, and whose judges faced accusations of bias and neo-colonialism.[60] Conversely, the civil parties appeared to be relying on the UN's involvement to guarantee fair proceedings, a reliance that appears to be influenced by a lack of faith in domestic law[61] and an awareness of the ongoing corruption that pervades the Cambodian legal system.[62] This reliance on international involvement has been noted in other contexts, such as amongst the Tamil victims in Sri Lanka, who rejected the concept of a domestically led inquiry into alleged war crimes during Sri Lanka's civil war, calling instead for an internationally led mechanism.[63] Kutnjak Ivković and Hagan's study in the former Yugoslavia further suggests an inverse correlation between faith in domestic courts and support for international courts, with an increase in support for domestic courts being mirrored by a decrease in support for the ICTY.[64] It may be that if faith in the Cambodian legal system was stronger, the international presence would not be so welcome. As it is, there appears to be an expectation that UN staff will not only deliver justice to victims but will also support and provide, as one civil party interviewee framed it, 'a model for the Cambodians'.[65]

The reliance on international actors is possibly also partly attributable to the prevalence within Cambodia of foreign-funded organisations, who have often taken over the role of the state in the provision of services and development. Indeed, Ear's study into aid dependence in Cambodia argued that 'donor projects have stifled government initiative, placing foreign agencies largely in charge of the government's service provision responsibilities'.[66] While the UNTAC mission finished over 20 years ago, a strong international presence remains, including a number of organisations who specifically engage with rule-of-law issues.[67] If Cambodians have repeatedly been fed a narrative that international actors will assist in the delivery of services, implementation of the rule of law and development of governance, it is perhaps unsurprising that such attitudes and expectations are found amongst the population with regards to the ECCC. Yet, such expectations risk subsequent disappointment and secondary victimisation. As others have argued, it is irresponsible to raise victims' hopes that transitional justice processes can 'end impunity, deliver justice, establish the truth or lead to healing and reconciliation'.[68] It is arguable that the raised hopes of the civil parties with regards to the ECCC's deliverance of 'justice' reflect an 'overselling' of ICL. Such hopes highlight the need for accurate information provision to victim populations and a more honest and humble reflection by those involved in the court's work on what the ECCC and the international community can actually deliver to victim populations.[69]

Other elements of procedural justice identified as contributing to 'quality of decision making' in the literature, such as consistency and correctability, were not discussed by the interviewees. However, one factor was frequently mentioned which has not often appeared in the literature, and this was expediency.[70] Expediency can be understood as the notion that a process should not be unduly time-consuming but should be speedy and without unnecessary bureaucracy.[71] Although not often considered within the procedural justice literature, expediency is considered an important factor within ICL practice; Whiting has spoken of the consensus that war criminals should be charged, arrested, and tried more expeditiously as 'unexceptional'.[72] The death of Slobodan Milošević before a verdict could be issued by the ICTY[73] brought into sharp relief the fact that, as argued by Zacklin, justice delayed can be justice denied for victim populations.[74] Furthermore, long trials are criticised for the risk they pose of infringing the rights of the accused, particularly if they are detained, reducing the deterrent value of prosecutions and allowing impunity.[75] The result has been a significant focus within the literature on how to ensure expedient investigations and trials.[76] Yet, this focus on expediency has been criticised as occasionally opposing the interests of victims, for example when it is used to justify the acceptance of plea bargains[77] or the pursuit of selective prosecutions which fail to address all alleged crimes.[78] This argument claims that an over-prizing of expediency sacrifices the full pursuit of accountability and truth for victims.[79] Many of these concerns find traction at the ECCC; the time that has passed since the crimes were committed and the advanced age of the victims and perpetrators make the risks of inefficiency all the greater, while the severance of Case 002 and the failure to adequately investigate and prosecute certain crimes demonstrate the trade-offs that can occur as courts attempt to pursue efficient proceedings. As was explored in Chapter 5, a judicial focus on expediency can also result in the curtailment of victims' rights, inhibiting other aspects of procedural justice such as voice and representation.

Despite the risks associated with a focus on expediency, the fear of justice delayed becoming justice denied was frequently expressed by interviewees. I was repeatedly asked when the court would finish its work, and interviewees drew attention to the advancing age of the defendants and victims.[80] Many individuals voiced their frustration at having had to wait so long for a judgement, and their fear that the other defendants would also die, meaning that the court 'will have been a failure'.[81] The delay was considered particularly baffling because of their belief that the judges 'already have the evidence, they already have the evidence of the people who died, they have the pictures of the victims'.[82] Although the civil parties had declared their general support and approval for the court, it was evident that the longer Case 002 took, the more frustrated they grew and the less inclined they felt to participate in its work:

> The thing is I don't like it when I go five or six times and have to waste my time travelling but get nothing as a result. I want to request the Court to quickly finish because I need to support my family and can't waste more time travelling back and forward from the Court.[83]

This was by far the most frequently raised point throughout the interviews[84] and appeared to have been voiced to the VSS and civil party legal teams with similar frequency:

> Most of the time I hear 'what's happening, why isn't there a judgment yet, why is it taking so long?'[85]
>
> They question why does the trial take so long, they say 'now I am too old'.[86]

It appears that civil parties supported the structure of the court and wished for fair procedures, but not to the extent that they risk receiving no judgement at all.[87]

This focus on expediency can be compared to the attitudes of those engaged in the work of the court, where there appears to be a general awareness that civil parties and Cambodian society are unhappy with the time the court is taking. Indeed, as noted in Chapter 5, expediency has become a major concern within the ECCC. However, the view expressed amongst practitioners was often a mixture of acknowledgement that the court was not progressing expediently, and a defiant claim that 'this is how long this stuff takes'.[88] Thus, civil parties simply did not understand or were mistaken:

> The thing the civil parties don't understand . . . and nobody could blame them. Seven years from start to finish, sadly in international criminal law is not that long.[89]
>
> So many people are criticising that this court is very slow, that the cases have been delayed too much. But that is not 100% correct . . . I think all the judges and officers have always tried to handle the cases in an efficient way.[90]

Such a divergence in perspective speaks to the distance that can exist between reality within a courtroom, where legal elites are well versed in the time-consuming processes of a trial and reality in the Cambodian provinces, where survivors of atrocity have lived for four decades without clear progress on perpetrators being held to account.[91] These differing discourses have been noted within other contexts; Robins's study in Nepal brought the vast difference between the needs-based discourse amongst victims, and legalistic discourse of elite civil society, into sharp relief.[92] Certainly, the civil parties' desire for expediency and the delivery of a (guilty) verdict illustrates that the standards by which international(ised) criminal courts are assessed by victim populations may differ from those used by elites. Such a divergence has also been noted within other contexts, Palmer's study of the ICTR demonstrated that while ICTR practitioners understood their work as being a contribution to ICL jurisprudence, their work was being assessed within Rwanda according to its perceived contribution to 'the truth'.[93] Palmer has argued that much could be gained in terms of moral and sociological legitimacy of courts if attention were paid to what subordinate groups are actually asking for.[94] Yet, it is arguable that expediency cannot be promised to civil parties; to do so would risk the fair trial rights of the accused. Indeed, the pursuit of legitimacy must be distinguished from the 'appeasement' of those from whom perceived legitimacy is sought.[95] In order to ensure the normative requirements of legitimacy, authority must also be exercised with reference to standards that can be defended externally in moral and political argument.[96] As noted by a civil party lawyer,

> For the Cambodian population, from what I hear so far, the court is rather a failure than a success because of the length of the proceedings, because everyone is complaining that it is taking too long, and of course the accused has died, but that again is a problem of expectation management, because you can't tell the people an international trial of this complexity will be finished in one year.[97]

These issues demonstrate the difficulties which can arise when the procedural justice factors by which an institution is judged conflict within one another; the court cannot guarantee expediency without sacrificing ethicality and instead must attempt to find a balance between the competing interests of accountability and due process.[98] In such a situation, it is arguable that the procedural justice factors of notification and information provision become more important, in order to manage expectations as to how long trials of this nature can take and when a judgement might reasonably be expected. The importance of information provision and the potential for 'cushioning' will be returned to in the following.

4. Quality of interpersonal treatment

The procedural justice literature frequently highlights the importance of interpersonal treatment to assessments of institutions.[99] Judgements about an institution may be strongly influenced by interpersonal experiences, and how individuals *feel* they are treated in and by the institution.[100] In the context of victims of crime, the importance of being treated with dignity and respect and provided with information has been particularly stressed.[101] More recently, the concept of victim participation through the exercising of voice and representation has moved to the centre of such discussions, with academics and practitioners alike citing the importance of incorporating the victim's voice into the proceedings.[102] Danieli has argued that 'the ability to participate actively in the proceedings . . . may assist victims to take back control of their lives and to ensure that their voices are heard, respected, and understood',[103] while Alvarez submits that ICL proceedings should 'afford opportunities for victims to tell their stories [and] find psychological comfort from their participation at trial'.[104] Doak has further argued that in granting such opportunities, in some cases, '[s]hame and humiliation can be transformed to dignity and virtue, and individuals can be instilled with a sense of empowerment and control'.[105] Advocates of victim participation argue that an increased role for victims will also enhance the victims' satisfaction and thus acceptance of the court.[106] On the other hand, critics of increased victim participation have argued that there is a risk that increasing victim involvement could lead to raised expectations, disappointment, the burden of feeling obliged to participate and even re-traumatisation.[107] It is therefore worth exploring the value victims themselves place on participation.

The civil parties interviewed for this study spoke with approval of being involved in the court's proceedings. They considered participating important, with many even considering it a duty, in order to seek justice for their dead relatives, and gain recognition of the loss and suffering of their families.[108] Such motivations are in keeping with the work of survivor and psychoanalyst Dori Laub, who has spoken of the need for survivors to tell and thus come to know one's story. In his view, survivors need two listeners, the external listener who acknowledges the survivor's experience, and the internal listener, who exercises agency and comes to understand their experience.[109] Similarly, the civil parties sought recognition of their experiences and to share the stories of their deceased relatives. Similar motivations have been expressed to other researchers.[110] Indeed, the importance placed on participation has been illustrated by the distress experienced by rejected civil party applicants, who have reported feelings of anger, sadness, disappointment, injustice and helplessness and of having let down their deceased loved ones and lost face in the eyes of their community.[111]

When asked about their experiences of participating at the court, the respondents reported a generally positive experience. They had been treated with respect and spoke approvingly of being welcomed by both national and international staff and provided with food and accommodation. The educational value of attendance was mentioned, although several admitted that they found the proceedings hard to understand. Nevertheless, having the chance to attend was still prized, if only because it involved a chance to see Phnom Penh, the building of the court, and the accused in person:

> It's exciting because we have a chance to talk, to hear the voice of the Khmer Rouge leader, and know what the court looks like.[112]
>
> I feel like when I attend the Court, it's exciting, I never knew before.[113]

The value placed on being treated with respect and provided with food and accommodation appears to be widely held by civil parties, according to a staff member within the VSS:

> The civil parties who come here, they enjoy something that surrounds the trials. From their home they got a free bus, eating a free lunch, staying in the hotels, there is a lot of services, for example TPO provide psychological services . . . The court is used as the root of the tree, and then what happens here is like the fruit and the flower . . . The positive thing is, more civil parties can receive important information and they can know that they are part of the proceedings. So this is a kind of respect.[114]

Interviewees who had not been invited to attend in some time would hint to the author that they would like to be asked again.[115] Others had attended and valued the experience but had decided that they would not attend again, either because they were too busy with their work and family or because they felt the proceedings were going on too long.[116] Again, these reactions speak to the distance between the legal world of Court professionals, and the needs-based world of civil parties.[117] The prizing of services can be understood as a natural reflection of limited access to those services, while a limited understanding of the trials is to be expected amongst those without legal training or education. As noted by a civil party lawyer,

> There is very very little legal understanding. There are a few civil parties who are well educated and they follow the trial and they have a very keen interest in it, and I think they will understand. But the majority will not understand.[118]

In an attempt to enhance the experience, the court's VSS have established procedures which allow civil parties to speak with their lawyers before and after the proceedings.[119] Yet, as explained by a former civil party lawyer,

> [i]f you hold meetings like the Victim Support Section does with 250 people and one morning session where court officials appear and talk a little bit, this is meaningless. Everyone sits there looking at them and nodding and smiling and they are polite, you can ask 'do you understand' and everybody would say yes. And then you ask a question on content and you can see they didn't get it. And then you have to start again and explain again in another manner to make it really accessible, or give examples so they understand what you're talking about.[120]

The large numbers of civil parties and the lack of resources available to the VSS naturally limit the extent to which such meetings are able to address all civil parties' questions and fully explain the proceedings. The implications of this will be returned to later, as this combination of low education amongst civil parties and the lack of resources to assist them in their understanding of the court has further implications for their assessments of procedural justice.

In terms of exercising voice, three civil party interviewees had addressed the court and were pleased to have had the opportunity to do so. Reactions to the experiences varied amongst the three, with one describing the experience as a 'positive feeling' because 'the court replied with what he wanted to know',[121] one saying it made her feel 'brave' and that she appreciated being given 'time and opportunity' to speak,[122] and one speaking of feeling a large amount of 'fear' on actually seeing the accused within the courtroom.[123] Mixed reactions to participation were also noted by a civil party lawyer, who noted that their clients often reported feelings of fear and distress as a result of cross-examination.[124] However, they noted that such a reaction was a natural response to the feeling of being doubted, and dismissed the idea that their clients would be re-traumatised by the experience.[125] Similarly, TPO councillors who provided support for civil parties during participation noted that civil parties were often pleased to testify but sometimes experienced negative feelings as a result of seeing the accused denying crimes[126] or from having to talk about their experiences during the regime.[127]

Trial transcripts demonstrate that several civil parties who testified spoke of feeling a sense of psychological relief,[128] with those who were given an opportunity to provide 'statements of suffering', describing that experience as particularly psychologically beneficial.[129] Bates's interviews with civil parties who had participated in Case 001 similarly found that a number spoke with satisfaction of having shared their story in public.[130] The value placed on statements of suffering is comparable to the experience of victims within domestic systems who have been given the opportunity to provide victim impact statements.[131] Van Camp and De Mesmaecker have found that this process, while sometimes criticised by victims for the limitations placed on their ability to freely express themselves, is appreciated in principle.[132]

Some civil parties also found the experience of asking the accused questions empowering and meaningful.[133] This is comparable to reactions noted within domestic systems with regard to restorative justice practices.[134] While a trial differs significantly from such practices, the process of addressing the accused may provide some of the same benefits noted in restorative justice research. For example, allowing civil parties to address the accused may have addressed their 'expressive need' to vocalise the consequences of victimisation to the offender.[135] Studies have suggested that the experience of being heard by the offender can be liberating and empowering.[136] However, one interviewee described their reaction of asking Duch a question as being one predominantly of fear 'because Mr Duch had experience to kill many people in Cambodia that's why I feel fear'.[137] Similar reactions have been noted by Stover et al., with civil parties finding Duch's confrontational behaviour in the courtroom and 'false' apologies upsetting.[138] As with testifying, it appears that confronting the accused resulted in complex reactions but was an opportunity that was often appreciated in principle.[139]

Very few interviewees expressed a wish for greater participatory rights or control over the court proceedings. While some wished to be given the chance to address the court themselves, all considered civil parties in general as having sufficient opportunity to express themselves within the courtroom. Indeed, some interviewees spoke of having no wish to address the court, for example 'I don't know how to ask, how to speak, because I have a low education I don't know how to talk to the Court'[140] and 'We don't have any idea and don't know how to speak or ask at the Court, we just want to listen to what's happening'.[141] This lack of inclination for enhanced voice or agency could be interpreted as evidence of the heterogeneous nature of victim populations and the need to be wary of assuming that enhanced participation rights are always sought;[142] victims may wish to have a role in proceedings, but the desire may not always be for greater participatory rights or individual voice.[143] However, it is also worth placing this reaction within the context of the capacity and agency of the individual civil parties interviewed, as it is possible that this disinclination is a reflection of the cultural and contextual relativity of procedural justice judgements.[144] A large number of those interviewed had received little in the way of education. The lack of education amongst interviewees was not surprising; most were from farming communities who would have had limited access to education even prior to the Khmer Rouge regime.[145] Many were living in severe poverty in the provinces, and a number belonged to ethnic minority groups who had faced prolonged and continued discrimination within Cambodia since the end of the Khmer Rouge. Furthermore, survivors of the Khmer Rouge regime have spoken of maintaining a life of secrecy in order to survive, a history that may not encourage a willingness to testify.[146] Indeed, having endured lives of hardship and deprivation, to expect civil parties to have the confidence to travel to Phnom Penh and address a courtroom of lawyers and judges is to ignore the power imbalance that exists between civil parties and transitional justice elites.[147] Cambodia continues to have a society based on status, wealth and a complicated social framework which emphasises patronage and social hierarchies;[148] such a culture may exacerbate this power imbalance and discourage civil parties living without wealth or status from feeling that they have a right to speak. Indeed, the civil parties interviewed were acutely aware of their own lack of education:

> When I attend the ECCC I am afraid to ask the lawyer, because I think the lawyer is very well educated and I am low educated, and I don't understand much but try to understand.[149]

The lack of intellectual and educational self-confidence amongst the interviewees, combined with their history of trauma and secrecy, may explain why there was a desire to participate, but few wishes to enhance their own role in the proceedings.[150] As noted by McEvoy and McConnachie, victims 'may be traumatised, lack relevant skills or capacity, have little access to power, resources and so forth'.[151] As such, victims may require representation and assistance, and prefer not to participate directly in proceedings. Drawing on Alcoff, McEvoy and McConnachie argue that in such cases, those who purport to represent and assist victims should keep in mind 'the particular power relations and discursive effects involved' in representing others.[152] Yet it is also important to note the possibility that with ongoing support and assistance, more individuals would wish to express themselves. As noted by a former civil party lawyer,

> One of my clients stood up in a meeting and said (without being asked to comment): 'So much has changed for me. At the beginning I did not dare to say anything. Now I learned to stand up and to speak. I want to thank you for that'.[153]

A staff member from the VSS noted a similar phenomenon:

> When the civil parties see the other civil parties talk about it, they cry, but they feel release, they want to share their story, they want to speak out, they want the other people to know.[154]

Such practices suggest a 'legal empowerment' potential of civil party participation at the ECCC.[155] Legal empowerment can be defined as attempts to increase 'the capacity of ordinary people to exercise their human and civil rights as individuals or as members of a community'.[156] Although the principle emerged from development discourse, it has increasingly been used in transitional justice scholarship[157] and particularly in conversations surrounding victim participation.[158] Indeed, a number of civil society actors, such as Cambodian Defenders Project (CDP) and The Cambodian Human Rights and Development Association (ADHOC), have adopted legal empowerment strategies in their work with civil parties, seeking to increase their clients' confidence and legal understanding.[159] Such projects have yielded positive results, ADHOC has noted growing confidence amongst its clients both inside and outside the courtroom, for example through its arrangement of a press conference to voice displeasure over the court's slow pace.[160] Other interviewees spoke of witnessing such empowerment, for example citing the collectivising of the civil parties through an association – 'which is also something that is almost impossible to create in this country'[161] – and their protests surrounding the curtailment of their rights in Case 001: 'The ability to stand up and to speak, and how they reflected on their own development and personal growth, that was amazing to see'.[162]

While these developments were noted by a number of interviewees who worked with the civil parties, it was also acknowledged that such developments were in part dictated by access to those actors and programmes geared towards furthering such empowerment:

> The civil parties see that they have rights, but not all . . . there are many in the provinces and I know that they have not been reached in the same way as the civil parties working here in Phnom Penh.[163]

It is possible that this is a relevant factor in the current study; as will be seen in the following, a number of the interviewees spoke of the lack of contact they had had with their representatives and of not being kept informed as to developments at the court. It is also worth noting that civil parties living within Phnom Penh may have greater access to their basic needs, making them more able to engage with the court.[164] A rights-based discourse such as that utilised in legal empowerment programmes can often overlook the prioritisation of basic needs amongst the relevant populations.[165] This is explored in greater detail later, in the context of substantive justice. I would not wish to make assumptions as to the motivations of civil parties, who may have a variety of personal reasons behind their disinclination to seek enhanced rights or voice within the proceedings. Nevertheless, with evidence of growing confidence amongst civil parties through their participation in the court and access to assistance and representation, it is possible that the interviewee's feelings that they 'don't know how to ask, how to speak' are a reflection of their specific context and situation, which could be changed through appropriate encouragement and support.[166]

Such developments and possibilities of empowerment mirror the growth of victims' advocacy within domestic systems, whereby engagement with civil society enabled victims to form associations and begin to lobby on their own behalf.[167] The Case 001 boycott,[168] the release of critical press statements[169] and the protests over reparations[170] are examples of civil parties attempting to exercise their own voice. Such occurrences also demonstrate that increased empowerment may lead not only to an increased wish to participate but also an increased wish to challenge the court. These developments tie into issues identified throughout this book related to the privileging of voice and the difference between the 'imagined victim' and actual victims. While Palmer has argued that courts can gain much in terms of legitimacy by listening to what victims actually want,[171] there is limited evidence to suggest the court is actually hearing and acting upon the views of these critical voices. Rather, there appears to be a preference for the professionalised civil society voices over those of the civil parties' themselves.[172] Furthermore, despite evidence that victims have specific complaints to make about the court, Chapter 6 demonstrated the continued use of the 'imagined victim' in legitimising practices, echoing Kendall and Nouwen's critique of the ICC, in which they argue that the support of the broad symbolic notion of the victim can be cited even to counter the criticisms of victim populations.[173]

In relation to procedural justice through representation, interviewees generally spoke positively of their lawyers, a view that has been reflected in quantitative studies.[174] Not all interviewees were aware of the change in representation in Case 002, a fact that mirrors Kirchenbauer et al.'s study, in which only one third of the civil parties interviewed identified the LCLs as their representatives in the courtroom.[175] Those who were aware of the introduction of the LCLs were happy for them to represent all the civil parties: 'Only two, international and national, are enough, because I believe they will give justice to me'.[176] However, it should be noted that this does not appear to be a uniformly held belief; one civil party lawyer spoke of the clients' dissatisfaction with the change,[177] while other studies have shown that civil parties have been unhappy with the change in the modes of participation in Case 002.[178] This divergence in opinion may in part be attributed to the fact that civil parties are not a homogenous group; different opinions are to be expected.[179] However, it is also possible that my own interviewees did not have a thorough enough knowledge of the court's process to understand the implications of the change in representation. Indeed, the issue of inadequate or misinformation being delivered to victims was a common theme during my research; the opinions of the civil parties with regards to the amount of information received are therefore worth exploring.

Procedural justice research has repeatedly highlighted the importance victims place on being kept informed about the progress of their case[180] and the negative impact that a lack of information can have on feelings of justice[181] and empowerment.[182] In the context of the ECCC, a lack of up-to-date information, and a more general lack of understanding about the court and its work, has been repeatedly commented on by civil society[183] and arose as an issue in many other studies.[184] Indeed, this lack of information was clearly illustrated during the course of my fieldwork, by the number of key facts civil parties were unaware of. One interviewee had been unaware that the charges against Ieng Thirith and Ieng Sary had been dropped until it was brought up during her interview – 'I feel like I don't know what has changed in the past until now because now I didn't get update from the court because when Ieng Thirith die [*sic*] I didn't know'[185] – and several were unclear as to which case they were involved in or who was representing them. Many of the civil parties who were interviewed during the second stage of fieldwork, which happened after the first judgement was released in Case 002/01, were unaware that a judgement had been rendered.[186] Such a finding is extremely problematic when one considers the strong desire for a judgement as explored earlier. In one troubling case, the long silence from the court and his lawyer, followed by an invitation to attend the proceedings, had caused a civil party real alarm and fear that this was a summons of the kind issued by the Khmer Rouge:

> The court invite me several times and I decide to attend but I . . . don't know the purpose, and I feel worried that someone want to kill me.[187]

With such important information failing to reach civil parties, and such fear-inducing misunderstandings occurring, their irritation is easy to comprehend, and the need for up-to-date information provision clearly highlighted. However, this lack of understanding is clearly tied to the lack of adequate resources earmarked for victim-centric measures. As bemoaned by a former civil party lawyer,

> You need legal assistants, or qualified people who understand the trial, who understand what is going on and who are able to translate information and to get them involved. If you don't have these people, if you don't have the resources to do this on a regular basis then this results in . . . asking the civil parties and they didn't know anything.[188]

Overall, it appears that many of the factors identified in the procedural justice literature featured in the judgements about the ECCC being made by civil parties, including ethicality and neutrality, participation, voice, being treated with dignity and respect and having access to representation and information.[189] While certain factors therefore appeared to be uniformly important, and it appears that civil parties were appreciative of the rights given to them in principle, attitudes about how well these had been delivered by the ECCC in practice varied. The extent to which these factors influenced overall judgements about the court is considered subsequently, following an analysis of civil parties' attitudes towards the court's deliverance of substantive justice.

5. Substantive justice

Substantive justice refers to the outcomes of the decision-making bodies and to the perceived fairness of those outcomes. Two factors appear to influence the judgements made by participants about outcomes: whether the result is positive and whether it was what was deserved by those involved.[190] Indeed, even positive outcomes can be considered unfair if different from what the individual believed was deserved,[191] while negative outcomes can result in intense feelings of disappointment and upset amongst victims of crime in particular.[192] Victims may have strong feelings with regards to the expected outcome; they may wish for retribution, acknowledgement of the severity of the offence and assured security through the incarceration of the accused.[193] However, procedural justice theorists have posited that while these outcomes are important, procedural justice is often considered more important,[194] and indeed, may even cushion the impact of negative decisions.[195] If indeed this is the case, then this would be of significant importance to the ECCC, which is limited by politics, a lack of resources and time in its ability to guarantee substantive justice.[196]

In the context of victims of international crime, substantive justice amounts to redressing their harm and the causes of their victimisation.[197] This is commonly held to incorporate three main outcomes: accountability, truth and reparations.[198] The civil party interviewees expressed strong views on all three aspects. In relation to 'accountability', there was not only a general agreement that the defendants were guilty but also an expectation that the court would find them so, and an understanding that if they did not, the court would be a 'failure'.[199] Furthermore, the defendants should be severely punished. When asked what should happen to the accused in Case 002, some expressed a wish for incarceration: 'They should be in jail for their whole life';[200] 'It's enough for me, for them to go to jail';[201] 'They should go to jail'.[202] However, some participants expressed their wish for the death penalty, or even personal vengeance, but were aware that this was not an option and that a life sentence was the most that could be hoped for:

> If I had the chance, I would want to kill, because I lost all my family members. But I am concerned that when I kill those persons, I become, I commit a crime, so I will be happy for them to stay in jail instead.[203]

This 'urge to punish' has been noted in other studies[204] and must be understood within the context of the atrocities committed during the Khmer Rouge regime and the long period of impunity that followed. These perspectives are also evidence that retributive theories of justice can go some way towards delivering justice to victim populations.[205] Indeed, evidence has suggested that the more serious the crime, the more likely that both the victim and the wider community will wish for some form of retribution.[206] However, the nature of international crimes make pursuing proportionate retribution 'inadequate and absurd'.[207] As Drumbl has noted, to pursue true proportionality in such cases might involve acts of torture and murder (indeed, both were mentioned by the civil parties), leading to the victims becoming as culpable as the original perpetrators.[208] Thus, retributive justice cannot be the sole means of addressing mass crimes.[209]

In a similar retributive vein, several civil parties expressed their wish for lower-level Khmer Rouge cadres to also be held accountable, a wish that is unlikely to come true because of the lack of political will within Cambodia, the already stretched resources of the court and the restricted personal jurisdiction of the court.[210] Indeed, prosecutions of mass violence are by their nature selective; resources will be dedicated to pursuing the cases that are most possible and politically preferable, rather than those that might be considered most worthy of pursuing.[211] These limitations demonstrate the inevitable failure of ICL in providing complete retributive justice to victims: the multitude of perpetrators, mass victimisation, state involvement, finite resources and specific mandates of courts all prevent an entirely retributive focused system from fully delivering a sense of justice.[212]

The civil parties' resignation that their notion of retribution was not possible suggests a limited form of the 'cushioning effect'[213] of procedural justice identified in the literature: the provision of information as to what sentences could be reasonably expected from the ECCC resulted in acceptance that certain desired outcomes would not be forthcoming. However, it seems unlikely that the cushioning effect would continue to be as effective in the case of a non-guilty verdict, or a sentence that was seen as overly lenient. While this can only be a speculation with regards to the present study due to the current status of the sentences against the three accused (a life sentence following appeal), the severe distress amongst the civil parties following Duch's initial sentence in Case 001 appears to support this conclusion:[214]

> Crimes against humanity has been reduced to 11 hours per life. Besides shock, what else can one feel at the moment?
>
> I ask if Cambodians are happy and the world is happy that millions of people died, a lot of money has been spent on the court – and the perpetrator is free [in 19 years]? I am not happy with that.[215]

Speaking with civil parties in the weeks following the judgement, Stover et al. found considerable disappointment and some anger about the sentence.[216] A civil party lawyer expressed their belief that a similar reaction would follow a lenient sentence in subsequent sub-trials:

> I think there is still very high expectations amongst all the civil parties, especially in terms of conviction, so for them, a life sentence. An acquittal would be unacceptable, there would be an outcry, and anything below a life sentence, as was the case with Duch would also cause an outcry.[217]

This perspective demonstrates that the importance placed on the neutrality and ethicality of the decision maker, as explored earlier, may not extend to a wish for a fair trial outweighing the desire for retribution. However, while procedural justice may not cushion light sentences or acquittals, Stover et al. noted that the civil parties in the immediate aftermath of Case 001's trial judgement often continued to consider the trial overall as fair, despite their dissatisfaction with the sentence.[218] This suggests that the procedural justice premise that procedures can strongly influence overall fairness judgements has traction.[219] Yet, as also argued within the literature, there may be a need for actual participation for this to be the case.[220] The civil parties in Case 002 are less likely to have been directly involved in the court's proceedings than those involved in Case 001, the sheer number of civil parties means that there are fewer opportunities to attend hearings, let alone participate within the courtroom.[221] In such cases, it may be that civil parties in Case 002 are more outcomes focused. As opined by one civil party lawyer,

> They don't understand the process, the only thing they see is what is the judgment, or how long do they have to be in prison. For me that's a big

> issue, but I feel like in the outreach activities by the court and by the civil societies don't seem to see that as a problem.[222]

It seems that this issue is tied to the provision of information to civil parties, and the resource limitations which restrict the ability of civil party lawyers, the court and civil society to meaningfully engage with civil parties and explain aspects of court process and procedure. As argued by Herman, it may be that through greater education on the rights of the accused and the need to ensure a fair trial, the relative importance placed on procedure and retribution could be altered.[223] However, it is also possible that the nature of the offences charged mean that for many people, retribution will always remain a key concern.[224]

In addition to the successful prosecution and imprisonment of perpetrators, a desire for reparations and truth were also expressed by many of the civil parties I interviewed. With regards to reparations, the majority were aware that individual compensation was not possible and thus worded their requests in more collective terms. The court's inability to provide individual reparations is not unproblematic: purely collective reparations risk compromising the victims' individual rights to a remedy, may result in the marginalisation of victims with additional needs and may allow for the continuation of the specific harms associated with criminally induced poverty, for example through the loss of a breadwinner.[225] However, given that the court has repeatedly asserted that it will not deliver individual reparations, the acceptance of this fact by civil parties could be interpreted as a positive result of information dissemination and the managing of victim expectations; many civil parties who participated in Case 001 had believed that they were entitled to individual monetary reparations and had been extremely distressed to find they were to receive nothing more than recognition of their harm and the publication of Duch's apologies and acknowledgements of responsibility.[226] Nevertheless, it seemed that some interviewees still believed that they could receive compensation:

> Not only me, but other people, that suffer from the Khmer Rouge regime, they expect that they will get compensation, to help their family improvement . . . they should give money in compensation to help them. I don't know how much, or how fully, but compensation is satisfactory for them.[227]

Indeed, contrary to the general approach within civil society, which appears geared towards managing victim expectations, one former civil party lawyer asserted that they had encouraged their clients to continue fighting for their right to individual reparations:

> With reparations for example, to insist that this is their right to have financial compensation. This is not granted of course, but this is bullshit what they [the judges] did.[228]

Certainly, while other studies have suggested a growth in resignation amongst civil parties with regards to reparations,[229] this has not been universal, and many continue to express a wish for individual reparations.[230] Indeed, many victims have found it hard to understand how so much money has been spent funding the court, without any provision being made for individual reparations.[231] With so many of the population living in poverty, the idea of spending millions on prosecuting elderly perpetrators without enabling some form of compensation to be given to those in need was unfathomable to many.[232]

Amongst the civil parties I interviewed, other reparation requests varied from being given Cambodian citizenship (for the ethnically Vietnamese)[233] to the building of memorials and religious buildings to education programmes to health care for survivors of the Khmer Rouge regime:

> I hope that I get compensation such as build a hospital, school or pagoda. Hospital for the villages health services . . . for the school I hope that the next generation might get their education . . . for the pagoda I think that maybe have a monk or stupa to pray for those that died . . . and I hope that the Court maybe build road for everyone.[234]

The requests for health care and education reflect the profile of the interviewees as individuals living in remote areas of the provinces, often in poverty, without easy access to health care or education provision. The frequent wish for a place of worship or memorial is also illustrative of the continuing strength of the Buddhist faith amongst Cambodian society and the importance placed on honouring the dead.[235] Thus, views on substantive justice, just as with procedural justice, are shaped by contexts. However, it is also worth noting a point raised by a former civil party lawyer:

> Imagine a person who has never been asked or never been in the situation to express what he or she wants . . . so the NGO workers think 'okay, what do we need here in Cambodia, we need hospitals, schools and roads. That is a development need, we don't have this' so then the victim says, oh yes it would be great to have a road, and yes a school would be nice and also a hospital would be nice.[236]

The lawyer's argument was that such reparation requests were not a true reflection of what civil parties might wish for, and that such requests focus on development rather than specifically addressing the harm experienced by civil parties, and therefore are not truly 'reparations'.[237] As they argued, 'the perpetrators use the road'.[238] Yet such development needs may also be important to civil parties, with the court representing a way of accessing services that they may not otherwise obtain. As noted by Roht-Arriaza and Orlovsky, victims' demands for reparations and development can often arise simultaneously.[239] Thus, while problematic from a perspective which would seek to distinguish reparations from development,[240] it may be precipitous to assume that these requests were not a genuine reflection of at least some of the civil parties' wishes.

The wish for schools and education programmes also appeared to be linked to the third element of substantive justice: truth. This right entails the determination not only of what happened but why and by whom. Ascertaining these truths can help alleviate suffering by acknowledging the harm and experiences of the victims.[241] This was reflected in the wishes of the interviewees, who expressed a desire for greater acknowledgement and information from the defendants, who should explain 'why they killed a lot of people',[242] 'apologise to the victims'[243] and 'know that they were the people who killed people during that, time, for them to know themselves. I want them to acknowledge what they did'.[244] It was hoped that through this acknowledgement 'the next generation [would] knowing about that feeling, about the killing fields', leading to 'peace and security so the people can live free from the Khmer Rouge'.[245] Thus, truth was tied to a desire to understand what happened, to understand why it happened, to receive acknowledgement and to prevent re-occurrence of violence.

These requests are reflected in other studies,[246] while the desire for acknowledgement and apology is reflective of the broader literature, within which there is evidence that victims place a high value on receiving apologies.[247] The desire for truth is also indicative of the local context. With little chance of a truth commission being formed within Cambodia, the court represents one of the few ways in which civil parties can access information about what happened and why.[248] Yet, criminal trials are not necessarily the best forum in which to pursue such goals.[249] The focus on the facts most relevant to determining the guilt or innocence of the accused necessarily limits the truth told,[250] while the adversarial approach does little to encourage admissions of responsibility. Certainly, Case 001 featured many statements of acknowledgement from Duch, and although few accepted his apologies, a number of civil parties have suggested that Duch's cooperation and truth telling were of some value and have praised the court for establishing a historical record and allowing Duch to provide a direct account of what happened.[251] In contrast, NGO staff interviewees highlighted the anger civil parties felt when the defendants in Case 002 refused to acknowledge their guilt.[252] This has also been reflected in other studies; Herman noted feelings of disappointment and anger amongst civil parties when the accused failed to take responsibility for crimes.[253] These concerns can be linked to those regarding the provision of information and enhancement of understanding amongst civil parties. It is possible that with an enhanced understanding of fair-trial rights, the disappointment associated with such denials might be lessened.[254]

It is evident that even within the small number of civil parties interviewed, there were a variety of different needs and wishes with regards to what the court should do for survivors of the Khmer Rouge regime. All three elements of substantive justice, accountability, reparations and truth, were of immense importance to the civil parties, an understandable consequence of the hardships and harms they have endured. In light of the wishes and views expressed by the civil parties, it is worth concluding by revisiting the claims made by procedural justice theorists and examining what, if any, impact the role granted to civil parties has had on their overall perceptions of the court.

6. Conclusion: The perceived legitimacy of the ECCC

In terms of the overall support voiced for the Court, all interviewees expressed satisfaction with the Court as a mechanism for dealing with the crimes of the Khmer Rouge. Furthermore, many expressed their belief that this support was commonly held within Cambodia: 'I think that all the Cambodian people support the court, and they have many religions such as Chinese, Vietnam, Laos, Islam and minority, and they all support it'.[255] This assumption has been supported by other studies, which have consistently shown relatively high levels of support amongst civil parties and the broader public.[256] Civil parties have certainly challenged the court on a number of issues, yet this does not appear to suggest that they consider the court as lacking legitimacy, rather, they are demonstrating a wish to engage with the court by expressing their own interests and confronting its limitations.

Victim perceptions of justice will often change over time, and one must therefore be wary of over-generalising. However, what is interesting about this study is the suggestion that civil parties were influenced by procedural justice as well as substantive when making their assessments of the ECCC. Many of the aspects of procedural justice identified within the literature featured in their evaluations, relating to both the quality of the decision making and the quality of the interaction. The additional factor of expediency also had a marked (negative) influence on the satisfaction they felt with the court's work. Thus, there appears to be evidence to support the theory that procedural justice judgements will influence victim perceptions of a court. With regard to how well the civil parties considered these factors as delivered by the ECCC, opinions were undoubtedly mixed and reveal more complex attitudes towards the ECCC than demonstrated by their initial statements of support. On one hand, there appeared to be a general sense of satisfaction with the opportunities they were given to participate, access representation and exercise voice within the proceedings, while the hybrid structure of the court appeared to provide reassurance of the court's neutrality. On the other hand, the time taken over the court's work and the low level of information provision were identified as particularly unsatisfactory aspects of the court's procedure.

The importance of social context and legal culture as highlighted in the literature is also supported by the evidence.[257] For example, the support that UN involvement received amongst the civil parties is in sharp juxtaposition to the suspicion occasionally demonstrated towards other international or hybrid tribunals and appears to reflect a lack of faith in the domestic legal system, as well as high expectations as to what the UN can deliver. The reluctance of some of the interviewees to speak before the court may also reflect the social context; civil parties were highly aware of their perceived intellectual inferiority to court staff. Such a finding demonstrates the need for engagement with victim populations, in order to ensure that modes of victim participation are reflective of the specific context in which the justice mechanism is operating and that civil parties receive the support and assistance they need in order to feel confident in their ability to participate. With evidence emerging of growing confidence amongst civil parties through their participation in the court and access to assistance and representation, it is possible that the interviewee's feelings that they 'don't know how to ask, how to speak' are a reflection of their specific context and situation, which could be changed through appropriate encouragement and support.

In addition to contributing to a sense of justice amongst participants, elements of procedural justice, particularly voice and representation, contribute to ensuring the interests of those participants are heard.[258] This was of natural importance to civil parties, who had expectations that the ECCC would provide them with substantive justice in the form of accountability, truth and reparations. Indeed, while procedural justice considerations played a role in their overall perceptions of justice, they primarily focused on outcomes, and the distress that has been witnessed in the aftermath of Case 001's judgement and limited reparations suggest that procedural justice may do little to 'cushion' unwelcome outcomes. Wemmers has attributed this focus on outcomes amongst victims of international crime to the severity of the harm done to them, and to their continued struggle for survival.[259] She points to Maslow's hierarchy of needs[260] and argues that victims need to feel safe and secure before they can consider issues such as procedural justice. Similarly, Robins has highlighted the distance that can exist between the legalistic discourses of transitional justice professionals, and those victims who continue to struggle to meet their basic needs.[261] In such a situation, access to services through reparations, and access to security through accountability, can assume greater importance than less tangible aspects of 'justice'. I agree that these may be significant contributing factors; certainly all civil parties interviewed were living in extreme poverty, many expressed their wish for increased peace and security, and some still displayed a very real sense of fear and insecurity. In such a situation, a focus on what a process can provide in terms of physical benefits is understandable. Indeed, it is notable that even when discussing procedural justice and their experiences of participating in the court's procedures, many civil parties dwelled with particular pleasure on the practical benefits, such as food and access to services, which accompanied that process.

However, attention should be given to the recurring theme that has emerged throughout this chapter: that amongst many of the interviewees, there was a demonstrable lack of accurate knowledge about the court, with significant facts such as the conclusion of Case 002/01 and the death of defendants being unknown. It is highly probable that for procedures to have a real impact on overall judgements, there is a need to ensure up-to-date and accurate information about the process of the justice mechanism. Certainly, the acceptance amongst some of the interviewees of the sentencing and reparations restrictions placed on the court suggests that the provision of information can at least provide some 'cushioning' of unpalatable outcomes and enhance to some extent the level of acceptance amongst the affected population. Such a finding demonstrates the importance of allocating space within court budgets to allow for meaningful participation and information provision. Indeed, the frequency with which the issue of notification and information provision arose during this analysis is unsurprising given the limited resources made available by the ECCC for victim-centric measures. It is possible that with greater resource allocation towards victim representation, outreach and information provision, some of the negative feelings expressed by the civil parties might have been avoided.

Thus, courts must be aware of the many needs of victims of mass atrocity. These may incorporate procedural justice elements, such as a wish to be acknowledged, represented, treated with dignity and kept informed of the progress of proceedings. However, the long-reaching impact of mass victimisation may mean that victims continue to prioritise the more substantive aspects of justice, such as truth, accountability and reparations. This does not mean procedural justice has no value; indeed, the reactions of the civil parties to procedures at the ECCC and their role within it are strong encouragement for those arguing for increasing levels of victim participation within international criminal courts. But caution should be used before assuming that enhanced participation can be a means of bringing 'justice' to victims; victims' conceptions of justice are complex and multifaceted, as was clearly illustrated by the civil parties. Thus, it may be more realistic to say that procedural justice can provide a way of incorporating the views of those most affected, allowing international(ised) criminal courts to become more relevant and responsive to the needs of victims of mass crimes.

Notes

1 C. Geertz, 'Thick Descriptions: Toward an Interpretive Theory of Culture' in C. Geertz (ed.), *The Interpretation of Cultures: Selected Essays* (Fontana Press, 1973) 3–30 at 7.

2 Ibid.; K. McEvoy, 'Beyond Legalism: Towards a Thicker Understanding of Transitional Justice' 24 *Journal of Law and Society* (2007) 411; M. Coppedge, 'Thickening Thin Concepts and Theories: Combining Large-N and Small-N in Comparative Politics' 31 *Comparative Politics* (1999) 465.

3 See Chapter 1.

4 Including J. Herman, *Local Voices in Internationalised Justice: The Experience of Civil Parties at the Extraordinary Chambers in the Courts of Cambodia* (Centre on Human Rights in Conflict, University of East London, May 2014); E. Hoven, M. Feiler and S. Scheibel, 'Victims in Trials of Mass Crimes: A Multi-Perspective Study of Civil Party Participation at the Extraordinary Chambers in the Courts of Cambodia' 3 *Cologne Occasional Papers on International Peace and Security Law* (2013); P. Pham et al., *After the First Trial: A Population-Based Survey on Knowledge and Perception of Justice and the Extraordinary Chambers in the Courts of Cambodia* (Human Rights Center, Berkeley, 2011); N. Stammel et al., *The Survivors' Voices: Attitudes on the ECCC, the Former Khmer Rouge and Civil Party Participation* (Berlin Center for the Treatment of Torture Victims, December 2010); P. Pham et al., *So We Will Never Forget: A Population-Based Survey on Attitudes About Social Reconstruction and the Extraordinary Chambers in the Courts of Cambodia* (Human Rights Center, Berkeley, 2009).

5 N. Palmer, *Courts in Conflict* (Oxford University Press, 2015).

6 R. Rhodes and M. Bevir, 'Defending Interpretation' 5 *European Political Science* (2006) 69. See also H. Rombouts, 'Importance and Difficulties of Victim-Based Research in Post-Conflict Societies' 10 *European Journal of Crime, Criminal Law and Criminal Justice* (2002) 216.

7 K. McEvoy and L. McGregor (eds.), *Transitional Justice from Below: Grassroots Activism and the Struggle for Change* (Hart Publishing, 2007).
8 Palmer, n.5 at 16.
9 J. Thibaut and L. Walker, *Procedural Justice: A Psychological Analysis* (Erlbaum, 1975).
10 T. Tyler, 'Procedural Justice, Legitimacy, and the Effective Rule of Law' 30 *Crime and Justice* (2003) 283.
11 T. Tyler, 'Social justice: Outcome and Procedure' 35(2) *International Journal of Psychology* (2000) 117; K. Leung and E.A. Lind, 'Procedural Justice and Culture: Effects of Culture, Gender, and Investigator Status on Procedural Preferences' 50(6) *Journal of Personality and Social Psychology* (1986) 1134; G. Leventhal, 'What Should be Done with Equity Theory' in K.J. Gergen et al. (eds.), *Social Exchange: Advances in Theory and Research* (Plenum, 1980); G. Leventhal, J. Karuza and W. Fry, 'Beyond Fairness: a Theory of Allocation Preferences' in G. Miluka (ed.), *Justice and Social Interaction* (Springer-Verlag, 1980) 167–218.
12 Tyler, n.10; Leventhal, n.11; J. Shapland, 'Victims, the Criminal Justice System and Compensation' 24(2) *British Journal of Criminology* (1984) 136 at 136–137.
13 Tyler, n.10; J. Wemmers, *Victims in the Criminal Justice System* (Kugler Publications, 1996); L. Musante, M.A. Gilbert and J. Thibaut, 'The Effects of Control on Perceived Fairness of Procedure and Outcome' 19 *Journal of Experimental Social Psychology* (1983) 223.
14 L. Moffett, *Justice for Victims at the International Criminal Court* (Routledge, 2014) 35; E. Kiza, C. Rathgeber and H. Rohne, *Victims of War: An Empirical Study on War Victimization and Victims' Attitudes towards Addressing Atrocities* (Hamburger Edition, 2006).
15 D. Beetham, *The Legitimation of Power*, P. Jones and A. Weale (eds.) (MacMillan, 1991).
16 J. Doak, 'Enriching Trial Justice for Crime Victims in Common Law Systems: Lessons from Transitional Environments' 21(2) *International Review of Victimology* (2015) 139.
17 H. Pitkin, 'Obligation and Consent – II' 60(1) *American Political Science Review* (1996) 39.
18 A. Liebling (assisted by H. Arnold), *Prisons and their Moral Performance* (Oxford University Press, 2004) 454–492.
19 D. Bodansky, 'The Legitimacy of International Governance: A Coming Challenge for International Environmental Law?' 93(3) *The American Journal of International Law* (1999) 596 at 601.
20 Beetham, n.15 at 15–16. See also Palmer, n.5 at 159.
21 S. Ford, 'A Social Psychology Model of the Perceived Legitimacy of International Criminal Courts: Implications for the Success of Transitional Justice Mechanisms' 45 *Vanderbilt Journal Transnational Law* (2012) 405; J. Ramji-Nogales, 'Designing Bespoke Transitional Justice: A Pluralist Process Approach' 32(1) *Michigan Journal of International Law* (2010) 1; J.E. Stromseth, 'Pursuing Accountability for Atrocities after Conflict: What Impact on Building the Rule of Law?' 38 *Georgetown Journal of International Law* (2007) 251.
22 See Chapter 6.
23 U. Orth, 'Secondary Victimization of Crime Victims by Criminal Proceedings' 15(4) *Social Justice Research* (2002) 313.
24 Y. Huo and T. Tyler, *Trust in the Law: Encouraging Public Cooperation with the Police and Courts* (Russell-Sage Foundation, 2002); Thibaut and Walker, n.9.
25 Orth, n.23.
26 E.A. Lind et al., 'Procedure and Outcome Effects on Reactions to Adjudicated Resolution of Conflicts of Interests' 39 *Journal of Personality and Social Psychology*

(1980) 643; S. LaTour, 'Determinants of Participant and Observer Satisfaction with Adversary and Inquisitorial Modes of Adjudication' 36(12) *Journal of Personality and Social Psychology* (1978) 1531.

27 E.A. Lind and K. Van den Bos, 'When Fairness Works: Toward a General Theory of Uncertainty Management' 24 *Research in Organisation Behavior* (2002) 181.

28 T. Tyler and S.L. Blader, 'The Group Engagement Model: Procedural Justice, Social Identity, and Cooperative Behaviour' 7(4) *Personality and Social Psychology Review* (2003) 349.

29 M. Osiel, *Mass Atrocity, Collective Memory and the Law* (New Brunswick, 1997) 225–226.

30 D. Taylor, 'Victim Participation in Transitional Justice Mechanisms: Real Power or Empty Ritual' *Impunity Watch Discussion Paper* (2014); Y. Danieli, 'Massive Trauma and the Healing Role of Reparative Justice' in C. Ferstman, M. Goetz and A. Stephens (eds.), *Reparations for Victims of Genocide, Crimes Against Humanity and War Crimes: Systems in Place and Systems in the Making* (Martinus Nijhoff, 2009); J. Wemmers, 'Victims and the International Criminal Court: Evaluating the Success of the ICC with Respect to Victims' 16 *International Review of Victimology* (2009) 221.

31 Moffett, n.14.

32 Ibid., at 32.

33 Case 001, Testimony given by expert witness Dr. Chhim Sotheara, a psychologist working with the Transcultural Psychosocial Organisation, Trial Transcript, 25 August 2009, at 8–10; M Witzel, *Understanding Trauma in Cambodia* (Centre for Social Development, 2007).

34 C. Kunst, *The Protection of Victims and Witnesses at International and Internationalized Criminal Courts – The Example of the ECCC* (Wolf Legal Publishers, 2013) 39–40.

35 One civil party in Case 001 informed the TC in July 2009 that she could not attend as she was 'too traumatized' to testify; see KRT Trial Monitor, 'Report No. 12: Week Ending July 9, 2009' *Monitoring Program of the War Crimes Studies Center* (UC Berkeley, July 2009) 6.

36 Kiza, Rathgeber and Rohne, n.14.

37 M. Klinkner and H. Davis, 'A Right to Truth: Victims and the International Criminal Court' 3 *Torture – Asian and Global Perspectives, Asian Human Rights Commission* (2014) 55.

38 Doak, n.16 at 144.

39 K. McEvoy and L. Mallinder, 'Amnesties in Transition: Punishment, Restoration, and the Governance of Mercy' 39(3) *Journal of Law and Society* (2012) 410.

40 Doak, n.16.

41 S. Kutnjak Ivković and J. Hagan, *Reclaiming Justice: The International Tribunal for the Former Yugoslavia and Local Courts* (Oxford University Press, 2011); A. Carcano, 'Sentencing and the Gravity of the Offence in International Criminal Law' 51(3) *The International and Comparative Law Quarterly* (2002) 583.

42 Moffett, n.14 at 151; L. Zegveld, 'Victims' Reparations Claims and International Criminal Courts: Incompatible Values?' 8 *Journal of International Criminal Justice* (2010) 79.

43 Danieli, n.30; Moffett, n.14; Wemmers, n.30 at 221; B. McGonigle Leyh, *Procedural Justice? Victim Participation in International Criminal Proceedings* (Intersentia, 2011); J. Wemmers, 'Victims' Need for Justice: Individual versus Collective Justice' in R. Letschert et al. (eds.), *Victimological Approaches to International Crimes: Africa* (Intersentia, 2011) 145–153.

44 Wemmers, n.30 and ibid. See also M. Pena and G. Carayon, 'Is the ICC making the Most of Victim Participation?' 7(3) *International Journal of Transitional Justice* (2013) 518 at 534.

45 Exceptions include Kutnjak Ivković and Hagan, n.41 at 138; E. Stover, M. Balthazard and K.A. Koenig, 'Confronting Duch: Civil Party Participation in Case 001 at the ECCC' 93(882) *International Review of the Red Cross* (2011); S. Cody, 'Procedural Justice, Legitimacy and Victim Participation in Uganda' in N. Hayashi, C. Bailliet and J. Nicholson, *The Legitimacy of International Criminal Tribunals* (Cambridge University Press, 2017) 376–398.
46 E.A. Lind and T.R. Tyler, *The Social Psychology of Procedural Justice* (Springer, 1988) 97.
47 B. Sheppard, 'Justice is no Simple Matter: Case for Elaborating our Model of Procedural Fairness' 49(4) *Journal of Personality and Social Psychology* (1985) 953.
48 Shapland, n.12.
49 T. Tyler, 'What is Procedural Justice?: Criteria Used by Citizens to Assess the Fairness of Legal Procedures' 22(1) *Law and Society Review* (1988); Leventhal, n.11.
50 T. Tyler, 'Procedural Justice and the Courts' 44 *Court Review* (2008) 26.
51 Wemmers, n.30.
52 Moffett, n.14 at 31.
53 Kutnjak Ivkovićh and Hagan, n.41.
54 Interview with CP1, 19 December 2013.
55 Interview with CP 9, 20 December 2013.
56 Interview with CP 10, 20 December 2013.
57 Interview with Lawyer 2 (CP Team), 26 September 2015.
58 Stover, Balthazard and Koenig, n.45 at 31; N. Kirchenbauer et al., 'Victims Participation before the Extraordinary Chambers in the Courts of Cambodia', *Baseline Study of the Cambodian Human Rights and Development Association's Civil Party Scheme for Case 002* (2013) 32; Herman, n.2. at 3.
59 Tyler, n.11 at 117.
60 R. Hodžić, 'Living the Legacy of Mass Atrocities: Victims' Perspectives on War Crimes Trials' 8(1) *Journal of International Criminal Justice* (2010) 113; A. Des Forges and T. Longman, 'Legal Response to Genocide in Rwanda' in H. Weinstein and E. Stover (eds.), *My Neighbor, My Enemy: Justice and Social Reconstruction in Rwanda and the Former Yugoslavia* (Cambridge University Press, 2004) 49–68; J. Kamatali, 'From the ICTR to ICC: Learning from the ICTR Experience in Bringing Justice to Rwandans' 12 *New England Journal of International and Comparative Law* (2005) 89.
61 Respondents in Pham et al., *So We Will Never Forget*, n.2 expressed distrust for judges and courts in general.
62 Report of the Special Representative of the Secretary-General for Human Rights in Cambodia, Yash Ghai, E/CN.4/2006/110, 24 January 2006.
63 'How Can We Have Peace?' War Survivors and Human Rights Defenders from Northern Sri Lanka in collaboration with Sri Lanka Campaign for Peace and Justice, March 2015, www.srilankacampaign.org/ (accessed 22/02/18).
64 Kutnjak Ivković and Hagan, n.41 at 50.
65 Interview with CP10, 19 December 2013.
66 S. Ear, 'The Political Economy of Aid and Governance in Cambodia' 15(1) *Asian Journal of Political Science* (2007) 68 at 75.
67 For example Destination Justice; UNOHCHR; American Bar Association; US Aid.
68 K. McEvoy and K. McConnachie, 'Victims and Transitional Justice: Voice, Agency and Blame' 22 *Social and Legal Studies* (2013) 489; McEvoy, n.2.
69 Ibid.
70 Although see T. Hresko, 'Restoration and Relief: Procedural Justice and the September 11th Victim Compensation Fund' 42(1) *Gonzaga Law Review* (2006–2007) 95.
71 Ibid., at 107.

72 A. Whiting 'In International Criminal Prosecutions, Justice Delayed Can Be Justice Delivered' 50(2) *Harvard International Law Journal* (2009) 323.
73 S. Darehshori, 'Weighing the Evidence: Lessons from the Slobodan Milošević Trial' *Human Rights Watch*, Volume 18, No. 10(D) (December 2006).
74 R. Zacklin, 'The Failings of Ad Hoc Tribunals' 2 *Journal of International Criminal Justice* (2004) 541 at 544.
75 Whiting, n.72 at 326.
76 E. Husketh, 'Pole Pole: Hastening Justice at UNICTR' 3(1) *Northwestern Journal of International Human Rights* (2005); A. Cassese, 'Is the ICC Still Having Teething Problems?' 4 *Journal of International Criminal Justice* (2006) 434; M.B. Harmon, 'The Pre-Trial Process at the ICTY as a Means of Ensuring Expeditious Trials' 5 *Journal of International Criminal Justice* (2007) 377.
77 R.E. Rauxloh, 'Plea Bargaining in International Criminal Justice: Can the international Criminal Court Afford to Avoid Trials' 1(2) *Journal of criminal Justice Research* (2011) 1; L. Burens, 'Plea Bargaining in International Criminal Tribunals: The End of Truth-Seeking in International Courts?' *Zeitschrift für Internationale Strafrechtsdogmatik* (2013).
78 S.M. Pritchett, 'Entrenched Hegemony, Efficient Procedure, or Selective Justice?: An Inquiry into Charges for Gender-Based Violence at the International Criminal Court' 17 *Transnational Law and Contemporary Problems* (2008) 265.
79 Burens, n.77.
80 This was the case during both stages of the interviews, despite the fact that a judgement had been issued in the interim, which is discussed in greater detail later.
81 Interview with CP27, 30 October 2014. This feeling has been expressed publicly by civil parties, through the organisation of a press conference in 2013. 'Civil Party Representatives Voices Regarding the Current State of Affairs at the ECCC' *ADHOC Press Release*, 25 March 2013.
82 Interview with CP1, 18 December 2013.
83 Interview with CP2, 18 December 2013.
84 Mentioned by 15 out of the 27 interviewed.
85 Interview with Lawyer 1 (CP Team), 11 November 2013.
86 Interview with VSS Staff 1, 27 November 2013.
87 *So We Will Never Forget*, n.2; Herman, n.2 at 4.
88 Interview with Lawyer 3 (Defence), 29 October 2014.
89 Ibid.
90 Interview with Judge 2, 11 November 2013.
91 S. Robins, 'Transitional Justice as an Elite Discourse' 44(1) *Critical Asian Studies* (2012) 3.
92 Ibid.
93 Palmer, n.5 at 172–177.
94 Ibid., at 171.
95 Liebling, n.18 at 472–473.
96 Ibid.
97 Interview with Lawyer 1 (CP Team), 11 November 2013.
98 R. Henham, 'Procedural Justice and Human Rights in International Sentencing' 4 *International Criminal Law Review* (2004) 185 at 186.
99 Tyler, n.10 at 283; Lind and Tyler, n.46 at 111; T.R. Tyler, *Why People Obey the Law: Procedural Justice, Legitimacy, and Compliance* (Yale University Press, 1990).
100 Liebling, n.18 at 473.
101 McGonigle Leyh, n.43 at 47–48; Wemmers, n.13; Shapland, n.12 136–137.
102 L. Moffett, 'Meaningful and Effective? Considering Victims' Interests through Participation at the International Criminal Court' 26 *Criminal Law Forum* (2015) 255; C. Hoyle and L. Ullrich, 'New Court, New Justice? The Evolution

of "Justice for Victims' at Domestic Courts and at the International Criminal Court' 12 *Journal of International Criminal Justice* (2014) 681; McGonigle Leyh, n.43 at 47–48; Wemmers, n.30; Danieli, n.30.

103 Y. Danieli, 'Victims: Essential Voices at the Court' *Victims' Rights Working Group Bulletin,* Issue 1, September 2004 at 1.

104 J. Alvarez, 'Rush to Closure: Lessons of the Tadić Judgment' 96 *Michigan Law Review* (1998) 2036 at 2038.

105 J. Doak, 'The Therapeutic Dimension of Transitional Justice: Emotional Repair and Victim Satisfaction in International Trials and Truth Commissions' 11 *International Criminal Law Review* (2011) 263 at 271.

106 Hoyle and Ullrich, n.102 at 686.

107 H. Reeves and P. Dunn, 'The Status of Crime Victims and Witnesses in the Twenty-First Century' in A. Bottoms and J. Roberts (eds.), *Hearing the Victim: Adversarial Justice, Crime Victims and the State* (Routledge, 2012) 46–71; P. Tobolowsky, 'Victim Participation in the Criminal Justice Process: Fifteen Years After the President's Task Force on Victims of Crime' 25 *New England Journal on Criminal and Civil Confinement* (1999) 21; A. Ashworth, 'Victim Impact Statements and Sentencing' *Criminal Law Review* (1993) 498.

108 Twenty-two of the 27 specifically mentioned seeking justice for their family.

109 D. Laub, 'An Event Without a Witness: Truth, Testimony and Survival' in S. Felman and D. Laub (eds.), *Testimony: Crisis of Witnessing in Literature, Psychoanalysis, and History* (Routledge, 1992) 75–93.

110 Herman, n.2 at 4–5; Hoven, Feiler and Scheibel, n.2; Stover, Balthazard and Koenig, n.45.

111 Stover, Balthazard and Koenig, ibid., at 36.

112 Interview with CP16, 29 October 2014. Speaking on behalf of herself and the four other women in the room.

113 Interview with CP11, 20 December 2013.

114 Interview with VSS Staff 2, 13 January 2014.

115 Interview with CP15, 20 December 2013; Interview with CP 1–4, 5 and 6, 19 December 2013. This wish amongst civil parties was also reported by VSS Staff 1, 27 November 2013 and TPO Staff 1, 26 November 2013.

116 Interview with CPs 7 and 8, 19 December 2013; Interview with CP11, 20 December 2013 and 15, 20 December 2013.

117 Robins, n.92.

118 Interview with Lawyer (CP Team), 11 November 2013.

119 Interview with VSS Staff 1, 27 November 2013.

120 Interview with Lawyer (Former CP Team member), 11 September 2015.

121 Interview with CP9, 19 December 2013.

122 Interview with CP 22, 27 October 2014.

123 Interview with CP13, 20 December 2013.

124 Interview with Lawyer 1 (CP Team), 11 November 2013.

125 Interview with Lawyer 1 (CP Team), 11 November 2013.

126 Interview with TPO Staff 2, 26 November 2013.

127 Interview with TPO Staff 1, 26 November 2013.

128 For example Case 001 civil party Chum Mey spoke of feeling happiness and relief, see Trial Transcript, 30 June 2009 at 67; Case 001 civil party Bou Meng also spoke of feeling lighter and better, Trial Transcript, 1 July 2009 at 85. See also Herman, n.2 at 6.

129 J.D. Ciorciari and A. Heindel, 'Victim Testimony in International and Hybrid Criminal Courts: Narrative Opportunities, Challenges and Fair Trial Demands' 56(2) *Virginia Journal of International Law* (2016).

130 A. Bates, *Transitional Justice in Cambodia: Analytical Report* (Atlas Project, October 2010) 66; R. Jeffery, 'The Forgiveness Dilemma: Emotions and Justice

at the Khmer Rouge Tribunal' 69(1) *Australian Journal of International Affairs* (2015) 35.

131 J.C. Karremans and P. Van Lange, 'Does Activating Justice Help or Hurt in Promoting Forgiveness?' 41 *Journal of Experimental Social Psychology* (2005) 290.

132 T. Van Camp and V. De Mesmaecker 'Procedural Justice for Victims of Crime: Are Victim Impact Statements and Victim-Offender Mediation Rising to the Challenge?' in I. Vanfraechem, A. Pemberton and F.M. Ndahinda (eds.), *Justice for Victims: Perspective on Rights, Transition and Reconciliation* (Routledge, 2014) 277–300. See also S.J. Szmania and M.L. Gracyalny, 'Addressing the Court, the Offender and the Community: A Communication Analysis of Victim Impact Statements in a Non-Capital Sentencing Hearing' 13(3) *International Review of Victimology* (2006) 231; J. Roberts and M. Manikis, *Victim Personal Statements at Sentencing: A Review of the Empirical Research* (Office of the Commissioner for Victims and Witnesses of England and Wales, 2011).

133 See for example Case 001, Trial Transcript, 19 August 2009 at 86; Ciorciari and Heindel, n.129 at 11–12.

134 Van Camp and De Mesmaecker, n.132 at 289; J. Shapland, G. Robinson and A. Sorsby, *Restorative Justice in Practice* (Routledge, 2011).

135 Ibid.

136 L.W. Sherman and H. Strang, *Restorative Justice: The Evidence* (Smith Institute, 2007).

137 Interview with CP13, 20 December 2013.

138 Stover, Balthazard and Koenig, n.45.

139 Ibid.

140 Interview with CP5, 18 December 2014.

141 Interview with CP7 and 8, 19 December 2014.

142 M.S. Groenhuijsen and A. Pemberton, 'Genocide, Crimes against Humanity and War Crimes: A Victimological Perspective on International Criminal Justice' in R. Letschert et al. (eds.), *Victimological Approaches to International Crimes: Africa* (Intersentia, 2011) 9–34.

143 J. Shapland, J. Willmore and P. Duff, *Victims in the Criminal Justice System* (Gower, 1985) 2.

144 Tyler, n.11 at 117; Leung and Lind, n.11; Lind and Tyler, n.46; Leventhal, Karuza and Fry, n.11.

145 D. Chandler, B. Kiernan, and C. Boua (eds.), *Pol Pot Plans the Future: Confidential Leadership Documents from Democratic Kampuchea, 1976–1977* (Yale University Southeast Asian Studies Monograph Series 33, 1988).

146 Stover, Balthazard and Koenig, n.45 at 15.

147 A. Kurze, C. Lamont and S. Robins, 'Contested Spaces of Transitional Justice: Legal Empowerment in Global Post-Conflict Contexts Revisited' 19(3) *The International Journal of Human Rights* (2015) 260; Robins, n.92.

148 T. Jacobsen and M. Stuart-Fox 'Power and Political Culture in Cambodia' 200 *Asia Research Institute Working Paper Series* (2013); J. Ledgerwood, 'Understanding Cambodia: Social Hierarchy and Patron-Client Relationships' *Cambodian Recent History and Contemporary: An Introductory Course*, Department of Anthropology and Center for Southeast Asian Studies, Northern Illinois University, 2002, www.seasite.niu.edu/khmer/ledgerwood/patrons.htm (accessed 22/02/18).

149 Interview with CP14, 20 December 2013.

150 This is not a uniformly held view within civil parties; see for example M. Mohan, 'The Paradox of Victim-Centrism: Victim Participation at the Khmer Rouge Tribunal' 9 *International Criminal Law Review* (2009) 733 for a discussion on civil party Theary Seng's wish for greater participation.

151 McEvoy and McConnachie, n.68 at 499.
152 L. Alcoff, 'The Problem of Speaking for Others' 20 *Cultural Critique* (1991–1992) 24.
153 Interview with Lawyer (Former CP Team member), 11 September 2015.
154 Interview with VSS Staff 1, 27 November 2013.
155 For the associations between procedural justice and victim empowerment see K. Cyr and J. Wemmers, 'Empowerment des victimes d'actes criminels' 44(2) *Criminologie* (2011) 125.
156 G. Soros, 'Legal Empowerment, Justice and Development' in *Case Studies in Legal Empowerment: From Land Rights to Healthcare* (Open Society Institute, 2013).
157 Kurze, Lamont and Robins, n.147; P. Lundy and M. McGovern, 'Whose Justice? Rethinking Transitional Justice from the Bottom Up' 35(2) *Journal of Law and Society* (2008) 265.
158 N. Roht-Arriaza (ed.), *Impunity and Human Rights in International Law and Practice* (Oxford University Press, 1995).
159 M. Balthazard, *Gender-Based Violence during The Khmer Rouge: A Forgotten Issue? Cambodian Defenders Project Gender-Based Violence Project, 2010–2012 Evaluation Report* (CDP, 2013).
160 M. Balthazard, *Khmer Rouge Tribunal Justice Project Evaluation Report, 2010–2012* (ADHOC, 2013).
161 Interview with Lawyer 2 (LCL Office), 21 November 2013.
162 Interview with Lawyer (Former CP Team member), 11 September 2015.
163 Interview with Lawyer 2 (LCL Office), 21 November 2013.
164 Ninety per cent of Cambodia's poor live in rural areas; see Asian Development Bank, *Cambodia: Country Poverty Analysis*, December 2014.
165 Kurze, Lamont and Robins, n.147.
166 Interview with Lawyer (Former CP Team member), 11 September 2015.
167 See Chapter 2.
168 M. Saliba, 'Civil Parties Boycott Start of Character Witness Testimony While Experts Offer Psychological Assessment of Duch' *Cambodia Tribunal Monitor*, 31 August 2009.
169 Balthazard, n.160.
170 K. Naren and H. Robertson, 'Victims Call for Money from ECCC' *The Cambodia Daily*, 17 October 2014; J. Herman, 'Uncooked Rice: Justice and Victimhood at the Extraordinary Chambers in the Courts of Cambodia and Beyond' in V. Druliolle and R. Brett (eds.), *The Politics of Victimhood in Post-Conflict Societies* (Palgrave MacMillan, 2018) 187–209.
171 Palmer, n.5.
172 McEvoy and McConnachie, n.68.
173 S. Kendall and S. Nouwen, 'Representational Practices at the International Criminal Court: The Gap between Juridified and Abstract Victimhood' 76 *Law and Contemporary Problems* (2013) 235.
174 Stammel et al., n.2 at 44.
175 Kirchenbauer et al., n.58 at 21.
176 Interview with CP10, 19 December 2013.
177 Interview with Lawyer (Former CP Team member), 11 September 2015.
178 Hoven, Feiler and Scheibel, n.2 at 72.
179 Groenhuijsen and Pemberton, n.142.
180 Van Camp and V. De Mesmaecker, n.132 at 278; Shapland, n.12 at 132–135; J. Goodey, *Victims and Victimology: Research, Policy and Practice* (Pearson Education Limited, 2005); H. Strang, *Repair or Revenge: Victims and Restorative Justice* (Oxford University Press, 2002).

181 Wemmers, n.13 at 126. This finding has been confirmed in subsequent studies, for an overview see J. Wemmers, 'Victims' Rights and the International Criminal Court: Perceptions within the Court Regarding the Victims' Right to Participate' 23 *Leiden Journal of International Law* (2010) 629.
182 Cyr and Wemmers, n.155.
183 M. Guiraud, *Victims' Rights before the Extraordinary Chambers in the Courts of Cambodia (ECCC): A Mixed Record for Civil Parties* (FIDH, November 2012); J. Herman, 'Realities of Victim Participation: The Civil Party System in Practice at the Extraordinary Chambers in the Courts of Cambodia (ECCC)' 16(4) *Contemporary Justice Review: Issues in Criminal, Social, and Restorative Justice* (2013) 461 at 474, citing interviews with international and national NGOs'.
184 Hoven, Feiler and Scheibel, n.2; Herman, n.2 at 7; Kirchenbauer et al. n.58; Stammel et al., n.2; Stover, Balthazard and Koenig, n.45.
185 Interview with CP9, 19 December 2013.
186 'Do you know there was a judgment in August?'; 'We didn't know and every time they call, and have a meeting and we come to join, it seemed like everyone don't know about this'. Interview with CPs 16–21, 24 October 2014.
187 Interview with CP13, 20 December 2013.
188 Interview with Lawyer (Former CP Team member), 11 September 2015.
189 Tyler, n.10; Wemmers, n.13; Shapland, n.12; Musante, Gilbert and Thibaut, n.13.
190 L. Walker, E.A. Lind and J. Thibaut, 'The Relation between Procedural and Distributive Justice' 65(8) *Virginia Law Review* (1979) 1401.
191 Ibid.
192 Orth, n.23 at 314.
193 Ibid., at 215.
194 K. Van den Bos and E.A. Lind, 'Uncertainty Management by Means of Fairness Judgments' 32 *Advances in Experimental Social Psychology* (2002) 1.
195 Lind and Tyler, n.46; LaTour, n.26.
196 J.D. Ciorciari and A. Heindel, *Hybrid Justice: The Extraordinary Chambers in the Courts of Cambodia* (University of Michigan Press, 2014).
197 Wemmers, n.43.
198 *Universal Declaration of Human Rights*, UNGA Res. 217 A (III), 10 December 1948, Article 8; Council of Europe, *European Convention for the Protection of Human Rights and Fundamental Freedoms, as amended by Protocols Nos. 11 and 14*, ETS 5, 4 November 1950, Article 13; UNGA, *International Covenant on Civil and Political Rights*, UNGA Resolution 2200A (XXI), 16 December 1966, Article 2(3); Organization of American States, *American Convention on Human Rights*, 'Pact of San Jose', Costa Rica, 22 November 1969, Article 25.
199 Interview with CP27, 30 October 2014.
200 Expressed unanimously by CPs22–26, 29 October 2014.
201 Interview with CP11, 20 December 2013.
202 Interview with CP9, 19 December 2013.
203 Interview with CP16, 29 October 2014.
204 J.P. Bair, 'From the Numbers Who Died to Those Who Survived: Victim Participation in the Extraordinary Chambers in the Court of Cambodia' 31 *University of Hawaii Law Review* (2008–2009) 508 at 536. See also J. Simon and R. Sparks, *The SAGE Handbook of Punishment and Society* (SAGE, 2013); Mohan, n.150; Hoven, Feiler and Scheibel, n.2 at 26. Pham et al., *So We Will Never Forget*, n.2 found a similar focus on the punishment of perpetrators amongst the broader Cambodian society.
205 A. Cassese, 'Reflections on International Criminal Justice' 60 *Modern Law Review* (1998) 1.

206 D. Gromet and J. Darley, 'Restoration and Retribution: How Including Retributive Components Affects the Acceptability of Restorative Justice Procedures' 19(4) *Social Justice Research* (2006) 395; N. Vidmar, 'Retribution and Revenge' in J. Sanders and V.L. Hamilton (eds.), *Handbook of Justice Research in Law* (Kluwer, 2000).
207 H. Arendt, *The Origins of Totalitarianism* (Harcourt, 1973) 439.
208 M. Drumbl, *Atrocity, Punishment and International Law* (Cambridge University Press, 2007) 157.
209 McEvoy and Mallinder, n.39 at 421.
210 Ciorciari and Heindel, n.196.
211 McEvoy and Mallinder, n.39 at 420.
212 Moffett, n.14; Groenhuijsen and Pemberton, n.142.
213 Tyler, n.99 Lind et al., n.26; LaTour, n.26; Thibaut and Walker, n.9.
214 D. McCargo, 'Politics by Other Means? The Virtual Trials of the Khmer Rouge Tribunal' 87(3) *International Affairs* (2011).
215 Civil Parties Theary Seng and Chum Mey, quoted in G. De Launey, 'Tears and Disbelief at Duch Verdict' *BBC News*, 26 July 2010, www.bbc.co.uk/news/world-asia-pacific-10763409 (accessed 20/02/18).
216 Stover, Balthazard and Koenig, n.45 at 36–37.
217 Interview with Lawyer 1 (CP Team), 12 November 2013.
218 Stover, Balthazard and Koenig, n.45 at 37.
219 Orth, n.23.
220 Walker, Lind and Thibaut, n.190.
221 Stover, Balthazard and Koenig, n.45 at 41, noting the possibility that participation in Case 002 will be more 'formulaic'.
222 Interview with Lawyer (CP Team), 12 November 2013.
223 Herman, n.2.
224 Gromet and Darley, n.206.
225 Moffett, n.14 at 179.
226 J. Herman, 'Reaching for Justice: The Participation of Victims at the Extraordinary Chambers in the Courts of Cambodia' *Centre on Human Rights in Conflict Policy Paper No. 5*, September 2010.
227 Interview with CP16, 20 December 2013.
228 Interview with Lawyer (Former CP Team member), 11 September 2015.
229 Herman, n.2.
230 Hoven, Feiler and Scheibel, n.2; Stammel et al., n.2 at 35.
231 Mohan, n.150; Bair, n.204 at 537.
232 Bair, n.204.
233 See also L. Nguyen and C. Sperfeldt, *A Boat Without Anchors: A Report on the Legal Status of Ethnic Vietnamese Minority Populations in Cambodia under Domestic and International Laws Governing Nationality and Statelessness* (Jesuit Refugee Service, 2012).
234 Interview with CP 9, 20 December 2013. Note: Pagodas and stupas are Buddhist places of worship.
235 J. Holt, 'Caring for the Dead Ritually in Cambodia' 1(1) *Southeast Asian Studies* (2012) 3; I. Harris, *Cambodian Buddhism: History and Practice* (University of Hawai'i Press, 2005).
236 Interview with Lawyer (Former CP Team member), 11 September 2015.
237 Ibid.
238 Ibid.
239 N. Roht-Arriaza and K. Orlovsky, 'A Complementary Relationship: Reparations and Development' *International Centre for Transitional Justice: Research Brief* (July 2009).

240 F. Iliff, F. Maitre-Muhl and A. Sirel, 'Adverse Consequences of Reparations' *Briefing Paper No.6* (University of Essex Reparations Unit, August 2011).
241 R. Aldana-Pindell, 'In Vindication of Justiciable Victims' Rights to Truth and Justice for State Sponsored Crimes' 35(5) *Vanderbilt Journal of Transnational Law* (2002) 1399 at 1439.
242 Interview with CP9, 19 December 2013.
243 Interview with CP13, 20 December 2103.
244 Interview with CP1, 18 December 2013.
245 Interview with CP17, 29 October 2014.
246 Kirchenbauer et al. n.58 at 19.
247 Doak, n.16; Strang, n.180; C. Fercello and M. Umbreit, *Client Evaluation of Family Group Conferencing in 12 Sites in the First Judicial District of Minnesota* (Center for Restorative Justice and Mediation, 1998).
248 J.D. Ciorciari and J. Ramji-Nogales, 'Lessons from the Cambodian Experience with Truth and Reconciliation' 19 *Buffalo Human Rights Law Review* (2012–2013) 193.
249 Ibid.
250 R. Mani, 'Reparation as a Component of Transitional Justice: Pursuing "Reparative Justice" in the Aftermath of Violent Conflict' in K. De Feyter et al. (eds.) *Out of the Ashes: Reparation for Victims of Gross and Systemic Human Rights Violations* (Intersentia, 2005) 53–82; J. Doak, *Victims' Rights, Human Rights and Criminal Justice: Reconceiving the Role of Third Parties* (Hart Publishing, 2008) 118–119.
251 P. Pham et al., 'Victim Participation and the Trial of Duch at the Extraordinary Chambers in the Courts of Cambodia' 3(3) *Journal of Human Rights Practice* (2011) 264.
252 Interview with NGO Staff 1, 15 November 2013; Interview with TPO Staff 2, 26 November 2013.
253 Herman, n.2 at 3.
254 Ibid., at 8.
255 Interview with CP1, 18 December 2013.
256 Pham et al., So we will Never Forget, n.2; Stover, Balthazard and Koenig, n.45; Stammel et al., n.2.
257 Tyler, n.11.
258 Moffett, n.14.
259 Wemmers, n.30.
260 A. Maslow, *Towards a Psychology of Being* (2nd edn) (Van Nostrand Reinhold, 1968).
261 Robins, n.92.

9 Lessons learned from Cambodia

This book has critically examined the alleged rise of a more 'victim-orientated justice' within ICL, through an examination of the ECCC's civil party participation system. In doing so, it has pursued three goals. First, it has aimed to shed light on the way in which both the ECCC and the role of victims within it were shaped by specific political, economic and legal contexts. Second, it has provided an empirical contribution to the discussion surrounding the perceived 'gap' between the legitimising value of the abstract 'imagined victim' and the extent to which victims are able to further their interests within international criminal courts. Third, it has analysed the impact, if any, that victim participation has had on the ECCC's ability to deliver 'justice' and garner legitimacy in the eyes of civil parties. This final chapter offers some brief conclusions with regards to each of these.

Shaping victimhood

In relation to the first goal, and drawing in particular from critical victimological literature, this book has explored how in Cambodia, as in other contexts, terms such as *victim* and *victimisation* are contested and open to manipulation by heterogeneous actors pursuing a range of other political or legal goals. Many groups and individuals can claim the label of 'victim', but the key questions for a critical victimologist are who has the power to apply the label and what considerations are significant in that determination.[1] The political history of both Cambodia, in general, and its responses to atrocity, in particular, show that not all experiences of victimhood have been equally acknowledged. In the Cambodian context, it is both the international community and the RGC who apply the label of 'victim', insofar as they identify whose victimisations deserve attention through criminal accountability mechanisms. The considerations which are significant in determining victimhood may relate at least in part to the severity of the harm; there is no denying that DK constituted a period of Cambodia's history characterised by atrocity and deprivation. However, they may also relate to broader political motivations and the desire to limit the grounds for liability and accountability. The claim that international(ised) criminal courts are political tools is not one that is unique to the ECCC, recurring attacks on international criminal trials as political show trials are reproduced throughout international criminal courtrooms and within the international legal literature.[2] Yet the agendas of political elites have had real and significant implications for those most affected by mass atrocity: the victims themselves. Responses to victimisation in Cambodia have been shown to be deeply entrenched in specific political, legal and economic contexts. The result has been the exclusion of broader forms of truth recovery, a limitation on the court's jurisdiction which precludes consideration of a multitude of harms perpetrated within Cambodia, and a court structure which allows political agendas to create continued obstacles to accountability.

In a classic example of Christie's 'theft of the conflict',[3] responses to the Khmer Rouge's crimes have been shaped first by political elites, and then by criminal justice professionals. The ECCC has gone further than many international(ised) criminal trials in incorporating a role for victims within its proceedings, with one of the most significant developments in the court's ability to deliver justice to victims being the creation of the civil party participation system. This system is unique from victim participation mechanisms within other international(ised) criminal courts, in that its creation was not envisioned by those responsible for its creation. Rather, it has been created and subsequently amended by those actively engaged in the work of the court. As a result, legal practitioners, identified within the literature as having influenced the role of victims within criminal courts at both a domestic and international level, have had a significant role in shaping victim participation within the ECCC. The initial creation of the civil party system can be attributed to judicial activism. In Chapter 4, this decision was found to have been influenced by a variety of factors, ranging from the international growth in victims' rights and advocacy to the pressure applied by civil society actors to the domestic legal system within which the court operates to the particular agendas and legal cultures of the judges themselves. As a result, a unique system was created that attempted to balance a role for victims with the external realities within which the court operated, particularly the vast scale of victimisation, limited court funding and a government unlikely to allow the court to step on its toes. This system has been subsequently subjected to modification and restriction, demonstrating the continued influence of court practitioners over the procedural and substantive 'justice' offered to victims.

Court practitioners have not been the only professional actors to influence the delivery of justice to victims. Just as civil society played a crucial role in the development of victims' rights in domestic contexts, there is no doubt that the involvement of civil society has greatly enhanced the ability of victims to pursue procedural and substantive justice within the ECCC. This enhancement has resulted from civil society's cooperation with the court, through the provision of representation, information, reparations and non-judicial measures, as well as civil society's confrontations with the court, through the highlighting of 'elitist blind spots'.[4] Yet the involvement of civil society actors raises its own challenges, particularly in relation to the ability of donors to influence and direct projects, as well as broader ethical concerns about what Alcoff famously described as the 'problem of speaking for others'.[5] Indeed, arguably one price which has been paid for more structured engagement with civil society actors is that the voices of professionalised civil society are given precedence over those of the victim populations themselves. Such findings support Haslam's observation that international criminal institutions show a tendency to investigate and determine the interests of affected communities through 'experts'.[6] The risks that such prioritisation will overlook the needs and wishes of victims themselves arguably support McEvoy and McConnachie's submission that transitional justice should be done 'in a way that is aware of and informed by' the dynamics that exist between professional civil society and victim populations.[7] It should be noted, of course, that much of civil society's involvement would have been unnecessary had adequate provision been made within the ECCC's budget for its victim-orientated measures. Therefore, international(ised) criminal courts seeking to involve victims within their processes should ensure that they have the funds and resources to meaningfully engage with those populations, a point that will be returned to below.

In light of the analysis within this book, I argue that there is a need within ICL scholarship and practice to greater acknowledge the role of actors and contexts in shaping responses to victimisation. Such responses are sites of contestation, in which the agendas of different transitional justice practitioners and other elites often play a significant role in demarcating the extent to which the real needs of victim populations in the aftermath of atrocity are addressed by transitional justice mechanisms. This can lead to restrictions being placed on victims' access to substantive and procedural justice, for example through the limitations placed on the court's jurisdiction. However, it can also lead to innovative processes and an enhancement of that same access, for example through the creation of the civil party system and the work of civil society in expanding the court's investigations and prosecutions. Thus, contest is not to be avoided but acknowledged, an acknowledgement that may contribute to not only greater humility, as advocated by McEvoy,[8] but greater honesty in the discourse surrounding transitional justice. For courts wishing to 'prove their victim-centeredness',[9] there is a further need to ensure that victims themselves are able to express voice and contribute to such contests rather than allowing their wishes to be primarily expressed by intermediaries. This appears to have been lacking at the ECCC, an observation which also links to the second and third conclusions of this thesis.

The imagined victim

The second aim of this book was to provide an empirical contribution to the literature surrounding the 'gap' between the 'imagined victim' and the 'actual victims' of international crimes. This 'gap' has been theorised through the work of Fletcher, Nouwen and Kendall and others,[10] who have argued that while the 'imagined victim' constitutes a valuable legitimising tool, 'actual victims' continue to have their ability to exercise rights within the court restricted. The 'imagined victim' as a legitimising tool has been demonstrated as present throughout the court's inception and work, from the language utilised by the Group of Experts in their initial report to that used by the court practitioners themselves.

Just as international criminal institutions are at least, in part, premised on, and draw legitimacy from, pursuing justice for victims, it appears practitioners, within the ECCC at least, utilise 'justice for victims' rhetoric in their self-legitimising practices. The 'imagined victim' appears in the language of legal practitioners as a beneficiary of justice, as a constituent of the court and as a symbol of personal and collective suffering. Delivering 'justice to victims' was identified by practitioners as a key goal of both the ECCC and the ICL more generally, as well as a personal motivator.

In practice, there has been a normative progression from the Nuremberg trials and the desire to keep victims out of the courtroom.[11] Practitioners spoke with approval of hearing civil parties' testimonies and questions to the accused, suggesting support for a role for victims beyond that of 'passive objects'.[12] However, while a number of civil parties have been given opportunities to exercise voice by directly addressing the court, it appears that there remains a desire to see this voice amplified, directed or indeed in some instances silenced to suit the other goals of the trial. This has been evident for example in the TC president's requests that civil parties curtail their testimony, and in the negative responses to civil parties who attempted to communicate more directly with the court. These examples suggest a preference for a more 'sanitized and innocuous'[13] form of participation, with the result that victims have had their ability to address the court directly restricted. Thus, while victims are a welcome 'human face',[14] there appears to be a continued preference for the primacy of the lawyer within the courtroom, with the victims' voice limited to allow for the furthering of the other goals of the institution.[15] This has also been reflected in the resistance to the originally expansive rights given to the civil parties' legal representatives, and subsequent curtailments of those rights. The introduction of the LCLs has constituted the most dramatic restriction: civil parties no longer exercise the right of attorney over their courtroom representatives. While this resistance seems to have at least, in part, been a reaction to the logistical and court management challenges associated with having increased numbers of legal representatives within the courtroom, it has inevitably had an impact on the ability of victims to have their interests accurately represented.

It therefore appears that while the 'imagined victim' and the notion of delivering 'justice to victims' has a significant role within the legitimising practices of the court, the actual victims of the Khmer Rouge are frequently denied ownership over the process. Thus, the theoretical 'gap' between the 'imagined victim' and the actual victims of atrocity finds support within the data collected for this study. The 'victim' in the context of the ECCC continues to be as Clarke has previously described: 'both central and marginal to the process'.[16] Indeed, by exploring this dichotomy within the attitudes of practitioners, I would argue that ICL practitioners' understandings with regards to who may claim 'ownership' of ICL trials may constitute a practical barrier to an enhancement of the rights of victims within international(ised) criminal courts. This is reflective of tendencies noted within the literature; practitioners working within domestic jurisdictions (both civil and common),[17] and within international(ised) criminal courts have demonstrated a continued belief that the provision of justice is the work of professional elites,[18] as well as an ability to oppose the introduction of measures that infringe upon their interests. While Chapters 2 and 3 also illustrated a rise in victim-centric theories of justice, particularly within the context of ICL, implementation remains greatly dependent on the attitudes of professionals. Furthermore, as noted in Chapter 6, ICL practitioners are granted an influence that would not often be found within domestic jurisdictions, potentially enhancing their ability to shape the role of victims within current and future international(ised) criminal courts.[19] This has been particularly evident in the case of the ECCC, where the fluid nature of the judge-made Internal Rules has facilitated the significant restriction of civil parties' rights. Thus, while transitional justice discourse may be increasingly victim-focused, the sustained belief amongst practitioners that justice processes are the domain of legal elites may see victims continue to be instrumentalised within those processes.

Civil party perceptions of justice and legitimacy

The third goal of the book has been to assess the impact, if any, that victim participation has had on the ECCC's ability to deliver 'justice' and garner legitimacy in the eyes of civil parties. While acknowledging that there is an inherent gap between 'law in books and law in action',[20] I have utilised procedural and substantive justice theories to assess the influence of different actors and contexts on the ECCC's ability to respond to the needs and interests of victims and have tested the argument that the perceived legitimacy of a court in the eyes of the victim population can be enhanced through the deliverance of procedural justice,[21] even when outcomes are unfavourable.[22] I also considered the overall assessments made about the ECCC by those civil parties engaged in its work, finding that despite the limitations of the civil party system, aspects of it are viewed with satisfaction by those who have participated. Drawing on domestic procedural justice theories, civil parties were asked about their perceptions as to the 'quality of decision making'[23] and 'quality of interpersonal treatment' at the ECCC.[24] Certain aspects of both were identified as important to the civil parties. The ability to express themselves and to address the accused was valued, demonstrating that some forms of participation gained support from victims and court practitioners alike. The civil parties spoke with approval of having access to legal representatives, although satisfaction with those representatives has been shown to vary amongst civil parties. Certain aspects of the court's work were viewed with significantly less satisfaction. Issues such as the time the court took to deliver a judgement in Case 002, the inability of the court to deliver individual reparations, and the lack of information provided to civil parties, arose as particularly important to the civil parties interviewed.

The civil parties' opinions suggested that elements of procedural justice theory can find traction in an international criminal context, such as Orth's argument that procedural justice will impact on overall judgements about an institution's legitimacy,[25] and Tyler's argument that cultural and social context will influence the specific procedural justice elements that are sought out by victim participants.[26] Yet, it seems that some of the underlying assumptions of procedural justice may require revisions in the international criminal context. For example, it appeared that fair procedures were unlikely to have the same 'cushioning' effect as has been observed within domestic contexts[27] and that substantive justice was of significantly greater importance to many of the civil parties than fair procedures. However, I would argue that the value of procedural justice is also largely dependent on meaningful engagement with participants, which, as explored within this book, has not always transpired within the ECCC.

One of the interesting results of civil party participation has been the empowerment of those who have participated. Although life for many civil parties has been characterised by poverty, a lack of education and, in many cases, ongoing discrimination and hardship, it seems that engagement with their legal representatives and the ECCC's processes has, in some cases, led to an increased sense of empowerment and agency. Indeed, a number of civil parties have shown themselves to be increasingly able to exercise voice and agency, and to challenge the aspects of the court's work that they consider unsatisfactory. While only limited evidence of this was observed, such findings contribute some limited support for the arguments of advocates of victim participation, such as Doak, who posit that participation can lead to a 'sense of empowerment and control'.[28] Victims are not the only constituent of the court, and their wishes cannot be catered to in every instance without sacrificing the court's ability to pursue fair trials and due process, yet dialogue between the court and civil parties could do much to enhance the impact of procedural justice on the perceived legitimacy of the ECCC in the eyes of those civil parties. Such a dialogue would recognise victims as valuable stakeholders in ICL processes and allow those most affected by international crimes to exert greater influence over the ways in which their harms are addressed. While enhanced participation may not necessarily lead to unwavering 'support' for courts, as demonstrated by the increased readiness to challenge the court exhibited by some civil parties, this does not necessarily undermine a court's legitimacy. Indeed, the development of more genuine dialogue with victim communities could arguably contribute to greater humility and honesty within the ICL discourse as argued for earlier and provide a balance to the power exercised by elites in shaping responses to victimisation.

Genuine consultation with victim communities requires resources as well as willingness. If international(ised) criminal courts are going to pursue a system of enhanced victim participation, there is a need to, first, fully consider the implications of such a process for trial management and, second, to ensure adequate resources are made available in order to implement the system effectively. It is submitted that the civil party system was created without adequate consideration of these two issues, with a number of adverse consequences resulting. The lack of consideration which was given to the creation of a system which allowed civil parties' individual representation led to frustration within the courtroom and a subsequent restriction being placed on the rights of the direct representatives of civil parties. Yet, it is possible that the implementation of trial management techniques from the beginning, for example through the imposition of pre-warned time limits, could have negated the need for such drastic restrictions.

Similarly, the creation of the civil party system was not accompanied by an adequate allocation of resources, leading to three main adverse consequences. First, the lack of legal aid inevitably impacted on the quality of legal representation available to civil parties. International civil party lawyers were often balancing their ECCC work with other modes of employment, with implications for their trial performance. Yet adequate planning and resource allocation may have enabled full time, fully prepared legal representatives. Second, the lack of resources available for outreach activities resulted in misinformation spreading, a lack of up-to-date knowledge about the court amongst civil parties, and corresponding frustrations and disenchantment. Finally, the implementation of a reparations mandate without considering plausible funding sources has caused significant distress to civil parties. While the subsequent amendments to the rules have allowed for a number of innovative civil society projects to be recognised as reparations, this places the onus on external actors to provide what the court cannot and removes the responsibility to provide reparations from both those accused of crimes and the state of Cambodia.

Thus, I argue that there is much to be learned from both the ECCC's successes and its failures. International criminal institutions will inevitably be shaped by political, social and legal contexts and a variety of different actors. However, a more critical engagement with this reality could open up space for creativity, as well as a more honest discussion about what a court can achieve. A move away from an elitist discourse, and an engagement with civil society actors, both as the 'subject' and the 'object' of ICL,[29] could assist in grounding ICL institutions more effectively within the specific contexts of the harm experienced. Indeed, if the move towards a victim-centric ICL discourse is to be reflected in practice, then there is a need to engage more genuinely with victim communities, both inside and outside of the courtroom. Finally, international(ised) criminal courts should ensure that they have the funds and resources to deliver what they set out to do. The raised expectations of victim communities, if left unfulfilled, can lead to secondary victimisation and disenchantment with ICL mechanisms. Yet the current study suggests that with greater engagement, and an acknowledgement of the specific interests and needs of victim groups, much can be done to address the harms experienced by these populations.

Notes

1 D. Miers, 'Positivist Victimology: a Critique Part 2' 1(3) *International Review of Victimology* (1990) 219 at 219.
2 See Chapter 4.
3 N. Christie, 'Conflict as Property' 17(1) *British Journal of Criminology* (1977) 1.
4 B. Rajagopal, 'International Law and Social Movements: Challenges of Theorizing Resistance' 41 *Colombia Journal of Transnational Law* (2003) 397 at 406.
5 L. Alcoff, 'The Problem of Speaking for Others' 20 *Cultural Critique* (1991–1992).

6 E. Haslam, 'Subjects and Objects: International Criminal Law and the Institutionalization of Civil Society' 5(2) *International Journal of Transitional Justice* (2011) 221.
7 K. McEvoy and K. McConnachie, 'Victims and Transitional Justice: Voice, Agency and Blame' 22 *Social and Legal Studies* (2013) 489.
8 K. McEvoy, 'Beyond Legalism: Towards a Thicker Understanding of Transitional Justice' 24 *Journal of Law and Society* (2007) 411.
9 McEvoy and McConnachie, n.7.
10 For example L.E. Fletcher, 'Refracted Justice: The Imagined Victim and the International Criminal Court' in C. De Vos, S. Kendall and C. Stahn (eds.), *Contested Justice: the Politics and Practice of International Criminal Court Interventions* (Cambridge University Press, 2015); S. Kendall and S. Nouwen, 'Representational Practices at the International Criminal Court: The Gap between Juridified and Abstract Victimhood' 76 *Law and Contemporary Problems* (2013) 235; McEvoy and McConnachie, ibid.
11 See Chapter 3.
12 C. Jorda and J. de Hemptinne, 'The Status and Role of the Victim' in A. Cassese, P. Gaeta and R.W. Jones (eds.), *The Rome Statute of the International Criminal Court: A Commentary* (Oxford University Press, 2002) 1387–1419 at 1389.
13 J. Doak, 'Enriching Trial Justice for Crime Victims in Common Law Systems: Lessons from Transitional Environments' 21(2) *International Review of Victimology* (2015) 139 at 149.
14 Interview with Lawyer 2 (LCL Office), 21 November 2013.
15 E. Haslam and R. Edmunds, 'Victim Participation, Politics and the Construction of Victims at the International Criminal Court: Reflections on Proceedings in Banda and Jerbo' 14 *Melbourne Journal of International Law* (2013) 727 at 745.
16 K.M. Clarke, *Fictions of Justice: The International Criminal Court and the Challenge of Legal Pluralism in Sub-Saharan Africa* (Cambridge University Press, 2009).
17 J. Doak, 'Victims' Rights in Criminal Trials: Prospects for Participation' 32(2) *Journal of Law and Society* (2005) 294; I. Bacik, C. Maunsell and S. Grogan, *The Legal Process and Victims of Rape* (Dublin Rape Crisis Centre, 1998); H. Kury and M. Kaiser, 'The Victim's Position within the Criminal Proceedings – An Empirical Study' in G. Kaiser, H. Kury and H.J. Albrecht (eds.), *Victims and Criminal Justice: Legal Protection, Restitution and Support* (Max-Planck Institute for Foreign and International Law, 1991) 579–628.
18 M.R. Maurrus, 'A Jewish Lobby at Nuremberg: Jacob Robinson and the Institute for Jewish Affairs 1945–1946' 27 *Cardozo Law Review* (2006) 1651; H. Cobban, *Amnesty after Atrocity? Healing Nations after Genocide and War Crimes* (Paradigm Publishers, 2006); *Situation in the DRC*, Prosecution's Reply on the Applications for Participation 01/04–1/dp to 01/04–6/dp, ICC-01/04–84-Conf, 15 August 2005.
19 L. Vinjamuri and J. Snyder, 'Advocacy and Scholarship in the Study of International War Crime Tribunals and Transitional Justice' 7 *Annual Review of Political Science* (2004) 345.
20 R. Pound, 'Law in Books and Law in Action' 44 *America Law Review* (1910) 12.
21 Y. Huo and T. Tyler, *Trust in the Law: Encouraging Public Cooperation with the Police and Courts* (Russell-Sage Foundation, 2002); J. Thibaut and L. Walker, *Procedural Justice: A Psychological Analysis* (Erlbaum, 1975).
22 E.A. Lind et al., 'Procedure and Outcome Effects on Reactions to Adjudicated Resolution of Conflicts of Interests' 39 *Journal of Personality and Social Psychology* (1980) 643; S. LaTour, 'Determinants of Participant and Observer Satisfaction with Adversary and Inquisitorial Modes of Adjudication' 36(12) *Journal of Personality and Social Psychology* (1978) 1531.

23 T. Tyler, 'Procedural Justice, Legitimacy, and the Effective Rule of Law' 30 *Crime and Justice* (2003) 283; J. Shapland, 'Victims, the Criminal Justice System and Compensation' 24(2) *British Journal of Criminology* (1984) 136; G. Leventhal, 'What Should be Done with Equity Theory' in K.J. Gergen et al. (eds.), *Social Exchange: Advances in Theory and Research* (Plenum, 1980).

24 J. Wemmers, *Victims in the Criminal Justice System* (Kugler Publications, 1996); L. Musante, M.A. Gilbert and J. Thibaut, 'The Effects of Control on Perceived Fairness of Procedure and Outcome' 19 *Journal of Experimental Social Psychology* (1983) 223.

25 U. Orth, 'Secondary Victimization of Crime Victims by Criminal Proceedings' 15(4) *Social Justice Research* (2002) 313.

26 T. Tyler, 'Social justice: Outcome and Procedure' 35(2) *International Journal of Psychology* (2000) 117.

27 Lind et al., n.22; LaTour, n.22; T.R. Tyler, *Why People Obey the Law: Procedural Justice, Legitimacy, and Compliance* (Yale University Press, 1990); J. Thibaut and L. Walker, *Procedural Justice: A Psychological Analysis* (Erlbaum, 1975).

28 J. Doak, 'The Therapeutic Dimension of Transitional Justice: Emotional Repair and Victim Satisfaction in International Trials and Truth Commissions' 11 *International Criminal Law Review* (2011) 263 at 271.

29 Haslam, n.6.

Appendix

Interview schedule

Judge 1, 7 November 2013
Lawyer 1 (LCL Office), 8 November 2013
Lawyer 1 (Defence), 8 November 2013
Lawyer 2 (Defence) 8 November 2013
Lawyer 3 (Defence) 8 November 2013 and 29 October 2014
Lawyer 1 (Co-Prosecutors' Office) 8 November 2013
Lawyer 2 (Co-Prosecutors' Office) 8 November 2013
Lawyer 1 (Chambers) 11 November 2013
Lawyer 2 (Chambers) 11 November 2013
Judge 2, 11 November 2013
Judge 3, 11 November 2013
Lawyer 3 (Chambers), 11 November 2013
Lawyer 1 (CP Team), 11 November 2013
NGO Staff 1, 15 November 2013.
Lawyer 2 (LCL Office), 21 November 2013
TPO Staff 1, 26 November 2013
TPO Staff 2, 26 November 2013.
VSS Staff 1, 27 November 2013
Legal Assistant (CP Team), 10 December 2013
Lawyer 4 (Defence), 13 December 2013
CP1, 18 December 2013
CP2, 18 December 2013
CP3, 18 December 2013
CP4, 18 December 2013
CP5, 18 December 2013
CP6, 18 December 2013
CP7, 19 December 2013
CP8, 19 December 2013
CP9, 19 December 2013
CP10, 19 December 2013
CP11, 20 December 2013
CP12, 20 December 2013
CP13, 20 December 2013

CP14, 20 December 2013
CP15, 20 December 2013
VSS Staff 2, 13 January 2014
Judge 4, 13 January 2014
CP16, 29 October 2014
CP17, 29 October 2014
CP18, 29 October 2014
CP19, 29 October 2014
CP20, 29 October 2014
CP21, 29 October 2014
CP22, 29 October 2014
CP23, 29 October 2014
CP24, 29 October 2014
CP25, 29 October 2014
CP26, 29 October 2014
CP27, 30 October 2014
Lawyer (Former CP Team member), 11 September 2015
Lawyer 2 (CP Team), 26 September 2015

Bibliography

Acquaviva, G., 'New Paths in International Criminal Justice? The Internal Rules of the Cambodian Extraordinary Chambers' 6 *Journal of International Criminal Justice* (2008) 129.

ADHOC, 'Civil Party Representatives Voices Regarding the Current State of Affairs at the ECCC' Press Release, 25 March 2013.

Aglioby, J., 'Khmer Rouge 'butcher' Dies Waiting to be Tried' *The Guardian*, 22 July 2006, www.theguardian.com/world/2006/jul/22/cambodia (accessed 09/02/18).

Ainley, K., 'Transitional Justice in Cambodia: the Coincidence of Power and Principle' in R. Jeffery (ed.) *Transitional Justice in the Asia-Pacific* (Cambridge University Press, 2014) 125–156.

Akhavan, P., 'Beyond Impunity: Can International Criminal Justice Prevent Future Atrocities?' 95(7) *American Journal of International Law* (2001).

Alcoff, L., 'The Problem of Speaking for Others' 20 *Cultural Critique* (1991–1992).

Aldana-Pindell, R., 'In Vindication of Justiciable Victims' Rights to Truth and Justice for State Sponsored Crimes' 35(5) *Vanderbilt Journal of Transnational Law* (2002) 1399.

Aldana-Pindell, R., 'An Emerging Universality of Justiciable Victims' Rights in the Criminal Process to Curtail Impunity for State-Sponsored Crimes' 26(3) *Human Rights Quarterly* (2004) 605.

Alvarez, J., 'Rush to Closure: Lessons of the Tadić Judgment' 96 *Michigan Law Review* (1998) 2036.

Anders, D.E., 'The Therapeutic Turn in International Humanitarian Law: War Crimes Tribunals as Sites of "Healing"?' *UC Berkeley Electronic Theses and Dissertations*, 2012.

Aptel, C, 'Prosecutorial Discretion at the ICC and Victims' Right to Remedy: Narrowing the Impunity Gap' 10 *Journal of International Criminal Justice* (2012) 1357.

Arajärvi, N, 'The Role of the International Criminal Judge in the Formation of the Customary International Law' 1(2) *European Journal of Legal Studies* (2007).

Arendt, H., *Eichmann in Jerusalem: A Report on the Banality of Evil* (Penguin, 1963).

Arendt, H., *The Origins of Totalitarianism* (Harcourt, 1973).

Arzt, D.E., 'Views on the Ground: The Local Perception of International Criminal Tribunals in the Former Yugoslavia and Sierra Leone' 603 *Annals of the American Academy of Political and Social Science, Law, Society, and Democracy: Comparative Perspectives* (2006) 226.

Ashworth, A., 'Victim Impact Statements and Sentencing' *Criminal Law Review* (1993) 498.

Ashworth, A., 'Victims' Rights, Defendants' Rights and Criminal Procedure' in A. Crawford and J. Goodey (eds.) *Integrating a Victim Perspective within Criminal Justice* (Ashgate, 2000) 185–204.

Asian Development Bank, *Cambodia: Country Poverty Analysis*, December 2014.

Bacik, I., C. Maunsell and S. Grogan, *The Legal Process and Victims of Rape* (Dublin Rape Crisis Centre, 1998).

Bair, J.P., 'From the Numbers Who Died to Those Who Survived: Victim Participation in the Extraordinary Chambers in the Court of Cambodia' 31 *University of Hawaii Law Review* (2008–2009) 508.

Balthazard, M., *Khmer Rouge Tribunal Justice Project Evaluation Report, 2010–2012* (ADHOC, 2013).

Balthazard, M., *Gender-Based Violence During The Khmer Rouge: A Forgotten Issue? Cambodian Defenders Project Gender-Based Violence Project, 2010–2012 Evaluation Report* (CDP, 2013).

Barbaret, R., 'Feminist Victimology' in B.S. Fisher and S.P. Lab (eds.) *Encyclopaedia of Victimology and Crime Prevention* (SAGE Publications, 2010) 407–409.

Barker, R., *Legitimating Identities: The Self-Presentation of Rulers and Subjects* (Cambridge University Press, 2001).

Barnett, R.E., 'Restitution: A New Paradigm of Criminal Justice' 87 *Ethics* (1977) 279.

Bassoiuni, M.C., 'International Recognition of Victims' Rights' 6(2) *Human Rights Law Review* (2006) 203.

Bassiouni, M.C., *Introduction to International Criminal Law* (Martinus Nijhoff Publishers, 2012).

Bates, A., 'Cambodia's Extraordinary Chamber: Is it the Most Effective and Appropriate Means of Addressing the Crimes of the Khmer Rouge?' in R. Henham and P. Behrens (eds.) *The Criminal Law of Genocide: International, Comparative, and Contextual Aspects* (Ashgate, 2007) 185–197.

Bates, A., *Transitional Justice in Cambodia: Analytical Report* (Atlas Project, October 2010).

Baum, L., 'Electing Judges' in L Epstein (ed.) *Contemplating Courts* (SAGE, 1995).

Baum, L., *The Puzzle of Judicial Behaviour* (University of Michigan, 1997).

Baum, L., *Judges and Their Audiences: A Perspective on Judicial Behaviour* (Princeton University Press, 2007).

BBC News, 'Khmer Rouge "Butcher" Captured' 6 March 1999, news.bbc.co.uk/1/hi/world/asia-pacific/291566.stm (accessed 09/02/18).

BBC News, 'UN Official to Meet Khmer Rouge Killer' 10 May 1999, news.bbc.co.uk/1/hi/world/asia-pacific/340151.stm (accessed 09/02/18).

Beetham, D., *The Legitimation of Power*, P. Jones and A. Weale (eds.) (MacMillan, 1991).

Beetham, D., 'Revisiting Legitimacy, Twenty Years On' in J. Tankebe and A. Liebling (eds.) *Legitimacy and Criminal Justice* (Oxford University Press, 2015) 19–37.

Beigbeder, Y., *Judging War Crimes and Torture: French Justice and International Criminal Tribunals and Commissions (1940–2005)* (Martinus Nijhoff, 2006).

Benvenisti, E., 'Customary International law as a Judicial Tool for Promoting Efficiency' in E. Benvenisti and M. Hirsh (eds.) *The Impact of International Law on International Cooperation* (2004) 85–116.

Birchall, J., Concerns Over Bid to Wrap up Outstanding Investigations at Cambodia's ECCC' *International Justice Monitor*, 16 June 2017.

Bodansky, D., 'The Legitimacy of International Governance: A Coming Challenge for International Environmental Law?' 93(3) *The American Journal of International Law* (1999) 596.

Bonacker, T., A. Oettler and C. Safferling, 'Valorising Victims' Ambivalences in Contemporary Trends in Transitional Justice' in T. Bonacker and C. Safferling (eds.) *Victims of International Crimes: An Interdisciplinary Discourse* (Asser Press, 2013) 275–279.

Bonacker, T., and C. Safferling, 'Introduction' in T Bonacker and C Safferling (eds.) *Victims of International Crimes: An Interdisciplinary Discourse* (Asser Press, 2013).

Booth, T., and K. Carrington, 'A Comparative Analysis of the Victim Policies across the Anglo-Speaking World' in S. Walklate (ed.) *Handbook of Victims and Victimology* (Routledge, 2007) 380–417.

Boulet, R.C., 'The World's First Genocide Trial, 30 Years on' *The Phnom Penh Post*, 19 August 2009.

Boyle, A., and C. Chinkin, *The Making of International Law* (Oxford University Press, 2006).

Boyle, D., 'The Rights of Victims: Participation, Representation, Protection, Reparation' 4 *Journal of International Criminal Justice* (2006) 307.

Breen, O.B., 'Allies or Adversaries? Foundation Responses to Government Policing of Cross-Border Charity' 17(1) *International Journal of Non-for-Profit Law* (2015) 45.

Brienen, M., and E. Hoegen, *Victims of Crime in 22 European Criminal Justice Systems* (Wolf Legal Productions, 2000).

Brubacher, M.R., 'Prosecutorial Discretion within the International Criminal Court' 2 *Journal of International Criminal Justice* (2004) 71.

Bueno, I., 'The Colombian Conflict and Restorative Justice' in D.L. Rothe and D. Kauzlarich (eds.) *Towards a Victimology of State Crime* (Routledge, 2014).

Burens, L., 'Plea Bargaining in International Criminal Tribunals: The End of Truth-Seeking in International Courts?' *Zeitschrift für Internationale Strafrechtsdogmatik* (2013).

Burrage, M., 'Revolution and the Collective Action of the French, American, and English Legal Professions' 13 *Law and Social Inquiry* (1988) 225.

Burton, M., R. Evans and A. Sanders, 'Vulnerable and Intimidation Witnesses and the Adversarial Process in England and Wales' 11(1) *The International Journal of Evidence and Proof* (2007).

Buyanunda, M., 'The Khmer Rouge on Trial: Whither the Defense?' 74 *Southern California Law Review* (2001) 1581.

Cahnman, W.J., 'Ideal Type Theory: Max Weber's Concept and Some of Its Derivations' 6(3) *The Sociology Quarterly* (1965) 268.

Cambodia Tribunal Monitor, 'Hearing Debates Delay, Scope, of Case 002/02' 11 November 2014, www.cambodiatribunal.org/2014/02/11/hearing-debates-delay-scope-for-case-00202/ (accessed 16/02/18).

Cambodian Committee of Women, *The Cambodian NGO Committee on CEDAW (NGO-CEDAW) Shadow Report (2013)* cambow.org/2013/11/14/we-are-expecting-new-donors/. (accessed 26/11/15).

Cambodian Defenders Projects, 'GBV under the Khmer Rouge Information Platform' gbvkr.org (accessed 16/11/18).

Carcano, A., 'Sentencing and the Gravity of the Offence in International Criminal Law' 51(3) *The International and Comparative Law Quarterly* (2002) 583.

Carothers T., and S. Brechenmacher, *Closing Space: Democracy and Human Rights Support Under Fire* (Carnegie Endowment for International Peace, 2014).

Carrabine, E. et al., *Criminology: A Sociological Introduction* (Routledge, 2004).

Cassese, A., 'Reflections on International Criminal Justice' 60 *Modern Law Review* (1998) 1.

Cassese, A., 'Is the ICC Still Having Teething Problems?' 4 *Journal of International Criminal Justice* (2006) 434.

Catani, L., 'Victims at the International Criminal Court' 10 *Journal of International Criminal Justice* (2012) 905.

Chakravarti, S., 'More than "Cheap Sentimentality": Victim Testimony at Nuremberg, the Eichmann Trial, and Truth Commissions' 15 *Constellations* 2 (2008) 223.

Chambers, G., and A. Millar, *Investigating Sexual Assault* (HMSO, 1983).

Chandler, D., B. Kiernan, and C. Boua (eds.) *Pol Pot Plans the Future: Confidential Leadership Documents from Democratic Kampuchea, 1976–1977* (Yale University Southeast Asian Studies Monograph Series 33, 1988).

Chandler, D.P., *The Tragedy of Cambodian History* (Yale University Press, 1991).

Charnovitz, S., 'Nongovernmental Organizations and International Law' 100 *American Journal of International Law* (2006) 348.

Chhang, Y., 'The Thief of History – Cambodia and the Special Court' 1(1) *The International Journal of Transitional Justice* (2007) 157.

Chinkin, C.M., 'Women's International Tribunal on Japanese Military Sexual Slavery' 95 *American Journal of International Law* (2001) 335.

Chouliaras, A., 'The Victimological Concern as the Driving Force in the Quest for Justice for State-Sponsored International Crimes' in R. Letschert et al. (eds.) *Victimological Approaches to International Crimes: Africa* (Intersentia, 2011) 35–64.

CHRAC, 'Civil Society Deeply Concerned about the ECCC Draft Internal Rules' 24 January 2007, www.licadho-cambodia.org/pressrelease.php?perm=138 (accessed 24/02/18).

CHRAC, 'Civil Society Calls for Investigation of Further Suspects by the ECCC' 14 January 2009, ki-media.blogspot.co.uk/2009/01/civil-society-calls-for-investigation.html (accessed 16/02/18).

CHRAC and ECCC Victims Unit, *Reparations for Victims of the Khmer Rouge Regime, Report of a Conference Held in Phnom Penh from 26–27 November 2008*, Phnom Penh, 2009.

Christensen, R., 'Getting to Peace by Reconciling Notions of Justice: The Importance of Considering Discrepancies Between Civil and Common Legal Systems in the Formation of the International Criminal Court' 6 *UCLA Journal of International Law and Foreign Affairs* (2004) 391.

Christie, N., 'Conflict as Property' 17(1) *British Journal of Criminology* (1977) 1.

Christie, N., 'The Ideal Victim' in E. Fattah (ed.) *From Crime Policy to Victim Policy* (St. Martin's Press, 1986) 17–30.

Chung, C., 'Victims' Participation at the International Criminal Court: Are Concessions of the Court Clouding the Promise?' 6(3) *Northwestern Journal of International Human Rights* (2008) 459.

Chy, T., *When the Criminal Laughs* (DC-Cam, 2014).

Ciorciari J.D. (ed.), *The Khmer Rouge Tribunal* (DC-Cam, 2006).

Ciorciari, J.D., 'History and Politics Behind the Khmer Rouge Trials' in J.D. Ciorciari and A. Heindel (eds.) *On Trial: the Khmer Rouge Accountability Process* (DC-Cam, 2009).

Ciorciari, J.D., 'The Duch Verdict' *Cambodia Tribunal Monitor*, 28 July 2010.

Ciorciari, J.D., and A. Heindel, *Hybrid Justice: The Extraordinary Chambers in the Courts of Cambodia* (University of Michigan Press, 2014).

Ciorciari, J.D., and A. Heindel, 'Experiments in International Criminal Justice: Lessons from the Khmer Rouge Tribunal' 35(2) *Michigan Journal of International Law* (2014) 369.

Ciorciari, J.D., and A. Heindel, 'Victim Testimony in International and Hybrid Criminal Courts: Narrative Opportunities, Challenges and Fair Trial Demands' 56(2) *Virginia Journal of International Law* (2016).

Ciorciari, J.D., and J. Ramji-Nogales, 'Lessons from the Cambodian Experience with Truth and Reconciliation' 19 *Buffalo Human Rights Law Review* (2012–2013) 193.

Cisse, C., 'The International Tribunals for the Former Yugoslavia and Rwanda: Some Elements of Comparison' 7 *Transnational Law and Contemporary Problems* (1997) 103.

Clark, P. and N. Palmer, *Testifying to Genocide: Victim and Witness Protection in Rwanda* (REDRESS, 2013).

Clarke, K.M., *Fictions of Justice: The International Criminal Court and the Challenge of Legal Pluralism in Sub-Saharan Africa* (Cambridge University Press, 2009).

Cody, S., 'Procedural Justice, Legitimacy and Victim Participation in Uganda' in N. Hayashi, C. Bailliet and J. Nicholson (eds.) *The Legitimacy of International Criminal Tribunals* (Cambridge University Press, 2017) 376–398.

Cohen, D., M. Hyde and P. van Tuyl, *A Well-Reasoned Opinion? Critical Analysis of the First Case Against the Alleged Senior Leaders of the Khmer Rouge (Case 002/01)* (East West Centre, 2015).

Cohen, S., *States of Denial: Knowing about Atrocities and Suffering* (Polity Press, 2001).

Copelon, R., 'Gender Crimes as War Crimes: Integrating Crimes against Women into International Criminal Law' 46 *McGill Law Journal* (2000) 217.

Coppedge, M., 'Thickening Thin Concepts and Theories: Combining Large-N and Small-N in Comparative Politics' 31 *Comparative Politics* (1999) 465.

Cornwall, A., and C. Nyamu-Musembi, 'Putting the "Rights-Based Approach" to Development into Perspective' 25 *Third World Quarterly* (2004) 1415.

Crawford, A., and J. Enterkin, 'Victim Contact Work in the Probation Service: Paradigm Shift or Pandora's Box?' 41 *British Journal of Criminology* (2001) 707.

Cryer, R., *Prosecuting International Crimes: Selectivity and the International Criminal Law Regime* (Cambridge University Press, 2005).

Cuddy, A., 'Victim Lawyers Stung by Cuts' *The Phnom Penh Post*, 11 May 2015, www.phnompenhpost.com/national/victim-lawyers-stung-cuts (accessed 16/02/18).

Cyr, K., and J. Wemmers, 'Empowerment des victimes d'actes criminels' 44(2) *Criminologie* (2011) 125.

Dahl, R.A., and B. Stinebrickner, *Modern Political Analysis* (6th edn) (Pearson, 2002).

Danieli, Y., 'Victims: Essential Voices at the Court' *Victims' Rights Working Group Bulletin*, Issue 1, September 2004.

Danieli, Y., 'Reappraising the Nuremberg Trials and their Legacy: The Role of Victims in International Law' 27(4) *Cardozo Law Review* (2006) 1633.

Damaska, M., 'What is the Point of International Criminal Justice?' 83 *Chicago Kent Law Review* (2008) 329.Danieli, Y., 'Massive Trauma and the Healing Role of Reparative Justice' in C. Ferstman, M. Goetz and A. Stephens (eds.) *Reparations for Victims of Genocide, Crimes Against Humanity and War Crimes: Systems in Place and Systems in the Making* (Martinus Nijhoff, 2009) 41–78.

Darehshori, S., 'Weighing the Evidence: Lessons from the Slobodan Milošević Trial' *Human Rights Watch*, Volume 18, No. 10(D), December 2006.

Daymon, D., 'Culture Formation in a New Television Station: A Multi-Perspective Analysis' 11 *British Journal of Management* (2000) 121.

DC-Cam, *Villagers React to Verdict in Case 002/01*, 7 August 2014, www.d.dccam.org/Projects/Living_Doc/pdf/Villagers_React_to_Verdict_in_Case_002-01.pdf. (accessed 16/02/18).

DC-Cam, 'A Response Team for the Khmer Rouge Tribunal', www.d.dccam.org/Projects/Tribunal_Response_Team/Tribunal_response.htm (accessed 16/02/18).

De Bertodano, S., 'Current Developments in Internationalized Courts' 1(1) *Journal of International Criminal Justice* (2003) 226.

DeFalco, R.C., 'Cases 003 and 004 at the Khmer Rouge Tribunal: The Definition of "Most Responsible" Individuals According to International Criminal Law' 8(2) *Genocide Studies and Prevention: An International Journal* (2014) 45.

De Hemptinne, J., 'Challenges Raised by Victims' Participation in the Proceedings of the Special Tribunal for Lebanon' 8(1) *Journal of International Criminal Justice* (2010) 16.

De Langis, T., *Final Results for ECCC Baseline Study on Gender Sensitivity in Transitional Justice Processes in Cambodia* (ECCC VSS, 2012).

De Langis, T., 'A Missed Opportunity, A Last Hope? Prosecuting Sexual Crimes under the Khmer Rouge Regime' 2 *Cambodia Law and Policy Journal* (2014) 39.

De Langis, T., ' "This Is Now the Most Important Trial in the World": A New Reading of Code #6, the Rule against Immoral Offenses Under the Khmer Rouge Regime' 3 *The Cambodia Law and Policy Journal* (2014) 39.

Dembour, M., and E. Haslam, 'Silencing Hearings? Victim-Witnesses at War Crimes Trials' 15(1) *European Journal of International Law* (2004).

De Nike, H., et al. (eds.), *Genocide in Cambodia: Documents from the Trial of Pol Pot and Ieng Sary* (University of Pennsylvania, 2000).

Des Forges, A., and T. Longman, 'Legal Response to Genocide in Rwanda' in H. Weinstein and E. Stover (eds.) *My Neighbor, My Enemy: Justice and Social Reconstruction in Rwanda and the Former Yugoslavia* (Cambridge University Press, 2004) 49–68.

Diamond, A.F., Esq., 'Victims Once Again? Civil Party Participation before the Extraordinary Chambers in the Courts of Cambodia' 38 *Rutgers Law Record* (2010–2011).

Dickinson, L.A., 'The Promise of Hybrid Courts' 97 *American Journal of International Law* (2003) 295.

Dignan, J., *Understanding Victims and Restorative Justice* (Oxford University Press, 2005).

Dignan, J., 'The Victim in Restorative Justice' in S. Walklate (ed.) *Handbook of Victims and Victimology* (Routledge, 2007) 309–333.

Doak, J., 'The Victim and the Criminal Process: An Analysis of Recent Trends in Regional and International Tribunals' 23(1) *Legal Studies* (2003) 1.

Doak, J., 'Victims' Rights in Criminal Trials: Prospects for Participation' 32(2) *Journal of Law and Society* (2005) 294.

Doak, J., *Victims' Rights, Human Rights and Criminal Justice: Reconceiving the Role of Third Parties* (Hart Publishing, 2008).

Doak, J., 'The Therapeutic Dimension of Transitional Justice: Emotional Repair and Victim Satisfaction in International Trials and Truth Commissions' 11 *International Criminal Law Review* (2011) 263.

Doak, J., 'Participatory Rights for Victims of Crime: In Search of International Consensus' 15(1) *Canadian Criminal Law Review* (2011) 43.

Doak, J., 'Enriching Trial Justice for Crime Victims in Common Law Systems: Lessons from Transitional Environments' 21(2) *International Review of Victimology* (2015) 139.

Doerner, W.G., and S.P. Lab, *Victimology* (3rd edn) (Anderson, 2002).

Dosch, J., 'The Role of Civil Society in Cambodia's Peace-building Process: Have Foreign Donors Made a Difference?' 52 *Asian Survey* (2012) 1067.

Dosch, J., D. Virorth, and K. Sedara, *The German Civil Peace Service: Case Study of Cambodia* (Federal Ministry for Economic Cooperation and Development, 2010).

Douglas, M., *How Institutions Think* (Routledge and Kegan Paul Ltd, 1987).

Douzinos, C., *The End of Human Rights: Critical Legal Thought at the Turn of the Century* (Hart Publishing, 2002).

Drumbl, M., *Atrocity, Punishment and International Law* (Cambridge University Press, 2007).

Dubler, R., 'Kaing Guek Eav (alias Duch), Judgement, ECCC, Case No 001/18–07–2007/ECCC/TC (26 July 2010)' *Australian International Law Journal* (2010).

Duman, D., 'The Creation and Diffusion of a Professional Ideology in Nineteenth Century England' 27 *Sociological Review* (1979) 113.

Dumont, H., 'Requirements for Victim Participation' in K. Tibor-Szabó and M. Hirst (eds.) *Victim Participation in International Criminal Justice* (Asser Press, 2017).

Dunn, P., 'Matching Service Delivery to Need' in S. Walklate (ed.) *Handbook of Victims and Victimology* (Routledge, 2007) 255–282.

Dunn, P., and E. Shepherd, 'Oral Testimony from the Witness's Perspective – Psychology and Forensic Considerations' in A. Heaton-Armstrong et al. (eds.) *Witness Testimony: Psychological, Investigative and Evidential Perspectives* (Oxford University, 2006).

Ear, S., 'The Political Economy of Aid and Governance in Cambodia' 15(1) *Asian Journal of Political Science* (2007) 68.

Easterly, W., *The White Man's Burden: Why the West's Efforts to Aid the Rest Have Done So Much Ill and So Little Good* (Oxford University Press, 2007).

Easterly, W., *The Tyranny of Experts: Economists, Dictators, and the Forgotten Rights of the Poor* (Basic Books, 2014).

ECCC, 'Amicus Curiae Briefs' www.eccc.gov.kh/en/topic/333 (accessed 16/02/18).

ECCC, 'Case 004', ECCC Website, www.eccc.gov.kh/en/case/topic/120 (accessed 14/02/18).

ECCC, 'The Purpose of Hearing Victims' Suffering' www.ecccc.gov.kh/en/blog/2013/07/07/purpose-hearing-victims-suffering (accessed 16/02/18).

ECCC, 'United Nations Mission Led by Mr. Mohammed Said, Coordinator for UN Assistance to the Khmer Rouge Tribunal (UNAKRT) to Phnom Penh Finalize the Budget for the EC. The Budget is Set at USD 56.3 Million' 12 August 2004, www.eccc.gov.kh/en/United%20Nations%20Mission%20led%20by%20Mr.%20Mohammed%20Said%2C%20Coordinator%20for%20UN%20Assistance%20to%20the%20Khmer%20Rouge%20Tribunal%20%28UNAKRT%29%20%2C%20to%20Phnom%20P (accessed 09/02/18).

ECCC, 'Joint Statement by Judicial Officers: ECCC Plenary Session Unanimously Adopts Internal Rules' 13 June 2007, www.eccc.gov.kh/sites/default/files/media/Joint_Press_Statement__on_internal_rules_eng_fr_13_june_2007.pdf (accessed 16/02/18).

ECCC, 'Historic Achievement in International Criminal Law: Victims of Khmer Rouge Crimes Fully Involved in Proceedings of the ECCC' Statement by the Victims Unit, 4 February 2008, www.eccc.gov.kh/sites/default/files/media/Victim_Unit_Press_Release.pdf (accessed 09/02/18).

ECCC, 'Statement of the Co-Prosecutors' 5 January 2009, www.eccc.gov.kh/sites/default/files/media/Statement_OCP_05-01-09_EN.pdf (accessed 14/02/18).

ECCC, 7th Plenary Session of the ECCC Concludes, 9 February 2010, www.eccc.gov.kh/sites/default/files/media/Press_Release_Conclusion_7th_Plenary_Session_(ENG).pdf (accessed 16/02/18).

ECCC, 'Germany Pledges More Financial Support to Maximise Victims' Participation in KR Trials' 17 June 2010, www.eccc.gov.kh/en/articles/germany-pledges-more-financial-support-maximise-victims-participation-kr-trials (accessed 09/02/18).

ECCC, 'Statement by the International Co-Investigating Judge' ECCC Website, 10 October 2011, www.eccc.gov.kh/en/articles/statement-international-co-investigating-judge (accessed 14/02/18).

ECCC, 'Press Release of the National Co-Investigating Judge' 6 December 2011, www.eccc.gov.kh/sites/default/files/media/ECCC%20IntRCIJ%206%20Dec%202011%20En.pdf (accessed 14/02/18).

ECCC, 'Press Release by the International Reserve Co-Investigating Judge' 19 March 2012, www.eccc.gov.kh/en/articles/press-release-international-reserve-co-investigating-judge (accessed 14/02/18).

ECCC, 'International Co-Prosecutor Requests Investigation of Alleged Sexual and Gender-based Violence in Case 004' 24 April 2014, www.eccc.gov.kh/en/articles/international-co-prosecutor-requests-investigation-alleged-sexual-and-gender-based (accessed 16/02/18).

ECCC, 'International Co-Prosecutor Files Supplementary Submission in Case 003' 4 November 2014, www.eccc.gov.kh/en/articles/international-co-prosecutor-files-supplementary-submission-case-003 (accessed 16/02/18).

ECCC, 'Statement by the Principal Donors Group for the Extraordinary Chambers in the Courts of Cambodia' 27 June 2014, www.eccc.gov.kh/en/articles/statement-principal-donors-group-extraordinary-chambers-courts-cambodia (accessed 09/02/18).

ECCC, 'The International Co-Investigating Judge Charges Ao An in Case 004', ECCC Website, 27 March 2015, www.eccc.gov.kh/en/document/public-affair/international-co-investigating-judge-charges-ao-case-004 (accessed 14/02/18).

ECCC, 'Mr Meas Muth Charged in Case 003', ECCC Website, 14 December 2015, www.eccc.gov.kh/en/articles/mr-meas-muth-charged-case-003, (accessed 14/02/18).

ECCC, 'How Is the Court Financed?' ECCC Website, 8th August 2017, www.eccc.gov.kh/en/faq/how-court-financed (accessed 09/02/18).

Eisenstein, J., and H. Jacob, *Felony justice: An Organizational Analysis of Criminal Courts* (Little, Brown and Company, 1977).

Elander, E., 'The Victim's Address: Expressivism and the Victim at the Extra-ordinary Chambers in the Courts of Cambodia' 7(1) *International Journal of Transitional Justice* (2013) 91.

Elias, E., *The Politics of Victimization – Victims, Victimology and Human Rights* (Oxford University Press, 1986).

Elias, E., *Victims Still: The Political Manipulation of Crime Victims* (Sage, 1993).

Ellis, M., *The ECCC-A Failure of Credibility* (International Bar Association, February 2012).

Englebrecht, C.M., 'The Struggle for "Ownership of the Conflict": An Exploration of Victim Participation and Voice in the Criminal Justice System' 36 *Criminal Justice Review* (2011) 129.

Epstein, L., and J. Knight, *The Choices Judges Make* (CQ Press, 1998).

Erez, E., and E. Bienkowska, 'Victim Participation in Proceedings and Satisfaction with Justice in the Continental Systems: The Case of Poland' 21 *Journal of Criminal Justice* (1993) 47.

Etcheson, C., *Retribution and Reconciliation: Healing What Ails Cambodia* (Project Report to the US Institute of Peace, October 2002).

Etcheson, C., 'The Politics of Genocide in Cambodia' in CPR Romano et al. (eds.) *Internationalized Criminal Courts: Sierra Leone, East Timor, Kosovo, and Cambodia* (Oxford University Press, 2004) 181–201.

Etcheson, C., *After the Killing Fields: Lessons from the Cambodian Genocide* (Praeger, 2005).

Evenson, E., *Unfinished Business: Closing Gaps in the Selection of ICC Cases* (Human Rights Watch, 2011).

Fardel, M., and N. Vehils Olarra, 'The Application Process: Procedure and Players' in K. Tibori-Szabó and M. Hirst (eds.) *Victim Participation in International Criminal Justice* (Asser Press, 2017) 11–43.

Fattah, E.A., 'Victims and Victimology: the Facts and the Rhetoric' 1(1) *International Review of Victimology* (1989) 43.

Fawthrop, T., and H. Jarvis, *Getting Away With Genocide?* (University of South Wales, 2005).

Fercello, C., and M. Umbreit, 'Client Evaluation of Family Group Conferencing in 12 Sites in the First Judicial District of Minnesota' *Center for Restorative Justice and Mediation* (1998).

Ferstman, C., 'Reparations, Assistance and Support' in K. Tibor-Szabó and M. Hirst (eds.) *Victim Participation in International Criminal* Justice (Asser Press, 2017).

FIDH, ADHOC, LICADHO and the Collective for Khmer Rouge Victims, *Key Comments and Proposals on ECCC Draft Internal Rules*, 17 November 2006, www.fidh.org/IMG/pdf/Key_Comments_FIDH-ADHOC-LICADHO-ADHOC.pdf (accessed 16/02/18).

Fifth Plenary Session of Judicial Officers, Closing Press Statement, 6 March 2009, www.eccc.gov.kh/sites/default/files/media/closing_plenary_session_EN.pdf (accessed 23/02/18).

Findlay, M., 'Activating a Victim Constituency in International Criminal Justice' 3 *International Journal of Transitional Justice* (2009) 183.

Fletcher, L.E., 'Refracted Justice: The Imagined Victim and the International Criminal Court' in C. De Vos, S. Kendall and C. Stahn (eds.) *Contested Justice: the Politics and Practice of International Criminal Court Interventions* (Cambridge University Press, 2015) 302–326.

Fletcher, L.E., and H.M. Weinstein, 'Transitional Justice and the "plight" of Victimhood' in C. Lawther et al. (eds.) *Research Handbook on Transitonal Justice* (Elgar, 2017) 244–266.

Fogelman, E., *Conscience and Courage: Rescuers of Jews During the Holocaust* (Anchor Books, 1995).

Fontaine, C., 'Cambodia Premier Says No to Trial' *Associated Press*, 28 December 1998.

Ford, S., 'A Social Psychology Model of the Perceived Legitimacy of International Criminal Courts: Implications for the Success of Transitional Justice Mechanisms' 45 *Vanderbilt Journal Transnational Law* (2012) 405.

Form, W., 'Justice 30 Years Later? The Cambodian Special Tribunal for the Punishment of Crimes against Humanity by the Khmer Rouge' 37(6) *Nationalities Papers* (2009).

Foucault, M., *Power/Knowledge: Selected Interviews and Other Writings 1972–1977* (Harvester Press, 1980).

Freeman, M., (ed.) *Overcoming Child Abuse: A Window on a World Problem* (Aldershort, 2000).

Friman, H., 'Procedural Law of Internationalized Criminal Courts' in C.P.R. Romano (ed.) *Internationalized Criminal Courts: Sierra Leone, East Timor, Kosovo, and Cambodia* (Oxford University Press, 2004) 317–358.

Funk, T.M., *Victims' Rights and Advocacy at the International Criminal Court* (Oxford University Press, 2010).

Galtung, J., 'Violence, Peace and Peace Research' 6(3) *Journal of Peace Research* (1969) 167.

Garkawe, S., 'Victims and the International Criminal Court: Three Major Issues' 3 *International Criminal Law Review* (2003) 345.

Garkawe, S., 'The Role and Rights of Victims at the Nuremberg International Military Tribunal' in H. Reginbogin, C. Safferling and W. Hippel (eds.) *The Nuremberg Trials: International Criminal Law since 1945* (Kluwer, 2006) 86–94.

Garland, D., *Punishment and Modern Society: A Study in Social Theory* (Oxford University Press, 1990).

Garland, D., and R. Sparks, 'Criminology, Social Theory and the Challenge of Our Times' in D. Garland and R. Sparks (eds.) *Criminology and Social Theory* (Oxford University, 2000).

Garoupa, T., and T. Ginsburg 'Judicial Audiences and Reputation: Perspectives from Comparative Law' 47 *Columbia Journal of Transnational Law* (2008) 451.

Geertz, C., 'Thick Descriptions: Toward an Interpretive Theory of Culture' in C. Geertz (ed.) *The Interpretation of Cultures: Selected Essays* (Fontana Press, 1973) 3–30.

Genn, H., 'Multiple Victimisation' in M. Maguire and J. Pointing (eds.) *Victims of Crime* (Open University Press, 1988) 90–100.

Gillison, D., 'Duch Denies Teaching to Kill; Also Denies Personally Killing' *Cambodia Daily*, 18 June 2009.

Ginsburg, T., *Judicial Review in New Democracies; Constitutional Courts in Asian Cases* (Cambridge University Press, 2003).

Gioia, D. and E. Pitre, 'Multiparadigm Perspectives on Theory Building' 15 *Academy of Management Review* (1990) 584.

Glasius, M., *The International Criminal Court: A Global Civil Society Achievement* (Routledge, 2006).

Glaspy, J., 'Justice Delayed? Recent Developments at the Extraordinary Chambers in the Courts of Cambodia' 21 *Harvard Human Rights Journal* (2008) 143.

Glenn, H.P., *Comparative Legal Families and Comparative Legal Traditions, the Oxford Handbook of Comparative Law* (Oxford University Press, 2006).

Goodey, J., *Victims and Victimology: Research, Policy and Practice* (Pearson Education Limited, 2005).

Graber, M.A., 'Legal, Strategic, or Legal Strategy: Deciding to Decide during the Civil War and Reconstruction' in R. Kahn and K. Kersch (eds.) *The Supreme Court and American Political Development* (University Press of Kansas, 2006).

Gray, D., 'An Excuse-Centered Approach to Transitional Justice' 74 *Fordham Law Review* (2005) 2621.

Green, P.J., and T. Ward, 'State Crime, Human Rights, and the Limits of Criminology' 27 *Social Justice* (2000) 101.

Green, P., and T. Ward, *Governments, Violence and Corruption* (Pluto Press, 2004) 7–8.

Green, S., 'Crime, Victimisation and Vulnerability' in S. Walklate (ed.) *Handbook of Victims and Victimology* (Routledge, 2007) 91–119.

Groenhuijsen, M.S., and A. Pemberton, 'Genocide, Crimes against Humanity and War Crimes: A Victimological Perspective on International Criminal Justice' in R. Letschert et al. (eds.) *Victimological Approaches to International Crimes: Africa* (Intersentia, 2011) 9–34.

Gromet, D. and J. Darley, 'Restoration and Retribution: How Including Retributive Components Affects the Acceptability of Restorative Justice Procedures' 19(4) *Social Justice Research* (2006) 395.

Guhr, A.H., 'Victim Participation during the Pre-Trial Stage at the International Criminal Court' 8 *International Criminal Law Review* (2008) 109.

Guiraud, M., *Victims' Rights before the Extraordinary Chambers in the Courts of Cambodia (ECCC): A Mixed Record for Civil Parties* (FIDH, November 2012).

Habermas, J., *Communication and the Evolution of Society, Unitarian Universalist Association* (Beacon Press, 1979).

Hall, J.A., 'Court Administration at the ECCC' in J.D. Ciorciari and A. Heindel (eds.) *On Trial: The Khmer Rouge Accountability Process* (DC-Cam, 2009) 172–213.

Halliday, T., *Beyond Monopoly: Lawyers, State Crises and Professional Empowerment* (University of Chicago Press, 1987).

Hamlyn, B., et al., 'Are Special Measures Working? Evidence from Surveys of Vulnerable and Intimidated Witnesses' *Home Office Research Study 283* (UK Home Office, 2004).

Hammarberg, T., 'How the Khmer Rouge Tribunal was Agreed: Discussions Between the Cambodian Government and the UN, Part 1: March 1997–March 1999' *Searching for the Truth* (DC-Cam, 2011).

Haniffa, F., *In the Pursuit of Democracy in Post Colonia Sri Lanka: Local Human Rights Approaches to Transitional Justice* (Law and Trust Society, 2006).

Hanlon, G., 'Lawyers, the Market and Significant Others' 60 *Modern Law Review* (1997) 798.

Hansen, T.O., 'The Vertical and Horizontal Expansion of Transitional Justice' in S. Buckley-Zistel et al. (eds.) *Transitional Justice Theories* (Routledge, 2014) 105–124.

Harmon, M.B., 'The Pre-Trial Process at the ICTY as a Means of Ensuring Expeditious Trials' 5 *Journal of International Criminal Justice* (2007) 377.

Haslam, E., 'Victim Participation at the International Criminal Court: A Triumph of Hope Over Experience' in D. McGoldrick et al. (eds.) *The Permanent International Criminal Court: Legal And Policy Issues* (Hart Publishing, 2004) 315–334.

Haslam, E., 'Law, Civil Society and Contested Justice' in M. Dembour and T. Kelly (eds.) *Paths to International Justice: Social and Legal Perspectives* (Cambridge University Press, 2007) 57–82.

Haslam, E., 'Subjects and Objects: International Criminal Law and the Institutionalization of Civil Society' 5(2) *International Journal of Transitional Justice* (2011) 221.

Haslam, E., and R. Edmunds, 'Common Legal Representation at the International Criminal Court: More Symbolic than Real?' 12 *International Criminal Law Review* (2012) 871.

Haslam, E., and R Edmunds, 'Managing a New "Partnership": "Professionalization", Intermediaries and the International Criminal Court' 24 *Criminal Law Forum* (2013) 49.

Haslam, E., and R. Edmunds, 'Victim Participation, Politics and the Construction of Victims at the International Criminal Court: Reflections on Proceedings in Banda and Jerbo' 14 *Melbourne Journal of International Law* (2013) 727.

Haynes, P., 'Victims' Lawyers in the Courtroom: Opening and Closing Statements, Questioning Witnesses, Challenging and Presenting Evidence' in K. Tibori-Szabó and M. Hirst (eds.) *Victim Participation in International Criminal Justice* (Asser, 2017) 243–281.

Hebert-Dolbec, M., 'Towards Bureaucratization: An Analysis of Common Legal Representation Practices before the International Criminal Court' 23(3) *Revue québécoise de droit international* (2015) 34.

Heder, S., 'A Review of the Negotiations Leading to the Establishment of the Personal Jurisdiction of the Extraordinary Chambers in the Courts of Cambodia' *Cambodia Tribunal Monitor*, 2 August 2011.

Heilbroner, R.L., *The Nature and Logic of Capitalism* (WW Norton, 1985).

Heindel, A., 'Impact of Severance on Individual Civil Parties' Legal Status and Right to Reparations' *Cambodian Tribunal Monitor*, 23 February 2013, www.cambodiatribunal.org/wp-content/uploads/2013/08/commentary_130223-english.pdf (accessed 16/02/18).

Helfer, L.R. and G.B. Dinwoodie, 'Designing Non-National Systems: The Case of the Uniform Domain Name Dispute Resolution Policy' 43 *William and Mary Law Review* (2001) 141.

Henham, R., 'Procedural Justice and Human Rights in International Sentencing' 4 *International Criminal Law Review* (2004) 185.

Henham, R., and M. Findlay, 'Introduction: Rethinking International Criminal Justice' in R. Henham and M. Findlay (eds.) *Exploring the Boundaries of International Criminal Justice* (Ashgate Publishing, 2011) 1–27.

Herman, J., 'Reaching for Justice: The Participation of Victims at the Extraordinary Chambers in the Courts of Cambodia' *Centre on Human Rights in Conflict Policy Paper No. 5*, September 2010.

Herman, J., 'Realities of Victim Participation: The Civil Party System in Practice at the Extraordinary Chambers in the Courts of Cambodia (ECCC)' 16(4) *Contemporary Justice Review: Issues in Criminal, Social, and Restorative Justice* (2013) 461.

Herman, J., *Local Voices in Internationalised Justice: The Experience of Civil Parties at the Extraordinary Chambers in the Courts of Cambodia* (Centre on Human Rights in Conflict, University of East London, May 2014).

Herman, J., 'Uncooked Rice: Justice and Victimhood at the Extraordinary Chambers in the Courts of Cambodia and Beyond' in V. Druliolle and R. Brett (eds.) *The Politics of Victimhood in Post-Conflict Societies* (Palgrave MacMillan, 2018) 187–209.

Hillyard, P., et al. (eds.), *Beyond Criminology: Taking Harm Seriously* (Pluto Press, 2004).

Hindelang, M., et al., *Victims of Personal Crime: An Empirical Foundation for a Theory of Personal Victimization* (MA Ballinger, 1978).

Hinton, A.L., 'Why Did You Kill?: The Cambodian Genocide and the Dark Side of Face and Honor' 57(1) *The Journal of Asian Studies* (1998).

Hirst, M., 'Legal Representation of Participating Victims' in K. Tibori-Szabó and M. Hirst (eds.) *Victim Participation in International Criminal Justice* (Asser Press, 2017) 111–169.

Hobbs, H., 'Victim Participation in International Criminal Proceedings: Problems and Potential Solutions in Implementing an Effective and Vital Component of Justice' 49 *Texas International Law Journal* (2014).

Hodgson, J., *French Criminal Justice: A Comparative Account of the Investigation and Prosecution of Crime in France* (Hart Publishing, 2005).

Hodžić, R., 'Living the Legacy of Mass Atrocities: Victims' Perspectives on War Crimes Trials' 8(1) *Journal of International Criminal Justice* (2010) 113.

Holstein, J.A., and G. Miller, 'Rethinking Victimisation: An Interactionist Approach to Victimology' 3 *Symbolic Interaction* (1990).

Holt, J., 'Caring for the Dead Ritually in Cambodia' 1(1) *Southeast Asian Studies* (2012) 3.

Hopkins, R., 'The Case 002/01 Trial Judgment: A Stepping Stone from Nuremberg to the Present?' in S. Meisenberg and I. Stegmiller (eds.) *The Extraordinary Chambers in the Courts of Cambodia* (Asser Press, 2016).

Hoven, E., 'Civil Party Participation in Trials of Mass Crimes: A Qualitative Study at the Extraordinary Chambers in the Courts of Cambodia' 12(1) *Journal of International Criminal Justice* (2014) 81.

Hoven, E., M. Feiler and S. Scheibel, 'Victims in Trials of Mass Crimes: A Multi-Perspective Study of Civil Party Participation at the Extraordinary Chambers in the Courts of Cambodia' 3 *Cologne Occasional Papers on International Peace and Security Law* (2013).

Hovil, L., and J. Quinn, *Peace First, Justice Later: Traditional Justice in Northern Uganda* (Refugee Law Project, 2005).

Hoyle, C., *An Evaluation of the One-Stop Shop and Victim Statement Pilot Projects* (UK Home Office, 1998).

Hoyle, C., R. Morgan and A. Sanders, *The Victim's Charter – An Evaluation of Pilot Projects' Home Office Research, Development and Statistics Directorate, Research Findings 107* (Home Office, 1999).

Hoyle, C., and L. Ullrich, 'New Court, New Justice? The Evolution of 'Justice for Victims' at Domestic Courts and at the International Criminal Court' 12 *Journal of International Criminal Justice* (2014) 681.

Hresko, T., 'Restoration and Relief: Procedural Justice and the September 11th Victim Compensation Fund' 42(1) *Gonzaga Law Review* (2006–2007) 95.

Hudson, C., *The Killing Fields* (Dell Publishing Co. 1984).

Hughes, C., *The Political Economy of the Cambodian Transition, 1991–2001* (Routledge Curzon, 2003).

Human Rights Watch, Comments on ECCC Internal Rules, 17 November 2006, www.hrw.org/news/2006/11/17/extraordinary-chambers-courts-cambodia (accessed 16/02/18).

Human Rights Watch, 'Cambodia: Judges Investigating Khmer Rouge Crimes Should Resign', 3 October 2011, www.hrw.org/news/2011/10/03/cambodia-judges-investigating-khmer-rouge-crimes-should-resign (accessed 14/02/18).

Human Rights Watch, 'Cambodia: Withdraw Fundamentally Flawed Judiciary Laws' 3 May 2014, www.hrw.org/news/2014/05/03/cambodia-withdraw-fundamentally-flawed-judiciary-laws (accessed 16/02/18).

Human Rights Watch, 'Cambodia: Stop Blocking Justice for Khmer Rouge Crimes', 22 March 2015, www.hrw.org/news/2015/03/22/cambodia-stop-blocking-justice-khmer-rouge-crimes (accessed 24/02/18).

Huo, Y., and T. Tyler, *Trust in the Law: Encouraging Public Cooperation with the Police and Courts* (Russell-Sage Foundation, 2002).

Hurd, I., *After Anarchy: Legitimacy and Power in the United Nations Security Council* (Princeton University Press, 2007).

Husketh, E., 'Pole Pole: Hastening Justice at UNICTR' 3(1) *Northwestern Journal of International Human Rights* (2005).

ICC, 'Statement to the Press by the Prosecutor of the International Criminal Court' Abidjan, Côte d'Ivoire, 20 July 2013.

ICTR, 'Statement by Justice Hassan B Jallow, Chief Prosecutor, ICTR & MICT on the Commemoration of the 20th Anniversary of the Rwandan Genocide' *ICTR Website*, 10 April 2014, unictr.unmict.org/en/news/statement-justice-hassan-b-jallow-chief-prosecutor-ictr-mict-commemmoration-20th-anniversary (accessed 09/02/2018).

Ignatieff, M., *Whose Universal Values? The Crisis in Human Rights* (Praemium Erasmianum Foundation, 1999).

Iliff, F., F. Maitre-Muhl and A. Sirel, 'Adverse Consequences of Reparations' *University of Essex Reparations Unit, Briefing Paper No.6* (August 2011).

International Center for Transitional Justice, Comments on Draft Internal Rules for the ECCC, 17 November 2006, www.ictj.org/publications?page=36 (accessed 26/11/15).

International Center for Transitional Justice, Victims Unit and Cambodian Human Rights Action Committee, 'Leaving a Lasting Legacy for Victims: Practical Workshop for ECCC Victims' Representatives' *Workshop Report*, Phnom Penh, 10 March 2009.

International Center for Transitional Justice, 'Outreach Strategies in International and Hybrid Courts' *Workshop Report*, Phnom Penh, 3–5 March 2010.

'The International Co-Investigating Judge Charges Im Chaem in Absentia in Case 004', *ECCC Website*, 3 March 2015, www.eccc.gov.kh/en/document/public-affair/international-co-investigating-judge-charges-im-chaem-absentia-case-004–0 (accessed 14/02/18).

Iontcheva Turner, J., 'Transnational Networks and International Criminal Justice' 105(5) *Michigan Law Review* (2007) 985.

Jackson, K.D., *Cambodia 1975–1978: Rendezvous with Death* (Princeton University Press, 1992).

Jacobsen, T. and M. Stuart-Fox, 'Power and Political Culture in Cambodia' 200 *Asia Research Institute Working Paper Series* (2013).

Jamieson, R. and K. McEvoy, 'State Crime by Proxy and Juridical Othering' 45 *British Journal of Criminology* (2005) 504.

Jarvis, H., '"Justice for the deceased": Victims' Participation in the Extraordinary Chambers in the Courts of Cambodia' 8(2) *Genocide Studies and Prevention: An International Journal* (2013) 19.

Jarvis, H., 'Trials and Tribulations: The Long Quest for Justice for the Cambodian Genocide' in S. Meisenberg and I. Stegmiller (eds.) *The Extraordinary Chambers in the Courts of Cambodia* (Asser Press, 2016).

Jeffery, R., 'Beyond Repair?: Collective and Moral Reparations at the Khmer Rouge Tribunal' 13 *Journal of Human Rights* (2014) 103.
Jeffery, R., and H. Joon Kim (eds.), *Transitional Justice in the Asia Pacific* (Cambridge University Press, 2013).
Jodoin, J., 'Understanding the Behaviour of International Courts: An Examination of Decision-Making at the ad hoc International Criminal Tribunals' 6(1) *Journal of International Law and International Relations* (2010) 1.
Johansen, K., *The Actual Impact of the International Criminal Tribunal for the Former Yugoslavia on the Reconciliation Process in Bosnia-Herzegovina*, Master Thesis for the Master of Philosophy in Peace and Conflict Studies, Department of Political Sciences, University of Oslo, 15 July 2011.
Johnstone, G., and D. Van Ness, *Handbook of Restorative Justice* (Taylor and Francis, 2007).
Jorda, C., and J. de Hemptinne 'The Status and Role of the Victim' in A. Cassesse, P. Gaeta and R.W. Jones (eds.) *The Rome Statute of the International Criminal Court: A Commentary* (Oxford University Press, 2002) 1387–1419.
Jouet, M., 'Reconciling the Conflicting Rights of Victims and Defendants at the International Criminal Court' 26 *Saint Louis University Public Law Review* (2007) 249.
Judge Sylvia Cartwright, 'Opening Speech to the ECCC 7th Plenary Session' ECCC Website, 2 February 2010, www.eccc.gov.kh/sites/default/files/media/02Feb2010Plenary-VicePresident-speech(Eng)_.pdf (accessed 16/02/18).
Judicial Solutions, 'Some "do's" and "don'ts" of Communicating with Victims' www.justicesolutions.org/art_pub_communicating_with_victims.pdf (accessed 16/02/18).
Kaldor, M., *Global Society: An Answer to War* (Polity Press, 2003).
Kamatali, J., 'From the ICTR to ICC: Learning from the ICTR Experience in Bringing Justice to Rwandans' 12 *New England Journal of International and Comparative Law* (2005) 89.
Kapur, R., 'The Tragedy of Victimization Rhetoric: Resurrecting the "Native" Subject in International/Post-Colonial Feminist Legal Politics' 15 *Harvard Human Rights Journal* (2002) 1.
Karremans, J.C., and P. Van Lange, 'Does Activating Justice Help or Hurt in Promoting Forgiveness?' 41 *Journal of Experimental Social Psychology* (2005) 290.
Kauzlarich, D., R.A. Matthews and W.J. Miller, 'Towards a Victimology of State Crime' 10 *Critical Criminology* (2001) 173.
Kay, F., 'Professionalism and Exclusionary Practices: Shifting the Terrain of Privilege and Professional Monopoly' 11 *International Journal of the Legal Profession* (2004) 11.
Kean, J., *Global Civil Society?* (Cambridge University Press, 2003).
Kearon, T. and B. Godfrey, 'Setting the Scene: A Question of History' in S. Walklate (ed.) *Handbook of Victims and Victimology* (Routledge, 2007) 17–37.
Kelly, M.G.E., *The Political Philosophy of Michel Foucault* (Routledge, 2009).
Kelsall, M.S., et al., 'Lessons Learned from the "Duch" Trial: A Comprehensive Review of the First Case before the Extraordinary Chambers in the Courts of Cambodia' *Asian International Justice Initiative, KRT Trial Monitoring Group*, 22 December 2009.
Kendall, S., 'Donors' Justice: Recasting International Criminal Accountability' 24 *Leiden Journal of International Law* (2011) 585.

Kendall, S., 'Commodifying Global Justice: Economies of Accountability at the International Criminal Court' 13(1) *Journal of International Criminal Justice* (2015) 113.

Kendall, S., and S. Nouwen, 'Representational Practices at the International Criminal Court: The Gap between Juridified and Abstract Victimhood' 76 *Law and Contemporary Problems* (2013) 235.

Kennedy, D., *Dark Sides of Virtue: Reassessing International Humanitarianism* (Princeton University Press, 2004).

Khmer Rouge Tribunal Monitor, *Report No. 12: Week Ending July 9, 2009* (UC Berkeley, July 2009).

Khmer Rouge Tribunal Monitor, 'Case 002, Issue No.62, Hearing on Evidence Week 57', 3–7 June 2013, krtmonitor.org/2013/06/07/krt-trial-monitor-c002-issue-62–3–7-june-2013/ (accessed 16/02/18).

Khmer Rouge Tribunal Monitor, 'Highlights of Issues Related to Civil Party Participation', 9 October 2013, krtmonitor.org/2013/10/09/highlights-civil-party-participation/ (accessed 16/02/18).

Khmer Rouge Tribunal Monitor, 'KRT Monitor Case 002/02 – Issue 79 (9–11 January 2017)', 9 February 2017, krtmonitor.org/2017/02/09/krt-monitor-case-00202-issue-79–9–11-january-2017/ (accessed 16/02/18).

Kiernan, B., *The Pol Pot Regime* (Yale University Press, 1996).

Kiernan, B., 'Background to the Conflict in Cambodia' in K Ambos and M Othman (eds.) *New Approaches in International Criminal Justice* (Max-Planck Institute, 2003) 173–188.

Kiernan, B., 'The Demography of Genocide in Southeast Asia' 35(4) *Critical Asian Studies* (2003).

Killean, R., 'An Incomplete Narrative: Prosecuting Sexual Violence at the ECCC' 3(1) *Journal of International Criminal Justice* (2015) 331.

Killean, R., 'Exposing Coercive Control in the Commission of Forced Marriage: A Cambodian Case Study' 14(2) *Contemporary Issues in Law* (2017) 95–118.

Killean, R., 'Pursuing Retributive and Reparative Justice within Cambodia' in C. Lawther, L. Moffett and D. Jacobs (eds.) *Research Handbook on Transitional Justice* (Elgar, 2017) 466–488.

Killean, R., 'Constructing Victimhood at the Khmer Rouge Tribunal: Visibility, Selectivity and Participation' *International Review of Victimology* (2018).

Killean, R. and L. Moffett, 'Victim Legal Representations before the ICC and ECCC' 15(4) *Journal of International Criminal Justice* (2017) 713.

Kirchenbauer, N., et al., 'Victims Participation before the Extraordinary Chambers in the Courts of Cambodia' *Baseline Study of the Cambodian Human Rights and Development Association's Civil Party Scheme for Case 002* (2013).

Kissinger, K., *White House Years* (Little Brown, 1979).

Kiza, E., C. Rathgeber and H. Rohne, *Victims of War: An Empirical Study on War Victimization and Victims' Attitudes towards Addressing Atrocities* (Hamburger Edition, 2006).

Klein, K.M., 'Bringing the Khmer Rouge to Justice: The Challenges and Risks Facing the Joint Tribunal in Cambodia' 4(3) *Northwestern Journal of International Human Rights* (2006).

Klinkner, M., and H. Davis, 'A Right to Truth: Victims and the International Criminal Court' 3 *Torture – Asian and Global Perspectives, Asian Human Rights Commission* (2014) 55.

Klosterman, T., 'The Feasibility and Propriety of a Truth Commission in Cambodia: Too Little? Too Late?' 15(3) *Arizona Journal of International and Comparative Law* (1998) 833.

Klug, F., 'Human Rights and Victims' in E. Cape (ed.) *Reconcilable Rights? Analysing the Tension between Victims and Defendants* (Legal Action Group, 2004) 111–124.

Knaus, G., and F. Martin, '"Travails of the European Raj" Lessons from Bosnia Herzegovina' 14 *Journal of Democracy* (2003) 60.

Koller, D.S., 'The Faith of the International Criminal Lawyer' 40 *New York University Journal of International law and Politics* (2008) 1019.

Koskenniemi, M., 'Between Impunity and Show Trials' 6 *Max Planck Yearbook of United Nations Law* (2002).

Kramer, A., and R. Killean 'Security Council Referrals to the ICC: A Politicised System' *The Irish Yearbook of International Law* (2012) 117.

Kress, C., 'The Procedural Law of the International Criminal Court in Outline: Anatomy of Unique Compromises' 1 *Journal of International Criminal Justice* (2003) 603.

Kroker, P., 'Transitional Justice Policy in Practice: Victim Participation in the Khmer Rouge Tribunal' 53 *German Yearbook of International Law* (2010) 753.

Kunst, C., *The Protection of Victims and Witnesses at International and Internationalized Criminal Courts – The Example of the ECCC* (Wolf Legal Publishers, 2013).

Kury, H., and M. Kaiser, 'The Victim's Position within the Criminal Proceedings – An Empirical Study' in G. Kaiser, H. Kury and H.J. Albrecht (eds.) *Victims and Criminal Justice: Legal Protection, Restitution and Support* (Max-Planck Institute for Foreign and International Law, 1991) 579–628.

Kurze, A., C. Lamont and S. Robins, 'Contested Spaces of Transitional Justice: Legal Empowerment in Global Post-Conflict Contexts Revisited' 19(3) *The International Journal of Human Rights* (2015).

Kutnjak Ivković, S., and J. Hagan, *Reclaiming Justice: The International Tribunal for the Former Yugoslavia and Local Courts* (Oxford University Press, 2011).

LaTour, S., 'Determinants of Participant and Observer Satisfaction with Adversary and Inquisitorial Modes of Adjudication' 36(12) *Journal of Personality and Social Psychology* (1978) 1531.

Laub, D., 'An Event without a Witness: Truth, Testimony and Survival' in S Felman and D Laub, *Testimony: Crisis of Witnessing in Literature, Psychoanalysis, and History* (Routledge, 1992) 75–93.

Lawrence-Lightfood, S., *I've Known Rivers: Lives of Loss and Liberation* (Basic Books, 1994).

Lawther, C., 'The Construction and Politicisation of Victimhood' in O Lynch and J Argomaniz (eds.) *Victims of Terrorism: A Comparative and Interdisciplinary Study* (Routledge, 2015) 10–31.

Lawther, C., 'Victims Needs and Dealing with the Past' in O Lynch and J Argomaniz (eds.) *Victims of Terrorism: A Comparative and Interdisciplinary Study* (Routledge, 2015) 31–58.

Ledgerwood, J., 'Understanding Cambodia: Social Hierarchy and Patron-Client Relationships' *Cambodian Recent History and Contemporary: An Introductory Course*, Department of Anthropology and Center for Southeast Asian Studies, Northern Illinois University, 2002, www.seasite.niu.edu/khmer/ledgerwood/patrons.htm (accessed 22/02/18).

Lee, R., (ed.) *The International Criminal Court: The Making of the Rome Statute-Issues, Negotiations, Results* (Kluwer Law International, 1999).

Liebling, A., (assisted by H Arnold), *Prisons and Their Moral Performance: A Study of Values, Quality and Prison Life* (Oxford University Press, 2004).

Letschert, R., et al. (eds.) *Victimological Approaches to International Crimes: Africa* (Intersentia, 2011).

Leung, K., and E.A. Lind, 'Procedural Justice and Culture: Effects of Culture, Gender, and Investigator Status on Procedural Preferences' 50(6) *Journal of Personality and Social Psychology* (1986) 1134.

Leventhal, G., 'What Should be Done with Equity Theory' in K.J. Gergen et al. (eds.) *Social Exchange: Advances in Theory and Research* (Plenum, 1980) 27–55.

Leventhal, G., J. Karuza and W. Fry, 'Beyond Fairness: a Theory of Allocation Preferences' in G. Miluka (ed.) *Justice and Social Interaction* (Springer-Verlag, 1980) 167–218.

Lewis, M.W., and A.J. Grimes, 'Metatriangulation: Building Theory from Multiple Paradigms' 24(4) *Academy of Management Review* (1999) 67.

Lilja, M., *Resisting Gendered Norms: Civil Society, the Juridical and Political Space in Cambodia* (Ashgate, 2013).

Lind, E.A., and T.R. Tyler, *The Social Psychology of Procedural Justice* (Springer, 1988).

Lind, E.A. and K. Van den Bos, 'When Fairness Works: Toward a General Theory of Uncertainty Management' 24 *Research in Organization Behavior* (2002) 181.

Lind, E.A., et al., 'Procedure and Outcome Effects on Reactions to Adjudicated Resolution of Conflicts of Interests' 39 *Journal of Personality and Social Psychology* (1980) 643.

Linton, S., 'New Approaches to International Justice in Cambodia and East Timor' 84 *International Review of the Red Cross* (2002) 845.

Linton, S., *Reconciliation in Cambodia* (Documentation Center of Cambodia, 2004).

Lipsky, M., and D. Olson, *Commission Politics: The Processing of Racial Crisis in America* (Transaction, 1977).

Lis, J., 'Yisrael Beiteinu Renews Bid to Brand Foreign-funded NGOs as Foreign Agents' *Haaretz*, 11 June 2015, www.haaretz.com/news/israel/.premium-1.660648 (accessed 16/02/18).

Loader, I., and A Mulcahy, *Policing and the Condition of England: Memory, Politics and Culture* (Oxford University Press, 2003).

Lobwein, W., 'Experiences of the Victims and Witnesses at the ICTY' in U Ewald and K Turkovic (eds.) *Large-Scale Victimisation as a Potential Source of Terrorist Activities: Importance of Regaining Security in Post-Conflict Societies* (IOS Press 2006) 197–208.

Long, N., 'From Paradigm Lost to Paradigm Regained? The Case for an Actor-Oriented Sociology of Development' 49 *European Review of Latin American and Caribbean Studies* (1990) 3.

Long, N. and A. Long, (eds.), *Battlefields of Knowledge: the Interlocking of Theory and Practice in Social Research and Development* (Routledge, 1992).

Luftglass, S., 'Crossroads in Cambodia: the United Nation's Responsibility to Withdraw Involvement from the Establishment of a Cambodian Tribunal to Prosecute the Khmer Rouge' 90 *Virginia Law Review* (2004) 893.

Luna, E., 'Punishment, Holism, and the Procedural Conception of Restorative Justice' 1 *Utah Law Review* (2003) 205.

Lundy, P. and M. McGovern, 'The Role of Community in Participatory Transitional Justice' in K McEvoy and L McGregor (eds.) *Transitional Justice from Below: Grassroots Activism and the Struggle for Change* (Hart Publishing, 2008) 99–120.

Lundy, P. and M. McGovern, 'Whose Justice? Rethinking Transitional Justice from the Bottom Up' 35(2) *Journal of Law and Society* (2008) 265.

MacKinnon, I., 'Prosecutor Wants to Indict Five More Khmer Rouge' *Financial Times*, 7 September 2009.
Madlingozi, T., 'On Transitional Justice Entrepreneurs and the Production of Victims' 2 *Journal of Human Rights Practice* (2010) 208.
Magliveras, K.D., 'Difficulties and Status of Efforts to Create an International Criminal Court in Cambodia' 3(2) *Asia-Pacific Journal on Human Rights and the Law* (2002) 105.
Maguire, M., 'The Needs and Rights of Victims of Crime' 14 *Crime and Justice* (1991) 363.
Maguire, M., and T. Bennett, *Burglary in a Dwelling* (Heinemann, 1982).
Mahoney, C., *The Justice Sector Afterthought: Witness Protection in Africa* (Institute for Security Studies, 2001).
Mallinder, L., *Amnesty, Human Rights and Political Transitions: Bridging the Peace and Justice Divide* (Hart Publishing, 2008).
Malmström, S., 'Restitution of Property and Compensation to Victims' in R. May (ed.) *Essays on ICTY Procedure and Evidence* (Kulwer Law International, 2001) 373–384.
Mani, R., 'Reparation as a Component of Transitional Justice: Pursuing "Reparative Justice" in the Aftermath of Violent Conflict' in K. De Feyter et al. (eds.) *Out of the Ashes: Reparation for Victims of Gross and Systemic Human Rights Violations* (Intersentia, 2005) 53–82.
Martens, K., 'Professionalised Representation of Human Rights NGOs to the United Nations' 10(1) *The International Journal of Human Rights* (2006) 19.
Maslow, A., *Towards a Psychology of Being* (2nd edn) (Van Nostrand Reinhold, 1968).
Massidda, P. and S. Pellet, 'Role and Practice of the Office of Public Counsel for Victims' in C. Stahn and G. Sluiter (eds.) *The Emerging Practice of the International Criminal Court* (Brill, 2009) 691–706.
Matthews, R.A. and D. Kauzlarich, 'State Crimes and State Harms: A Tale of Two Definitions Frameworks' 48 *Cime, Law and Social Change* (2007) 43.
Matza, D., *Delinquency and Drift* (Wiley, 1964).
Maurrus, M.R., 'A Jewish Lobby at Nuremberg: Jacob Robinson and the Institute for Jewish Affairs 1945–1946' 27 *Cardozo Law Review* (2006) 1651.
Mawby, R., 'Public Sector Services and the Victim of Crime' in S. Walklate (ed.) *Handbook of Victims and Victimology* (Routledge 2007) 209–240.
Mawby R., and S. Walklate, *Critical Victimology* (Sage, 1994).
McAlinden, A.M., 'Deconstructing Victim and Offender Identities in Discourses on Child Sexual Abuse: Hierarchies, Blame and the Good/Evil Dialectic' 54(2) *British Journal of Criminology* (2014) 180.
McCargo, D., 'Politics by Other Means? The Virtual Trials of the Khmer Rouge Tribunal' 87(3) *International Affairs* (2011).
McCarthy, C., 'Victim Redress and International Criminal Justice: Competing Paradigms, or Compatible Forms of Justice?' 10 *Journal of International Criminal Justice* (2012) 351.
McCormack, T.L.H., 'Selective Reaction to Atrocity: War Crimes and the Development of International Criminal Law' 60 *Albany Law Review* (1996–1997) 681.
McEvoy, K., 'Beyond Legalism: Towards a Thicker Understanding of Transitional Justice' 24 *Journal of Law and Society* (2007) 411.
McEvoy, K., 'Letting Go of Legalism: Developing a 'Thicker' Version of Transitional Justice' in K. McEvoy and L. McGregor (eds.) *Transitional Justice from Below: Grassroots Activism and the Struggle for Change* (Hart Publishing, 2008).

McEvoy, K., and B. Gormally, '"Seeing" Is Believing: Positivist Terrorology, Peacemaking Criminology, and the Northern Ireland Peace Process' 8(1) *Critical Criminology* (1997) 9.

McEvoy, K., and L. Mallinder, 'Amnesties in Transition: Punishment, Restoration, and the Governance of Mercy' 39(3) *Journal of Law and Society* (2012) 410.

McEvoy, K., and K. McConnachie, 'Victimology in Transitional Justice: Victimhood, Innocence and Hierarchy' 9(5) *European Journal of Criminology* (2012) 527.

McEvoy, K., and K. McConnachie, 'Victims and Transitional Justice: Voice, Agency and Blame' 22 *Social and Legal Studies* (2013) 489.

McEvoy, K., and L. McGregor (eds.), *Transitional Justice from Below: Grassroots Activism and the Struggle for Change* (Hart Publishing, 2008).

McEvoy, K., and R. Rebouche, 'Mobilising the Professions?: Lawyers, Politics and the Collective Legal Conscience' in J. Morison, K. McEvoy and G. Anthony (eds.) *Judges, Human Rights and Transition* (Oxford University Press, 2007) 275–314.

McGonigle, B., 'Two for the Price of One: Attempts by the Extraordinary Chambers in the Courts of Cambodia to Combine Retributive and Restorative Justice Principles' 2(1) *Leiden Journal of International Law* (2009) 127.

McGonigle Leyh, B., *Procedural Justice? Victim Participation in International Criminal Proceedings* (Intersentia, 2011).

McGonigle Leyh, B., 'Victim-Oriented Measures at International Criminal Institutions: Participation and its Pitfalls' 12 *International Criminal Law Review* (2012) 375.

McGregor, L., 'International Law as a "Tiered Process"' in K McEvoy and L McGregor (eds.) *Transitional Justice from Below: Grassroots Activism and the Struggle for Change* (Hart Publishing, 2008) 47–75.

McKay, F., *REDRESS Statement on behalf of the Victims Rights Working Group*, Rome Conference, 16 June 1998.

McKinlay J., 'On the Professional Regulation of Change' in P Halmos (ed.) *Professionalization and Social Change* (The Sociological Review, 1973) 61–84.

Meernick, J., 'Victors' Justice or the Law? Judging and Punishing at the International Criminal Tribunal for the Former Yugoslavia' *Journal of Conflict Resolution* (2003) 140.

Meernik, J., 'Justice and Peace? How the International Criminal Tribunal Affects Societal Peace in Bosnia' 42 *Journal of Peace Research* 30 (2005).

Mendelsohn, B., 'Rape in Criminology' *Giustizia Penale* (1940).

Mendelsohn, B., 'Une nouvelle branche de la science bio-psycho-sociale, la victimologie' *Etudes Internationales de Psycho-Sociologie Criminelle* (1956).

Menkel-Meadow, C., 'The Causes of Cause Lawyering: Toward and Understanding of the Motivation and Commitment of Social Justice Lawyers' in A. Sarat and S Scheigold (eds.) *Cause Lawyering: Political Commitments and Professional Responsibilities* (Oxford University Press, 1998) 31–68.

Mettraux, G., 'Victims' Participation in International Criminal Law' 8(1) *Journal of International Criminal Justice* (2010) 75.

Mettraux, G., et al., *Expert Initiative on Promoting Effectiveness at the International Criminal Court* (University of Amsterdam, 2014).

Metzl, J.F., *Western Responses to Human Rights Abuses in Cambodia, 1975–80* (Palgrave McMillan, 1996).

Mey, C., *Survivor* (DC-Cam, 2012).

Miceli, T.J., and M.M. Cogel 'Reputation and Judicial Decision-Making' 23 *Journal of Economic Behavior and Organization* (1994) 31.

Michalowski, R. 'All or Nothing: An Inquiry into the (Im)possibility of Cause Lawyering under Cuban Socialism' in A. Sarat and S Scheigold (eds.) *Cause Lawyering: Political Commitments and Professional Responsibilities* (Oxford University Press, 1998).

Miers, D., 'Positivist Victimology: a Critique Part 1' 1 *International Review of Victimology* (1989) 1.

Miers, D., 'Positivist Victimology: a Critique Part 2' 1(3) *International Review of Victimology* (1990) 219.

Miers, D., 'Looking beyond Great Britain: the Development of Criminal Injuries Compensation' in S. Walklate (ed.) *Handbook of Victims and Victimology* (Routledge, 2007) 337–362.

Minority Rights Organisation, www.mirocambodia.org.

Moffett, L., 'The Role of Victims in the International Criminal Tribunals of the Second World War' 12(2) *International Criminal Law Review* (2012) 245.

Moffett, L., *Justice for Victims at the International Criminal Court* (Routledge, 2014).

Moffett, L., 'Meaningful and Effective? Considering Victims' Interests through Participation at the International Criminal Court' 26 *Criminal Law Forum* (2015) 255.

Moffett, L., 'Reparations for Victims at the International Criminal Court: A New Way Forward?' 21(9) *The International Journal of Human Rights* (2017) 1204.

Mohan, G., 'Not so Distant, Not so Strange: the Personal and the Political in Participatory Research' 2 *Ethics, Place and the Environment* (1999) 41.

Mohan, M., 'The Paradox of Victim-Centrism: Victim Participation at the Khmer Rouge Tribunal' 9 *International Criminal Law Review* (2009) 733.

Mohan, M., 'Reconstituting the "Un-Person": The Khmer Krom and the Khmer Rouge Tribunal' 12 *Singapore Yearbook of International Law* (2010) 43.

Morgan, R., and A. Sanders, *The Uses of Victim Statements* (UK Home Office, 1999).

Morris, A., and L. Gelsthorpe, 'Re-visioning Men's Violence against Female Partners' 39(3) *Howard Journal of Criminal Justice* (2000) 412.

Moyo, D., *Dead Aid: Why Aid Is Not Working and How There Is a Better Way for Africa* (FSG, 2010).

Muck, W., and E. Wiebelhaus-Brahm, 'Patterns of Transitional Justice Assistance among the International Community' *Paper Presented at Sixth European Consortium for Political Research General Conference* (Reykjavik, 25–27 August 2011).

Muleefu, A., 'The Role of Civil Society in Addressing Problems Faced by Victims in Post-Genocide Rwanda' in R. Letschert et al. (eds.) *Victimological Approaches to International Crimes: Africa* (Intersentia, 2011) 411–436.

Munck, R., and D. O'Hearn (eds.), *Critical Development Theory: Contributions to a New Paradigm* (Zed Books, 2009).

Musante, L., M.A. Gilbert and J. Thibaut, 'The Effects of Control on Perceived Fairness of Procedure and Outcome' 19 *Journal of Experimental Social Psychology* (1983) 223.

Musila, G., *Rethinking International Criminal Law: Restorative Justice and the Rights of Victims in the International Criminal Court* (Lambert Academic Publishing, 2010).

Mydans, S., 'Cambodia is Swept by Reports Saying that Pol Pot has Died' *New York Times*, 16 April 1998.

Mysliweic, E., *Punishing the Poor: The International Isolation of Kampuchea* (Oxfam Professional, 1988).

Nagel, W., 'Structural Victimization' 2 *International Journal of Criminology* (1975) 99.

Naren, K. and H. Robertson, 'Victims Call for Money from ECCC' *The Cambodia Daily*, 17 October 2014, www.cambodiadaily.com/news/victims-call-for-compensation-from-eccc-70135/ (accessed 22/02/18).

Newton, E., 'A Study of the Policies and Procedures Implemented by the Probation Service with Respect to Victims of Serious Crime' 2(1) *British Journal of Community Justice* (2003) 25.

Nguyen, L., and C. Sperfeldt, *A Boat Without Anchors: A Report on the Legal Status of Ethnic Vietnamese Minority Populations in Cambodia under Domestic and International Laws Governing Nationality and Statelessness* (Jesuit Refugee Service, 2012).

Nguyen, L., and C. Sperfeldt, 'Victim Participation and Minorities in Internationalised Criminal Trials: Ethnic Vietnamese Civil Parties at the Extraordinary Chambers in the Courts of Cambodia' 14 *Macquarie Law Journal* (2014) 97.

Nohlen, D., et al., *Elections in Asia: A Data Handbook, Volume II* (Oxford University Press, 2001).

Nouwen, S., 'Justifying Justice' in J Crawford and M. Koskennieme (eds.) *The Cambridge Companion to International Law* (Cambridge University Press, 2012) 327–352.

Nowrojee, B., '"Your Justice is Too Slow": Will the ICTR Fail Rwanda's Rape Victims?' *Occasional Paper No. 10, UN Research Institute for Social Devlopment* (2005).

Nyamu-Musembi, C., 'Towards an Actor-Oriented Perspective on Human Rights' *Working Paper 169, Surrey Institute of Development Studies* (2002).

Oomen, B., 'Donor-Driven Justice and its Discontents: The Case of Rwanda' 36(5) *Development and Change* (2005) 887.

Open Society Justice Initiative, *Recent Developments at the Extraordinary Chambers in the Courts of Cambodia* (May 2008).

Open Society Justice Initiative, *Recent Developments at the Extraordinary Chambers in the Courts of Cambodia* (November 2009).

Open Society Justice Initiative, *Recent Initiatives at the Extraordinary Chambers in the Courts of Cambodia* (March 2010).

Open Society Justice Initiative, *Political Interference at the Extraordinary Chambers in the Courts of Cambodia* (July 2010).

Open Society Justice Initiative, *Recent Developments at the Extraordinary Chamber in the Courts of Cambodia* (September 2010).

Open Society Justice Initiative, 'Funding Reparations for Victims in Case 002 is Critical to the Legacy of the Extraordinary Chambers in the Courts of Cambodia (ECCC)' *Position Paper*, September 2013.

Opening Speech by the Plenary's President Judge KONG Srim, 13 September 2010, www.eccc.gov.kh/sites/default/files/media/8th_plenary_president_speech_EN.pdf (accessed 16/02/18).

Orentlicher, D., 'Settling Accounts' Revisited: Reconciling Global Norms with Local Agency' 1 *International Journal of Transitional Justice* (2007) 10.

Orentlicher, D., *That Someone Guilty Be Punished: Impact of the ICTY in Bosnia* (Open Society Justice Initiative and International Center for Transitional Justice, 2010).

Organisation for Security and Cooperation in Europe, *Trial Monitoring: A Reference Manual for Practitioners* (OSCE, Office for Democratic Institutions and Human Rights, 2012).

Orth, U., 'Secondary Victimization of Crime Victims by Criminal Proceedings' 15(4) *Social Justice Research* (2002) 313.

Osiel, M., *Mass Atrocity, Collective Memory and the Law* (Transaction Publishers, 1997).

Osiel, M., *Making Sense of Mass Atrocity* (Cambridge University Press, 2009).

O'Toole, J., 'ECCC Officials to Seek Funds in US' *The Phnom Penh Post*, 20 May 2010, www.phnompenhpost.com/national/eccc-officials-seek-funds-us (accessed 16/02/18).

O'Toole, J., 'Reparations Remain a Key Issue' *The Phnom Penh Post*, 27 July 2010.

Owen, T., and Kernan, B., 'Bombs over Cambodia' *The Walrus Magazine*, October 2006.

Palmer, N., *Courts in Conflict* (Oxford University Press, 2015).

Papic, Z., et al., *International Support Policies to South East European Counties – Lessons (Not) Learned in Bosnia-Herzegovina* (Open Society Fund, 2001).

Paris, R., 'International Peacebuilding and the "Mission Civilisatrice"' 28 *Review of International Studies* (2002) 637.

Parks, T., 'The Rise and Fall of Donor Funding for Advocacy NGOs: Understanding the Impact' 18(2) *Development in Practice* (2008) 213.

Pasqualucci, J.M., 'Victim Reparations in the Inter-American Human Rights System: A Critical Assessment of Current Practice and Procedure' 32 *Michigan Journal of International Law* (1996–1997) 1.

Pearson, Z., 'Non-Governmental Organizations and the International Criminal Court: Changing Landscapes of International Law' 39 *Cornell International Law Journal* (2006).

Pena, M., 'Victim Participation at the International Criminal Court: Achievements Made and Challenges Lying Ahead' 16 *ILSA Journal of International and Comparative Law* (2009–2010) 497.

Pena, M., and G. Carayon, 'Is the ICC making the Most of Victim Participation?' 7(3) *International Journal of Transitional Justice* (2013) 518.

Peou, S., *International Democracy Assistance for Peacebuilding: The Cambodian Experience* (Palgrave Macmillan, 2007).

Petit, R., 'Lawfare and International Tribunals: A Question of Definition? A Reflection on the Creation of the "Khmer Rouge Tribunal"' 43 *Case Western Reserve Journal of International Law* (2010–2011) 189.

Pham, P., et al., *So We Will Never Forget: A Population-Based Survey on Attitudes About Social Reconstruction and the Extraordinary Chambers in the Courts of Cambodia* (Human Rights Center, Berkeley, 2009).

Pham, P., et al., *After the First Trial: A Population-Based Survey on Knowledge and Perception of Justice and the Extraordinary Chambers in the Courts of Cambodia* (Human Rights Center, Berkeley, 2011).

Pham, P., et al. 'Victim Participation and the Trial of Duch at the Extraordinary Chambers in the Courts of Cambodia' 3 *Journal of Human Rights Practice* (2011) 264.

Picker, C., 'International Law's Mixed Heritage: A Common/Civil Law Jurisdiction' 41 *Vanderbilt Journal of Transnational Law* (2008).

Pitkin, H., 'Obligation and Consent – II' 60(1) *American Political Science Review* (1996) 39.

Pizzi, W., *Trials Without Truth: Why Our System of Criminal Trials Has Become an Expensive Failure and What We Need to Do to Rebuild It* (New York University Press, 1999).

Polikoff, N.D., 'Am I My Client?: The Role Confusion of a Lawyer Activist' 31 *Harvard Civil Rights-Civil Liberties Law Review* (1996) 443.
Ponchaud, F., *Cambodia Year Zero* (Henry Holt & Co, 1978).
Posner, R.A., *How Judges Think* (Harvard University Press, 2008).
Pritchett, S.M., 'Entrenched Hegemony, Efficient Procedure, or Selective Justice?: An Inquiry into Charges for Gender-Based Violence at the International Criminal Court' 17 *Transnational Law and Contemporary Problems* (2008) 265.
Rajagopal, B., 'International Law and Social Movements: Challenges of Theorizing Resistance' 41 *Colombia Journal of Transnational Law* (2003) 397.
Rajagopal, B., *International Law from Below: Development, Social Movements and Third World Resistance* (Cambridge University Press, 2003).
Rajalakshmi, V., 'Targeting NGOs' *Frontline*, 11 July 2014, www.frontline.in/cover-story/targeting-ngos/article6141097.ece (accessed 16/02/18).
Ramirez, R., 'Stakeholder Analysis and Conflict Management' in D Buckles (ed.) *Cultivating Peace: Conflict and Collaboration in Natural Resource Management* (World Bank, 1999) 101–129.
Ramji-Nogales, J., 'Designing Bespoke Transitional Justice: A Pluralist Process Approach' 32(1) *Michigan Journal of International Law* (2010) 1.
Ramsay, P., 'Overcriminalization as Vulnerable Citizenship' 13(2) *New Criminal Law Review* (2010) 262.
Rasmussen, H., *On Law and Policy in the European Court of Justice: A Comparative Study in Judicial Policymaking* (Martinus Nijhoff, 1986).
Ratner, S.R., 'The United Nations Group of Experts for Cambodia' 93 *American Journal of International Law* (1999) 948.
Raub, L., 'Positioning Hybrid Tribunals in International Criminal Justice' *41 International Law and Politics* (2009).
Rauschenbach, M., and D. Scalia, 'Victims and International Criminal Justice: a Vexed Question?' 870 *International Review of the Red Cross* (2008).
Rauxloh, R.E., 'Plea Bargaining in International Criminal Justice: Can the international Criminal Court Afford to Avoid Trials' 1(2) *Journal of criminal Justice Research* (2011) 1.
REDRESS, *Justice for Victims. The ICC's Reparations Mandate* (REDRESS Trust, 2011).
REDRESS, *The Participation of Victims in International Criminal Court Proceedings: A Review of the Practice and Consideration of Options for the Future* (REDRESS Trust, 2012).
Reeves, H., and P. Dunn, 'The Status of Crime Victims and Witnesses in the Twenty-First Century' in A. Bottoms and J. Roberts (eds.) *Hearing the Victim: Adversarial Justice, Crime Victims and the State* (Routledge, 2012) 46–71.
Renzetti, C., 'Feminist Perspectives on Victimisation' in J.K. Wilson (ed.) *The Praeger Handbook of Victimology* (Greenwood Press, 2009).
Rhodes, R., and M. Bevir, 'Defending Interpretation' 5 *European Political Science* (2006) 69.
Roberts, J., and M. Manikis, '*Victim Personal Statements at Sentencing: A Review of the Empirical Research* (Office of the Commissioner for Victims and Witnesses of England and Wales, 2011).
Robins, S., 'Towards a Victim-Centred Transitional Justice: Understanding the Needs of Families of the Disappeared in Postconflict Nepal' 5 *The International Journal of Transitional Justice* (2011) 75.

Robins, S., 'Transitional Justice as an Elite Discourse' 44(1) *Critical Asian Studies* (2012) 3.

Robinson, W., *Promoting Polyarchy: Globalisation, US Intervention, and Hegemony* (Cambridge University Press, 1996).

Rock, P., *A View from the Shadows: The Ministry of the Solicitor General of Canada and the Justice for Victims of Crime Initiative* (Clarendon Press, 1986).

Rock, P., *Helping Victims of Crime: The Home Office and the Rise of the Victim in England and Wales* (Clarendon Press, 1990).

Rock, P., 'On Becoming a Victim' in C. Hoyle and R. Young (eds.) *New Visions of Crime and Victims* (Hart Publishing, 2002) 1–22.

Rogers, G., 'Provision of Post-sentence Advice to Victims of Serious Crime: Perceptions in one British Probation Service' 1(4) *Crime Prevention and Community Safety: An International Journal* (1999).

Roht-Arriaza, N. (ed.), *Impunity and Human Rights in International Law and Practice* (Oxford University Press, 1995).

Roht-Arriaza, N., and K. Orlovsky, 'A Complementary Relationship: Reparations and Development' *International Centre for Transitional Justice: Research Brief* (July 2009).

Rombouts, H., 'Importance and Difficulties of Victim-Based Research in Post-Conflict Societies' 10 *European Journal of Crime, Criminal Law and Criminal Justice* (2002) 216.

Rosenfeld, F., 'Collective Reparations for Victims of Armed Conflict' 92 *International Review of the Red Cross* (2010) 731.

Rothe, D.L. and D. Kauzlarich, 'A Victimology of State Crime' in D.L. Rothe and D. Kauzlarich (eds.) *Towards a Victimology of state Crime* (Routledge, 2014) 3–15.

Rudy, D., and M. Hirst, 'Victims Appearing in Person before a Chamber' in K. Tibori-Szabó and M. Hirst (eds.) *Victim Participation in International Criminal Justice* (Asser, 2017) 283–281.

SáCouto, S., and K. Cleary, 'Victims' Participation in the Investigations of the International Criminal Court' 17 *Transnational Law and Contemporary Problems* (2008) 73.

Sagan, S., 'African Criminals/African Victims: The Institutionalised Production of Cultural Narratives in International Criminal Law' 39(3) *Millennium Journal of International Studies* (2010) 12.

Saliba, M., 'Civil Parties Boycott Start of Character Witness Testimony while Experts Offer Psychological Assessment of Duch' *Cambodia Tribunal Monitor*, 31 August 2009.

Saliba, M., 'Civil Party Participation at ECCC: Overview' *Cambodia Tribunal Monitor*, 6 November 2009.

Samset, I., S.S. Petersen and V. Wang, 'Maintaining the Process? Aid to Transitional Justice in Rwanda and Guatemala, 1995–2005' *Paper Presented at 'Building a Future on Peace and Justice'* (Nuremberg, 25–27 June 2007).

Samuel, G., *A Short Introduction to the Common Law* (Edward Elgar, 2014).

Sanders, A., et al., 'Victim Impact Statements: Don't Work, Can't Work' *Criminal Law Review* (June 2001) 447.

Sarat, A., 'Vengeance, Victims and the Identities of Law' 6(2) *Social and Legal Studies* (1997) 163.

Sarat, A., and S. Scheigold (eds.), *Cause Lawyering: Political Commitments and Professional Responsibilities* (Oxford University Press, 1998).

Sarat, A., and S. Scheingold (eds.), *Cause Lawyering and the State in a Global Era* (Oxford University Press, 2001).

Sarat, A. and S. Scheingold (eds.), *The Worlds Cause Lawyers Make: Structure and Agency in Legal Practice* (Stanford University Press, 2005).

Sarat., A. and S. Scheingold (eds.) *Cause Lawyering and Social Movements* (Stanford University Press, 2006).

Sarat, A., and S. Scheingold (eds.) *The Cultural Lives of Cause Lawyers* (Cambridge University Press, 2008).

Schabas, W.A., 'Victor's Justice: Selecting "Situations" at the International Criminal Court' 42 *The John Marshall Law Review* (2009–2010) 535.

Schafer, S., *Victimology: The Victim and His Criminal* (Reston Publishing Company, 1977).

Schauer, F., 'Incentives, Reputation, and the Inglorious Determinants of Judicial Behavior' 68 *University of Cincinnati Law Review* (1999) 615.

Scheffer, D., 'The Extraordinary Chambers in the Courts of Cambodia' in M.C. Bassiouni (ed.) *International Criminal Law* (3rd edn) (Martinus Nijhoff Publishers, 2008) 219–256.

Scheffer, D., 'The Negotiating History of the ECCC's Personal Jurisdiction' *Cambodia Tribunal Monitor*, 22 May 2011.

Scheffer, D., *All the Missing Souls: A Personal History of the War Crimes Tribunals* (Princeton University Press, 2012).

Scheingold, S., and A. Sarat, *Something to Believe In: Politics, Professionalism, and Cause Lawyering* (Stanford University Press, 2004).

Scully, S., 'Judging the Successes and Failures of the Extraordinary Chambers of the Courts of Cambodia' 13 *Asian-Pacific Law and Policy Journal* (2011–2012) 300.

Se, S., 'Cambodian PM Says No Third Khmer Rouge Trial' *Agence France-Presse*, 27 October 2010.

Segal, J.A., and H.J. Spaeth, *The Supreme Court and the Attitudinal Model Revisited* (Cambridge University Press, 2002).

Shapland, J., 'Victims, the Criminal Justice System and Compensation' 24(2) *British Journal of Criminology* (1984) 136.

Shapland, J., 'Monitoring Victim Needs and Victim Programmes' in A. Alvazzi del Frate, U. Zvekic and J.J.M. Van Dijk (eds.) *Understanding Crime: Experiences of Crime and Crime Control*, Acts of the International Conference, Rome, 18–20 November 1992 (UNICRI, 1992) 241–250.

Shapland, J. (ed.), *Justice, Community and Civil Society: A Contested Terrain* (Willan Publishing, 2008).

Shapland, J., and D. Cohen 'Facilities for Victims: The Role of the Police and the Courts' 28 *Criminal Law Review* (1987).

Shapland, J., J. Willmore and P. Duff, *Victims in the Criminal Justice System* (Gower, 1985).

Sheppard, B., 'Justice is no Simple Matter: Case for Elaborating our Model of Procedural Fairness' 49(4) *Journal of Personality and Social Psychology* (1985) 953.

Sherman, L.W., and H. Strang, *Restorative Justice: The Evidence* (Smith Institute, 2007).

Sherwood, H., 'Human Rights Groups Face Global Crackdown "Not Seen in a Generation"' *The Guardian*, 26 August 2015, www.theguardian.com/law/2015/aug/26/ngos-face-restrictions-laws-human-rights-generation (accessed 26/11/15).

Shklar, J., *Legalism: Law, Morals, and Political Trials* (Harvard University Press, 1964).

Simon, J., and R. Sparks, *The SAGE Handbook of Punishment and Society* (SAGE, 2013).

Skilbeck, R., 'Defending the Khmer Rouge' 8 *International Criminal Law Review* (2008) 423.

Smart, C., *Feminism and the Power of Law* (Routledge, 1989).

Smith, D., and J. Gray, *Police and People in London: the PSI Report, Vol 1* (Gower, 1985).

Smith, E., 'Victims in the Witness Stand: Socio-Cultural and Psychological Challenges in Eliciting Victim Testimony' in K. Tibori-Szabó and M. Hirst (eds.) *Victim Participation in International Criminal Justice* (Asser Press, 2017) 315–341.

Sokol, D.S., 'Reduced Victim Participation: A Misstep by the Extraordinary Chambers in the Courts of Cambodia' 10 *Washington University Global Studies Law Review* (2011).

Sommerlad, H., 'Managerialism and the Legal Profession: A New Professional Paradigm' 2 *International Journal of the Legal Profession* (1995) 159.

Soros, G., 'Legal Empowerment, Justice and Development' in *Case Studies in Legal Empowerment: From Land Rights to Healthcare* (Open Society Institute, 2013).

Spalek, B., *Crime Victims: Theory, Policy and Practice* (Palgrave Macmillan, 2006).

Sparks R., et al., *Surveying Witnesses* (John Wiley, 1977).

Sperfeldt, C., 'Cambodian Civil Society and the Khmer Rouge Tribunal' 6(1) *International Journal of Transitional Justice* (2012) 149.

Sperfeldt, C. 'The Trial Against Hissène Habré: networked justice and reparations at the Extraordinary African Chambers' 21(9) *The International Journal of Human Rights* (2017) 1243.

Spiga, V., 'No Redress without Justice: Victims and International Criminal Law' 10 *Journal of International Criminal Justice* (2012) 1377.

Stammel, N., et al., *The Survivors' Voices: Attitudes on the ECCC, the Former Khmer Rouge and Civil Party Participation* (Berlin Center for the Treatment of Torture Victims, December 2010).

Starygin, S., 'Internal Rules of the Extraordinary Chambers in the Courts of Cambodia (ECCC): Setting an Example of the Rule of Law by Breaking the Law?' 3(2) *Journal of Law and Conflict Resolution* (2011) 20.

Stegmiller, I., 'Legal Developments in Civil Party Participation at the Extraordinary Chambers in the Courts of Cambodia' 27 *Leiden Journal of International Law* (2014) 465.

Stensrud, E.E., 'New Dilemmas in Transitional Justice: Lessons from the Mixed Courts in Sierra Leone and Cambodia' 46(1) *Journal of Peace Research* (2009) 5.

Stover, E., *The Witnesses: War Crimes and the Promise of Justice in The Hague* (University of Pennsylvania Press, 2005).

Stover, E., et al., 'The Medical and Social Consequences of Land Mines in Cambodia' 272(5) *Journal of the American Medical Association* (1994).

Stover, E., M. Balthazard and K.A. Koenig, 'Confronting Duch: Civil Party Participation in Case 001 at the ECCC' 93(882) *International Review of the Red Cross* (2011).

Stover, E., and H. Weinstein, 'Conclusion: A Common Objective, a Universe of Alternatives' in H. Weinstein and E. Stover (eds.) *My Neighbor, My Enemy: Justice and Social Reconstruction in Rwanda and the Former Yugoslavia* (Cambridge University Press, 2004) 323–343.

Stover, R. and H.S. Erlanger, *Making It and Breaking It: The Fate of Public Interest Commitment during Law School* (University of Illinois Press, 1989).

Strang, H., *Repair or Revenge: Victims and Restorative Justice* (Oxford University Press, 2002).

Strangio, S., *Hun Sen's Cambodia* (Yale University Press, 2014).

Stromseth, J.E., 'Pursuing Accountability for Atrocities after Conflict: What Impact on Building the Rule of Law?' 38 *Georgetown Journal of International Law* (2007) 251.

Studzinsky, S., 'Victim Participation before the Extraordinary Chambers in the Courts of Cambodia' 6 *Zeitschrift fur Internationale Strafrechtdogmati* (2011) 997.

Studzinsky, S., 'Participation Rights of Victims as Civil Parties and the Challenges' in T. Bonacker and C. Safferling (eds.) *Victims of International Crimes: An Interdisciplinary Discourse* (Asser Press, 2013) 175–189.

Szmania, S.J., and M.L. Gracyalny, 'Addressing the Court, the Offender and the Community: A Communication Analysis of Victim Impact Statements in a Non-Capital Sentencing Hearing' 13(3) *International Review of Victimology* (2006) 231.

Tallgren, I., 'The Sensibility and Sense of International Criminal Law' 13(3) *European Journal of International Law* (2002) 561.

Tankebe, J., and A. Liebling (eds.), *Legitimacy and Criminal Justice* (Oxford University Press, 2015).

Tarr, G.A., *Judicial Process and Judicial Policy Making* (Wadsworth, 2003).

Taylor, D., 'Victim Participation in Transitional Justice Mechanisms: Real Power or Empty Ritual' *Impunity Watch Discussion Paper* (2014).

Taylor, R.S., 'Better Late Than Never' in J.E. Stromseth (ed.) *International and Comparative Criminal Law Series, Accountability for Atrocities: National and International Responses* (Transnational Publishers, 2003) 237–270.

Taylor, T., *The Anatomy of the Nuremberg Trials: A Personal Memoir* (Alfred A. Knopf, 1992).Teitel, R.G., 'Transitional Justice Genealogy' 16 *Harvard Human Rights Journal* (2003) 69.

Thibaut, J., and L. Walker, *Procedural Justice: A Psychological Analysis* (Erlbaum, 1975).

Thumula, A., B. Goold and I. Loader, 'A Tainted Trade? Moral Ambivalence and Legitimation Work in the Private Security Industry' 62 *British Journal of Sociology* (2011) 283.

Tibori-Szabó, K., et al., 'Communication Between Victims' Lawyers and Their Clients' in K Tibori-Szabó and M. Hirst (eds.) *Victim Participation in International Criminal Justice* (Asser Press, 2017) 433–465.

Tiefenbrun, S.W., 'The Paradox of International Adjudication: Developments in the International Criminal Tribunals for the Former Yugoslavia and Rwanda, The World Court and the International Criminal Court' 25 *North Carolina Journal of International Law and Commercial Regulation* (2000).

Tobolowsky, P., 'Victim Participation in the Criminal Justice Process: Fifteen Years after the President's Task Force on Victims of Crime' 25 *New England Journal on Criminal and Civil Confinement* (1999) 21.

Torrens, S.M.'Allegations of Political Interference, Bias and Corruption at the ECCC' in S. Meisenberg and I. Stegmiller (eds.) *The Extraordinary Chambers in the Courts of Cambodia* (Asser Press, 2016) 45–75.

Transcultural Psychosocial Organisation, *2014 Annual Report*, tpocambodia.org/annual-reports/ (accessed 16/02/18).

Transcultural Psychosocial Organisations, 'Promoting Gender Equality and Improving Justice for Female Survivors and Victims of Gender-Based Violence under the Khmer Rouge Regime', tpocambodia.org/index.php?id=134 (accessed 16/02/18).
Treves T., et al. (eds.), *Civil Society, International Courts and Compliance Bodies* (Asser Press, 2005).
Trombetta-Panigadi, F., 'NGOs and the Activities of the International Criminal Court' in T Treves et al. (eds.) *Civil Society, International Courts and Compliance Bodies* (Asser Press, 2005) 121–129.
Trumbull IV, C., 'The Victims of Victim Participation in International Criminal Proceedings' 29(4) *Michigan Journal of International* Law (2008) 777.
Tulloch, J., *One Day in July: Experiencing 7/7* (Little Brown, 2006).
Turchi, E.A. 'Victims' Attendance in the Courtroom to Observe Proceedings' in K. Tibori-Szabó and M. Hirst (eds.) *Victim Participation in International Criminal Justice* (Asser, 2017) 341–356.
Tyler, T., 'What is Procedural Justice?: Criteria Used by Citizens to Assess the Fairness of Legal Procedures' 22(1) *Law and Society Review* (1988).
Tyler, T., *Why People Obey the Law: Procedural Justice, Legitimacy, and Compliance* (Yale University Press, 1990).
Tyler, T., 'Social Justice: Outcome and Procedure' 35(2) *International Journal of Psychology* (2000) 117.
Tyler, T., 'Procedural Justice, Legitimacy, and the Effective Rule of Law' 30 *Crime and Justice* (2003) 283.
Tyler, T., 'Procedural Justice and the Courts' 44 *Court Review* (2008) 26.
Tyler, T. and S.L. Blader, 'The Group Engagement Model: Procedural Justice, Social Identity, and Cooperative Behaviour' 7(4) *Personality and Social Psychology Review* (2003) 349.
UN, 'UN Ends Negotiations with Cambodia for Proposed Court to Try Former Khmer Rouge' UN News Centre, www.un.org/apps/news/story.asp?NewsID=2829#.Wn2x0macZTY (accessed 09/02/18).
Ung, L., *First They Killed My Father* (Mainstream Publishing, 2001).
Valier, C., *Crime and Punishment in Contemporary Culture* (Routledge, 2004).
Van Camp, T., and V. De Mesmaecker, 'Procedural Justice for Victims of Crime: Are Victim Impact Statements and Victim-Offender Mediation Rising to the Challenge?' in I. Vanfraechem, A. Pemberton and F.M. Ndahinda (eds.) *Justice for Victims: Perspective on Rights, Transition and Reconciliation* (Routledge, 2014) 277–300.
Van den Wyngaert, C., 'Victims before International Criminal Courts. Some Views and Concerns of an ICC Trial Judge' 44 *Case Western Reserve Journal of International Law* (2011) 475.
Vannak, H., *Bou Meng* (DC-Cam, 2010).
Vannarin, N., and D. Gillison, 'Hun Sen Again Warns ECCC of Civil War' *The Cambodia Daily*, 8 September 2009, www.cambodiadaily.com/archives/hun-sen-again-warns-eccc-of-civil-war-1451/ (accessed 09/02/18).
Van Ness, D.W. and K.H. Strong, *Restorative Justice: An Introduction to Restorative Justice* (3rd edn) (LexisNexis/Anderson Publishing, 2006).
Van Rooy, A., *The Global Legitimacy Game: Civil Society, Globalization and Protest* (Palgrave Macmillan, 2004).
Van Wijk, J., 'Who is the "Little old Lady" of International Crimes? Christie's Concept of the Ideal Victim Reinterpreted' 19(2) *International Review of Victimology* (2013) 159.

Vasiliev, S., 'Article 68(3) and the Personal Interests of Victims in the Emerging Practice of the ICC' in C. Stahn and G. Sluiter (eds.) *The Emerging Practice of the International Criminal Court* (Brill, 2009) 635–691.

Vasiliev, S., 'Trial Process at the ECCC: The Rise and Fall of the Inquisitorial Paradigm in International Criminal Law?' in S. Meisenberg and I. Stegmiller (eds.) *The Extraordinary Chambers in the Courts of Cambodia: Hybrid Contributions to International Criminal Law* (Asser Press, 2016).

Veltmeyer, H., *The Critical Development Studies Handbook: Tools For Change* (Pluto Press, 2011).

Veneciano, J.D., and A. Hinton (eds.), *Night of the Khmer Rouge: Genocide and Justice in Cambodia* (Paul Robeson Gallery, 2007).

Vinjamuri, L., and J. Snyder, 'Advocacy and Scholarship in the Study of International War Crime Tribunals and Transitional Justice' 7 *Annual Review of Political Science* (2004) 345.

Von Hentig, H., *The Criminal and His Victim* (Yale University Press, 1948).

Walgrave, L., 'Restorative Justice: An Alternative for Responding to Crime?' in O.B. Shoham and M. Kett (eds.) *International Handbook of Penology and Criminal Justice* (CRC Press, 2008) 613–691.

Walker, L., E.A. Lind and J. Thibaut, 'The Relation between Procedural and Distributive Justice' 65(8) *Virginia Law Review* (1979) 1401.

Walklate, S., *Victimology: The Victim and the Criminal Justice Process* (Unwin Hyman, 1989).

Walklate, S., *Imagining the Victim of Crime* (McGraw-Hill, 2006).

Walklate, S. (ed.), *Handbook of Victims and Victimology* (Routledge, 2007).

Walklate, S., 'Victims, Policy and Delivery' in S. Walklate (ed.) *Handbook of Victims and Victimology* (Routledge, 2007) 203–209.

Wallace, J., 'The Bucolic Life of a Cambodian Grandmother Accused of Mass Killings', *New York Times*, 24 February 2017.

Wallace, J., and K. Naren, 'Khmer Rouge Victims Seek Cash Damages to Honour their Dead' *International Justice Tribune*, 14 January 2015.

Waller, I., 'International Standards, National Trail Blazing and the Next Steps' in M. Maguire and J. Pointing (eds.) *Victims of Crime: A New Deal?* (Open University Press, 1988) 195–203.

Weinstein, H. and E. Stover (eds.), *My Neighbor, My Enemy: Justice and Social Reconstruction in Rwanda and the Former Yugoslavia* (Cambridge University Press, 2004).

Wemmers, J., *Victims in the Criminal Justice System* (Kugler Publications, 1996).

Wemmers, J., 'Victims and the International Criminal Court: Evaluating the Success of the ICC with Respect to Victims' 16 *International Review of Victimology* (2009) 221.

Wemmers, J., 'Victims' Rights and the International Criminal Court: Perceptions within the Court Regarding the Victims' Right to Participate' 23 *Leiden Journal of International Law* (2010) 629.

Wemmers, J., 'Victims' Need for Justice: Individual versus Collective Justice' in R. Letschert et al. (eds.) *Victimological Approaches to International Crimes: Africa* (Intersentia, 2011) 145–289.

Werner, A., and D. Rudy, 'Civil Party Representation at the ECCC: Sounding the Retreat in International Criminal Law?' 8(3) *Northwestern Journal of International Human Rights* (2010) 301.

Wessel, J., 'Judicial Policy-Making at the International Criminal Court: An Institutional Guide to Analyzing International Adjudication' 44 *Columbia Journal of Transnational Law* (2006) 377.

Westad, A., and S. Quinn-Judge (eds.) *The Third Indochina War: Conflict between China, Vietnam and Cambodia, 1972–79* (Routledge, 2006).

White, C., *Bridging Divides in Transitional Justice* (Intersentia, 2017).

Whiting, A., 'In International Criminal Prosecutions, Justice Delayed Can Be Justice Delivered' 50(2) *Harvard International Law Journal* (2009) 323.

Wilkins, D.B., 'Two Paths to the Mountain Top? The Role of Legal Education in Shaping the Values of Black Corporate Lawyers' 45 *Stanford Law Review* (1993) 1981.

Williams, B., and H. Goodman, 'The Role of the Voluntary Sector' in S. Walklate (ed.) *Handbook of Victims and Victimology* (Routledge, 2007) 240–255.

Wilson, R.A., *Writing History in International Criminal Trials* (Cambridge University Press, 2011).

Wolfe-Robinson, M., 'Cambodia Court hearing Khmer Rouge Trials Close to Bankruptcy' *The Guardian*, 4 December 2012, www.theguardian.com/law/2012/dec/04/cambodia-khmer-rouge-court-bankruptcy (accessed 16/02/18).

Wolhuter, L., N. Olley and D. Denham, *Victimology: Victimisation and Victims' Rights* (Routledge, 2009).

World Bank, 'Cambodia Statistics' data.worldbank.org/country/Cambodia (accessed 16/02/18).

Yathay, P., *Stay Alive My Son* (Cornell University Press, 2000).

Yesberg, K., 'Accessing Justice Through Victim Participation at the Khmer Rouge Tribunal' 40 *Victoria University of Wellington Law Review* (2009) 555.

Zacklin, R., 'The Failings of Ad Hoc Tribunals' 2 *Journal of International Criminal Justice* (2004) 541.

Zappalà, S., 'The Rights of Victims v. the Rights of the Accused' 8 *Journal of International Criminal Justice* (2010) 137.

Zasloff, J., and M. Brown, *Cambodia Confounds the Peacemakers 1979–1998* (Cornell University Press, 1998).

Zedner, L., 'Victims' in M. Maguire, R. Morgan and R. Reiner (eds.) *The Oxford Handbook of Criminology* (3rd edn) (Oxford University Press, 2002) 419–456.

Zegveld, L., 'Victims' Reparations Claims and International Criminal Courts: Incompatible Values?' 8 *Journal of International Criminal Justice* (2010) 79.

Table of cases

Extraordinary chambers in the courts of Cambodia

Case 001

Separation Order, 002/14–08–2006, 19 September 2007
Decision on Appeal against Detention Order of Kaing Guek Eav, 001/18–07–2007-ECCC-OCIJ, 3 December 2007
Closing Order indicting Kaing Guek Eav alias "Duch", 001/18–07–2007-ECCC-OCIJ, 8 August 2008
Decision on Appeal against Closing Order Indicting Kaing Guek Eav alias "Duch", 001/18–07–2007-ECCC-PTC, 5 December 2008
Decision of the Trial Chamber Concerning Proof of Identity for Civil Party Applicants, 001/18–07–2007-ECCC/TC, 26 February 2009
Direction on the Scheduling of the Trial, 001/18–07–2007/ECCC/TC, 20 March 2009
Decision on the Request of the Co-Lawyers for Civil Parties Group 2 to Make an Opening Statement During the Substantive Hearing, 001/18–7–2007-ECCC/TC, 27 March 2009
Decision on Civil Party Co-lawyers' joint request for a ruling on the standing of Civil Party lawyers to make submissions on sentencing and directions concerning the questioning of the accused, experts and witnesses testifying on character, and accompanying Dissenting Opinion of Judge Lavergne, 001/18–07–2007/ECCC/TC, 9 October 2009
Supreme Court Chamber, Decision on the Appeals Filed by Lawyers for Civil Parties (Groups 2 and 4) against the Trial Chamber's Oral Decisions of 27 August 2009, 001/18–07–2007/ECCC/SC, 24 December 2009
Trial Judgement, 001/18–07–2007-ECCC/TC, 26 July 2010
Appeal of the Co-Lawyers from the Group 3 Civil Parties against the Judgment of 26 July 2010, Supreme Court Chamber, 5 October 2010
Co-Prosecutors' Appeal against the Trial Chamber Judgement of 26 July 2010, 001/18–07–2007-ECCC/SC, 13 October 2010
Appeal against Rejection of Civil Party Applicants in the Judgement (Civil Party Group 2), 001/18–07–2007-ECCC/SC, 22 October 2010

Appeal against Judgement on Reparations (Civil Party Group 2) 001/18–07–2007-ECCC/SC, 2 November 2010

Appeal Brief by the Co-Lawyers for Kaing Guek Eav alias "Duch" against the Trial Chamber Judgement of 26 July 2010, 001/18–07–2007-ECCC/SC, 18 November 2010

Case 001, Appeal Judgement, 001/18–07–2007-ECCC/SC, 3 February 2012

Trial transcripts: 31 March 2009; 20 June 2009; 22 June 2009; 30 June 2009; 1 July 2009; 6 July 2009; 13 July 2009; 22 July 2009; 29 July 2009; 12 August 2009; 24 August 2009; 27 August 2009; 23 November 2009

Case 002

Introductory Submission, Office of the Co-Prosecutor (confidential) 18 July 2007

Decision on Civil Party Participation in Provisional Detention Appeals, 002/19–09–2007-ECCC/OCIJ, 20 March 2008

Written Version of Oral Decision of 1 July 2008 on the Civil Party's Request to Address the Court in Person, Pre-Trial Chamber, 002/19–09–2007-ECCC/OCIJ, 3 July 2008

Decision on Nuon Chea's Appeal against Order Refusing Request for Annulment, 002/19–09–2007-ECCC/OCIJ, 26 August 2008

Decision on Application for Reconsideration of Civil Party's Right to Address Pre-Trial Chamber in Person, 002/19–09–2007-ECCC/OCIJ, 28 August 2008

Order on the Admissibility of Civil Party Applicants from Current Residents of Oddar Meanchey Province, 002/19–09–2007-ECCC-OCIJ, 26 August 2010

Closing Order, 002/19–09–2007-ECCC-OCIJ, 15 September 2010

Decision on Appeals against Orders of the Co-Investigating Judges on the Admissibility of Civil Party Applications, 002/19–09–2007-ECCC/PTC, 24 June 2011

Decision on Appeals Against Orders of the Co-Investigating Judges on the Admissibility of Civil Party Applications, Separate and Partially Dissenting Opinion of Judge Marchi-Uhel, 002/19–09–2007-ECCC/PTC, 24 June 2011

Severance Order Pursuant to Internal Rule 89ter, 002/19–09–2007-ECCC/TC, 22 September 2011

Response to Co-Prosecutors' Request for Reconsideration of the Severance Order, 002/19–09–2007-ECCC/TC, 11 October 2011

Lead Co-Lawyers and Civil Party Lawyers Request for Reconsideration of the Terms of the Severance Order, 002/19–09–2007-ECCC/TC, 18 October 2011

Lead Co-Lawyers and Civil Party Lawyers' Request to Make Brief Preliminary Remarks on Behalf of Civil Parties After Co-Prosecutors' Opening Statement, 002/19–9–2007-ECCC/TC, 2 November 2011

Trial Chamber Response to Lead Co-Lawyers and Civil Party Lawyers' Request to Make a Brief Preliminary Remarks on Behalf of Civil Parties, 002/19–9–2007-ECCC/TC, 15 November 2011

Decision on IENG Thirith's Fitness to Stand Trial, 002/19–09–2007/ECCC/TC, 17 November 2011
Termination of the Proceedings against the Accused IENG Sary, ECCC Trial Chamber, 002/19–09–2007/ECCC/TC, 14 March 2013
Decision on Severance of Case 002/01 following Supreme Court Chamber Decision of 8 February 2013, 002/19–09–2007/ECCC/TC, 26 April 2013
Decision on Additional Severance of Case 002/02 and Scope of Case 002/02, 002/19–09–2007-ECCC/TC, 4 April 2014
Case 002/01, Trial Judgement, 002/19–09–2007/ECCC/TC, 7 August 2014
Case 002/02, Decision on Civil Party Lead Co-Lawyers' Request to Make Opening Remarks, 002/19–9–2007-ECCC/TC, 14 October 2014
NUON Chea's Appeal against the Judgement in Case 002/01, 002/19–09–2007/ECCC/SC, 29 December 2014
Mr Khieu Samphân's Defence Appeal Brief against the Judgement in Case 002/01, 002/19–09–2007/ECCC/SC, 29 December 2014
Termination of the Proceedings against the Accused IENG Thirith, 002/19–09–2007/ECCC/TC, 27 August 2015
Case 002/01, Appeals Judgement, 002/19–09–2007/ECCC/SC, 23 November 2016
Trial transcripts: 30 June 2011; 2 February 2012; 11 January 2012; 29 August 2012

Cases 003 and 004

Considerations of the Pre-Trial Chamber Regarding the Disagreement between the Co-Prosecutors Pursuant to Internal Rule 71, 001/18–11–2008-ECCC/PTC, 18 August 2009
Notice of Conclusion of Judicial Investigation, 002/19–09–2007-ECCC-OCIJ, 29 April 2011
Considerations of the Pre-Trial Chamber Regarding the International Co-Prosecutor's Appeal Against the Co-Investigating Judges' Order on International Co-Prosecutor's Public Statement Regarding Case 003, 003/07–09–2009-ECCC/OCIJ, 24 October 2011
Opinion of the Pre-Trial Chamber Judges Downing and Chung on the Disagreement between the Co-Investigating Judges Pursuant to Internal Rule 72, 003/16–12–2011-ECCC/PTC, 10 February 2012
Decision to Charge Meas Muth in Abstentia, Case File No: 003/07–09–2009-ECCC-OCIJ, 3 March 2015
Closing Order on Case 004/01, 004/1/07–09–2009-ECCC-OCIJ, 22 February 2017

International Tribunal for the Former Yugoslavia

Prosecutor v. Nikolić, Judgment, IT-02–60/1, 2 December 2003

International Criminal Court

Prosecutor v. Gbagbo, Organization of the Participation of Victims, ICC-02/11-01/11-29-Red, 6 February 2012.

The Prosecutor v. Kenyatta, Decision on Prosecution's Application for a Finding of Non-Compliance under Article 87(7) of the Statute, ICC-01/09-02/11-982, 3 December 2014.

Prosecutor v. Lubanga Dyilo, Judgment on the Appeals of The Prosecutor and The Defence against Trial Chamber I's Decision on Victims' Participation of 18 January 2008, ICC Appeal Chamber, ICC-01/04-01/06-1432, 11 July 2008.

Prosecutor v. Lubanga Dyilo, Decision Establishing the Principles and Procedures to be Applied to Reparations, ICC-01/04-01/06-2904, 7 August 2012.

Prosecutor v. Lubanga Dyilo, Judgment on the Appeals against the 'Decision establishing the Principles and Procedures to be applied to Reparations' ICC-01/04-01/06-3129, 7 August 2012 with AMENDED Order for Reparations (Annex A) and Public Annexes 1 and 2, ICC-01/04-01/06-3129, 3 March 2015.

Prosecutor v Ruto and Sang, Common Legal Representative for Victims' Comprehensive Report on the Withdrawal of Victims from the Turbo area by Letter dated 5 June 2013, ICC-01/09-01/11-896-Corr-Red, 5 September 2013.

European Court of Human Rights

Aksoy v. Turkey, Judgment, App. No. 21987/93, 18 December 1996.
Aydin v. Turkey, Judgment, App. No. 23178/94, 25 September 1997.
Bazorkina v. Russia, Judgment, App. No. 69481/01 27 June 2006.
Jordan v. United Kingdom, Judgment, App. No. 24746/94, 4 May 2001.
Perez v. France, Judgment, App. No. 47287/99, 12 February 2004.
Salman v. Turkey, Judgment, App. No. 21986/93, 27 June 2000.
Timurtus v. Turkey, Judgment, App. No. 23531/94, 13 June 2000.

Inter-American Court of Human Rights

Blake v. Guatemala, Judgment (Merits), 24 January 1998.

Moiwana Community v. Suriname, Preliminary Objections, Merits, Reparations and Costs, Series C, No. 124, 15 June 2005.

Plan de Sánchez Massacre v. Guatemala, Merits, Reparations and Costs, Series C, No. 116, 19 November 2004.

Velasquez-Rodriguez v. Honduras, Judgment, Series C, No. 4, 29 July 1988.

Villagran Morales et al. v. Guatemala, Judgment, 19 November 1999.

Table of legislation

International

Agreement for the Prosecution and Punishment of the Major War Criminals of the European Axis, and Charter of the International Military Tribunal, London, 8 August 1945.

Special Proclamation, Establishment of an International Military Tribunal for the Far East, TIAS No. 1589, 19 January 1946.

Agreements on a Comprehensive Political Settlement of the Cambodia Conflict, Paris, 23 October 1991.

Statute of the International Tribunal for the Prosecution of Persons Responsible for Serious Violations of International Humanitarian Law Committed in the Territory of the former Yugoslavia since 1991, UNSC Res. 827, S/Res/827, 25 May 1993.

Statute of the International Criminal Tribunal for Rwanda ('ICTR Statute'), UNSC Resolution 955, S/Res/955, 8 November 1994.

Rome Statute of the International Criminal Court, 2149 UNTS 256, 17 July 1998.

Agreement between the UN and the Royal Government of Cambodia Concerning the Prosecution under Cambodian Law of Crimes Committed during the Period of Democratic Kampuchea, 6 June 2003, entered into force 29 April 2005, UN Doc. A/RES57/228B (Annex) 13 May 2003.

Statute for the Special Tribunal for Lebanon, UNSC Res. 1757, S/RES/1757, 31 January 2007.

Statute of the Extraordinary African Chambers within the Courts of Senegal Created to Prosecute International Crimes Committed in Chad between 7 June 1982 and 1 December 1990, February 2013.

National

Decree Law No. 1: Establishment of People's Revolutionary Tribunal at Phnom Penh to Try the Pol Pot-Ieng Sary Clique for the Crime of Genocide, Phnom Penh, 15 July 1979.

Law on Outlawing the Group of 'Democratic Kampuchea', KHM/30, 15 July 1994.

Law on the Establishment of Extraordinary Chambers in the Courts of Cambodia for the Prosecution of Crimes Committed during the Period of Democratic Kampuchea, Law NS/RKM/0801/12, 10 August 2001.

Russian Federation Laws on Introducing Amendments to Certain Legislative Acts of the Russian Federation 2006.

Code de Procédure Pénale du Royaume du Cambodie, 7 June 2007.

Introducing Amendments to Certain Legislative Acts of the Russian Federation Regarding the Regulation of Activities of Non-commercial Organizations Performing the Function of Foreign Agents 2012.

Statute of the Extraordinary African Chambers within the Courts of Senegal Created to Prosecute International Crimes Committed in Chad between 7 June 1982 and 1 December 1990, February 2013.

UN documents and other international instruments

Universal Declaration of Human Rights, UNGA Resolution 217 A (III), 10 December 1948.

Council of Europe, *European Convention for the Protection of Human Rights and Fundamental Freedoms, as amended by Protocols Nos. 11 and 14*, ETS 5, 4 November 1950.

International Covenant on Civil and Political Rights, UNGA Resolution 2200A (XXI), 16 December 1966.

Organization of American States, *American Convention on Human Rights*, "Pact of San Jose", Costa Rica, 22 November 1969.

Convention against Torture and Other Cruel, Inhuman or Degrading Treatment or Punishment, UNGA Resolution 39/46, 10 December 1984.

UN Declaration of Basic Principles of Justice for Victims of Crime and Abuse of Power, UNGA Resolution 40/34, 29 November 1985.

UN Basic Principles for the Treatment of Prisoners, UNGA Resolution 45/111, 14 December 1990.

UN Standard Minimum Rules for Non-Custodial Measures, UNGA Resolution 45/110, 14 December 1990.

UNSC Resolution 745, S/RES/745, 28 February 1992.

UNOHCHR, *The Right to Restitution, Compensation and Rehabilitation for Victims of Gross Violations of Human Rights and Fundamental Freedoms, Final Report of the Special Rapporteur, Mr M.Ch Bassiouni*, UN Doc. E/CN.4/2000/62, 5 March 1993.

UNSC, *Madeleine Albright Statement to the UN Security Council, Provisional Verbatim Record to the 3217th Meeting*, UN Doc. S/PV 3217, 25 May 1993.

ICTY, Annual Report to the UNGA, A/49/342, S/1994/1007, 29 August 1994.

ICTY, *Annual Report to the UNGA*, A/50/365-S/1995/728, 23 August 1995.

Letter from Norodom Ranariddh, Cambodian First Prime Minister, and Hun Sen, Cambodian Second Prime Minister, to Secretary General Annan, 21 June 1997.

Identical Letters dated 23 June 1997 from the Secretary-General addressed to the President of the General Assembly and to the President of the Security Council, A/51/930, S/1997/488, 24 June 1997.

UNGA Resolution A/RES/52/135, 27 February 1998.

ICTR, *Annual Report to the UNGA*, A/53/429-S/1998/857, 23 September 1998.

Report of the Group of Experts for Cambodia Established Pursuant to General Assembly Resolution 52/135, UN Doc. A/53/850, 15 March 1999.

UN Office on Drugs and Crime, *Handbook on Justice for Victims*, 1999.

Convention against Transnational Organised Crime, UNGA 55/25, 15 November 2000.

UN Principles on the Effective Investigation and Documentation of Torture and Other Cruel, Inhuman or Degrading Treatment or Punishment, UNGA Resolution 55/89, 4 December 2000.

Vienna Declaration on Crime and Justice: Meeting the Challenges of the 21st Century, UNGA Resolution 55/59, 4 December 2000.

International Law Commission, *Draft Articles on Responsibility of States for Internationally Wrongful Acts*, Supplement No. 10 (A/56/10), chp.IV.E.1, 1 November 2001.

UN High Commissioner for Human Rights, *Secretary-General Replies to the Cambodian Prime Minister's Letter on Trial of Khmer Rouge Leaders*, UN Doc. SG.S.8341, 20 August 2002, cambodia.ohchr.org/EN/PagesFiles/Statements/Statement2002.htm (accessed 26/11/2015).

UNGA Resolution A/RES/57/228, 27 February 2003.

Report of the Secretary-General on Khmer Rouge Trials, UN Doc A/57/769, 31 March 2003.

UN Press Office, *General Assembly Approves Draft Agreement Between UN, Cambodia on Khmer Rouge Trials*, UN Doc. GA/10135, 13 May 2003.

UNGA Resolution A/RES/57/228B, 22 May 2003.

Letter from Prime Minister Hun Sen to Mr. Kofi Annan, *UN Secretary-General, on the Adoption by the National Assembly of Cambodia of the Draft Law Approving the Agreement between the UN and the Royal Government of Cambodia Concerning the Prosecution under the Cambodian Law of Crimes Committed during the Period of Democratic Kampuchea*, 4 October 2004.

UNOHCHR, *Updated Set of Principles for the Protection and Promotion of Human Rights through Action to Combat Impunity*, UN Doc. E/CN.4/2005/102/Add.1, 18 February 2005.

UN Basic Principles and Guidelines on the Right to a Remedy and Reparation for Victims of Gross Violations of International Human Rights Law and Serious Violations of International Humanitarian Law, UNGA Resolution 60/147, 16 December 2005.

UNOHCHR, *Rule-of-Law Tools for Post-Conflict States: Maximizing the Legacy of Hybrid Courts*, HR/PUB/08/2 (2008).

UNSC Resolution 1932, S/RES/1932, 29 June 2010.

Rules of procedure and practice directives

ICC, Rules of Procedure and Evidence, ICC-ASP/1/3, 9 September 2002.

SCSL, Rule of Procedure and Evidence, adopted on 16 January 2002.

ECCC, Internal Rules, 12 June 2007.

ECCC, Practice Direction on Victim Participation, Revision 1, 27 October 2008.

ICC, Report of the Court on the Strategy in Relation to Victims, ICC-ASP/8/45, 10 November 2009.

ECCC, Lead Co-Lawyers and Civil Party Lawyers Administrative Internal Regulations, August 2011.

ICC, Guidelines Governing the Relations between the Court and Intermediaries: for the Organs and Units of the Court and Counsel working with intermediaries, March 2014.

ICTR, Rules of Procedure and Evidence, 29 June 1995, as amended 13 May 2015.

ICTY, Rules of Procedure and Evidence, Revision 50, 8 July 2015.

Index

FSC
www.fsc.org
MIX
Papier | Fördert
gute Waldnutzung
FSC® C083411

Kolibri 360 GmbH
Ferdinand-Jühlke-Straße 7
99095 Erfurt, Deutschland
produktsicherheit@kolibri360.de